Myth and Reality

in

Late-Eighteenth-Century British Politics

and Other Papers

IAN R. CHRISTIE

Professor of Modern British History,
University College, London

MACMILLAN

First published 1970 *by*
MACMILLAN AND CO LTD
Little Essex Street London WC2
and also at Bombay Calcutta and Madras
Macmillan South Africa (Publishers) Pty Ltd Johannesburg
The Macmillan Company of Australia Pty Ltd Melbourne
The Macmillan Company of Canada Ltd Toronto
Gill and Macmillan Ltd Dublin

Printed in Great Britain by
ROBERT MACLEHOSE AND CO LTD
The University Press, Glasgow

Contents

Acknowledgements

FOR leave to reprint a number of the essays in this volume I make grateful acknowledgement to the director of the Institute of Historical Research, and to the editors of the *English Historical Review*, the *Guildhall Miscellany*, the *Historical Journal*, *History Today*, the *Journal of British Studies* and *Norfolk Archaeology*. Constable and Company Limited kindly permitted the republication of the essay forming an introduction to the second impression of G. S. Veitch's *The Genesis of Parliamentary Reform*. One or two misprints and minor errors have been corrected, some footnotes have been adjusted to fit the juxtaposition of the papers in one volume and to eliminate an out-of-date set of references to Rockingham's papers, and a brief addition has been inserted in paper 6.

About half the contents of this volume have not appeared before, and in respect of these papers once again I owe thanks in many quarters. I have to acknowledge the gracious permission of Her Majesty the Queen to consult documents in the papers of George III and of George, Prince of Wales, in the Royal Archives at Windsor. I am also grateful to the following for their kind permission to make use of collections of family papers: The Marquess of Bath; the Duke of Bedford and the Trustees of the Bedford Settled Estates; the Duke of Devonshire; the Earl Fitzwilliam and the Trustees of the Wentworth Woodhouse Estate; and S. C. Whitbread Esquire of Southill Park. For help in supplying xeroxes of imprints and photocopies of documents, or in making documents accessible, I have great pleasure in thanking the staff of the manuscript department of the British Museum and of the National Library of Scotland, the librarians of the City Library, Sheffield, the William Salt Library, Stafford and the Aberdeen Public Library; the keeper, the department of western manuscripts, the Bodleian Library, the curator of manuscripts, the Public Library, Boston, Mass., the head of the department of palaeography and diplomatic at the University of Durham, the county archivist, Bedford Record Office, and Miss M. Draper at the office of the Bedford Settled Estates. Mr N. E. S. Norris of Brighton kindly supplied a transcript of a letter in his possession written by Lord North, which added materially to the contents of paper 6, and Professor Donald E. Ginter of Duke University, North Carolina, provided copies of transcripts of letters from James Perry to William Adam in his possession. I am also grateful to Mr E. L. C. Mullins, secretary to the History of Parliament Trust, for permission to check certain transcripts in the files of the Trust. Last but not least, my thanks are given to Dr Geoffrey Alderman, without whose help in his capacity of research assistant some of the hitherto unprinted papers in this volume could not have been completed at the present time.

I. R. C.

April 1969

Introduction

MOST of the papers reprinted or published for the first time in the following pages bear on one or other of three themes in the history of Great Britain in the late eighteenth century which have held my attention for a number of years: the central direction of government under the system of 'limited monarchy'; the working of the political system; and the nature of movements for constitutional reform prior to the impact of the French Revolution on British politics. All these themes have a common focal point in the political myth which is discussed in the title-paper of this volume. In connection with all of them a number of historians have been carrying forward a steady process of reinterpretation and reintegration, leading to a new, more harmonised and coherent presentation of the period, in the wake of the seismic demolition carried out at the end of the 1920s by Sir Lewis Namier. I hope that the following papers, when taken together, may make some contribution to this process.

I

With the publication of Namier's two major works on British eighteenth-century history, *The Structure of Politics at the Accession of George III*, and *England in the Age of the American Revolution*, the then accepted picture of the political world in the first half of George III's reign lay scattered in ruins. Schoolmasters, it has been said, hastily roped off the later eighteenth century and guided their charges through more simply charted periods.[1] Nor was it they only who fled from chaos. Namier himself had provided only a few foundations and guidelines for the new historical reconstructions made necessary by the levelling of the old. At that time his intention of carrying his work further was immediately precluded by the non-availability of vital manuscript collections containing the papers of

[1] E. N. Williams, reviewing *Eighteenth Century England*, by Dorothy Marshall (*History Today*, XIII (1963) 133).

George Grenville, the Marquis of Rockingham and Edmund Burke. In any case, perhaps there was more to be done than one man could do; and according to one story in circulation many years ago, Namier declined to teach later-eighteenth-century British history on taking up his professorial appointment at Manchester, because no books were available with which it could be correctly taught. The problem of outdated books, the lack of landmarks or of a general framework of reference for the politics of the period, and the resultant sense of confusion, were still very apparent when I began to cover this ground in university teaching some twenty years ago. Certain constitutional outlines had been firmly restated by Mark Alméras Thomson;[1] but many aspects of the history of the period had not yet been re-presented in a form congruent with the new constitutional interpretation. New answers had not yet been clearly and fully formulated to replace vanished responses to such leading questions as: How was the central direction of government being carried on after 1760, if it was not being exercised by the king himself and/or a secret cabal? What were the motivations of the parliamentary opposition led by the Marquis of Rockingham, and how were they to be accounted for, if the internal political situation postulated by the 'whig legend' did not exist? Also, how, in the light of this fact, were various movements aiming at reform of the constitution to be fitted into place? If politics could not be regarded as a battle of virtuous whigs against resurgent, authoritarian tories, what then was the nature of the groups and parties which played out their roles in the House of Commons? On all these questions scholars have been making gradual contributions to a new synthesis over the past twenty years, and some of its outlines have begun to emerge in such general surveys of the period as those given by Mr J. Steven Watson in *The Reign of George III* and Dr Dorothy Marshall in her *Eighteenth Century England.*

II

The most thorough post-Namier study of the central direction of government in the reign of George III is provided by Richard

[1] In *A Constitutional History of England, 1642 to 1801* (1938) part IV; in this connection, see especially pp. 367–78.

Pares's book, *King George III and the Politicians*. Pares devoted a close-packed chapter to a survey of the relations between the king and the cabinet. He showed that the reference of policy questions to the cabinet depended in principle on the king's discretion, but that in practice his freedom to exercise it was limited. In many situations individual ministers would not be willing to accept sole responsibility for acts of the crown. In such instances, and also in cases where they were in personal disagreement with the king, ministers would press for matters to be referred to the cabinet, and when this had been done the king was under a strong moral compulsion to accept the advice which was proffered. Pares pointed also to certain indications of a growing practice on the part of cabinet ministers to meet for informal discussions even although business had not been formally referred to them with the king's consent. He concluded also that when the cabinet made a recommendation, it was usual practice for the minister in charge of the business to draw up a minute, which either he or the prime minister transmitted to the king. All these things were indications that the role of the cabinet was becoming more regular and clear-cut. It might be thought that this also indicated a growing dominance in the field of policy. However, against these trends Pares set the conclusion that from about 1767 the correspondence of George III became fuller than before of administrative detail, and that this indicated that 'more and more' was 'submitted to the king's decision'.[1] Some aspects of cabinet history were not fully examined in this study. Pares did not concern himself closely with its evolution; nor did he undertake any detailed survey of the king's role in the making of policy.

Paper 2 is an attempt to push our knowledge of this subject somewhat further. Here I have tried to look more closely than has been done hitherto both at the evolution of the cabinet and of its business routine, and at the king's relationship with it in regard to the formulation of policy. The results of this investigation suggest both amplifications and modifications of Pares's findings. Some important new detail about cabinet routine emerges. Pares's assumption that the procedure of submitting advice to George III by means of cabinet minutes was followed from the beginning of

[1] Pares, *King George III and the Politicians* (Oxford, 1953) pp. 153–4, 159–60, 162–3, 168.

the reign is seen to be incorrect. This was not normally done until late in 1779. Previously the king received the advice either in a verbal report or in the form of draft dispatches submitted for his formal approval. The innovation, a response to a war situation, seems to have been an attempt to ensure, by the maintenance of a more formal record (kept by the king), that the cabinet was effectively discharging its reponsibilities. It had, however, the unforseen consequence of strengthening still further the cabinet's role in the process of decision: it is significant that the most regular use was made of this new procedure by the ministries of Rockingham and of Lord Grenville, which were the least comfortable in their relations with George III.[1]

Other additional evidence places still more stress on the positive role of the cabinet after 1760. There are considerable indications that its members at times came together regularly to talk about public affairs, whether or not specific matters had been referred to it. Colonial affairs, diplomacy and war created a press of important business of a kind for which no single minister could take upon himself to accept responsibility. Both circumstances helped to give the cabinet momentum, to emphasise its connections with parliament, and to reduce in practice the significance of its formal constitutional dependence upon the sovereign. Much of the specific evidence from which Pares deduced an increasing royal assumption of responsibility for decisions will not in fact bear this inference;[2] and a good deal of testimony from contemporaries also conflicts with it. Some modification of Pares's views seems warranted. It is evident that there was constant dialogue over policy between the king and the cabinet (as well as between the king and individual ministers); but this was more a process of participation than of direction. On some occasions George III got his way, but there

[1] This discovery raises the further important question whether George II had customarily received minutes of cabinet. In the absence of royal papers for that period this is not easily to be ascertained. My very cursory excursions into collections of ministerial papers before 1760 have not brought to light any references to minutes being submitted to him, but this question can only be answered by a historian with a very thorough knowledge, which I do not command, of the papers of Newcastle, Holdernesse, Henry Fox, William Pitt, Sir Thomas Robinson, the Duke of Bedford and other ministers.

[2] See pp. 106–7 below.

were other equally significant occasions when he failed to do so or swallowed an unpalatable recommendation. The 'mixed monarchy' of the eighteenth century presupposed an active king; but it seems an exaggeration to regard the nature and extent of George III's activity in the 1760s or 1770s as justifying the description 'personal rule'.

III

A number of the papers which follow relate to the changing pattern of parliamentary politics during the first half of George III's reign. Throughout this period the members of the House of Commons can in general be assigned to one or other of the three categories – independents, court and administration group, and party politicians – described in Namier's essay, 'Monarchy and the Party System', although for some individuals a clear distinction is hard to make;[1] but within this general framework, the system was by 1784 no longer what it had been around 1760. The court and administration party was diminishing in size, and the conditions which had sustained it were gradually changing. Some of the slow reductions in the links of patronage between the House of Commons and the executive government which were taking place in this period are traced in paper 14, and some additional information illustrative of the decline in the number of 'government boroughs' is provided in paper 9. Under the stress of events in the middle years of the reign, even so typical and fully committed a member of the court and administration group as John Robinson, whose political loyalties are discussed in paper 5, might suddenly find his political bearings destroyed.[2] A trend of greater importance, however, was the emergence of party; and in this connection it would perhaps be appropriate to discuss somewhat more fully the context of the material presented in papers 1 and 3.

I believe that there is now little disagreement among historians of this period over the fact that the evolution of the political party led first by Rockingham and then by the Duke of Portland is of key importance for the story of the development of party politics. At the most elementary level this importance emerges in terms of

[1] *Crossroads of Power* (1962) pp. 213–34.
[2] Pp. 164–6 below.

numbers of followers in the House of Commons. It is true that mere size was not always regarded as a criterion of party excellence in the late eighteenth century, or even later: one of Rockingham's chief lieutenants once 'wished the Opposition was reduced to six or seven, who could depend on each other';[1] and during the decade after the death of Pitt Canning, with a party of about sixteen, 'considered himself, with a few followers of character, as constituting a more influential party, and standing in a more commanding and freer position than if he had been a leader of fifty, each of whom would probably have felt they had a claim upon him'.[2] Even at the end of George III's reign the ministerial (also the largest) party did not comprise an absolute majority of the House, and between 1790 and 1820 there were checks and even retrogressions in the consolidation of parties.[3] But the emergence of an opposition party, vaguely comprising some seventy members in the late 1760s and with a more clearly defined membership of about eighty by 1780, rising after Fox's coalition with North to about 150, although not accompanied by a comparable consolidation on the government side of the House, marked a clear trend away from the conditions of group or faction politics which characterised the years immediately after 1760.[4]

Mere personal connection could hardly have kept such a formation together. Its appearance is symptomatic of other elements of change. A large party needs the bonds both of organisation and of ideas and policies, and in the period extending some two or three years either side of 1770 a transition was evident from an era of personal parties (among which personal competition for power was the driving force) to one of political parties (in which the pursuit or reversal of policies was the main ground of contention). Wilkes, America, and the affairs of the East India Company gave

[1] Horace Walpole, *Memoirs of the Reign of King George III*, ed. G. F. R. Barker, 4 vols (1894) II 96.

[2] MS. autobiography of E. J. Littleton, cited in C. R. Fay, *Huskisson and his Age* (1951) p. 79.

[3] Austin Mitchell, *The Whigs in Opposition, 1815–1830* (Oxford, 1967) ch. III, esp. pp. 59–67; F. O'Gorman, *The Whig Party and the French Revolution* (1967); Michael Roberts, *The Whig Party, 1807–12* (1939).

[4] John Brooke, *The Chatham Administration, 1766–1768* (1956) ch. VI; Ian R. Christie, *The End of North's Ministry, 1780–1782* (1958) pp. 196–230; Namier, *Crossroads of Power*, p. 229

the politicians vital issues on which to disagree.[1] A number of historians have elaborated on the nature of the change which came over Rockingham's associates at this time: the greater stress laid upon the merits of party; the concern with principle and consistency, to the point of having a programme, even if only a limited one, which it was genuinely intended to implement; and the development of an ideology which can, in a limited sense, be described as liberal.[2] But various features of this change still require elucidation.

Organisation came relatively late in the history of this party. Up till 1782 there was virtually none, save for the rather haphazard conclaves of the magnates who led its various connections and made their town houses available for party meetings, and the activity of one or two individuals as party whips and tellers.[3] In the next few years there was a distinct advance, perhaps not unconnected with the disappearance or eclipse of an older generation of leaders and the emergence of younger men – a process in which Edmund Burke, the man of ideas, was replaced in importance by the organisation man, William Adam.[4] The office of shadow secretary to the treasury assumed by Adam during the regency crisis of 1788–9, when it was thought the party was on the threshold of office, fostered a new and, as it proved, a permanent organisational framework, with a party manager, two different funds for general purposes and for elections, a permanent establishment for parliamentary canvassing and the issue of circular letters; and an extra-parliamentary basis in political clubs, set up with the object of broadening the party's electoral support not only in the metropolis but also in the provinces. By the early 1790s a situation had come into being very different from that in which Rockingham and his friends had first launched themselves into opposition in 1763.

[1] Sir Lewis Namier and John Brooke, *The History of Parliament: The House of Commons, 1754–1790*, 3 vols (1964) I 198–201.

[2] E.g. G. H. Guttridge, *English Whiggism and the American Revolution* (Berkeley and Los Angeles, 1963) *passim*; Carl B. Cone, *Burke and the Nature of Politics*, vol. I, *The Age of the American Revolution* (University of Kentucky, 1957) ch. VII; A. S. Foord, *His Majesty's Opposition, 1714–1830* (Oxford, 1964) pp. 338–50.

[3] Foord, *His Majesty's Opposition*, pp. 338–50.

[4] The matter which follows rests upon the valuable discussion in the introduction to Donald E. Ginter, *Whig Organization in the General Election of 1790* (Berkeley and Los Angeles, 1967).

Before 1782 it was policy and theory which chiefly held the Rockingham party together. Manuscript evidence which has become available within the last twenty years or so has made it possible to examine this circumstance at a new level of penetration,[1] and this is the main justification for paper 1. At the same time this paper attempts a reconsideration of the position of this party, holding its particular set of ideas, in relation to the general context of political events. This is a matter which has required more consideration than it has received ever since the publication of *The Structure of Politics*. The neglect shown towards it clearly worried Sir Herbert Butterfield in the 1950s, but though he pointed out the problem,[2] he did not himself attempt to present any new synthesis which might provide a line of escape from the Scylla and Charybdis of 'whig history' or of 'tory history' with the whigs left out. Nor, so far as I know, has any other historian done so; though within a few years of the appearance of *The Structure of Politics* there was a notable attempt to revivify 'whig history'. Professor G. H. Guttridge sought to restore some semblance of the old order by presenting a modified and reconstructed version of the whig–tory conflict.[3] The grounds on which I think this view unsatisfactory are detailed in paper 7. The suggestion there put forward, that ministerial politicians can be better understood as acting on principles of conservative pragmatism in home affairs, and not of tory ideology, and that the opposition completely misread the situation, is not intended, however, to entail the conclusion that the ideas of the opposition should be simply ignored. Indeed, the very brief mention which the whig myth discussed in paper 1 has received at the hands of Professors Guttridge and Foord[4] prompts the reflection that while some past generations of historians gave too much weight to Burke's political writings of this period, the present generation, including historians who cannot in any way be thought of as associated with Namier, may have been falling into the opposite error of giving them too little. This, perhaps, has

[1] Particularly the correspondence of Burke and of Rockingham, much of which has been admirably edited in the series of volumes of *The Correspondence of Edmund Burke*, under the general editorship of T. W. Copeland.

[2] Herbert Butterfield, *George III and the Historians* (1957) pp. 261–70.

[3] *English Whiggism and the American Revolution.*

[4] Ibid.; Foord, *His Majesty's Opposition*, pp. 344–5.

been due to a failure to envisage how they might be fitted into the general picture of the 1770s. Furthermore, in the light of the private correspondence of members of the Rockingham party it seems inadmissable to conclude that Burke in his published pamphlets was deliberately exaggerating for effect and did not mean what he said.[1] On the contrary, the circumstances of the Rockingham party's tenure of power and dismissal from office in 1765–6 gave rise among its leaders to a genuine conviction that power in the state had been captured by a sinister and would-be tyrannous cabal. The intellectual heritage of opposition politicians made it particularly easy, perhaps almost inevitable, for them to think in this way. Behind the formulation of the theory laý a whole pervasive inheritance of ideas reiterated by one generation after another of gifted pamphleteers. This literature focused to the point of obsession upon the processes of decay in free political societies. It laid continual stress upon the natural tendency in governments to encroach upon the freedom of individuals and upon the dangers of corruption, which might destroy the effectiveness of representative institutions as a shield of liberty.[2] Various elements of a conspiracy-theory about ministerial politics had for long been in the air, before particular events suggested to the Rockinghams that they were the latest victims of such a conspiracy, and formed a natural basis for their own elaboration of it as an explanation of their experiences.

It follows that the Rockingham party's theory of the secret cabal and the double cabinet, however mistaken, provides an important key to the evolution of British politics in the age of the American Revolution, and even beyond. Paper 1 is devoted to some examination of its development and of its consequences. The theory preceded, and in a sense absorbed, the issues of the Middlesex election and the coercion of the American colonies – events which are usually taken to be the cause of transition in the political life of

[1] This is the impression I get from the treatment of this point by Professor Carl B. Cone (*Burke and the Nature of Politics*, I 202), but perhaps I am misinterpreting him.

[2] On this subject see Caroline Robbins, *The Eighteenth-Century Commonwealthman* (Cambridge, Mass., 1959), and, for its connections with the revolutionary movement in the American colonies, Bernard Bailyn, *The Ideological Origins of the American Revolution* (Cambridge, Mass., 1967).

the 1770s – though from both it gathered additional momentum. The advantages of ideological cohesion and moral strength which it provided for the party which espoused it are obvious. Its devotees regarded themselves as defenders of the constitution against an insidious and malignant danger. The campaign against the supposed secret cabal was no mere pose to justify to the outer world a conduct in conflict with old-time prejudices against a formed opposition. These men believed in the danger; the campaign reflected their deeply-felt convictions; their conception of the situation provided a rational justification for their demand for a clean sweep of suspect elements from the administration and the rejection of compromises and coalitions, of which paper 3 presents an instance. The fact that their analysis of the political situation did not correspond with the realities, some of which are illustrated in papers 2, 7 and 14, in no way diminishes its significance as an explanation of the party's actions and of its fortunes. Moreover, not only is it an essential part of the history of the party, which cannot without it be properly understood, but it falls into place as part of the whole larger pattern of political events during the first half of the reign of George III; and it is probable that duly orientated investigation might reveal its reverberations in British politics for a far longer period – one stretching well into the nineteenth century.

How should we see this larger pattern of political events? In paper 7 I have set out my reasons for suggesting that both the aristocratic and the popular metropolitan oppositions to George III's governments are to be placed in a context completely different from that envisaged by the participants themselves, not as movements in resistance to a resurgent tory reaction but as a new phase in the trend towards a greater liberalism in British political institutions. One must doubt very strongly whether in general contemporaries themselves were aware of this. But in retrospect it is unmistakable that once again, in the later eighteenth century as so many times in earlier English history, those who defended the positions they sought by reference to ancient custom were in fact advancing new claims of a liberal and enlightened kind against old practices which no longer commanded general acquiescence. When the judges analysed and condemned eighteenth-century practice with regard to general warrants; when liberal elements in the legal profession conducted and won the sixty-year battle to deprive judges of their control over judgements on libel; when the House of Commons turned in revolt from the jurisdiction over parliamentary elections which it had exercised for a century and a half, often with cynical disregard for the views and rights of electors; and when both Houses were obliged perforce to admit that with coercive powers against the London newspaper press struck from their hands there was no practical alternative to suffering the publication of accounts of debates; then, it seems clear, the foundations of a new political world were being laid. In that generation, almost if not quite for the last time, reformers acted within a general conceptual framework – the appeal to a model in the past – which in pattern was essentially medieval. And because they did so they hid from themselves, and to some extent also from later generations, the nature of the processes in which they were taking part. In addition to this cause of misunderstanding, concentration of attention upon the unreal questions raised by the Rockingham party myth helped to conceal the real nature of the changes which were taking place at this time.

IV

The themes of constitutional reform running through British politics in the second half of the eighteenth century are variously touched upon in papers 1, 3, 8, 11, 12, 13 and 14. Investigation has shown that a great diversity of views on this question existed among various political groups, and that some of their ideas were neither reconcilable nor mutually acceptable. Burke's diagnosis of the situation, analysed in paper 1, provided a starting-point for right-wing reformers. Posing the existence of a threat simply to an aristocratically dominated political system, it gave rise to the carefully tailored programme of 'economical reform' enacted in 1782. Paper 12 presents detail about the remarkable, slightly less right-wing reform movement created by an important minority of the Yorkshire gentry. These men shared many of the misconceptions of the Rockingham party, but in addition they were motivated by some degree of suspicion and hostility towards its aristocratic leaders and so they believed in rather more sweeping reforms. Paper 11 gives a detailed account of one phase of the very different campaign mounted by metropolitan reformers, whose interpretation of the 'whig myth' was coloured by the point of view of a great urban community which felt itself the odd man out in a political society run by and in the interests of landowners. An example of the provincial urban attitude which helps to explain why none of these movements had a wider general appeal is provided by the short note on Great Yarmouth in paper 13. Opponents of the ruling corporation interest in this borough had no objection to government patronage, so long as they could secure control locally and exploit it in their own interest. Apart from this point of view, many contemporaries had a well-founded suspicion that the spectre of corruption paraded before their eyes in opposition propaganda was less grisly than the reformers alleged, a belief supported by the analysis of 'influence' in paper 14.

However abortive the reform agitation discussed in some of these papers, nevertheless reforms of different kinds were taking place; and papers 15 and 16 point the moral that in human societies it is often the unforeseen trains of development which may bring the important changes, while those sought by men's conscious purpose prove abortive or even recoil upon their authors. The growth and impact of the newspaper press as a factor in British politics during the reign of George III has not yet been fully assessed; nor will this be possible until a good deal more spadework has been done. Professor Arthur Aspinall's important pioneer study, *Politics and the Press, c. 1780–1850*, needs much further amplification, which will only be possible through the detailed study of a number of the important newspapers and a closer examination of the way in which the press as a whole was developing over these decades. During the course of sixty or seventy years the growth of the newspaper press was to produce a political world of depths and dimensions very different from that familiar to those who witnessed the accession of George III. Had they lived into the next reign, many of those witnesses would have recoiled from the press situation which they then encountered. There is a deep irony in the juxtaposition in time of Burke's publication of *Thoughts on the Cause of the Present Discontents* and his championship of those who supported liberty of the press in that nearest approximation to a filibuster ever perhaps seen in the eighteenth-century House of Commons, the unsuccessful campaign conducted by a small handful of members against the House's attempt to vindicate upon the person of the lord mayor of London its privilege of secrecy of debate. The failure of the House to defend its position marked a decisive stage in the development of the press and, consequently, of public opinion as a new, imponderable factor in the working of the British constitution. At that time Burke saw advantages in the free play of well-informed public opinion and had sought to cultivate public support for the Rockingham party. But in the long run the press was likely to be harmful to the dominance of the aristocracy, in which he believed; and in Burke's last years, as his remarks in 1791 about the *Morning Chronicle* and its owners show, the expression of radical opinions in the newspapers aroused his hatred and fear.[1]

In paper 15 I have attempted to draw together a concise summary of certain important developments during the reign of George III: the general increase in newspaper circulation; one or two salient innovations in business organisation and the increase in scale of newspaper businesses; the rising standards of the journalistic profession; the purposes which it served; and the influence upon these developments of the men who can justifiably be described as the first 'newspaper tycoons'. Paper 16 looks at one of these tycoons in more detail. James Perry was a portent and perhaps the greatest single formative influence among the journalists of his generation. No professional journalist before him had been accepted into the inner circles of a great political party, been intimate for many years with its leaders, and been made privy to the party's secret counsels. Under his aegis forthright political controversy was carried on at a level of intellect and of decorum rarely found in the newspapers of that day. A full-scale work on Perry, combining biography with a detailed study of his newspaper, the *Morning Chronicle*, is one of the most essential preliminaries to a full understanding of the development of the newspaper press in George III's time and of the impact which it had on political life.

Horace Walpole, the letter-writer and diarist, has been the subject of an admirable biography,[2] and one more such slight con-

[1] See pp. 345-6 below.

[2] R. W. Ketton Cremer, *Horace Walpole*, 2nd ed. (1946). See also the examination of various aspects of Walpole's activity in Wilmarth S. Lewis, *Horace Walpole* (1961).

tribution on him as paper 17 might well seem otiose. I hope, however, that this little sketch, which gave me much joy in the writing, may whet the appetites of readers who have not yet made fuller acquaintance with him. Perhaps, too, there is a certain fitness in having this book, which opens with a survey of the origins of the 'whig myth', close with some notice of the man whose posthumously published writings contributed so powerfully to the planting of it in mid-nineteenth-century British historical writing.

V

None of the papers in this volume bears directly on one of the most important episodes in the reign of George III, the American Revolution. Nevertheless many of them have an indirect relevance to it; and the thinking that lies behind them deeply colours my interpretation of events during that fateful crisis.[1] History is a seamless web, though this is something that we practitioners sometimes do not, perhaps at times cannot, keep in mind; but displacements in one sphere of historical scholarship can sometimes cause deep unforeseen disturbances elsewhere. As Professor Edmund S. Morgan pointed out a few years ago, in an illuminating address subsequently printed in the *William and Mary Quarterly*,[2] developments in the interpretation of British late-eighteenth-century domestic history during the past thirty years had destroyed the old framework of interpretation of the Revolution without substituting any alternative coherent framework in its place. British historians, he wrote, notably Sir Lewis Namier and Richard Pares, had abandoned any idea of the existence of parties 'with any principle or belief beyond that of serving selfish or local interests'; the effect of this was to discredit the 'whig interpretation' of the Revolution, and furthermore, 'the deflation of Fox and Burke, and the other Rockingham whigs, while accomplished with scarcely a glance in the direction of the colonies, nevertheless [deprived] the American revolutionists of a group of allies whose high-minded sympathy had been relied upon by earlier historians to help demonstrate the

[1] See my *Crisis of Empire: Great Britain and the American Colonies, 1754–1783* (1966).

[2] 'The American Revolution: Revisions in need of revising', *William and Mary Quarterly*, 3rd series, XIV (1957) 3–15.

justice of the American cause.' Also, he noted, 'the righteousness of the Americans is somewhat diminished through the loss of the principal villain of the piece [George III] . . . no longer the foe of liberty seeking to subvert the British constitution, but an earnest and responsible monarch, doing his job to the best of his abilities.'[1]

These findings, Morgan continued, had implications for developments in the colonies which had not, when he wrote in 1956, been either faced or explained. They appeared to force historians into the position of explaining the Revolution in terms of 'narrow or selfish views and . . . evil-minded agitators'. And yet, how is it possible to follow the logic of this position and explain men of the stature of George Washington, John Adams, Thomas Jefferson and Benjamin Franklin 'as agitators, or as the dupes of agitators, or as narrow-minded men without the vision to see beyond provincial borders'?[2]

Here, of course, Professor Morgan is perfectly right: one cannot do so. However this does not necessarily mean, as at one point he seems to suggest,[3] that the only way of escape is a return to the 'whig interpretation' of the Revolution. The same kind of re-orientation of the picture which some of the following papers suggest in respect of the Rockinghams can also be made for the leaders of the American Revolution. Professor Bernard Bailyn is surely right when he emphasises the extent to which a conviction of the existence of a malign conspiracy against the liberties of Englishmen had taken root in America just as it had in the ranks of the parliamentary opposition in Britain.[4] 'Dupe' is both too petty and too inadequate a word to use in such contexts of either Washington or Adams on the one hand or of Rockingham and Burke on the other. For just as the Revolution, to use Professor Morgan's phrase, is a 'brute fact', so also it is a brute fact that men are not in possession of total information about the political situation in which they move; their information is both incomplete and partially incorrect. No more than a military commander deploying for a battle can they know everything on the other side of the hill. The historical records of humanity are strewn with the wreckage of grand designs constructed without adequate information and born out of misconceptions. Indeed, the military analogy is not exact,

[1] Ibid., pp. 4–6. [2] Ibid., p. 7. [3] Ibid., p. 13.

[4] *Ideological Origins of the American Revolution, passim.*

because situations facing politicians may well be, probably are, more complex, profound and difficult to grasp. Another factor in the situation may be that if the politician's analysis is not pragmatic, but is guided to too great a degree by preconceived theory (this was as true of the British imperialists of the 1760s and 1770s as it was in a different way of their opponents), that very circumstance will itself catastrophically magnify the scale of error. Like the leaders of the Rockingham party, the leaders of the American Revolution were enmeshed in the trap of a false analysis: to assert this is not to deny their stature but merely to say they shared common human fallibility. That analysis was not, of course, a complete explanation of the drive towards revolution and independence; the resistance of maturing, largely self-governing political systems against a tightening imperial control provides an ample explanation in itself. But the analysis, false though it was, provided a powerful additional ideological drive. The recasting of the story of the Revolution in accordance with this line of argument may also be of assistance in another respect. It opens up a path for resolving the problem of the status and dignity of the American loyalists (otherwise dupes or villains?), concerning whom, it seems to me, the 'whig' interpretation of the American Revolution presents considerable difficulties.

From this starting-point, and in the light of the material presented in the papers which follow, some of the remaining questions posed by Professor Morgan may be less intractable than they appeared to him in 1956. The chasm which he contemplates between the two presentations by different groups of historians of an idealised imperial vision and the actual petty localism of British politicians certainly exists.[1] I think it can be closed a little as regards the British politicians; but I would go with him in holding that the imperial system lauded by Professor Gipson had certain serious flaws, and that British statesmen handling imperial questions in the period of the American Revolution lacked the imagination, vision and flexibility of mind to deal with the situation successfully.[2] They too were caught in the trap of a false analysis – the then current concept of the supremacy of parliament. The fact that they were at the same time being accused both by the

[1] *William and Mary Quarterly*, XIV 8.

[2] This point is stated more fully in my *Crisis of Empire*, pp. 111–14.

Rockingham party and by the American colonists of a deliberate plot against the principles of the British constitution, of which they were blameless, was probably no help to clarity of thought on their part. The investigation of the cabinet system in paper 2 suggests that George III should be regarded as carrying a share of the responsibility for the Revolution, though the modifications of interpretation which this paper puts forward would lead, I submit, to a rejection of Morgan's suggestion that 'he must bear most of the praise or blame'.[1] The idea – from which Morgan, in my view rightly, recoils – that 'the Whigs were hypocritical in their attack on George III and their support for the Americans'[2] has no basis in fact and need not be adduced as any part of an explanation of the facts of British politics in the age of the American Revolution.

[1] *William and Mary Quarterly*, XIV 13.
[2] Ibid.

ONE

*Myth and Reality in Late-Eighteenth-Century British Politics**

IT will never be thought, I hope, that myth is not a proper subject of concern for the historian. Belief in myths is so common a part of the human condition that these can hardly be neglected by those responsible for elucidating the human story. Conceivably the layman might take an oversimplified view of the historian's duty. It might seem to him that, faced with the diametrically opposed phenomena, 'myth' and 'reality', the historian has merely the simplest choice to make. His quest is the truth so far as he can attain it. What could be further removed from this than myth, which according to one common dictionary definition is 'purely fictitious narrative'? Perhaps we historians do write fiction at times, despite our better intentions. But this is hardly the purpose we set ourselves. That purpose has been commonly defined as 'a continuous methodical record of public events'; and the essence of an 'event' is that it is something real, something that has actually happened, something that has left its impress on the sands of time.

However, for the historian, the separation of 'myth' and 'reality' is less simple than appears on the surface. Behind every 'real' event lies the complex of human considerations which went into the making of it. We have to consider which opinions of the persons concerned with the event were true and which were false, which turn out to be congruous with all the available information we can lay hands on, which lack congruity and should therefore be adjudged to be 'myth'. But even then the separation cannot be achieved. We are faced with the ineluctable if paradoxical truth that in history a myth may be, indeed often is, a fact, a reality, in its own right. If people in a given historical situation firmly believed in a certain view of their circumstances and based their

* An inaugural lecture delivered at University College, London on 11 May, 1967.

actions upon it, then however mythical this view is proved to be, it becomes part of the data at the historian's command, by means of which he seeks to explain what happened. Indeed, the historian faced with a myth has at once two distinct but interrelated duties: to unravel the truth of the situation as distinct from the myth which is current about it; and, secondly, to examine the repercussions of the myth upon the situation.

I am not concerned in this lecture with latter-day myths which later generations of authors and editors have created in writing about the reign of George III. These have their own fascination, but this lecture is not an exercise in historiography, which has for this period been dealt with notably elsewhere.[1] Nor am I concerned with the myths which the men of the eighteenth century created about their own past or took over from their seventeenth-century predecessors, such as the myth of the Anglo-Saxon constitution. The eighteenth century provides enough myths of its own. There was the court myth of 'kings in chains'. There was the whig myth which identified whigdom with sole responsibility for the 'glorious revolution' of 1688.[2] Above all there was the particular myth with which I propose to concern myself here – the Rockingham party's concept of the 'king's friends' and the 'double cabinet'. This undoubtedly stands foremost in importance. An elucidation of it provides material information about the motivation of the parliamentary opposition through fifteen crucial years of the reign of George III. Such an investigation also provides insights for biographers of the leader of the chief opposition party, the Marquis of Rockingham, and of the party's outstanding spokesman in the House of Commons, Edmund Burke. Nevertheless, this myth has not been explored to any adequate extent in the work of present-day historians. This is presumably because most historians dealing with this period have been primarily occupied with the first of the two duties to which I have referred. They have been busy tracing the actual situation, a task which logically requires first priority, and they have therefore pushed to one side the incorrect representations of it. In the broad canvas of Mr J. Steven Watson's book, *The Reign of George III*, the myth of the double cabinet has a mere

[1] In Butterfield, *George III and the Historians*.

[2] On the whig myth see Foord, *His Majesty's Opposition*, pp. 67, 137, 152–3, 236 n., 312, 318, 327.

mention of three lines.[1] Professor G. H. Guttridge, the historiographer of the Rockingham party, though clearly not accepting the theory of the double cabinet, has not, in his monograph on the Rockinghams, given this idea as critical a study in relation to facts as it deserves.[2] Rather more space is found for the subject in Professor A. S. Foord's book, *His Majesty's Opposition*, and this author makes some stimulating observations, but his treatment of one detail in his very large canvas is inevitably brief.[3] Much the same observation holds good for Professor Butterfield's treatment of it in *George III and the Historians*.[4]

A full explanation of the origins of this myth awaits the completion of detailed studies, from all the documents now available, of the political history of the years 1763 to 1770. Over the two crucial years 1766 to 1768 the work has been done, and the context in which the myth developed is admirably described in Mr John Brooke's book, *The Chatham Administration*.[5] On this work I have relied a great deal. Still required are specialist studies of the periods of the Grenville and the first Rockingham administrations, spanning the period April 1763 to July 1766; and also of the years 1769 to 1770, on which the old detailed account by Winstanley, written without benefit of important collections of papers now available, is far from adequate in coverage or in analysis of motives and attitudes.[6] The present brief survey cannot make up for these gaps. However, the general conditions from which the myth arose are sufficiently clear and an outline of its growth can readily be traced.

The material of chief concern for this purpose is private correspondence. The spoken word in parliament may be an instrument of concealment as well as of revelation. It is in private letters that the inquirer may hope he is approaching the opinions of the men who are under investigation. In any case the surviving reports of parliamentary proceedings are very imperfect. For the period

[1] *The Reign of George III, 1760–1815* (Oxford, 1960) p. 126.

[2] *English Whiggism and the American Revolution.*

[3] *His Majesty's Opposition*, pp. 316–21.

[4] *George III and the Historians*, pp. 53–7.

[5] *The Chatham Administration, 1766–1768* (1956). For brief references to early stages of the myth, see pp. 47–8, 181–2, 186, 191, 199, and especially 210, 212, 214.

[6] D. A. Winstanley, *Lord Chatham and the Whig Opposition, 1766–1770* (Cambridge, 1912).

before 1770 they yield little evidence of the generalised theories about court power which the Rockinghams were developing, though the private correspondence occasionally shows that these ideas were being voiced in debate.[1] Letters provide both more reliable and also fuller information. They present, however, one outstanding semantic problem. Did a man, when he wrote the word 'court', mean it in the generally accepted sense of 'court and administration'; or did he use it in the specialised sense developed by the Rockinghams, of a party at court distinct from the administration and standing in some sort of sinister relationship with it? Sometimes this point can only be settled by taking each person's letters in the aggregate and getting the general sense of what he habitually meant by that term.[2]

A natural starting-point in this inquiry is in the writings of Edmund Burke. A word on Burke's qualities and role is therefore warranted. In many ways Burke commands my admiration. He had integrity and principle. A strong sense of moral purpose infused his politics. In his speeches and writings about colonial affairs in the years before the American Revolution he displayed, it seems to me, a grasp of political realities and an imaginative sensitivity of a very high order indeed. Imagination was his greatest strength. Without this there can be no genius. But the imagination is an unruly engine requiring a strong governor to control it, and this

[1] Thus, on 16 Dec 1768, according to Rockingham who was in the Commons gallery throughout the debate, Dowdeswell 'entered into the state of this country, *how* it had been distressed by the odious maxims pursued of late – of divide et impera . . . Dowdeswell said – till an administration could be framed on a strong basis etc – He thought an Office in Administration could be no man's ambition. He was sure it could not be the object of an honest man.' (B[ritish] M[useum] Add. MSS. 35430, fo. 139.) There is no hint of this in Sir Henry Cavendish's account (B.M. Egerton MSS. 216, pp. 16–20, printed in *Sir Henry Cavendish's Debates*, ed. J. Wright, 2 vols (1841–3) I 105–6). Again, the complaints made by Bute's son, cited below (p.45 n.2) suggest that the Houses of Parliament were treated to a good deal more denunciation of Bute's involvement in the 'double cabinet' in 1770–1 than is to be found on record now.

[2] For instance, there is a clear distinction between the usage in the letters of Edmund Burke and that in those of Thomas Whately, a follower of George Grenville whose party did not give credence to the myth of the double cabinet. For Burke's formal explanation of a change in usage, see Edmund Burke, *Works*, Bohn ed., 8 vols (1894–1900) I 320.

Burke's nature could not always provide. Imagination could carry him to the heights, as in his appreciation of the nature of the Anglo-American crisis. It could also lead him astray, as in his analysis of the working of the political system in the early years of the reign of George III. Here, however, let me hasten to say, the fault was not merely Burke's. As I shall make clear later, Burke's role was to interpret and restate for public consumption in his own inimitable style a theory in general currency among leaders of the Rockingham party.[1] If there is any criticism to be made of him, it is only that he lacked the clarity of mind to see the grave flaws in the theoretical structure which they and he together had elaborated.

The main public statement of the concept of the king's friends and the double cabinet is contained in Burke's well-known party manifesto, *Thoughts on the Cause of the Present Discontents*, published in April 1770. It had been foreshadowed, however, in February of the previous year, in the last pages of his polemic, *Observations on a Late Publication intituled 'The Present State of the Nation'*. There Burke wrote of ministers not buttressed by the phalanx of party as being 'delivered up into the hands of those who feel neither respect for their persons nor gratitude for their favours; who are put about them in appearance to serve, in reality to govern them; and when the signal is given, to abandon and destroy them in order to set up some new dupe of ambition, who in his turn, is to be abandoned and destroyed'.[2]

In the *Thoughts* this momentary vision is expanded and given the appearance of solid substance. The outlines are etched deep and a wealth of detail is applied to give the light and shadow of verisimilitude. It is postulated that a strange division of authority in central government had taken place. A ring of obscure men, variously designated as 'the court', the 'court faction', the 'king's men', or the 'king's friends', had set up an illegitimate focus of power, by exploiting on the one hand the patronage and prestige of the executive government – the 'influence of the crown' – and on the other the divisions between and within the various groups of politicians.[3] While evading responsibility, they had engrossed supreme direction of policy and an ample share of emolument. This shadowy power-group, Burke alleged, had been steadily at

[1] Pp. 40–1 below. [2] *Works*, I 297–8.
[3] Ibid., pp. 315–16.

work since the beginning of the reign ten years before; and with brilliant ingenuity he dovetailed into a narrative of its progress a whole series of political events which historians have since shown to have had other and very diverse explanations.[1] Good government, he concluded, would only be restored, 'if any considerable bodies of men' had 'honesty and resolution enough never to accept administration unless this garrison of *king's men*, which is stationed, as in a citadel, to control and enslave it, be entirely broken and disbanded'.[2] This was the role cast for themselves by the leaders of the Rockingham party, to whom Burke was counsellor and propagandist-in-chief.

This party myth arose out of two distinct types of circumstance – first, the general conditions of politics about the middle of the eighteenth century, and second, particular circumstances relating to the Rockingham party.

Foremost among the general conditions was the indeterminate interplay, within the system of 'limited monarchy', of the forces concerned with the establishment and survival of administrations. Theoretically the choice of ministers lay with the king. In practice his choice was circumscribed, because men appointed as ministers could not govern without the confidence of parliament. At any given moment the process of government-making reflected the balance between the strength of the king and the strength of the parliamentary politicians. That balance could move appreciably in favour of the one or the other without breaking the confines of the system. If a great part of the politicians could agree among themselves, they might attain a quasi-dictatorial position, as had occurred in the seventeen-forties; but there was nothing inherent in the system to secure to them the continuance of this position, and if anything the fissile tendencies of oligarchical politics worked against it.[3] If, on the other hand, the politicians were divided among themselves, the king's freedom of manœuvre in appointing ministers increased.

[1] Ibid., pp. 317–29. [2] Ibid., p. 371.

[3] For this reason I am doubtful whether there was anything so determinate as a 'drift of the constitution in a certain direction', which Pares suggests was arrested by George III (*King George III and the Politicians*, p. 61). It seems to me more apt to think of oscillations, purely political movements, within the confines of an unchanging and fairly elastic constitutional framework.

At all events – and this is the second of the general conditions – a fragmentation of political groups seems to have begun, for reasons outside the scope of this discussion, before the accession of George III in 1760. This trend was accelerated by the appearance of a new, young king, by the train of events which followed his accession, and to some extent also by a marked change of generation, as older politicians died or retired and younger men came to the fore during the seven-year period of George III's first parliament.[1] This circumstance, together with the fact that there then happened to be no competing member of the royal family who might act as the rallying point of a formidable parliamentary opposition, assured the king an exceptional freedom in choosing ministers. A further consequence was that administrations constructed to secure a sufficiently wide basis of support in parliament suffered even more than usual from the weaknesses to which coalitions are naturally prone.

This party fragmentation coincided with the appearance on the throne of a king anxious to assert and exercise his constitutional rights and duties, and this personal factor tended to exaggerate what may be seen as in any case a natural swing of the pendulum. Thus George III and the less favoured of the politicians looked back with very contrasted feelings upon the circumstances of the previous twenty-five years. Each emphasised the principle favouring their political aspirations, the king the rights of the crown, the politicians, in response, the rights of parliament. Involved in this third general precondition of the Rockingham party myth was the king's personal relationship with the Earl of Bute. The origin and nature of this relationship do not concern us, but its consequences do. For over three years after George III's accession, Bute was the

[1] About the beginning of 1767 Rockingham, leader of the most substantial of the parties in opposition, divided attendant members of the House of Commons into nine different groups, five of which, including his own, were personal 'connections' (Brooke, *The Chatham Administration*, p. 241). On the other side, Lord Northington, the lord president in Chatham's administration, referring only to the personal groupings and conflating those led by the Duke of Bedford and George Grenville, declared: 'There are four parties, Butes, Bedfords, Rockinghams, and Chathams, and we (the last) are the weakest of the four.' (Albemarle, *Memoirs of the Marquis of Rockingham and his Contemporaries*, 2 vols. (1852) II 34.)

only man he felt he could trust. Even after the king was obliged to give up his intimate connection with Bute, he still felt a special obligation towards Bute's brother and other minor politicians and placemen, who had formed a quasi-party round Bute after 1761. They did not constitute a party in the proper sense, for Bute refused to assume leadership and interpose himself between them and the king.[1] After 1763 he withdrew from active politics.[2] However, the 'friends of the king's friend' or 'king's friends' remained a recognisably distinct group till about 1767, and they were privileged to the extent that the king resented and resisted the attempts of ministers to exclude them from office and emolument. After July 1766, when Chatham's complaisance made this no longer a problem, they ceased to be a thorn in the flesh of ministers, and they soon became merged in the broader corps of courtiers and government servants who tended to remain in office regardless of changes of administration.[3]

Within this general political context particular experiences undergone during the twelve months of Lord Rockingham's first administration decisively shaped the thinking of the Marquis and his friends. This ministry, which endured from July 1765 to July 1766, was, like all other ministries of the time, a coalition, and in parliament it rested partly upon the support of minor placemen and private members who belonged to the Bute connection. Although

[1] Bute to George III, [Aug 1766], *Letters from George III to Lord Bute, 1756–1766*, ed. R. Sedgwick (1939) p. 257.

[2] It is clear, however, that for a year or so George III still turned to him as to a sort of father-figure who would bolster up his morale in his dealings with the politicians (ibid., pp. lxv–lxvi). The ministers had ground for irritation at times about this; but it is my impression – though only detailed studies of the kind mentioned above will show this – that the net effects were of little importance.

[3] Despite overlaps and transitions there was a clear separation in men's minds between Bute's king's friends, so long as they preserved any simulacrum of independent existence, and the corps of court and administration, which Rockingham opprobriously dubbed the 'Swiss' (Brooke, *The Chatham Administration*, p. 241). In July 1767 the lord president, Lord Northington, still thought of the 'king's friends' as one of the constituent groups of the Chatham administration and – significantly – as one which might go out with the others into opposition to a Bedford–Rockingham ministry – the last sort of conduct Bute would ever have thought suitable for them (*Autobiography and Political Correspondence of Augustus Henry. Third Duke of Grafton*, ed. Sir William Anson (1898) p. 149).

Bute was now in retirement, the momentum which had kept these men together had not yet subsided. They were still a party; and it was a grievance with some of them that the Rockinghams refused them what they regarded as an adequate share of court preferment.[1] Their cordial support was not secured. On the great American question dealt with by this ministry, the repeal of the Stamp Act, they were by conviction imperialists who thought concessions to the colonists ill-advised; and the king himself was not prepared to demand that they vote contrary to what both they and he himself believed.[2] The Rockinghams felt betrayed by the refusal of the minor place-holders in this group to vote in support of government and resented their self-assertion in various other matters. The normal reaction of ministers faced by a revolt of this kind was to have some rebels dismissed by way of example,[3] but on this point they encountered resistance from the king. In the early part of 1766 George III himself still looked on the old Bute connection as his 'friends', men on whom he could particularly rely, and he feared being left totally at the mercy of the political factions if they were proscribed and as a party destroyed.[4] Behind this attitude lay his deeply engrained conviction that an essential function of his kingly office was the choosing of ministers. This conviction was sharpened by a personal hatred of his late first minister, George Grenville, and a determination, if possible, not to have Grenville forced upon him again.[5] When Rockingham at the beginning of May 1766 refused to broaden his ministry by making a cordial partition of court places with Bute's friends, he himself seems to have thought it virtually doomed to extinction.[6] The king concluded that it could not long survive, declined to show it further positive marks of confidence,[7] and sought to escape the embarrassments of a ministerial crisis breaking upon him unawares by calling in William

[1] *Letters from George III to Lord Bute* p., 247.

[2] Ibid. Rockingham foresaw trouble with them over the repeal of the Stamp Act from the moment this measure was decided (to Charles Yorke, 25 Jan 1766, B.M. Add. MSS. 35430. fos. 37–8).

[3] *The Correspondence of King George III*, ed. Sir John Fortescue, 6 vols. (1927–8) [as corrected by Sir Lewis Namier, *Additions and Corrections to Sir John Fortescue's edition* . . . (Manchester, 1937)] I nos. 333, 335.

[4] *Letters from George III to Lord Bute*, p. 242.

[5] Ibid., pp. 244–5.

[6] Ibid., pp. 247, 249.

[7] Ibid., p. 251.

Pitt. Pitt he found prepared to be more complaisant towards some of Bute's friends, though determined not to treat with them as a party. In this determination George III acquiesced,[1] and this fact marked the start of the disappearance of the king's friends as a recognisable political group just at the moment when they were about to become the stuff of a legend. In bringing about this change of ministry the king seems to have relied on an opinion obtained privately from Bute that, Grenville being ruled out, only Pitt could establish a strong and stable ministry;[2] but Bute played no part in bringing about the arrangements with Pitt that followed.[3]

At this point one other contributory circumstance needs to be mentioned. No one who reads through the correspondence of the Rockingham–Newcastle connection during the later 1760s – especially the voluminous copies which the Duke of Newcastle kept of his own steady stream of letters – can fail to be impressed by the sheer ignorance of fact and the fog of rumour through which its leaders, once they were out of office, were trying to grope towards explanations of events. To give one example: at one moment in September 1766 Rockingham's supporter Lord Albemarle seems to have taken quite seriously an utterly baseless story that Rockingham's dismissal and the formation of the Chatham ministry had been due to pressure from George III's Hanoverian ministers. Frederick of Prussia, it was said, was threatening to foreclose on some Hanoverian territory, if debts he claimed as due to him were not paid. Only the thought of facing the Great Commoner would make him stay his hand.[4] Newcastle, who knew his political world better than the young hopefuls surrounding Rockingham, once wrote a budget of news to the Marquis with the warning: 'I send . . . these reports, not knowing any of them to be true.'[5] But even his fifty years' experience could not prevent him from misinterpreting the facts before him. It is no wonder that the historian familiar with the well-documented situation of the government side may feel that, in reading the correspondence of the opposition, he has somehow strayed into a Looking-Glass world.

[1] Ibid., pp. lxvii–lxviii. [2] Ibid., p. 250.

[3] Ibid., pp. 251–2. The first approaches to Pitt were made on the king's behalf by the lord chancellor, Northington.

[4] Albemarle to Rockingham, 15 Sept 1766, Rockingham MSS.

[5] 17 Dec 1767, B.M. Add. MSS. 32987, fo. 315.

To Rockingham and his immediate associates their removal from office, followed by favours done to one or two of Bute's friends, soon came to appear the effects of an intrigue on the part of the latter, if not on the part of Bute himself. On the eve of their dismissal the Earl of Hardwicke wrote to Rockingham:[1]

> I am surprized your Lordship has not more Court intelligence about the motions and intrigues of Carlton House, and the constant undermining practices of the Scotch *Thane*, who resides as little in the country this summer, as he has done for the 2 last.

And then the next day:

> I suppose you know by this time whence the source of this sudden resolution to send for Mr Pitt has arisen. I presume from that *quarter*, which has and will have the real *interior* influence and *weight* which hurried out the last Ministers, and will the present, let the outward instruments and actors change ever so often.

Subsequently, as the Rockinghams moved into association in opposition with the parties led by George Grenville and the Duke of Bedford, they compared experiences with the leaders of these groups, who, while in office, had had their own quarrels with the Bute connection. They also observed dissensions over policy within the new administration. And so what at first appeared an intrigue began to take on in their eyes the proportions of a conspiracy. Some six months later, in February 1767, another of Rockingham's friends, Sir George Savile, wrote to him:[2]

[1] 10, 11 July 1766, Albemarle, *Memoirs of the Marquis of Rockingham*, I 367, 363, printed in the wrong order; cf. Hardwicke's comments to his brother, ibid., pp. 365–6. Hardwicke, however, did not accept the later interpretations put upon these events by Rockingham, and in retrospect attributed Rockingham's difficulties to maladroitness: 'by his want of management for Lord Bute, he had lost all interest at Court' (ibid., p. 334).

[2] Albemarle, *Memoirs of the Marquis of Rockingham*, II 41–2. The way in which this line of argument was pursued even by members of the Bedford party, who did not follow it through to the same conclusions as the Rockinghams, is reflected in Thomas Bradshaw's report of a speech by Rigby in May 1767: 'Wished [Townshend] had disclosed to the House who was the former of all these short-lived Administrations, and what hidden influence raised and displaced them.' However Wedderburn, a member of the third opposition party led by George Grenville, 'denied the presence of any hidden influence' (*Autobiography of Grafton*, pp. 177–8). James West reported this speech to Newcastle in a similar sense (B.M. Add. MSS. 32981, fos. 375–81).

> You know I always said, with many more, that you – the last set – were humbugged. Granting this, we now have three things which all seem to point one way. G[eorge] G[renville], first; your set, second; and Lord Chatham last (which is precedence in matter of duping), all in turn made to believe that they should be supported; nay, in the last instance, actually ostensibly supported, yet all by hook or by crook let down, either by ineffectual support, or, as the case seems now, by admitting to a show of power on such previous conditions as shall sow the seeds of dissolution in the very establishment of a Ministry.

Five months later the suspicions hinted at by Savile were being restated with the force of an axiom. In July the Rockinghams professed to have discerned the prevalence of 'a political principle which says that the power of the Crown arises out of the weakness of the Administration'. In their view only a complete rout of the Bute group could bring this state of affairs to an end. On that ground Rockingham refused merely to accede to the Chatham ministry, declaring that on those terms his party would still be 'subject to the same power as we had been before'.[1] Commenting

[1] Memorandum by Dowdeswell, 23–4 July 1767, and Rockingham to Hardwicke, 26 July 1767, cited in Brooke, *The Chatham Administration*, pp. 214, 212. A week earlier Rockingham had been writing in letters about the maxim *divide et impera* as occasioning all the confusions of the past six years and the need to root out the 'mischievous power' which had applied it (to Charles Yorke, 18 July 1767, B.M. Add. MSS. 35430, fo. 84; to Conway, 19 July, cited in *The Chatham Administration*, p. 199). Cf. Rockingham's account of Dowdeswell's speech in the Commons on 16 Dec 1768, (to Charles Yorke, 17 Dec 1768, B.M. Add. MSS. 35430, fo. 139). Another echo of this attitude, which was evidently undergoing a process of growth and definition as the politicians talked and wrote, is contained in a letter of 13 July 1767 from Archbishop Thomas Secker to Newcastle: 'Matters go on very well thus far, but the better they go, the less likely they will be to meet with approbation in a certain place. The consequences of so strong an administration will be foreseen; and a negative will be put upon the admission of it; unless there appear to be hope of dividing it. And then all will be as bad as ever.' (B.M. Add. MSS. 33003, fo. 366, printed in Mary Bateson, *A Narrative of the Changes in the Ministry, 1765–1767, as told by the Duke of Newcastle in a series of letters to John White, M.P.* (1898) p. 138). The Duke of Richmond's gloss on this a year later was that 'they [the administration] are never changed but when they are getting strong enough to do the country some real service' (to Newcastle, B.M. Add. MSS. 32990, fo. 332, cited in Alison Gilbert Olson, *The Radical Duke* (1961) p. 27).

on this refusal Burke wrote: 'I am quite satisfied that if ever the Court had any real intention that your Lordship should come in, it was merely to office, and not to administration, to lower your Character, and entirely to disunite the party.'[1] Here the term 'court' was clearly used in that special meaning connoting something separate from and malevolently disposed towards the administration, which is one of the chief characteristics of the double-cabinet theory.[2]

Thus, by the summer of 1767, the essential outlines of the myth of the double cabinet were already in embryo. Some features were yet to be added, but it was only a short step to the full-dress expression of the theory three years later in Burke's *Thoughts on the Cause of the Present Discontents*. Party correspondence during these three years gives some indications of its growth. Up till July 1767 Newcastle looked upon the administration as a Bute–Chatham ministry.[3] As the party's negotiations during that month with Chatham's first lord of the treasury, the Duke of Grafton, made it quite clear that Chatham was out of action, he began henceforth to describe it as a 'Bute administration',[4] and the logical extension of this idea was that Grafton and the other ministers were simply forming a front for Bute. Even Bute's departure abroad could not open Newcastle's eyes; and to him Bute's supposed paramour, the Princess Dowager of Wales, remained a further target of suspicion. In September 1768 he wrote to Rockingham: 'I can make no judgment of the present situation of the Administration, nor even who are the Ministers. I suppose, they are the Duke of Bedford and the Duke of Grafton, as far as they are permitted to act by an Absent Lord and a present great Lady.'[5] Meanwhile Rockingham

[1] 1 Aug 1767, *The Correspondence of Edmund Burke*, ed. T. W. Copeland *et al.* (Cambridge, 1958, in progress), cited below as *Burke Correspondence*, I 316–17.

[2] This is not the first use of the term 'court' in this special sense. It appears previously in a letter from Lord Hardwicke to Charles Yorke of 3 May 1767, and in one from Rockingham of 10 June 1767 (B.M. Add. MSS. 35362, fo. 95; 32982, fos. 279–80). By August, presumably, it was current coin.

[3] E.g. B.M. Add. MSS. 32980, fo. 430; 32981, fo. 2; 32985, fo. 13.

[4] E.g. B.M. Add. MSS. 32985, fos. 39, 65, 70, 358; 32986, fos. 331, 378, 391–2; 32987, fos. 257, 378, 398.

[5] B.M. Add. MSS. 32991 A, fo. 94. Cf. Lord Albemarle's comment on the replacement of Amherst as governor of Virginia by Botetourt just at

himself at the beginning of 1768 was expressing fears 'lest the whole Constitution should be lost and absorbed, by the further extension of the already overgrown influence of the Crown', and was discussing what he then described as 'my ideas' regarding the disfranchisement of revenue officers.[1] He too saw Grafton as little more than a puppet. 'Our home politics', he wrote in May 1769 to a connection at Boston, 'continue amongst us as heretofore an Administration without the confidence of the people and supported by nothing, but from their obtaining the support *of a party*, whose views are arbitrary everywhere and to whom the Administration pay almost implicit obedience.'[2]

Thus when, in June 1769, Burke began to browse systematically over 'the Papers of the system of the last 9 years',[3] it is clear that he approached them with an already established elaborate framework of ideas which had been discussed *ad nauseam* among the leaders of the Rockingham party. Moreover, he had talked over the general scheme of his forthcoming pamphlet with Rockingham while composition was still at an early stage and Rockingham in turn discussed it with others before any draft had reached him. Early in November Rockingham wrote to Burke: 'I know pretty well from the conversations I have had with several – that the Idea totally corresponds as much with their *present sentiments*, as it does with all their *past* conduct.'[4] If ever a pamphlet reflected the thoughts of a party and not merely of its author, it was this; and the purpose of the circulation of a major part of the draft among the leaders during the autumn before its publication was not so much to obtain their agreement to a work originating from his own mind as

---

the time when Bute was setting out for the Continent: 'The E. of Bute who I suppose has given his order to the D. of Grafton upon this unjust, iniquitous act left London yesterday'; and also that of Rockingham: 'I cannot account for Lord Botetourt being made governor etc. but by the desire of Ld Bute – and I can see no other policy in it than in the tenor of his Lordship's constant conduct – which ever has seemed to have in view the extending and keeping up confusion.' (B.M. Add. MSS. 32990, fos. 378, 407.)

[1] To Charles Yorke, 17 Jan 1768, B.M. Add. MSS. 35430, fo. 96. This letter seems to indicate that Rockingham himself was responsible for the development of this idea as a plank of his party's programme over the next fourteen years.

[2] To Joseph Harrison, collector of customs at Boston, 19 May 1769, Rockingham MSS.

[3] Burke Correspondence, II 39–40.

[4] Ibid., 104.

to ensure that he had stated their consensus to their satisfaction.[1]

One of the most striking features of the double-cabinet myth was its comprehensiveness and adaptability. As Burke showed in the *Thoughts*, almost any aberration could be attributed to the machinations of the court party: the resignation of William Pitt in 1761 and of the Duke of Newcastle in 1762; the changes of ministry in 1765 and 1766; the coalition-type nature of all the administrations of the period (all these as applications of the principle *divide et impera*);[2] the attack by Sir James Lowther, Bute's son-in-law, upon the Duke of Portland's territorial and political interest in Cumberland;[3] the ousting of Lord Shelburne from the office of secretary of state in 1768;[4] and the government's mishandling the next year of the affair of John Wilkes and the Middlesex election.[5] All this was generalising from insufficient premises. In these instances the Rockinghams misinterpreted, ignored or were unaware of a whole series of important factors: the cabinet divisions over war and peace after 1760; the retirement of Bute; George III's inveterate dislike of George Grenville, which was a key motive in the ministerial changes of 1765 and 1766;[6] his irritation at their own clumsy

[1] Rockingham and Dowdeswell together went through this draft, while the latter was staying at Wentworth Woodhouse during the latter part of November; it then went to Sir George Savile, who returned it to Rockingham with his comments; and on 23 December Rockingham referred it to Dowdeswell again together with written notes of the observations he had made when they were together. Dowdeswell was asked to pass the whole to Burke and go over the observations with him. 'I wish', Rockingham wrote, 'it was possible that this work could soon make its appearance.' (Savile to Rockingham, Dec 1769, *Burke Correspondence*, II 118–21; Rockingham to Dowdeswell, 23 Dec 1769, Albemarle, *Memoirs of the Marquis of Rockingham*, II 144–5).

[2] *Works*, I 318–19, 325–6, 329–30.

[3] Ibid., p. 326.

[4] Ibid., pp. 339–40.

[5] Ibid., pp. 350–5.

[6] George III's memoranda, *The Correspondence of King George III*, I nos. 100, 139, 142, 140, 141; George III to Bute, [10 Jan, 3 May, 12 July 1766], *Letters from George III to Lord Bute*, pp. 244–5, 248, 250. The prolonged convalescent period of weakness and irritability following the severe attack of porphyria from which the king suffered in the early weeks of 1765 may have contributed materially to worsen his personal relations with Grenville, though these were already not cordial (Richard Hunter and Ida Macalpine, 'A Clinical Reassessment of the "Insanity" of George III and some of its Historical Implications,' *Bulletin of the Institute of Historical Research*, XL (1967) 166–85).

handling of the question of his brothers' establishments in the spring of 1766;[1] the disruptive effect on any ministry of the anarchic personality of Charles Townshend; the lack of confidence between Shelburne and the Duke of Grafton, and the tensions between him and the Bedfords, when they secured a commanding position in the ministry at the end of 1767;[2] and the ministerial concern in 1769 for public order and governmental as well as personal prestige which motivated the campaign against John Wilkes.[3]

Less familiar, because the full documentation has only recently become available, is the way in which Burke, and presumably other members of the party also, applied the concept to the explanation of particular occurrences in the years after the publication of the *Thoughts*.[4] From the year 1770 onwards, the double cabinet furnished a perfect *diabolus ex machina* for any untoward event. For instance, when, early in 1771, the ministry became involved in an abortive struggle with the London printers, backed by the City authorities, over the preservation of the parliamentary privilege of secrecy of debate, here are Burke's comments in letters to one of his oldest private friends in Ireland: 'Carleton House has kicked up one of its annual disturbances, in order to render the

[1] *The Correspondence of King George III*, I no. 319.

[2] Brooke, *The Chatham Administration*, pp. 363–4, 375–83; *Autobiography of Grafton*, p. 220.

[3] Ibid., pp. 195–6.

[4] Here are some further examples from the months after the appearance of the *Thoughts*. Burke to O'Hara, 15 Aug 1770: 'I do not know whether the apparent ministers triumph or not. They may last some time for the interiour managers have nothing to fear from them; and they are in that thorough state of weakness and disunion that answers fully the purposes of their appointment.' Burke to Shackleton, same date: 'As to our affairs they remain as they have been. The people in general dissatisfied. Government feeble, hated, and insulted – but a dread of pushing things to a dangerous extreme, while we are seeking for a remedy to distempers which all confess, brings many to the support and most to a sort of ill-humoured acquiescence in the present Court System of administration.' Burke to Rockingham, 7, 8 Sept 1770: 'I have seen but few people this summer. Among those few, were some of the Courtiers. The Court is fully resolved to adhere to its present System; but that if, contrary to their expectation it should be found impossible to go on with the present instruments, they will send to Lord Chatham, not to your Lordship, or to the Grenvilles.' (*Burke Correspondence*, II 148, 150, 157.)

ministry odious to the publick and subservient to themselves'; and again: 'The Ministers bring on such things they know not how; being impelled forward by powers that they neither see nor understand.'[1] When in 1772 a conflict within the cabinet over land speculation on the Ohio led to the resignation of the colonial secretary, Lord Hillsborough, and his replacement by Lord North's stepbrother, Lord Dartmouth, Burke guessed:

> I am far from sure, that the influence which governs everything, and in order to do so takes care to keep up a ballance of power in the Ministry, did not think, that the Bedford people were already so [too] strong, and that Lord North, who had not a Man in the Cabinet he could call his own, was rather too naked, for that ostensible Lead they give him in publick Business; Now two capital departments both for figure and patronage are on that side, and consequently so much is detracted from the consequence of those other Factions, which are to be preserved in a state of humble existence in the Ministry.[2]

An occasion in May 1773, when North failed to rally a majority in the House of Commons drew the comment: 'He is not a good shepherd and the flock has no regard to his Voice; because he is an hireling, and the Sheep are not his own.'[3] Of the debate in February 1775 on North's conciliatory offers to the colonists, which many government supporters criticised as too generous, Burke wrote: 'They were like to fall in pieces upon it among themselves and would have done it, so as to leave Lord N. in a minority, if Sir Gilbert Elliot had not given the signal of union from powers higher than ministry.'[4] Rockingham read the signs in the same way. In the autumn of 1779 Lord Gower and Lord Weymouth, two chiefs of the Bedford party, resigned from the government on account of North's failure to deal energetically with the pressing problem of Irish trade, seriously crippled by the American War of Independence. This proved, in Rockingham's view, 'that Mr Rigby and Co

[1] *Burke Correspondence*, II 206–7.

[2] Ibid., pp. 327–8. On this episode see Peter Marshall, 'Lord Hillsborough, Samuel Wharton and the Ohio Grant, 1769–1775', *English Historical Review*, LXXX (1965) 717–39, esp. 731.

[3] *Burke Correspondence*, II 435.

[4] *Burke Correspondence*, III 118. Still other examples could be cited from Burke's printed letters of the years 1770–80.

are in no degree in the Secrets of the Interior Cabinet or in the interior recesses of His Majesty's thoughts'.[1] And when a vacant secretaryship of state was filled by Lord Stormont, a nephew of Lord Chief Justice Mansfield, whom the Rockinghams now regarded as one of the secret councillors, Rockingham commented: 'The probability of Lord Mansfield's superintendence will not gain any additional confidence in his support, nor will it be deemed a *new acquisition* of wisdom to his Majesty's *secret* or nominal Cabinet Council.'[2] When North fell and the way to power was at last open in the spring of 1782, Rockingham was still acting on the theory proclaimed in the *Thoughts* twelve years before. He stipulated that the king should not 'mean to preserve any of the persons who had been considered as *obnoxious Ministers*, or of those who were deemed as belonging to a sort of secret system, from which many attributed all the evils of the reign'.[3] So firmly had the conviction become entrenched that for years afterwards Burke continued to attribute the misfortunes of his party to the 'court system'.[4]

I turn now to some premises of the double-cabinet theory. These to my mind have only to be stated to reveal its inherent implausibility. The initial premise was that political conditions of the kind then existing had bred and always would breed a knot of intriguers seeking illicit power. These men, as Burke phrased it in the *Thoughts*, 'thought they now beheld an opportunity (by a certain sort of statesman never long undiscovered or [un]employed) of drawing to themselves, by the aggrandisement of a court faction, a degree of power which they could never hope to derive from natural influence or from honourable service.' This opportunity was linked with the accession of George III. But by insisting on the universality of this tendency Burke, as in other instances, gave the concept flexibility and adaptability and set it free from the immediate circumstances to which it related:

[1] *Burke Correspondence*, IV 161.

[2] Rockingham to Admiral Keppel, 3 Nov 1779, Rockingham MSS., omitted from the letter as printed in Albemarle, *Memoirs of the Marquis of Rockingham*, II, at the foot of p. 388.

[3] Rockingham MSS., cited with slight inaccuracies in Albemarle, *Memoirs of the Marquis of Rockingham*, II 453.

[4] *Burke Correspondence*, V 35, 70, 94, 121–2, 294–5, 445, 448; *Works*, II 259, 274–5.

> It may appear somewhat affected [he wrote] that in so much discourse upon this extraordinary party, I should say so little of the Earl of Bute, who is the supposed head of it. But this was neither owing to affectation nor inadvertence. . . . Where there is a regular system of operations carried on, it is the system, and not any individual person who acts in it, that is truly dangerous. This system has not arisen solely from the ambition of Lord Bute, but from the circumstances which favoured it. . . . We should have been tried with it, if the Earl of Bute had never existed; and it will want neither an active head nor active members, when the Earl of Bute exists no longer. . . . Another motive [Burke added] induces me to put the personal considerations of Lord Bute wholly out of the question. He communicates very little in a direct manner with the greater part of our men of business. This has never been his custom. It is enough that he surrounds them with his creatures.[1]

With the theory formulated in these terms, its supposed validity was not in the least affected when Bute's deliberate, prolonged withdrawal abroad during 1769 and 1770 made it impracticable to continue regarding him as the chief villain of the piece. By December 1770 Burke himself was firmly convinced that Bute was 'no longer the adviser', but that 'his system' had fallen 'into firmer and abler hands'.[2] Henceforth suspicion tended to focus on one member

[1] *Works*, I 317–18.

[2] *Burke Correspondence*, II 176. This view seems to have gained general acceptance. Early in 1772 Bute's eldest son, Lord Mountstuart, wrote to a friend: 'In one respect my father may be more at his ease; he is no longer abused in print, nor tormented with people desiring his interest . . . ambiguous expressions of secret influence, double cabinet, etc. no longer amuse the House of Lords and Commons in the mouths of Lrds Chatham and Mr Burke.' (Namier and Brooke, *History of Parliament*, III 502.) But the cloud of suspicion remained. In a letter of 3 July 1779 soliciting employment abroad, Mountstuart observed to Lord Weymouth: 'You are no stranger to the uncommon and unaccountable dislike that the whole country in a manner either bear or affect to bear to my family, or what (so long as he lives) is the same thing, to my father; it is such that very effectually shuts the door against my rising in the state. The minister durst not do it, or if he would, I cannot suppose him so inclined. . . . I carry from this unpopularity such a pest about me that the Opposition was even alarmed at the idea of my joining them.' (Bath MSS. – I have to acknowledge the kind permission of the Marquess of Bath to make use of this material in his family papers.) In December 1783 Pitt made the excuse

or another of the court and administration circle supporting North's ministry, who had had some kind of contact with Bute when he was a minister in the years 1761–3. By the beginning of 1775 it began to settle upon the hard-working and efficient government servant, Charles Jenkinson, and until the fall of North's ministry seven years later, and even after, opposition politicians tended to regard him as the secret, irresponsible director of events.[1]

It is fair comment at this point that the Rockinghams were not very good judges of the men whom they cast as villains. To carry through over a prolonged period a conspiracy for power of the kind outlined in the *Thoughts* would have required extraordinary force of personality, skill and tenacity. We can only be surprised that the Rockinghams should have thought such capabilities enjoyed by Bute, who had a nervous breakdown after little more than two years in high office; or by Charles Jenkinson, whose character displayed administrative abilities of a high order but who never rose above the second rank because he lacked the exuberant vitality and fertility of resource without which a man cannot become a great politician. But the real implausibility of the Rockinghams' first premise stands fully revealed when it is linked with the two others which formed the essential basis of the whole concept: the hoodwinking of the king and the hoodwinking of the ministers.

During the period when the strands of reflection eventually woven into Burke's *Thoughts* were first being spun out of the experiences of the Rockinghams, it came to be firmly believed that the 'court system' was operating unbeknown to the king. This idea clearly derived from the well-established gambit in opposition politics that the virtuous politicians must rescue the king out of the hands of wicked ministers who were misleading him or holding

for not offering office to Shelburne that 'at present it would not be much more alarming to many to bring Lord Bute forward.' (Thomas Orde to Shelburne, 18 Dec 1783, cited in Fitzmaurice, *Life of William, Earl of Shelburne*, 2 vols (1912) II 284.)

[1] *Burke Correspondence*, III 89; *The Jenkinson Papers, 1760–1766*, ed. Ninetta S. Jucker (1949) pp. xxiii–xxviii. In December 1778 Burke commented ironically upon Jenkinson's appointment to the war office: 'Our New Secretary at War has entered upon the Business of his department. He is a very great, a very grave, and a very gracious Minister.' (*Burke Correspondence*, IV 34.)

him in thrall.[1] In the summer of 1767 Rockingham's own opinion seems to have been rather ambiguous. Reporting a conversation with George III he wrote: 'I said that when I had the honour of being in his Majesty's service, the measures of Administration were thwarted and obstructed by men in office, acting like a corps; that I flattered myself it was not intirely with his Majesty's inclination.'[2] Two years later he had come down more firmly on the side of the king's innocence. Commenting on Junius's celebrated letter to the king of 19 December 1769, he wrote: 'I should have liked it better if the turn had not been so directly to have *charged* his Majesty, but to have *conjured him to think*, and no longer to have *been led*; and in general to have put it on the foot that it was Lord Bute and the Ministers' conduct against whom the public were so exasperated, and not so directly to have attacked his Majesty, whom the public regards only as misled.'[3] A few months earlier Burke, too, had written in terms which implied that matters would be mended if only the king's eyes were opened;[4] and when he described in the *Thoughts* the circumstances which first inspired

[1] Foord, *His Majesty's Opposition*, pp. 240, 261; *Letters from George III to Lord Bute*, pp. xvii–xviii. In July 1767, when Rockingham was associating with Bedford in a joint opposition aimed at overturning the Chatham ministry, Bedford in a letter to him described their groups as parties 'who had lately united themselves together in parliament, to rescue his Majesty and this country out of the hands of the Earl of Bute' (*Correspondence of John, Fourth Duke of Bedford*, ed. Lord John Russell, 3 vols (1842–6) cited below as *Bedford Correspondence*, III 373).

[2] Brooke, *The Chatham Administration*, p. 210.

[3] To Dowdeswell, 23 Dec 1769, Albemarle, *Memoirs of the Marquis of Rockingham*, II 147.

[4] To Rockingham, 2 July 1769: 'I observe, that the Court cares very little what becomes of the people in Ministerial situations; whether they are odious or not; or whether they go through their Business easily and gracefully or struggle with the most embarrassing and scandalous difficulties. What they suffer makes no impression. But I observe them to be much alarmed with whatever is brought directly into the K[ing]'s presence. Nothing can tend more to bring the whole System into disrepute and disgust with him, than to see with his own Eyes and hear with his own Ears the Effect it has upon the people. His feeling in this manner the ill-consequences of the System will, I am persuaded, be the only means of bringing on, that *only* change which can do good, I mean the change of the whole scheme of weak, divided and dependent administrations.' (*Burke Correspondence*, II 41.) Burke was writing to justify a campaign of petitions against the recent seating of Luttrell for Middlesex.

the supposed conspiracy against the constitution, he was careful to draw a distinction between the 'court system' and George III.[1]

Concurrent with this view of the king's position was the idea that the ministers themselves were hoodwinked and led on without their knowledge, were the manipulated puppets of a hidden power. In the *Thoughts* the opinion expressed in 1767 by Sir George Savile, that the Rockinghams and other groups had been 'humbugged', reappeared, elaborated and systematised in Burke's sonorous prose:[2]

> In the beginning of each arrangement no professions of confidence and support are wanting, to induce the leading men to engage. But while the ministers of the day appear in all the pomp and pride of power, while they have all their canvass spread out to the wind, and every sail filled with the fair and prosperous gale of royal favour, in a short time they find, they know not how, a current which sets directly against them; which prevents all progress; and even drives them backwards. They grow ashamed and mortified in a situation, which, by its vicinity to power, only serves to remind them the more strongly of their insignificance. They are obliged either to execute the orders of their inferiors, or to see themselves opposed by the natural instruments of their office.

Rockingham's own short-sighted move in leaving some of his friends in office under Chatham on the assumption that they would form a party cave in the ministry was twisted into a further denunciation:[3]

> When any adverse connexion is to be destroyed, the cabal seldom appear in the work themselves. They find out some person of whom the party entertains a high opinion. Such a person they endeavour to delude with various pretences. They teach him first to distrust, and then to quarrel with, his friends; among whom, by the same arts, they excite a similar diffidence of him; so that in this mutual fear and distrust, he may suffer himself to be employed as the instrument in the change which is brought about....
>
> When such a person has broke in this manner with his connexions, he is soon compelled to commit some flagrant act of iniquitous, personal hostility against some of them, (such as an

[1] *Works*, I 317. [2] Ibid., p. 325. [3] Ibid., p. 326.

attempt to strip a particular friend of his family estate), by which the cabal hope to render the parties utterly irreconcilable.

Very persuasive! But recall at whom it was aimed! No one familiar with the events of 1767 can fail to realise that the second of these passages was directed primarily to a particular address. General Henry Conway had been a secretary of state under Rockingham, and he agreed to continue in office under Chatham. When, a few months later, Rockingham decided the ministry ought to be overthrown, the one step he wanted but could not secure was Conway's resignation; and by the summer Conway's decision to stay in had become a source of bitter vexation. The animus in this passage is readily explained. But could the Rockinghams really believe that Conway, a man hypersensitive about honour and right dealing, would have been cozened in this way? And did they really consider as either dupes or as willing tools the leaders of the Bedford party, who took a predominant part in the administration after 1767, with whom, that summer, they had been prepared to divide the cabinet? Nonsensical as it now appears, they certainly did, but the fact is not flattering to their judgement of men.

One flaw in the original theory they eventually could not help seeing, but this did not shake their faith in it. As the years passed by and the king's eyes clearly were not opened, either by the party's printed propaganda or by its parliamentary campaigns, the Rockinghams seem to have moved towards what was, given their starting-point, the unavoidable conclusion that George III himself was a party to the conspiracy and that the cabinet ministers knowingly and unashamedly made themselves its tools.[1] The American war forced on this development in party thinking because it established, for a prolonged period, an unusual identity of purpose between the ministers and the king himself. Even so, the Rockinghams still saw the secret cabal as the essential feature of a triple-headed foe against which they were pitted.[2]

[1] When Rockingham wrote to Burke in November 1779 that the leaders of the Bedford party were 'in no degree in the Secrets of the Interior Cabinet or in the interior recesses of His Majesty's thoughts' (p. 44 above) he appears to have been coupling the king and the 'interior cabinet' as a single source of policy.

[2] Cf. Rockingham's terms for accepting office in 1782, cited on p. 44 above.

Finally, what were the consequences of this Rockingham party myth? The most important was that with it, and as an integral part of it, went a belief in a need for the party to secure a monoply of power in order to annihilate the supposed court system. This principle was formulated early in 1767.[1] From then on the Rockinghams rejected any idea of taking a share of places in an existing administration and insisted that they could only come into office in a new-formed administration of their own. This object entailed a series of further conditions: the formation of a durable coalition of all the parties in opposition and the reduction of the administration to impotence in parliament. Even if the atttitudes of the parties had made it possible (which it was not) for Rockingham to achieve the first of these conditions, the government-orientated character of eighteenth-century politics and the rudimentary nature of party groupings at that time did not and could not enable him to establish the second. The Bedford party's junction with the Chatham administration at the end of 1767 – later obliquely denounced as unprincipled in the *Thoughts*[2] – decisively reduced the parliamentary forces in opposition, and within a year of its publication, on the death of George Grenville, the members of his party were to do the same. In fact the Rockingham party's mistaken diagnosis of the condition of politics thus led them into a line of action which, in almost any other eventuality except the one which did occur, would have brought them to a political dead-end. There was no future before them. They were pricing themselves out of the political market. They had rejected as useless the more prosaic but realistic way to power of such earlier predecessors in opposition as Carteret or the elder Pitt or of their own more commonsensical contemporaries, the Bedfords. Only an exceptional convulsion, the

[1] By March 1767 Rockingham was determined that if he again came into office he would insist upon having a majority of cabinet posts given to his friends (B.M. Add. MSS. 32980, fo. 450).

[2] 'Those knots or cabals of men who have got together avowedly without any public principle, in order to sell their conjunct iniquity at the higher rate, and are therefore universally odious, ought never to be suffered to domineer in the state; because they have *no connexion with the sentiments and opinions of the people*. (*Works*, I 334.) Only when one has closely followed the story of the relations between the Rockinghams and the Bedfords during 1767 is it possible fully to savour this refined piece of abuse.

disaster of the American War of Independence, saved them from facing the ultimate choice of abandoning their principle or accepting the fact of lifelong exclusion from office.[1]

A second outcome, springing inevitably from the first, was the new insistence which Burke laid upon action by men as a party according to principles of public interest. This is so familiar that little need be said of it here. It is, however, necessary to point out that the claim of the Rockinghams to be the only party acting on principle was partisan and unjustified: the Bedfords, for instance, felt it a matter of principle to uphold British authority over the colonies to a degree which the Rockinghams would never have contemplated; and unfortunately the miscalculations of the Rockinghams enabled them to have their way, with results that future generations have learnt to deplore.[2] The limitation in the new doctrine of party also must be stressed. It was developed as a response to the belief that in a cabinet composed of two or more factions the 'court party' would always be able to dominate by causing contention.[3] Accordingly, its positive aspect did not entail much more than that all the chief cabinet posts should be in the hands of the Rockingham party if it took office. Other groups would be enlisted to give support in parliament and paid their price in posts of dignity which did not confer any responsibility or

[1] This was realised by Charles Fox, who was far more of a realist than Rockingham and his friends – indeed too much of a realist for the country gentlemen to stomach. Once Fox had begun to regard himself as an ally of Rockingham, he tried more than once between 1778 and 1782 to break down the self-excluding barrier which the Rockinghams had erected, urging acceptance of a coalition with some part of the North administration (e.g. Albemarle, *Memoirs of the Marquis of Rockingham*, II 371–4). He urged in vain. The further comment may perhaps be made that in view of the fact that the main corps of Rockingham's party only enjoyed office (in the coalition) for eight months out of the twelve years following his death on 1 July 1782, even the American disaster did not rescue them from the consequences of their misconceptions.

[2] Brooke, *The Chatham Administration*, p. 332. As Newcastle pointed out to Rockingham, the Bedford party's bargain with Grafton in December 1767 made them 'masters of the American Affairs' (20 Dec 1767, B.M. Add. MSS. 32987, fo. 360). Rockingham's preconception had prevented him from seeing that he and his friends might instead have achieved this position.

[3] *Works*, I 325–6.

power.[1] But this programme was not practicable in the 1760s, when the politicians were divided both by personal loyalties and by serious differences over American policy.[2] Even in 1782 Rockingham had to assemble a cabinet half the members of which did not belong to his party. The nearest his associates ever came to success was with the formation of the coalition ministry in 1783, when they were able to capture four out of seven cabinet posts for themselves.[3]

Thirdly, the Rockingham party's double-cabinet concept gave edge to the carefully limited programme of constitutional reform which the party developed between 1768 and 1782. Believing that the influence of the executive on parliament through placemen and through electors was on the increase, the Rockinghams sought to reduce it and redress the constitutional balance. There is much diversity and vagueness in their statements on this subject, but it seems evident, at any rate, that at some periods some of them were

[1] 'It is however false that the idea of a united administration carries with it that of a proscription of any other party. It does indeed imply the necessity of having the great strongholds of government in well-united hands, in order to secure the predominance of right and uniform principles; of having the capital offices of deliberation and execution of those who can deliberate with mutual confidence, and who will execute what is resolved with firmness and fidelity. . . . No system of that kind can be formed, which will not leave room fully sufficient for healing coalitions.' (*Observations on a Late Publication, 'The Present State of the Nation'*, *Works*, I 295.)

[2] What the Rockinghams failed to see was that in the circumstances of the 1760s this project was visionary. They did not accept the consequences of the situation which George III saw clearly enough in the spring of 1766 – that if on the one hand they would not compound with Pitt and on the other they would not compound with Bute's friends, their parliamentary position might become untenable if the latter withdrew into sullen abstention. Nor was it other than disingenuous when they came to assume after 1767 that the followers of Bedford and Grenville were not 'good men' because they had refused the preconditions of a 'healing coalition' – thus abating their pretensions to power (which were no less valid than those of the Rockinghams) and their views of what should constitute public policy.

[3] In 1782 six out of the eleven members of the cabinet did not belong to Rockingham's party. In 1783 Portland, Fox, Cavendish and Keppel formed one party in the cabinet, North, Stormont and Carlisle the other. That Carlisle was reckoned to stand with North at this time is apparent from Fox's undated note to him April 1783 (H[istorical] M[anuscripts] C[ommission], *Fifteenth Report, Appendix*, part VI, *Carlisle MSS.*, p. 635).

concerned not so much with the influence of the executive as such but with its exploitation by the secret cabals which they presumed existed. In this context abolition of sinecures and reform of the household could have as their ultimate purpose the destruction of the lucrative lodgements within the royal establishments, in which, it was assumed the 'king's friends' both took their personal profit and moved the secret levers of power, while remaining screened from responsibility.[1]

Fourthly, if we assume, as seems very justifiable, that British policy towards the American colonies would have followed a much more conciliatory course had the Rockinghams taken the share of office in Chatham's administration open to them in the summer of 1767, then we must conclude that the seed of suspicion, the first burgeoning of the myth, which prevented them from doing so, played its part in bringing about one of the greatest disasters in British history, the bloody quarrel with the American colonists.[2] It was small recompense, on the other side of the scale, that in 1782 their party was available to provide an alternative ministry when the American failures of the North administration destroyed its credit in the House of Commons.

The myth of the double cabinet thus has significance on several counts. However out of accord with the facts known to the men who were in power after July 1766, it became a central, dominating theme in the thought of the leaders of the most important and permanent political grouping in opposition. To them this 'double cabinet' was a real and menacing feature of the political scene in which they acted out their part. Upon their belief in its existence they based their speculations about the causes of particular events. Concern about it motivated their policies and the political strategy and tactics they pursued. As a result they abandoned those possibilities of obtaining office which were inherent in the actual political situation and pinned their hopes to a near-impossibility: the forcing their way into office as a block on an upsurge of parliamentary and public feeling. They hoped that a league of all good

[1] Linked up with this was the whole further corpus of myth which developed during the American War of Independence, to the effect that the 'court' was planning the extinction of English liberties in the colonies and would then exploit colonial resources for the purpose of extinguishing them at home also.

[2] Cf. p. 51 n. 2 above.

men might do the business. But the hard facts of the contemporary political situation were against them. In consequence, they threw away the chance that was in their hands to control the orderly peaceful evolution of Anglo-American relations; and they condemned themselves to a political sterility, out of which it is difficult to see how they could have escaped, had not the North ministry run into disaster over the American War of Independence.

TWO

The Cabinet in the Reign of George III, to 1790

IN 1937 Sir Lewis Namier wrote: 'While the outlines of the eighteenth-century Cabinet have by now been drawn, the detail, which in parts is of decisive importance, has still to be filled in; and the subject calls for a film, perhaps, rather than a picture to render the quick, fleeting changes.'[1] Cabinet practice is notoriously elusive. The more comparisons are made, even from one decade to the next of the period under review, or even within one decade, the more evident it becomes that while certain broad developments stand out, there were also fluctuations and discarded experiments in the working of cabinet machinery, which make the 'still-life' approach particularly inept.

Namier himself left no more than a fragment on what is perhaps the most elusive and the least clearly depicted facet of eighteenth-century government.[2] But the subject has by no means been neglected. A good deal of authoritative historical writing on various aspects of the first half of George III's reign touches in one way or another on the work of the cabinet. In particular, it can only be with trepidation that any scholar ventures to pursue a trail which Richard Pares blazed with such brilliant perspicuity a few years ago. No one reading his *King George III and the Politicians* can fail to be impressed by the marvellous combination of insight and breadth and depth of knowledge, such that some of the most important conclusions seem to be reached as if by instinct, to be emanations from a totality of awareness of the period rather than observations laboriously demonstrated. However this book provides the only full-scale frontal attack on the question in the last twenty years, and its author worked under certain limitations as regards material. On the basis of sources of information which were not available to him and also of more recent published work,

[1] 'The End of the Nominal Cabinet', *Crossroads of Power*, p. 118.
[2] 'The Ford Lectures, 1934, (ii) The Cabinet', ibid., pp. 93–110.

it is possible to modify or correct some aspects of the picture he drew and to amplify others; and there were some features of cabinet development in the later eighteenth century to which he paid little or no attention.

I

By the early years of George III's reign an 'effective cabinet' had completely supplanted the 'nominal cabinet' of earlier years as an instrument of political decision. The 'nominal cabinet' of some twenty members still had a shadowy existence, meeting to hear the text of the king's speech and the criminal reports of the recorder of London, but by 1760 it had become almost entirely divorced from the control of affairs of state.[1] These responsibilities had passed into the hands of a cabinet of between ten and twelve members. This body was larger than the inner councils or *conciliabula* which had been in operation during much of the reign of George II; and though its creation had been due in large measure to political accident,[2] once formed it would seem it was more likely to have the momentum necessary finally to displace the nominal cabinet than would an inner council composed of only five or six ministers. Another factor almost certainly operated powerfully in the same direction. This was the disappearance after 1755 of the lords justices. Virtually identical in membership with the nominal cabinet, the lords justices gave it at times a formal life, almost a legal status, which disappeared when the king of Great Britain ceased to visit his electorate of Hanover.[3]

For the opening five years of George III's reign there is a good deal of further information on the composition and working of the cabinet in collections of minutes and memoranda which were not available when Namier and Pares prepared their Ford Lectures – twenty in the papers of the second Earl of Egremont for the eighteen months (December 1761 to August 1763) when he was

[1] Namier, *Crossroads of Power*, pp. 119–20. 'Almost', because its last flickers of responsible political activity occurred during Bute's ascendancy: see pp. 59–61 below.

[2] See Ian R. Christie, 'The Cabinet during the Grenville Administration', *English Historical Review*, LXXIII (1958) 91–2.

[3] Attention is drawn to this important point in J. P. Mackintosh, *The British Cabinet* (1962) pp. 55–6.

secretary of state,[1] and over twenty in the papers of George Grenville, one or two of earlier date than April 1763, but mostly relating to the two years of his administration.[2] Another four lists of attendance for the end of 1761 and the early months of 1762 can be culled from the political diary of the fourth Duke of Devonshire.[3] From these and one or two other scattered records of attendance and other supporting documents, it is possible to discern certain tendencies in cabinet development beginning to take charge at this period, while others came to a halt.

The Pitt–Newcastle cabinet which was in existence in 1760, and the Bute cabinet into which this gradually evolved during the next two years, were rather larger than average by later-eighteenth-century standards. The reasons were primarily political. Initially the cabinet arose out of a coalition of the forces of Pitt and Newcastle, and each of its leaders insisted upon having the support of a group of friends.[4] After George III's accession the inclusion of Bute made this difficulty worse.[5] At the beginning of 1762, in addition to the three great officers of state, the lord keeper, the lord president, and the lord privy seal, and five departmental ministers, the first lord of the treasury, the two secretaries of state, the first lord of the admiralty and the commander-in-chief, who were the normal core of any later-eighteenth-century cabinet, Bute's cabinet included four political supernumeraries: the Duke of Devonshire (lord chamberlain); Lord Mansfield (lord chief justice); Lord Hardwicke (without any office); and George Grenville who, although holding only the quasi-sinecure office of treasurer of the navy, had been brought in to take the lead in the House of Commons. Bute did not take the opportunity to lessen

[1] Egremont MSS. [P.R.O. 30/47/21].

[2] Grenville MSS. in the possession of Sir John Murray. For some discussion of these see *English Historical Review*, LXXIII 86–91.

[3] I am indebted to the Duke of Devonshire for permission to use this material from the family papers at Chatsworth and to Mr John Brooke for allowing me to consult a copy of this diary in his possession.

[4] Christie, in *English Historical Review*, LXXIII 91–2.

[5] Namier, *Crossroads of Power*, p. 99: 'Newcastle was cowardly and ineffective, Bute was cowardly and inexperienced. Therefore Newcastle had to be attended by his political nurse, Hardwicke, who held no office, and by Devonshire, who was Lord Chamberlain; Bute hoped to find support in Bedford and Mansfield; while Pitt had his "second" in Temple.'

the size of this slightly unwieldy body offered by the withdrawal of Newcastle and his henchmen in the spring of 1762. The old Leicester House politician, Bubb Dodington, now Lord Melcombe, was promoted to it for the last few weeks of his life; and in the autumn, not only was Henry Fox brought in as leader in the Commons, but way was made for Earl Gower, the keeper of the great wardrobe – who seems to have been thought of as the Duke of Bedford's special representative in the cabinet while Bedford was negotiating peace terms in Paris[1] – and another old Leicester House man, Lord Egmont.

With a cabinet of such a size, and handling ticklish negotiations to end a great war, inevitably perhaps small inner groups made their appearance. Sometimes these were quite clearly confidential steering committees, created for political as well as administrative convenience, to deal with diplomatic questions on which secrecy was essential. At certain times Bute headed conclaves of three or four ministers, and it rather looks as if some of the decisions about the negotiations for peace with France in 1762 were made by him and the two secretaries of state alone.[2] During most of March 1762 the initial secret approaches to France through the Sardinian ambassadors, which began the negotiation of the peace of Paris, were handled at meetings of only six or seven ministers.[3] At a later stage they went before meetings of nine or ten.[4] A similar sequence of smaller meetings in July and September was followed by larger gatherings during the autumn.[5] Finally, there are three known meetings during 1762 and early 1763 to which the archbishop of Canterbury was invited, which stand in a separate category.

[1] On 8 Nov 1762 Bedford wrote from Paris, congratulating Gower on being called to the cabinet: 'I shall for my own particular be sure of having by your and Mr Fox's admission three or four friends in the Cabinet who will I hope for the future take care of my interests, and that I may not be again as ill used, as has been my fate, ever since my arrival in this country.' (Granville MSS. [P.R.O. 30/29/1].)

[2] Namier, *Crossroads of Power*, pp. 99–100; *Letters from George III to Lord Bute*, pp. 94, 119, 125.

[3] Cabinet minutes, 5, 9, 18 March 1762, Egremont MSS.

[4] Cabinet minutes, 8, 27, 30 April, ibid.; entry dated 10 April, Duke of Devonshire's political diary.

[5] Minutes for smaller meetings on 24 June, 30 July, 3 Sept; minutes for larger meetings on 22 and 25 Oct, 10 Nov, 2 Dec, Egremont MSS., Grenville MSS., and Egremont to Bedford, 26 Oct 1762, P.R.O. 30/47/5.

A certain degree of confusion among historians as to exactly what body was functioning at any given moment in 1762 is not to be wondered at, since contemporaries themselves had no single view of the matter. When was the full, that is, nominal, cabinet functioning, and when some body of lesser degree? On 2 January 1762 that experienced lawyer, Lord Hardwicke, wrote to the archbishop of Canterbury expressing the view that a meeting on the declaration of war with Spain which the archbishop had failed to attend that day was 'the first strictly proper Cabinet Council that has been summoned a great while, unless for the Recorder's report'.[1] Subsequently the archbishop attended two other meetings, on 10 November 1762 and on 16 February 1763, at each of which ten other ministers were also present.

How should these meetings be regarded? There are one or two other indications that contemporaries drew some distinction between less and more numerous meetings of ministers. It looks as if smaller meetings might be convened by any minister;[2] whereas the senior secretary of state had a particular responsibility for the convening of the cabinet proper.[3] And yet, except for the presence of the archbishop there was no difference in character between the composition of the meetings on 10 November and 16 February and at least nine other meetings between April 1762 and January 1763, for which lists of attendance are known, all of them attended by nine or ten ministers. In letters to the Duke of Bedford of late October 1762, both Bute and Henry Fox referred to two

[1] Lambeth Palace Library MS. 1130/1/no. 87. I am indebted for this reference to Professor R. W. Greaves. Unfortunately no list of those present is known to me.

[2] Devonshire, in his political diary under 6 Jan 1762, noted a meeting of seven ministers, to which he and Newcastle were summoned by Bute.

[3] On Tuesday, 1 June 1762, George III wrote to Bute in connection with a forthcoming cabinet meeting to hear the king's speech: 'I thank my D. Friend for having reminded me of Lord Melcombe, I will not fail to tell Ld Egremont when he comes, for he as segnior Secretary I understand from them both has the office of summoning.' (*Letters from George III to Lord Bute*, p. 112.) The archbishop's summons to the meeting of 2 Jan 1762 (which he did not attend owing to gout) came from Egremont (Lambeth Palace Library MS. 1130/1/no. 86). Earl Gower received from Egremont the notification that he was called to the cabinet (18 Oct 1762, Granville MSS., P.R.O. 30/29/1), and there are several acknowledgements of calls to meetings from various cabinet ministers in the Egremont MSS.

immediately preceding meetings of this kind as 'cabinets' (though Fox also used the term council), and Earl Gower referred to them, all in the space of three or four lines, as 'the effective or rather ineffective cabinet', 'the Council', and 'the Cabinet'.[1] Furthermore, Egremont, the senior secretary of state, does not seem to have recognised consistently any difference of definition between these and meetings of a smaller number of ministers, for his minutes are often docketed 'Minute of Cabinet Council' regardless of whether six or ten ministers were present. It has been suggested that at this time the nominal cabinet was 'a kind of reserve on which the king and his leading ministers could draw for their inner councils when a wider attendance was required',[2] and certainly this idea seems to have been in the minds of some people in the autumn of 1762. But the lists of attendance now available do not suggest that action was being taken on this principle. Henry Fox, Egmont and Gower were all brought into the functioning cabinet that autumn. None of them, before their summons, held a place on the strength of which they might be regarded as being already members of the nominal cabinet: and the correspondence concerning Gower's inclusion gives the impression that he was now for the first time brought into 'the cabinet'.[3] Perhaps, in a muddled way, Bute and his chief colleagues thought that by summoning the archbishop to join the group of working ministers they were in some way convening a body which was a more 'strictly proper' cabinet (as Hardwicke had put it). But these three particular instances of summoning one extra person hardly illustrate a drawing upon reserves. Although the archbishop attended, he could see no point in it – to the minute of the meeting of 10 November 1762 Egremont added: 'Mem:

[1] *Bedford Correspondence*, III 137, 140–1; Gower to Bedford, 25 Oct 1762, Bedford MSS.

[2] Namier, *Crossroads of Power*, pp. 102–3.

[3] On Gower, see p. 58, n. 1. As keeper of the great wardrobe he did not hold one of the great court offices normally associated with the nominal cabinet (see the list in Namier, *Crossroads of Power*, p. 119). Egmont's summons to the cabinet in Nov 1762 was in connection with a proposed reshuffle which would have opened the admiralty for him, and at one moment he believed he had got it (Egmont to Egremont, 20 Nov 1762, Egremont MSS., P.R.O. 30/47/27); but presumably arrangements to provide for Grenville elsewhere fell through, and Egmont became postmaster-general. Henry Fox's office of paymaster-general had no established connection with the cabinet, nominal or otherwise.

The Archbishop of Canterbury said that having no previous knowledge of the negotiation desired not to be comprehended in the advice offered to the king.'[1] In retrospect, whatever the intention at the time, it seems hardly appropriate to regard the meeting of 16 February 1763 as in any real sense the last meeting of the nominal cabinet. Save for the presence of the archbishop this body was the 'effective cabinet', in immediate and continuous lineal descent from 'the Committee of the Cabinet Council to meet on business', which Pitt and Newcastle had established in 1757.[2]

By the time of Bute's resignation in April 1763, it was as if the politicians had become fully accustomed to this form of cabinet organisation. Little change was made in the general structure, though by a natural process the number of members was slightly reduced. The positions of head of the government and spokesman in the Commons were united in the person of George Grenville. With the war over a military representative was no longer needed and the commander-in-chief, Ligonier, dropped out. The Earl of Sandwich replaced Grenville at the admiralty. Otherwise the cabinet remained as before; and as, for the time being, the office of lord president, vacant since the death of Granville in January, was held open, its number was reduced from ten to eight, including the lord chamberlain (Gower), the postmaster-general (Egmont), and the lord chief justice (Mansfield). During the late summer the weight of the honorific offices was reduced, for Egmont moved to the long-coveted admiralty in the reshuffle consequent upon Egremont's death. Mansfield withdrew and was replaced by another eminent lawyer, Lord Marchmont, and Bedford accepted the presidency of the Council. By September Grenville's cabinet had taken its final shape, as a body of eight meeting regularly on business. Midway through 1764, with the addition of the lord lieutenant of Ireland, the number was brought up to nine.

Even although this cabinet was rather smaller than its predecessor, it did not escape the development of concentric circles of confidence. At the outset Grenville and the two secretaries regarded themselves as the members of cabinet who would determine important decisions, and even the king himself referred to 'the

[1] Egremont MSS.

[2] B.M. Add. MSS. 32997, fo. 207; see p. 56 above.

Triumvirate'.[1] After four months Egremont's death broke up this formation, but by the beginning of 1764 a new inner ring had emerged, composed of Grenville, Bedford and the two secretaries of state, and its existence was formalised by the institution of a weekly dinner.[2] So far as business was concerned, however, this body remained an informal one. It never seems, for instance, to have put its views on record in formal minutes. The incomplete but probably representative collection of memoranda and minutes giving lists of attendance preserved in the Grenville papers indicates that the whole cabinet of eight or nine met regularly, and that except for the lord keeper, who did not get on with his colleagues, the attendance of individuals was also regular.[3] The institution of the weekly cabinet dinner, for which perhaps the convivial Sandwich was mainly responsible, helped to give a sustained existence to it, at a time when there was far less pressure of business to bring it together than there had been during the Seven Years War.[4]

Rockingham's first cabinet of 1765–6, initially with eight members and later with nine, made no departure from the pattern of the two previous years, and at first Chatham's cabinet, with nine members, continued in the same mould. However, Grafton's recruitment of the Bedford party in January 1768 forced the number up to eleven, for a third secretaryship of state was created for Lord Hillsborough, and General Conway, displaced as secretary by another Bedfordite, remained a member though no longer holding

[1] *Letters from George III to Lord Bute*, p. 228 and n.; Namier, *Crossroads of Power*, pp. 103–4.

[2] This dining arrangement was instituted on Sandwich's initiative at the end of January 1764; see *The Grenville Papers*, ed. W. J. Smith, 4 vols, (1852–3) II 256, 489 (the editor's comment on the first of these pages is misconceived).

[3] These documents are printed in *Additional Grenville Papers, 1763–1765*, ed. J. R. G. Tomlinson (Manchester, 1962) pp. 317–38, and a further minute, of 5 Apr 1765, appears in two printed collections, from different copies (*Grenville Papers*, III 15–16, and *The Correspondence of King George III*, I no. 48).

[4] An exchange of letters between Grenville and Halifax early in 1765 attests the concurrence at that time of both series of dinners, that of the inner ring of four ministers then normally taking place on a Thursday, while the cabinet dinners took place on Sundays (*Additional Grenville Papers*, pp. 244–5).

a cabinet office.[1] The first step to check this trend was taken when Chatham resigned the following autumn, when Grafton stipulated, as a measure to keep numbers down, that his successor as privy seal should not be in the cabinet.[2] The same argument provided Grafton himself with a tactful excuse when, in 1771, he succeeded Lord Suffolk in this office, but did not have enough confidence in the other ministers to wish to be associated with the direction of policy.[3] In 1770 Grafton's retirement enabled the two cabinet posts of first lord of the treasury and chancellor of the exchequer with the lead in the Commons to be united in the hands of a Commons' man, Lord North. About the same time the resignations of the military representatives, Conway and Granby, without replacements reduced the number of cabinet ministers to eight. The cabinet now consisted of the first lord of the treasury, the three secretaries of state, the lord chancellor, lord president, lord privy seal, and the first lord of the admiralty. Between 1771 and 1775 Grafton's refusal to sit as lord privy seal in cabinet reduced the number to seven; and it was this exceptionally small group that dealt with the early stages of the American revolutionary crisis in 1774–5. In 1775 the number increased to eight again, when Lord Dartmouth insisted upon taking the privy seal when he gave up the American department,[4] and his long tenure up to 1782 may have helped finally to fix the character of this office as a cabinet post. With the addition of a commander-in-chief in 1778 the number in the cabinet rose once more to nine, at which it remained till 1782.

After the fall of North, political pressures forced a brief return to something like the Bute pattern – a large cabinet with eleven

[1] Conway was lieutenant-general of the ordnance, second in command there to Lord Granby, who had been brought into the cabinet by Chatham and who continued to attend, though only irregularly, till 1770.

[2] George III to Lord North, 11 June 1771, *The Correspondence of King George III*, II no. 964.

[3] Ibid.; *Autobiography of Grafton*, p. 264. Lord Suffolk as lord privy seal in 1770–1 seems to have been in the cabinet. He certainly attended on the one occasion in this period for which a list of attendance is known (cabinet minute, 7 June 1771, Granville MSS., P.R.O. 30/29/3).

[4] On Dartmouth and the privy seal in 1775 see *The Correspondence of King George III*, III nos. 1740–6, 1748–50, 1752, 1755. Perhaps with the precedent of Bute in mind, Dartmouth rejected the king's proposal that he should retain his place in cabinet with the office of groom of the stole.

members. The political leaders who had been in opposition to North – Rockingham, Shelburne and Grafton – all wished for support and also recognition by the inclusion of their friends, and the appointment of a peer to the treasury made necessary the presence of a chancellor of the exchequer in the Commons, an addition which cancelled out the abolition of the colonial secretaryship.

The change of ministry in July 1782 made no change in the structure of the cabinet. It was a remarkable achievement of the Fox–North coalition in April 1783 to re-establish a small cabinet reminiscent in structure of that which had existed in the early years of North's own ministry. The departments represented in this cabinet were the treasury, the exchequer, the two secretaryships of state and the admiralty, with the great offices of lord president and lord privy seal. There was no lord chancellor: as the great seal was left in commission, power in this cabinet was concentrated once more in the hands of seven ministers. Save for the appointment of a lord chancellor in December 1783, the younger Pitt made no change in the general form of the cabinet, and its number was restricted to eight until after 1790.

Whereas in Bute's period of power household offices might still be associated with membership of the cabinet, by 1790 this was the case no longer. This development is one of the more obvious indications of the breaking of the links between the central directing body in the state and the old nominal cabinet. Bute himself had become a cabinet minister while groom of the stole, and Gower sat for two and a half years in the Bute and Grenville cabinets as keeper of the great wardrobe and then lord chamberlain. It seems likely that Dartmouth's refusal of the stole in 1775 was symptomatic of a change of outlook among the politicians; and after 1765 there was only one isolated instance of a household officer making a brief appearance in the cabinet – the Duke of Rutland, as lord steward in February and March 1783. Possibly personal factors may have contributed to associate two other posts with the cabinet. On several occasions leading ministers wanted to attach friends with military interests to their group in the cabinet. To this may be attributed the inclusion first of Lord Granby and then of the Duke of Richmond as masters-general of the ordnance (1766–70, 1782–3, 1784–95). Shelburne's concern to obtain a place for his legal friend,

John Dunning, now made Lord Ashburton, in 1782, led to the chancellor of the duchy of Lancaster being a cabinet minister, and this useful precedent was to be exploited by Pitt in 1791.[1] In general, between 1760 and 1790 the attitude had gained ground that, with the exception of the three great offices of state,[2] ministers in the cabinet should have active departmental responsibilities.

Although there were caves and factions at odds in the cabinets of the years 1766 to 1783, there seems to have been no return to the situation of concentric circles of confidence to be found in the cabinets headed by Bute and Grenville. A certain formal precedence was conceded to the head of the treasury and the secretaries of state. For instance, the office instruction about the circulation of papers coming into the northern department in the early 1770s restricted to these three the circulation of secret and confidential dispatches and reports.[3] But while it is likely that business sometimes received preliminary discussion at this level, there was no revival of an inner cabinet. The small size of the cabinet itself militated against this; so also, probably, did the faction divisions which often separated the secretaries of state from each other or from the head of the treasury.[4] In fact, in periods of crisis the cabinet as a whole was in constant control of developments. Detailed study of the government's reaction in early 1774 to the Boston tea-party shows the issues being handled at a series of meetings of the full cabinet – one at the end of January, five during February, and three more during March.[5] Even with a large cabinet and a ticklish peace negotiation in progress during 1782, when, if at any time, some of

[1] As head of the board of trade Lord Hawkesbury was given the duchy in 1786. He was brought into the cabinet in 1791.

[2] The offices of lord chancellor, lord president, and lord privy seal.

[3] K. Ellis, *The Post Office in the Eighteenth Century* (1958) pp. 152–3. The colonial colonial secretary was omtted from this circulation.

[4] On this see Pares, *King George III and the Politicians*, pp. 167–71.

[5] Cabinet minutes of 29 Jan, 4, 5, 16, 19, 28 Feb, 1 Mar, and notes of an agenda for 10 Mar, Dartmouth MSS., William Salt Library, Stafford; cabinet minute of 30 Mar 1774, Sandwich MSS., cited in C. R. Ritcheson, *British Politics and the American Revolution* (Norman, Okl., 1954) p. 161. For a full detailed study of the cabinet's activities during these weeks, see Bernard Donoughue, *British Politics and the American Revolution: The Path to War, 1773–75* (1964) pp. 34–72.

the features of cabinet life in 1762 might have been expected to recur, the records show no sign of a division between an inner ring of ministers and the rest. For this period there are particularly full files of cabinet minutes and memoranda, with lists of attendance, those of the king[1] being supplemented by the collections of Fox[2] and Grantham.[3] Rockingham's cabinet is shown by these to have been assembled at least fifteen times during the weeks from 28 March to 23 May 1782. Shelburne's cabinet had at least twenty-six meetings between 12 July and 19 December. For most of these meetings lists of attendance exist, and it is clear that while a few ministers took summer leave in August, their attendance was almost, if not completely, regular during the four crucial months which followed. The shifting peace terms were discussed *ad nauseam* and on one or two points, notably the proposed cession of Gibraltar, Shelburne was forced to yield his initial schemes in face of the general disapproval of his colleagues. On 3 December one cabinet meeting lasted for eight hours.[4] The cabinet minutes and the supporting correspondence[5] all indicate that there was full cabinet consultation at each major stage in the negotiation, that efforts were made to inform one or two ministers who were absent from particular meetings, and that no independent action beyond the essential needs of carrying on negotiations was taken by an inner ring.

Regularity and system are hall-marks of healthy governmental institutions. How far did the later-eighteenth-century cabinet measure by these standards?

Information about dates of meetings of the cabinet is extremely

[1] *The Correspondence of King George III*, v and vi *passim*.

[2] B.M. Add. MSS. 47559, which also contains Fox's correspondence with George III during 1782 and 1783, much of it duplicating *The Correspondence of King George III*.

[3] Grantham MSS., Bedford R.O. Grantham's copies of cabinet minutes are in bundle L 29 and include some items not now in the king's papers.

[4] *The Correspondence of King George III*, vi no. 4005.

[5] Correspondence between the members of Shelburne's cabinet in the papers of Shelburne (Lansdowne MSS. at Bowood), Grantham (Bedford Record Office), Grafton (West Suffolk Record Office, Bury St Edmunds); their correspondence with George III (*The Correspondence of King George III*, vi *passim*); and Grafton's own account in his *Autobiography*, pp. 346–54, which shows signs of having been written up from memoranda made at the time.

uneven. Sometimes it is full, at others scarce. However there is sufficient evidence to suggest that cabinet meetings were both regular and frequent. Thus, in the year 1762, for which the records are fairly good, dates of twenty-six meetings have been ascertained, including a number of meetings of six or seven ministers which Lord Egremont considered were meetings of cabinet. During one of the periods of greatest pressure, in March and April, there were eleven meetings within eight weeks. Evidence for a three-month period in the winter and early spring of 1768 indicates at least eleven meetings, and there were about the same number recorded for a similar period in 1774. The latter part of the period of the American War of Independence is more fully documented. There were at least twenty-one meetings in the first five months of 1778, twenty-eight during the second half of 1780, forty-five during the year 1781, and forty-six during the year 1782 (all but five of them after the formation of the Rockingham administration on 27 March). For certain limited periods the known records sometimes show an extraordinary frequency of meetings. There were eight during March 1778, five of them in a period of six days. There were nine during January 1781: two of these took place on one day. The Rockingham cabinet met seven times at least in April 1782 and another seven times in May. Between 12 July and 5 September 1782 Shelburne's cabinet held at least fourteen meetings, and on two of these days there may in fact have been two successive meetings.

This may be termed 'the argument from the maximum'; and for very few years in the period is it possible to pin down exactly a large number of days when the cabinet met. However, the problem can also be approached in another way. At least from early 1764, some time in Grenville's ministry, the system of weekly cabinet dinners was introduced, and also another series of weekly dinners for the inner ring. The days on which these were held are not known, save in one or two instances; but this information, taken together with the fact that the first four cabinet meetings of 1764 for which dates were known all took place on Tuesdays (2, 9, 23 Feb, 20 Mar), suggests that a custom of weekly meetings had become established. The spring of 1765 yields traces of a similar kind: of the four meetings known, those of 5 and 26 April were both held on Fridays, those of 22 May and 12 June both fell on Wednesdays. Such dates of meetings as are known suggest that no such regularity was observed for several years after the fall of Grenville's ministry, but at some stage which cannot be determined during North's administration, the system of weekly meetings was re-established. There is a hint of this in early 1774, when a string of meetings occurred on Fridays (29 Jan, 5 and 19 Feb). In the first five months of 1778, eight out of twenty-one known meetings took place on Saturdays, and so did six out of the nine known for the first half of 1779. The recorded meetings in the first half of 1780 are few; but in the summer and autumn of that year, over a period of five months, nine out of eighteen took place on Thursdays. Throughout the well-documented year 1781 the evidence is much less open to doubt. Out of seven recorded days of meeting in January, only one fell on a Saturday, but from February till June eleven out of sixteen known meetings took place on that day. In the second half of the year the day was changed: from 12 July to 8 November, ten out of fifteen known meetings took place on Thursdays. Of the six meetings in December five were held on Saturdays, and in January 1782 the cabinet reverted to Thursdays, holding meetings on the third, tenth and seventeenth. Not only is a standing arrangement of weekly meetings evident during the later years of North's administration, but it is clear that this regularity was connected with the cabinet dinners, which were business meetings.[1] Thus, in the summer of 1780 a meeting on 3 August 'at Ld Amherst's' was followed

[1] For instance Sandwich to North, 6 Mar 1778: 'As you say in your letter . . . that you join with me in opinion that our military preparations should be pressed with great diligence, and that you are ready to have our naval situation discussed in the cabinet without delay, I conclude you mean that should be part of our business at our dinner tomorrow.' (*The private papers of John, Earl of Sandwich, First Lord of the Admiralty, 1771–1782*, ed. G. R. Barnes and J. H. Owen, 4 vols (1932–8), cited below as *Sandwich Papers*, I 349.) In Sept 1779 Germain considered that a dinner meeting might reach a final decision on the question whether North America or the West Indies was to have first priority, but that if the business were not finished he would propose a meeting for the next morning, when the ministers would be less sleepy than after dinner (H.M.C., *Knox MSS.*, p. 162). On 24 June 1779 George III instructed Weymouth to bring up a point of military business at the dinner that evening (*The Correspondence of King George III*, IV no. 2681); see also his letter to Sandwich, 16 Dec 1781 (*Sandwich Papers*, IV 206).

on 10 August 'at Ld Sandwich's'. Dartmouth played host at the next known meeting which, unless the minute (as occasionally happened) was dated the morning after, took place on Friday 18th. The host at the meeting on 24 August is not known; at the next recorded meeting (also on a Thursday – 14 Sept) it was Germain. In the following year, 1781, a similar variation of the place of meeting can be traced through the cabinet minutes of February and March, and again from 30 August to 27 September. Meetings outside this weekly sequence were held as required, either in the ministers' houses or in their offices. In a case of urgent diplomatic business on 6 September 1781 a meeting was held in the morning although a routine meeting was to take place later in the day, both meetings giving rise to cabinet minutes.[1]

Except for the lord chancellor there was a complete break in the personnel of the cabinet when North resigned in March 1782, and departures of practice in more than one respect are evident. The custom of the weekly meeting was one of the casualties. Nor was it reintroduced for some time. The irregularity in the dates of meetings of Shelburne's cabinet of July 1782 and of the coalition cabinet which succeeded it the following spring makes it clear that there was no return to the system. Although its strength and convenience are obvious, none of the governments of 1782 and 1783 lasted long enough to come to terms with this fact; and the urgency of business imposed a need for so many and frequent meetings on the cabinets of both Rockingham and Shelburne that a return to it was the less likely. It is less easy to be sure about practice after December 1783. For the period from then up till the end of 1790 materials on the meetings of Pitt's cabinet are particularly scanty.[2] Dated meetings in close sequence are rare: three in nine days in January 1785;[3] three on three successive days in mid-October

[1] For this case, see *The Correspondence of King George III*, v nos. 3405–8.

[2] There are only eighteen cabinet minutes known for this period (printed in *The Later Correspondence of George III*, ed. A. Aspinall, vol. 1, *December 1783 to January 1793* (1962).) Mr J. Ehrman has told me that his detailed study of Pitt's administration during these years has thrown up references to only sixty-six meetings, exclusive of dinners, a few of these being proposals for meetings which may not in all cases have taken place.

[3] *The Later Correspondence of George III*, pp. 121, 126–7.

1787;[1] seven during the regency crisis, on 27 and 29 November and 1, 3, 6, 7 and 8 December, the first of which was an extraordinary assembly at Windsor to advise the Prince of Wales and the third an instance of this cabinet holding a dinner meeting for discussion of business.[2] However, at least for a period, Pitt's cabinet had adopted, within little over two years after its formation, a routine more exacting than any to be traced earlier in the reign, meeting regularly every Tuesday at one o'clock and every Friday at half past eight in the evening.[3] One might perhaps read into this change the implication that the members of the cabinet were already used to meeting regularly once a week but felt this to be insufficient in the existing circumstances; but the evidence is too thin for any firm conclusions to be drawn on this point for the whole period 1784–90.[4]

To the extent that the cabinet did meet regularly according to a predetermined routine, the questions who called it and how business came before it assume a lesser importance. Great numbers of papers were sent round to its members as a matter of course.[5]

[1] Ibid., pp. 342–3. Carmarthen's note of 5 p.m., 12 Oct 1787 to the king clearly implies, I think, that the cabinet had already looked that afternoon at the dispatches they intended to discuss more thoroughly on the thirteenth. Earlier in the year, too, so Lord Hardwicke learned from his correspondent, Aust, there had been almost daily meetings on the Dutch question (13 June 1787, B.M. Add. MSS. 35625, fo. 83).

[2] *The Diaries and Correspondence of . . . George Rose*, ed. L. V. Harcourt, 2 vols (1860) pp. 89, 91; *Political Memoranda of Francis, Fifth Duke of Leeds*, ed. Oscar Browning (1884) pp. 119–32.

[3] Carmarthen to George III, 30 Jan 1786: 'Lord Carmarthen begs leave . . . to transmit the papers . . . to your Majesty with the least possible delay, on account of the very interesting letter No 1 from Mr Liston, a copy of which Lord Carmarthen has directed to be made out for Mr Pitt, by which means the very important matters contained in it may be taken into consideration tomorrow, your Majesty's confidential servants having agreed to meet regularly every Tuesday at one o'clock, and every Fryday at half an hour after eight in the evening.' (*The Later Correspondence of George III*, p. 208.)

[4] 31 Jan 1786 (see previous note) was a Tuesday. The only other meeting for which a date is known to me during this year was also held on a Tuesday (17 June). Two of the three known meetings in the first half of 1787 also took place on Tuesdays (20 Feb, 5 June). But this evidence, which is suggestive, is too thin to be a basis for generalisation.

[5] Papers of this kind are to be found, for instance, in the Dartmouth MSS., and the Granville MSS. for the middle years of North's administration. On 7 Feb 1775 the Duke of Richmond observed in the House of

In addition, when important business came up in a minister's department, he would send out copies of papers and invite comment from colleagues unable to attend.[1] With the full emergence of the efficient cabinet as the only effective cabinet, any official function of summons which may have been exercised by the senior secretary of state fell into disuse. Any member who found urgent business arising could call it together.[2] In theory business was only referred to the cabinet if the king approved a minister's suggestion that this course be followed (or suggested it himself): there was no right of discussion with a view to a recommendation if neither king nor minister saw the necessity.[3] The formalities were fairly regularly observed; but whether the restriction meant much is another question. Throughout this period there were numerous important questions of diplomacy and war which no minister would have taken upon himself, or over which it would have gone

---

Lords: 'The correspondence with our foreign ministers, at a convenient time, is sent round in little blue boxes to the efficient cabinet ministers . . . each of them give their opinions on them in writing.' (*The Parliamentary History*, ed. Cobbett and Wright (1806–20) XVIII 278.) See also p. 65, n.3.

[1] For instance, in Nov 1772, Rochford circulated a memorandum on the general diplomatic situation, which from its style was clearly intended as a basis for vital decisions about foreign policy. Copies exist in the papers of Lord Dartmouth (Dartmouth MSS.) and of Lord Sandwich (*Sandwich Papers*, I 30–2).

[2] Camden to Gower, acknowledging a summons, 19 Apr 1768, Granville MSS., P.R.O. 30/29/1; Hillsborough, sending a summons to Gower, 13 July 1768, ibid., P.R.O. 30/29/3; Suffolk, acknowledging a summons from Dartmouth, 9 Jan 1775, North sending to Dartmouth, 10 Feb 1778, North to Dartmouth, stating Weymouth had sent out cards, 17 July 1778, Suffolk sending a summons to Dartmouth 14 Oct 1778, Dartmouth MSS. A letter from John Robinson to Sandwich dated 19 June 1779 makes it clear that North did not regard this as any part of his duty as 'the Minister': 'Lord North also thinks that there should not be a moment's time lost in the orders to be sent out to Sir Charles Hardy, and he says that he thinks you might collect a cabinet to consider this at St James's today.' (*Sandwich Papers*, III 24.) See also North to Sandwich, 21 July 1776, 27 Apr 1778 (ibid., I 214, II 35–6). It will not escape observation that these three notes imply that the ruling consideration was that one or more members wanted a meeting, therefore there would be one: leave from the king is not mentioned and it was evidently taken for granted that it would be given.

[3] For illustrations of this point, see Pares, *King George III and the Politicians*, p. 153.

hard with him among his colleagues had he tried to do so. For a minister to call a cabinet and refer business to it before taking the royal pleasure was contrary to rule. Known cases in this period are few and usually urgent. For this reason, perhaps, they seem to have passed without protest from the king;[1] but an attempt by Fox to raise a minor matter in this way soon after the formation of the Rockingham ministry of 1782 drew his adverse comment.[2] It seems likely that in many instances a minister made an arrangement with the king that in certain eventualities, such as the arrival of expected dispatches, he might, without further reference, bring the matter up at the next meeting, or call one specially for the purpose. It was probably in circumstances like this that the task of sending out the cards was delegated to an under-secretary.[3]

When the cabinet met it was the task of the minister (or ministers) concerned to set forth the business on which a decision, in the form of advice to the king, was required. His was the responsibility to propose a course of action if one was needed. After the business had thus been opened, the other ministers by a well-established

[1] North seems to have submitted the complaint of the opposition peers about the proposed Irish absentee land tax to the cabinet and sent back its answer without previous submission to the king in either case (*The Correspondence of King George III*, III nos. 1310, 1314). On 2 May 1776 Germain seems to have summoned a cabinet to consider newly arrived American dispatches and simply told the king: 'Lord George wishes to know the opinion of the cabinet, to be submitted to your Majesty, whether any alteration should be made in the destination of the Hessians.' (Ibid., III no. 1859.) Similar action is on record in 1778 by Weymouth (ibid., IV no. 2907, misplaced by the editor), in 1781 by Hillsborough and by Stormont (ibid., V nos. 3234 and 3340); by Sydney in 1785 (*The Later Correspondence of George III*, I 170), by Carmarthen in 1787 (ibid., p. 343). In June 1790 Chatham, as the only minister in town, seems to have convened a meeting on his own responsibility when Carmarthen's under-secretary went to him with urgent dispatches (B.M. Add. MSS. 28066, fo. 55). Most of the later cases were matters of urgency.

[2] George III to Shelburne, 29 Apr 1782, *The Correspondence of King George III*, V no. 3700.

[3] J. Pownall, endorsement on a letter from Sir Stanier Porten, 30 Nov 1774, Dartmouth MSS., cited in M. M. Spector, *The American Department of the British Government, 1768–1782* (1940) p. 47; P. O. Hutchinson, *Diary and letters of . . . Thomas Hutchinson*, 2 vols (1883–6), cited below as *Hutchinson Diary*, I 467–8, under 12 June 1775; on this occasion Dartmouth, if he had indeed given discretion to Pownall, seems to have regretted that it was used.

rule spoke in turn, beginning with the youngest.[1] There is little evidence that anyone played a chairman's role. Certainly North did not.[2] If anyone ever gave attention to the point, they may have thought it was normally a task for the lord president, for one or two ministers at any rate, in this period, thought of the cabinet as a committee of the privy council;[3] but such few descriptions as exist suggest that there was the least possible formality.

Most of the business dealt with by the cabinet fell within one or other of three or four fairly well defined categories, though there was some overlapping between them. A great deal of time was taken up with diplomatic business. Questions affecting the armed forces arose in peace time, partly in connection with foreign policy, partly in relation to colonial affairs; and in war time the number of meetings summoned to deal with questions both of strategy and defence administration increased very greatly. Colonial matters came before the cabinet from time to time, and these loomed larger as the crisis approached in the relations between Great Britain and the American colonies. The affairs of Ireland engrossed its attention almost continuously during the autumn and winter of 1767–8, and required discussion again on a number of occasions, notably in 1779 and in the opening weeks of 1785. Apart from these main fields of government activity, the cabinet dealt at times with a great miscellany of subjects: the proposed regency bill of 1765; John Wilkes and public order in 1768; the general election of 1774 and one or two of those which followed; the execution of press warrants in the City of London in 1776; the king's conduct in response to petitions from the City, from Lord

[1] *Autobiography of Grafton*, p. 230; H.M.C., *Various Collections*, VI, *Knox MSS.*, p. 272.

[2] North's habit of dozing in cabinet was notorious. William Knox, under-secretary in the colonial department, gave an account, which sounds almost too highly coloured to be true, of one cabinet meeting, when the country was on the verge of war with the United Provinces, at which North, Bathurst and Hillsborough all slept through the proceedings (H.M.C., VI *Knox MSS.*, p. 271).

[3] Rochford to Gower, 11 July 1772, Granville MSS., P.R.O. 30/29/1. Earl Gower declared in debate, in November 1779, that 'he had presided . . . for some years at The Council-table', in what is fairly clearly a reference to the cabinet (John Almon, *The Parliamentary Register*, XV (1780) 99–100)

George Gordon and so on. The affairs of the East India Company were certainly considered in cabinet in the early part of 1767. Presumably they were also before it on later occasions; though the available evidence for the legislation of 1773, for instance, puts stress not on any cabinet discussion but on the work of parliamentary committees. At times the defence of the Company's trading interests involved more general questions of diplomacy.

It is impossible to define any scale of impoıtance of questions which might or might not be discussed. Evidently ministers worked to some sort of yardstick. In 1775, when the Earl of Bristol challenged Lord Sandwich in the House of Lords to say whether he would feel justified in sending the whole force of ships of the line immediately available to relieve Gibraltar should the Spaniards attack it, Sandwich made answer:

> I can hardly think myself enabled, from my official situation, to answer the . . . question. That is a matter of state, not, in my opinion, at all connected with the immediate business of my department. If I was ordered to comply with such a requisition, I must certainly obey it; whatever might be my own private opinion, my sentiments in this House, or the arguments I might use elsewhere, when it came under deliberation as a matter of state. . . . The question would not turn on what I, in my official capacity, wished to do; but what the majority of his Majesty's servants had really decided.[1]

An agenda drawn up for the colonial secretary, Lord Dartmouth, before an interview with George III, illustrates again the distinction between the two types of business. The first six memoranda it contained concerned items on which Dartmouth considered it necessary to ask the king if the 'sense of the cabinet' should be taken: they included the withdrawal of British troops from Kaskaskia, the bishop of Quebec's appointment of a coadjutor, a report on the state of the fortifications at Placentia, the running by the Virginians of a boundary line which encroached upon the hunting grounds of the Cherokees, a crisis between a governor and his council, and a dispute between the Africa merchants and the Dutch West India Company. There followed six items which Dartmouth evidently did not consider appropriate for the attention

[1] *Parliamentary History*, ed. Cobbett and Wright, XVIII 670–1.

of the cabinet: approval of the dissolution of a colonial assembly and the issue of writs for new elections; and a series of colonial appointments, ranging from a new governor and lieutenant-governor of Barbados to a solicitor-general in the same colony.[1] Circumstances could bring important appointments into the category of 'matters of state'. The cabinet dealt with the establishment of three admiralty judgeships in North America in 1767,[2] though not, so far as is known, with the filling of the actual appointments. However, it was suggested to Lord Sandwich on one occasion that appointments of fleet commanders should not be made 'without the approbation of the cabinet', since several appointments had been the cause of disquiet.[3]

In general the cabinet seems to have dealt direct with business initiated by one of its members. There is no evidence of any standing committees on particular types of business and only one or two instances of an *ad hoc* committee dealing with some particular item. In 1769 a comprehensive survey of defence problems in Newfoundland, Nova Scotia and the West Indies was undertaken by the colonial secretary and the three service ministers in the cabinet, with the secretary-at-war in attendance.[4] In 1778 Lord North, Lord Sandwich and one of the secretaries of state seem to have acted together as a committee meeting with Lord Amherst, to take Amherst's views about future war strategy, these views being discussed at a full meeting of the cabinet the following day.[5] Since recorded instances are so scarce, it seems probable that this method was not often adopted.

In another way, however, cabinet practice was extremely adaptable and calculated to ensure that the cabinet received the fullest information before reaching decisions. In the early years after 1761 (until the creation of the third secretary of state for the colonies

[1] 'A memorandum of business upon which the King's Pleasure is to be taken', Dartmouth MSS., mentioned in H.M.C., *Fourteenth Report, Appendix*, part x, p. 121.

[2] Cabinet minute, 19 Aug 1767, Shelburne MSS., William L. Clements Library.

[3] John Robinson to Sandwich, 18 Aug 1777, *Sandwich Papers*, I 239–40.

[4] Hillsborough (colonies), Granby and Conway (board of ordnance), Hawke (admiralty), and Barrington (secretary-at-war); *The Correspondence of King George III*, III no 1658, misdated and misplaced by the editor.

[5] *The Correspondence of King George III*, IV nos. 2170, 2172, 2171.

made this unnecessary), the first commissioner of the board of trade was regularly summoned when colonial affairs were under discussion.[1] In 1767, when the cabinet ministers were engaged in one of their periodic frustrating discussions of French failure to demolish port facilities at Dunkirk in accordance with the peace treaty of 1763, arrangements were made for the engineer officers who had been concerned in the business to attend to give information.[2] In December 1770 the cabinet took special steps to inform itself about Irish affairs, and the same informant was again in attendance about a year later.[3] Written advice was demanded from the attorney and solicitor-general on several occasions when questions of possibly treasonable activity in the colonies were under discussion,[4] and sometimes these legal officers were summoned to give opinions in person.[5] In 1778 Lord Amherst was called upon to give advice before he was actually appointed commander-in-chief with a seat in the cabinet;[6] and on one occasion early in Pitt's ministry, when the Anglo-French diplomatic rivalry in the United Provinces was at a critical stage, the British ambassador at The Hague came over at his own request to represent the case and took part in cabinet discussions.[7]

When a cabinet meeting had reached a decision – that is to say, in form, a recommendation of advice to the king – it was normally recorded in one, or both, of two ways: in a dispatch or instruction, or in a cabinet minute. If a minute was drawn up, it was customary that this should be read over to the members present to ensure that it correctly expressed their agreed views.[8] The responsibility for drafting the minute fell upon the secretaries of state and on them

[1] Cabinet minutes, 8 July 1763, Egremont MSS., 23 Apr, 13 and 1 Dec 1764, and 21 Jan 1765, Grenville (John Murray) MSS.

[2] Cabinet minute, 14 Aug 1767, Shelburne MSS., William L. Clements Library.

[3] Thomas Allan to Macartney, 25 Dec 1770, to Lord Townshend, 24 Dec 1771, cited in Edith M. Johnston, *Great Britain and Ireland, 1760–1800* (1963) pp. 84, 92.

[4] Cabinet minutes, 20 Aug 1772, 4, 5, 19 Feb 1774, Dartmouth MSS.

[5] Cabinet minutes, 28 Feb, 1 Mar 1774, ibid.

[6] *The Correspondence of King George III*, IV nos. 2170–2, 2227, 2229.

[7] Alfred Cobban, *Ambassadors and Secret Agents: The Diplomacy of the First Earl of Malmesbury at The Hague* (1954) pp. 129, 132–3.

[8] *Calendar of Home Office Papers of the Reign of George III, 1766–1769*, ed. Joseph Redington (1879) p. 212.

alone. When George Grenville, in October 1762, was transferred from the secretaryship of state to the admiralty, Henry Fox reported that, though he was still in the cabinet, he would 'no longer have it in his power to guide and interline Lord Egremont's drafts';[1] and Admiral Keppel's submission of minutes to the king on naval business during 1782 seems to have been quite exceptional.

The recommendation was invariably submitted to the king for his approval. In many cases it was known that, as the king was in agreement with the policy, this was a pure formality, and in urgent cases, this formal completion of the process might be anticipated. And yet when, for instance, Carmarthen, as foreign secretary, deviated from the normal rule on ground of urgency, he clearly regarded this as exceptional and irregular. On 20 February 1787 he wrote to Sir James Harris:[2]

> The cabinet today agreed to the proposition of allowing the additional two per cent to the well disposed Friezlanders. The Minute I have sent to the King, and of course cannot in point of form give you notice of this determination till I have seen His Majesty; I would not however defer communicating it to you in a private letter as speedily as possible, in order that it may be carried into effect immediately.

Normal practice seems to have been for the secretary of state handling the business to communicate the recommendation to the king, but some evidence to be discussed below suggests that there may have been some concentration of this responsibility in the hands of the senior secretary of state during the last two years of North's administration – if this was so, it is another of the interesting pieces of wartime rationalisation of procedure

[1] *Bedford Correspondence*, III 141.

[2] B.M. Add. MSS. 28062, fo. 98 (copy). In December 1780 Stormont asked leave to send an urgent dispatch out straightway if the cabinet approved it, without laying it before the king again (*The Correspondence of King George III*, v no. 2935). In April 1782 the king, unasked, gave Keppel leave to take, without further reference back to him, such action as the cabinet should approve after discussing the dispatches which Keppel had laid before him, provided he sent a copy of the cabinet minute for his information; and he described this as a usual practice (ibid., nos. 3629, 3630).

which was abandoned upon the fall of North's administration.

By 1768 at least, and probably earlier, it was understood that drafts of important dispatches would be circulated to the cabinet ministers, to make sure that they agreed that these correctly stated the decisions they had reached. Hillsborough, then a newly fledged member of the cabinet as minister in charge of colonial affairs, was once instructed by George III that this was the method to be followed;[1] and a conspicuous instance a year later, when he failed properly to comply with it, marked a stage towards the breakdown of Grafton's ministry.[2] Evidence can be adduced that the practice continued to be followed during North's administration;[3] and clearly it was an essential precaution if a cabinet was to be preserved from collapse through lack of confidence and agreement among its members.

In 1765, soon after the formation of Rockingham's first administration, the veteran Duke of Newcastle wrote to one of the two then inexperienced secretaries of state, 'that the resolution of every meeting of the king's servants should be reduced to a minute. . . . Without that there is no security for the execution of what is agreed.[4]

From the evidence of various manuscript collections it is clear that a fair number of ministers – perhaps all those with executive responsibility – acted upon this principle. In 1767 Lord Shelburne stated that it was 'the indispensable custom' to take and read over a minute at cabinet meetings;[5] and so far as his own business as secretary of state from 1766 to 1768 is concerned, this is amply borne out by the string of minutes in his papers. To the minister in charge of the particular business the minute served two purposes: as an *aide-mémoire* and also as a warrant that he acted with the

[1] *The Correspondence of King George III*, II no. 598.

[2] *Autobiography of Grafton*, pp. 229–35.

[3] On 22 Jan 1776 Weymouth received a message from North: 'Lord North presents his compliments to Lord Weymouth and upon reading the draft of his Lordship's letter to the Lord Lieutenant of Ireland is of opinion that it agrees perfectly with the resolution of the cabinet.' (Bath MSS.)

[4] B.M. Add. MSS. 32969, fo. 321, cited in Namier, *Crossroads of Power*, p. 107.

[5] *Calendar of Home Office Papers of the reign of George III*, pp. 212–13, cited in Mackintosh, *The British Cabinet*, p. 59, n. 94.

collective support of his colleagues and could invoke their joint responsibility if he was attacked afterwards. The statement that 'George III kept these minutes – it is doubtful if anybody else did'[1] quite misrepresents the situation; for, although the record is far from complete, in most of the cases where private papers of departmental ministers exist (principally the secretaries of state), there copies of cabinet minutes are to be found;[2] and of over a hundred minutes known for the reign up to the end of 1777, only two are to be found in the king's papers.[3] A great number of these are obviously the ministers' own working copies; but one or two collections have a greater significance.

The nineteen cabinet memoranda and cabinet minutes preserved in George Grenville's papers for the period July 1763 to June 1765 relate in many cases to American or diplomatic questions for which Grenville, as head of the treasury, had no departmental responsibility – in a few instances only did they touch on matters with which he was particularly concerned, financial settlements under the Peace of Paris.[4] Most of them are in his hand, or that of his wife. Six, however, are written in a clerk's hand; and as one of them was sent to Grenville by Halifax, as Grenville had been

[1] Pares, *King George III and the Politicians*, p. 160 and n. 4.

[2] Egremont MSS. 20 (3 Dec 1761 – 8 July 1763); Grenville MSS. (a) 5 (29 Mar 1762 – 16 Feb 1763, four of them duplicated in the Astle MSS. in B.M. Add. MSS. 34713, fos. 106–14), (b) 19 (8 July 1763 – 12 June 1765); Shelburne MSS., William L. Clements Library, 18 (5 Aug 1766 – 23 Sept 1768); Granville MSS. 11 (18 Mar 1768 – 10 Jan 1777); Dartmouth MSS. 27 (18 Mar 1768 – 25 Feb 1777); Sandwich MSS., printed or noticed in *Sandwich Papers*, 5 (3 Oct 1774 – 25 Feb 1777). There are thirty more minutes in the Sandwich papers for the years 1778–82, and others are to be found in Bath MSS. 4 (15 Mar 1777 – 11 Apr 1778); Fox MSS. 14 (28 Mar 1782 – 13 Nov 1783); Grantham MSS. 19 (20 July 1782 – 24 Jan 1783); Leeds MSS., B.M. Add. MSS. 28064–8, 8 (24 Apr 1785 – 18 May 1790). Apart from these, copies of a few of them, and also one or two not otherwise known, have turned up in ministers' departmental papers in the Public Record Office.

[3] 5 Apr 1765 and 20 June 1776, *The Correspondence of King George III*, I no. 48 and III no. 1895. The first of these was exceptional in being called for by the king on his personal business, the proposals for a regency. The document at vol. III no. 1658 described by the editor as a minute of cabinet is, in fact, a minute by an advisory committee on military questions, and its correct date is 31 May 1769.

[4] See *Additional Grenville Papers*, pp. 317–38.

absent from that meeting, a question arises whether he may have been supplied with the other five from the same source.[1] The most interesting feature of this group of papers is the way in which it shows Grenville keeping track of the main decisions in a way which, so far as present information shows, no later head of the treasury did at any other time in George III's reign.

Earl Gower, as president of the council from 1768 to 1779, had virtually no departmental responsibilities. Nevertheless, in the surviving, obviously incomplete section of his papers now in the Public Record Office, there are eleven cabinet minutes and memoranda. Seven out of these documents relate to business transacted by Lord Rochford, secretary of state for the northern department. In three instances internal evidence shows that Rochford supplied them, and it seems likely that the same may have been the case with one or two of the others. During the same period Gower did not receive copies of any of the minutes for which Dartmouth was responsible at the colonial department. These circumstances may reflect either a loss of some papers or a special political connection between Rochford and Gower at this time.

The four remaining documents in this group raise even more interesting questions. All are concerned with American business. The earliest is dated (incorrectly a day early) 18 March 1768. The office file copy of the secretary of state (in this case, Hillsborough) is among the papers of the colonial department. The remaining three minutes are all to be found also in the papers of Lord Dartmouth who, by the time they were written, had retired from the colonial department and become lord privy seal. That of 30 May 1776 concerned supplies for the armed forces in North America and involved the responsibilities of the treasury, the admiralty, and the colonial secretary. The next, of 18 November 1776, related to obstruction to the execution of press warrants in the City of London; there is a third copy of this minute in the private papers of the first lord of the admiralty, Lord Sandwich. The third, of 10 January 1777, dealt with military business in Germain's department. The appearance of copies of these three minutes in the possession of two ministers who had no departmental responsibility for the business to which they related may be remaining evidence of a practice only partially adopted during the middle

[1] Ibid., p. 323.

years of North's ministry of a general circulation of minutes to members of the cabinet.[1] Cabinet minutes relating to the dissolution of parliament also raise a problem of distribution, for the surviving minute for 1774 is in Dartmouth's papers, and that for 1780 in those of Lord Sandwich as part of a long minute dealing with naval business.

The last two years of North's administration gave rise to two new developments, one permanent, one transient.

Up to the year 1778 the king's papers are almost devoid of cabinet minutes.[2] It is also a singular circumstance that two of the earliest minutes in his collection relating to North's administration, minutes of 17 and 18 January 1778, are copies in his own hand. This suggests that up to this time, and indeed for nearly two years to come, no regular practice of preparing a copy of a cabinet minute as a formal submission of advice to the king had yet been established. As regards the early years of the reign up to 1768, there is no doubt that this was in fact the situation. On 27 March of that year Hillsborough submitted an important dispatch for the king's approval; and he wrote: 'I have the honour also to send copies of the Minute and of the proposal laid before your Majesty,

[1] Gower was absent from one of these three meetings, but in no other instance was it a case of the record being sent to an absent minister. It is possible that the presence of cabinet minutes in his papers may have something to do with a formal role as chairman (see p. 73 n. 3), but in that case the absence of copies of at least some of the other minutes known for his years of office seems curious; and other lord presidents of the period do not seem to have accumulated minutes.

[2] Not only is there an absence of minutes, but there are no routine references to their being sent or received in the correspondence between king and the ministers. One minute of 5 Apr 1765, sent to the king by Sandwich, is peculiar in character, in that it related to a matter of personal concern to the king himself, the provision of a regency in the event of his death (*The Correspondence of King George III*, I no. 48). The next paper published by Sir John Fortescue under the description of a cabinet minute (vol. III no. 1658, misdated and misplaced, and actually of 31 May 1769) is a minute of a committee of four cabinet ministers with the secretary-at-war in attendance, dealing with military business which was the king's particular interest and responsibility. The next – a cabinet minute of 20 June 1776 in the handwriting of Philip Stephens, secretary to the admiralty – seems to have been inserted among other papers about the strength of the British and the French fleets and can be considered fairly exceptional in importance (vol. III nos. 1894–6).

in case your Majesty should wish to have recourse to them.'[1] The sentence could not possibly have been phrased int his way had the delivery of cabinet minutes to the king already become an established practice. The advice was communicated verbally or in the form of drafts. The minute still remained a working document for cabinet ministers, as its phraseology shows,[2] and at first no change in the style was made when copies began to be supplied for the king's use. The phrasing of North's letter forwarding one of the minutes of January 1778 also suggests that the practice was still unusual. When the new procedure had settled down, ministers' letters to the king forwarding minutes almost invariably refer to 'the minute of cabinet' or 'the minute of a meeting of the cabinet': North's letter refers to 'a minute of a cabinet'.[3] Furthermore in this case the king had specifically directed that a cabinet minute should be drawn up – but this was not stated to be for his own satisfaction but that the members of cabinet should have no excuse for speaking with divergent voices in parliament.[4]

These circumstances seem to point very clearly to the conclusion that the lack of cabinet minutes in the king's papers for the years before 1778, and the presence of only a handful in 1778 and 1779, does not reflect a partial destruction of the papers. Up to this point minutes simply had not been regularly passed over to him. But the growing pressures of the war, the need to regularise procedures and ensure the taking of decisions, and the cabinet reshuffle of late 1779, led to a change. Some years afterwards Lord Stormont, who in 1779 became northern, and also senior, secretary of state, wrote to an unidentified correspondent: 'I regularly delivered to the

[1] *The Correspondence of King George III*, II no. 597.

[2] It does not seem to have been regarded as exceptionable for copies of minutes to be supplied to diplomatic representatives abroad for their guidance. Thus Egremont, under cover of a letter of 26 Oct 1762, forwarded to Bedford at Paris a copy of the minute of 22 Oct (Egremont MSS. copy or draft, P.R.O. 30/47/5). For other instances, see *Correspondence of William Pitt, Earl of Chatham*, ed. W. S. Taylor and J. H. Pringle, 4 vols (1838–40) III 31; *Diaries and Correspondence of James Harris, First Earl of Malmesbury*, ed. by his grandson, 4 vols (1844), cited below as *Malmesbury Correspondence*, II 307.

[3] *The Correspondence of King George III*, IV no. 2171.

[4] Ibid., no. 2161.

King a copy of every minute of cabinet.'[1] This statement is borne out by the king's papers, for with one exception at the very beginning of this period, every minute there from 27 November 1779 to January 1782 is in Stormont's hand. About April 1780 Stormont introduced a hitherto unknown formula in order to escape the task of writing eight or nine names at the head of the minute. The minute of 22 April is headed simply 'Present/The whole Cabinet',[2] and on later occasions when only one or two ministers were absent, he used some such formula as 'The Whole Cabinet except the Chancellor who is indisposed'. The appearance of this type of heading in some of the minutes for the last two years of North's ministry which survive in Sandwich's papers suggests that their source was an original draft by Stormont. Moreover, it seems likely that Stormont's responsibility for communication on secretary's business with the king was not confined to minutes but extended more widely, for the king's papers for these two years contain very few letters from either of the other two secretaries of state.

The new system of regularly communicating cabinet minutes to the king not only survived the change of ministry in March 1782 but then passed through another phase of its evolution. It now became a formal tender of advice. The change is marked from the commencement of the flow of minutes submitted by members of the Rockingham administration. These invariably opened with some such phrase as 'It is humbly recommended to His Majesty'. Why did this occur? Various reasons suggest themselves. Perhaps in part it arose out of the diffidence of some of the ministers who were now serving for the first time; perhaps even more it was caused by the undercurrent of disagreement between the ministers and the king and the determination of the ministers to put their proposals for action on record in as formal a manner as possible – a circumstance which seems to have been repeated in

[1] H.M.C., *Laing MSS.*, II 527. Henceforth the king's collection of minutes is fairly complete, though occasionally it can be supplemented from ministers' papers. In the autumn of 1779 at least one minister, Sandwich, was concerned about the proper recording of cabinet decisions (*The Correspondence of King George III*, IV no. 2775) and the arrangement that the king should have them regularly may have been designed as a safeguard that this should be done.

[2] *The Correspondence of King George III*, V no. 3002.

1806–7.[1] Whatever the reason, once adopted, the new formula stuck and became the normal style thereafter.

However, no subsequent ministry repeated the radical experiment instituted by Stormont at the end of 1779, of communicating the minutes only through the senior secretary of state. Under Rockingham and Shelburne the two secretaries of state and the head of the admiralty all exercised the function in respect of the business of their departments, and Pitt's two secretaries of state continued to do so after December 1783. Perhaps this was a more natural system; and it seems likely that in any case the jealousies between Fox and Shelburne would have made it impossible for either to yield such primacy to the other during the brief tenure of the second Rockingham ministry.

II

From this survey of the size, evolution and routine of business of the cabinet, an impression emerges of a body which, however dependent it was in theory upon the king, had in fact a considerable momentum of its own. There remains the central problem: how was policy formed and to what degree did George III enter into the process?

The first question which arises is this: did George III reshape ministries with particular principles of policy in mind? In general the answer is in the negative. In the period under discussion the only evident instance of this was in December 1783, when concern for constitutional principle reinforced his hatred of Charles James Fox. In most of the cabinet changes of the period in which the king took any initiative he was more concerned with men than with measures. In 1760 he had a vague ideal before him of purity and good government, as contrasted with what he thought of as the corruption and mismanagement of his grandfather's ministers. He was also anxious not to be reduced by the then ministers into the state of thraldom which he assumed they had forced upon George II. I am not sure that these points are to be dignified with the

[1] See Pares, *King George III and the Politicans*, p. 163 and n. 1. The king's papers contain the very large number of thirty-seven minutes for the fourteen months during which the 'Talents' were in office, a much greater number than for any period after 1782.

description of 'policy'. In any case they had little to do with the transformations of the cabinet in 1761 and 1762, which arose out of the isolation within it on particular points of policy of first Pitt and then Newcastle. Grenville's succession to the treasury in 1763 was a further reshaping, not a change of the ministry, regretted by the king but forced upon him by Bute's refusal any longer to face the drudgery of office.

A clear ministerial break occurred when Grenville and his colleagues were replaced by the Rockinghams, but royal considerations of policy had little to do with it. There was little cordiality or trust between Grenville and George III. The unhappy days of their intercourse left a permanent scar on the king's mind.[1] Grenville and his colleagues fell foul of the king over issues which were personal or matters of political management rather than state policy, and they seem to have finally overstepped the mark in May 1765 in attempting to force him to make Lord Weymouth lord lieutenant of Ireland.[2] In these circumstances it was as a way of escape that the king accepted the services of Rockingham and Newcastle under the aegis of the Duke of Cumberland. No stipulations about policy were mentioned, save for the continued exclusion from influence of Bute. This government in its turn disobliged the king over the question of allowances for his brothers. More fatal, however, was its precarious weakness in parliament, so Chatham was brought in to create a ministry of talent led by his own genius. Again there were no stipulations about policy, though the king, against his own soundly formed judgement, acquiesced in the pursuit of a Prussian alliance.[3]

From 1766 to 1782 there was no clear break in administration, only a series of transformations, of which the first and most important was the introduction of the Bedford group in 1767. As Mr John Brooke has shown, this arrangement was carried through with very little attention to questions of high policy.[4] And yet this

[1] Many years afterwards, on 8 Apr 1782, the king wrote to Shelburne: 'Lord Shelburne will grow as averse to yellow and black boxes as I was to visits from the late G. Grenville.' (Lansdowne MSS.)

[2] The king's complaints against them are fully detailed in the longest of his memoranda on this change of ministry, *The Correspondence of King George III*, I no. 141. See too Harris, *Life of Lord Chancellor Hardwicke*, III 446.

[3] Pares, *King George III and the Politicians*, p. 114.

[4] Brooke, *The Chatham Administration*, pp. 295–333.

was a decisive turning-point. Instead of the cabinet being weighted in favour of the conciliatory colonial policy urged by the Rockinghams, power fell into the hands of the more imperialist-minded Bedford group and events flowed on inexorably to the Declaration of Independence.

The changes of ministry in 1782 and 1783, far from displaying royal influence, were exceptional in the extent to which the politicians, not the king, dictated terms on policy. With the triumph of Pitt over the coalition the king turned the tables. In this instance it can perhaps be said that he fought successfully for a principle of policy. Fox, as Pares has aptly said, 'had formed the intention of de-personalising the monarchy'.[1] In resisting him the king championed the policy of maintaining the existing constitutional system against innovations of that sort; and the whole tenor of Pitt's career shows that Pitt agreed with this intention. But with this point gained, the king appreciated that Pitt must have a certain latitude over more immediate political aims and allowed it over the question of parliamentary reform, much as in 1766 he had allowed latitude to Pitt's father over the attempt to secure a Prussian alliance.

If the arrangement of ministries had little connection with the making of policy – and this seems the right conclusion, provided the existence of occasional exceptions is recognised – the question then remains: how large was the role of the king in the shaping of policy decisions in face of circumstances as they arose? To what extent did he enter into the work of his administrations?

What is now perhaps to be described as the classic view of this matter has been stated by Pares:[2]

> George III did not try to control the everyday operations of government in person from beginning to end of his reign. . . . Unless the loss of part of his correspondence has created a misleading impression, he did not take a very active part in administration during the Ministry of Grenville, or even of the feeble Rockingham – still less during that of the superman Chatham, whom, in all probability, he was prepared genuinely to look up to.
>
> From some time between 1767 and 1770, however, his printed correspondence becomes much fuller of administrative detail,

[1] *King George III and the Politicians*, pp. 123–4.

[2] Ibid., pp. 173–4.

> and it is apparent that more and more is submitted to the king's decision. Probably he never claimed this, but it came about because Grafton was indolent and North unable to make up his mind. We find the king deciding what admiral shall command a squadron, and how many ships shall sail to the West Indies. He also acts, one might say, as Secretary-at-War: having approved a secret expedition against Goree, he undertakes to provide the soldiers, saying: 'I trust with a little consideration I shall be able to chalk out means of effecting what I look on as so essential a service.' He twice dismisses a Lord Chancellor when Grafton or North is unequal to the task. He composes quarrels in the Cabinet, and once conducts a Cabinet reshuffle, with the air of a householder distributing domestic tasks among some rather difficult servants with a special eye to the comfort and prestige of the major-domo. He gets North out of a difficulty about some law promotions and twice warns him not to promise offices without consulting him first. Some of his ministers treat him as one might treat a Prime Minister who did not happen to be at the Cabinet: Rochford sends him confidential reports of Cabinet discussions and primes him for his conferences in the closet, Lord George Germain (apparently) asks whether he has any particular commands as to the line he should take at a Cabinet meeting.
>
> Indeed, one might well ask, who was Prime Minister at this time – George III or Lord North?

As against this, there is the view put forward by Namier:[1]

> From pathologically indolent he turned pathologically industrious – and never again could let off working; but there was little sense of values, no perspective, no detachment. . . . His innumerable letters . . . contain some shrewd perceptions or remarks, evidence of 'very tolerable parts if . . . properly exercised'. But most of his letters merely repeat approvingly what some Minister, big or small, has suggested. 'Lord A. is very right . . .'; 'General B. has acted very properly . . . '; 'the minute of Cabinet meets with my fullest concurrence . . . '; 'Nothing can more deserve my approbation than' – whatever it was. But if a basic change is suggested, his obstinacy and prejudices appear.

Is either of these judgements correct, or do both overstate their case?

[1] Namier, *Crossroads of Power*, p. 137.

One way in which to approach this question is to ask, what did contemporaries think, or appear to think? Those who were in the know, that is, members of the cabinet and other chief officials, often made verbal or written observations which implied that the real momentum of government lay in the departments and the cabinet, and that it was what was decided in these places that really mattered. Perhaps too much weight should not be placed upon the views sometimes expressed by members of the cabinet, that a departmental minister should have plans to meet the situations which he caused to be brought before their attention.[1] More revealing are the turns of phrase sometimes used by ministers in correspondence with envoys and colonial governors, in the semi-official letters in which they dropped the formal mode of sending instructions by 'His Majesty's command'. For instance, on 3 August 1764, Lord Sandwich, then northern secretary, wrote to Buckinghamshire at Petersburg: 'As to the treaty of alliance, your Excellency has made all the advances which the dignity of the Crown will admit, or the rules of good policy can require, and it is the opinion of His Majesty's servants here that the showing too great eagerness in the pursuit of that object will more probably retard than forward the conclusion of it.' In a dispatch of the same day to Sir John Goodricke in Stockholm he used a similar phrase: 'It is incumbent upon the King's servants to inform themselves minutely of the conditions expected by Sweden . . . that they may not, by degrees, be drawn into measures which it might be extremely inconvenient for this country to carry into execution.'[2] A whole series of such examples can be culled from the correspondence of the commander-in-chief in America, General Gage. Hillsborough wrote to him on 12

[1] On 26 Sept 1764 the king told Grenville that both the chancellor and Bedford had complained to him of 'the deadness of Lord Halifax at Council'. Grenville agreed that it was wrong, 'and said that it was the part of the Secretary of State to open the subject on which the Council met; to deliver his own opinion, and then ask that of other Lords'. (*Grenville Papers*, II 515.) Rochford wrote to Sandwich on 10 Dec 1774: 'What surprises me, between you and I, is that the Minister of the Department, Lord Dartmouth, does not come with some plan to cabinet. I should think it only duty to do so, were there any dispute with France and Spain.' (*Sandwich Papers*, I 55–6.)

[2] *The Fourth Earl of Sandwich: Diplomatic Correspondence, 1763–1765*, ed. Frank Spencer (1961) pp. 187, 190.

March 1768: 'The orders contained in the Earl of Shelburne's despatch to Sir William Johnstone . . . will shew that His Majesty's servants have not been inattentive to the danger that threatens the colonies.'[1] In a private letter of 4 April Lord Barrington informed him that 'the ministers had met to consider in what manner the troops under [his] command should be disposed', related the proceedings of two cabinets and forwarded a copy of a minute which the second meeting had approved.[2] Here are other instances. Hillsborough, 24 December 1768: 'For my part I shall not fail to submit your observations upon the Mutiny Act to the consideration of the rest of His Majesty's servants, and shall be very happy if any alteration can be made therein, which, without giving up the principle, may render it more easy in the execution.'[3] 13 May 1769: 'The consideration of the state of the Illinois country and the forts will now I hope soon receive a final decision . . . [when] the King's servants shall have given their advice thereupon, I will not lose a moment in transmitting His Majesty's pleasure to you.'[4] In a letter of 19 July 1771 Hillsborough disclosed his intention of referring to the cabinet an outstanding problem, which as yet he had not been able to lay in full before the king.[5] In a letter of 2 January 1769 to Governor Bernard of Massachusetts, Barrington wrote: 'I wish there were a better prospect of such measures at home as will tend to preserve the obedience of the colonies and such have been proposed; I can moreover assure you that they have been relished by the majority of the cabinet; but by some fatal catastrophe two or three men there, with less ability, less credit, less authority, and less responsibility than the rest, have carry'd their point and produced that flimsy unavailing Address.'[6] Implicit in all these passages is the assumption that at the stage of referring a matter to the cabinet and at the stage of implementing its decision the

[1] *The correspondence of General Thomas Gage with the secretaries of state, 1763–1775*, ed. C. E. Carter, 2 vols (1931–4), cited below as *Gage Correspondence*, II 59.

[2] Ibid., p. 65.

[3] Ibid., p. 82.

[4] Ibid., p. 88. Cf. phrasing in Hillsborough's letter of 24 Mar 1769, no. 18, ibid., p. 84.

[5] Ibid., p. 135.

[6] *The Barrington–Bernard Correspondence*, ed. E. Channing and A. C. Coolidge (1912) p. 182.

approval of the sovereign was largely formal. However punctilious the care taken to obtain the royal pleasure – and it was punctilious – the king might be expected to follow the wishes or advice of the ministers. Most of these examples, it may be observed, are taken from the correspondence of ministers who in politics ranked themselves as 'king's men'.

Other ministerial correspondence yields evidence supporting this impression. On 17 August 1768 Lord Weymouth wrote a long letter to Gower, requesting his views on a point of policy regarding Corsica.[1] The two opinions between which a decision had to be made were championed by himself and the Duke of Grafton, and there was no mention of the king – though it appears that Grafton had interested the king in his point of view.[2] On 10 October 1772 Rochford wrote to Gower: 'Next Tuesday the cabinet is to meet again to decide whether the parliament shall meet before Christmas, it is the damned East India Company that will call us together and I'm afraid we must meet, Suffolk and Sandwich who are both out of town have left their sentiments with me.'[3] In September 1772, when Sandwich at the admiralty was pressed by North for economies, he replied immediately that he assumed North would wish 'to have a meeting of the King's servants', stated his strong objection, and concluded: 'I think you would choose that that matter and the whole of this important business should be fully discussed before any measure concerning it is adopted.'[4] In and after October 1774 ministers talked of the dissolution of parliament that autumn as very much their idea. Suffolk in the Lords declared himself a principal adviser of the measure,[5] and Lord North told Thomas Hutchinson: 'Parliament was dissolved on this account – that we might at the beginning of a parliament take such measures as we could depend upon a parliament to prosecute to effect.'[6] There are sundry other remarks scattered throughout Hutchinson's diary which reinforce the impression of the cabinet as the real

[1] Granville MSS., P.R.O. 30/20/1.
[2] *The Correspondence of King George III*, II nos. 642, 644.
[3] Granville MSS., P.R.O. 30/29/1.
[4] *Sandwich Papers*, I 25–6.
[5] *Parliamentary History*, ed. Cobbett and Wright, XVIII 161; cf. H.M.C., *Knox MSS.*, p. 257.
[6] *Hutchinson Diary*, I 298.

effective centre of decision – thus, on 28 June 1775, occurs the entry: 'Pownall [senior under-secretary in the colonial department] says the cabinet must meet tonight and must come to some decisive measures, and either wholly leave the colonies independent, or act more vigorously in reducing them to government.'[1] On two different occasions during the American war, two leading ministers, Sandwich and Germain, stated categorically that the planning of campaigns and naval expeditions was approved by the cabinet: each expedition was, in the words of Sandwich, 'the result of the collective wisdom of all His Majesty's confidential servants'.[2] The same habit of mind is equally traceable in the eighties. Carmarthen wrote on 7 January 1785, acknowledging despatches: 'His Majesty's confidential servants have not failed to take their contents into their most serious consideration.' To another envoy he wrote on 15 May 1785: 'It appears to the King's confidential servants highly necessary to be informed of the real point of view in which the system of Europe appears to his Prussian Majesty.'[3] Other instances from Carmarthen's correspondence could be cited.

In face of all this testimony one might well begin to wonder what was the king's position in the scheme of government.[4] Indeed, one or two direct ministerial explanations seem to belittle it. General Conway, secretary of state in the Rockingham and Chatham ministries, gave Horace Walpole to understand that the king

[1] Ibid., p. 480.

[2] Undated memo, Sandwich MSS., cited in G. Martelli, *Jemmy Twitcher* (1962) p. 183; Germain to Carleton, 10 July 1777, H.M.C., *Knox MSS.*, p. 132 – the circumstances of the dispatch were such that Germain's stress upon the king's 'mature deliberation' and judgement upon the recommendations of the cabinet should not be taken too seriously.

[3] B.M. Add. MSS. 28060, fos. 277, 333. Other instances are in B.M. Add. MSS. 28064, fos. 130, 132, 134, 140. N.B. also his letter of 20 Feb 1787 to Sir James Harris, cited above (p. 77).

[4] It is much more rare to encounter a phrase linking the king and the cabinet together in the process of decision. An example is in a letter from Conway to Gage of 17 Dec 1765: 'His majesty and the servants in his confidence have thought it advisable to lay the whole business of the late disturbances in America before parliament.' (*Gage Correspondence*, II 31.) On 2 June 1773 Dartmouth wrote concerning another cabinet decision: 'It is their unanimous opinion in which the King concurs, that . . . ' – a formula recognising the king's role but carrying once again the overtone of feeling that the cabinet was the more important (P.R.O., C.O. 5/765, fos. 260–1).

rarely interfered with his ministers.[1] Later – in a period when, so it has been argued, George III was taking a more active part in government – Lord Hillsborough, the former secretary of state for the colonies, declared that while the king would argue very sensibly, he would always leave his own sentiments and conform to his ministers'.[2]

In Hillsborough's view the king, if not dominant, was at least active; and there are plenty of examples of the dialogue carried on between him and the cabinet. In April 1768, in advance of a cabinet meeting, he sent Grafton suggestions about the control of riots – as this involved use of the military, he was himself particularly concerned.[3] A few months later, when the question of Corsica was coming before the cabinet, he was quick to inject into the discussion his view that open hostilities with the French should be avoided.[4] At the beginning of 1769 he prepared a memorandum counselling moderation in answer to some of Lord Hillsborough's proposals for reasserting British authority in North America.[5] In August 1772 he set himself to cool the attitude of the ministers towards a piece of French provocation.[6] In April 1773, the day a cabinet was to meet to discuss a threatened French intervention in Sweden, he stated his view that a partial naval mobilisation should take place immediately (it did).[7] Twelve months later,

[1] Walpole wrote: 'Whether hating or liking the persons he employed, he seemed to resign himself entirely to their conduct for the time. If what they proposed was very disagreeable to him, at most he avoided it by delay.' The period referred to includes the repeal of the Stamp Act. (Horace Walpole, *Memoirs of the Reign of King George III*, III 66.)

[2] This was in 1775; *Hutchinson Diary*, I 378.

[3] To Grafton, 9 Apr 1768, *The Correspondence of King George III*, II no. 607.

[4] To Grafton, 16 Sept 1768, ibid., no. 653.

[5] Hillsborough to George III, 15 Feb 1769; King's memorandum, ibid., nos. 701, 701A.

[6] George III to North, 1 Aug 1772, ibid., no. 1102.

[7] George III to North, 20 Apr 1773, ibid., no. 1228. A number of instances of George III's close involvement in the detailed stages of the Swedish crisis, adduced mainly from foreign sources, are given in Professor Michael Roberts's paper, 'Great Britain and the Swedish Revolution of 1772–73', *Historical Journal*, VII (1964) 1–46. A letter of 10 Oct 1772, in which Lord Rochford, the southern secretary, forwarding to the lord president a copy of a cabinet minute, observed: 'I am sure if we are *firm*

upon the receipt of news that the French were arming to protect their traffic against a Russian fleet engaged in operations against the Turks in the Mediterranean, he wrote both to Lord North and the southern secretary, Lord Rochford, stressing the need to proceed circumspectly and not provoke an open quarrel with the French.[1] None of his observations in these instances was particularly original, although they were certainly sensible; and there is no evidence as to whether or not they had any influence on the cabinet's decisions. Occasionally he could intervene usefully at a later stage. In 1779, after a cabinet instruction had been drawn up for the commander of the Channel fleet, he spotted a flaw and was able to secure its amendment by the cabinet.[2] But all this was relatively unimportant; it did not amount to directing the government. With regard to the later years of North's ministry, the author of an exhaustive study of the British war machine in the American War of Independence concluded: 'George III did not direct the war. He received ministers individually, and commented on their views; but beyond insisting in general terms on the subjugation of America, he made no attempt to steer strategy. . . . About the strategic movement of troops he was always punctiliously consulted . . . but though he was capable of rejecting Cabinet advice to send a regiment to Jamaica, it went there just the same.'[3]

Examples can also be cited of the cabinet rejecting royal suggestions in minor matters; not always, it may be said, with the happiest results. In the early summer of 1775 the cabinet ministers objected to the beating up of recruits in Ireland. The king pointed out at the end of August that if his proposal had been adopted, 'the army would have been at least 2 or 3000 men stronger at this

---

and *temperate* we may yet keep all quiet', suggests that knowledge of the very secret, temperate line of policy being followed with regard to France was not confined to so narrow an inner ring of ministers as Professor Roberts, following the views of the foreign agents, seems to think (Granville MSS., P.R.O. 30/29/1).

[1] *The Correspondence of King George III*, II nos. 1436–8.

[2] George III to Weymouth, 19 June 1779, Bath MSS., printed in J. H. Jesse, *Memoirs of the Life and Reign of George III*, 3 vols (1867) II 246; Weymouth to George III, 19 June 1779, *The Correspondence of King George III*, IV no. 2664.

[3] Piers Mackesy, *The War for America, 1775–1783* (1964) p. 23

hour'.[1] In February 1779, at the instance of Sandwich, they rejected his proposal (formulated on the basis of a line or two of advice he had requested from Weymouth) that Palliser, from whose charges Admiral Keppel had just been cleared, ought to be dismissed immediately. Within two or three days they were forced by parliamentary considerations to effect this by sending and begging Palliser to resign voluntarily from his employments.[2] George III commented dryly: 'Lord North cannot be surprised at my thinking the step I proposed of removing Sir Hugh Palliser last Saturday was not so improper as the majority of the cabinet seemed to think, when Lord Sandwich himself is forced to come now to a mean subterfuge to attain the same end.'[3]

Other cases of dialogue can be adduced, but on matters of greater importance which deserve fuller treatment. This leads on to a second fruitful line of approach to the problem – the examination of the part played by the king in the evolution and execution of various major strokes of policy. In a number of instances, some sort of a starting-point is supplied by a handful of studies, mostly recent, of particular aspects of British foreign policy. There is the difficulty, of course, that the writers have not usually been concerned to look at the part played by the king, but they do provide a detailed background for the review of other evidence bearing upon this special aspect of the question. Even then, however, this other evidence is often fragmentary, since vital stages in policy-making may have occurred in verbal discussions for which no written record survives. Still, a few suggestive indications do emerge. It becomes clear that the king's position was one of closer involvement than the evidence just cited might tend to suggest.

The biggest major issue of policy at the beginning of George III's reign was the conclusion of peace with France. In the early part of 1762 secret *pourparlers* were carried on through the medium of the Sardinian envoys in London and Paris. The negotiations were placed on a formal basis in May and the preliminaries were signed at the beginning of November.[4] In the period from April to

[1] To North, 26 Aug 1775, *The Correspondence of King George III*, II no. 1702.

[2] Ibid., IV nos. 2539, 2540, 2542, 2547, 2548.

[3] Ibid., no. 2549.

[4] Zenab Esmat Rashed, *The Peace of Paris, 1763* (1951) pp. 118–91.

December 1762 George III mentioned the peace negotiations thirty-seven times in letters to Bute.[1] During the same eight months the southern secretary, Lord Egremont, was in the closet for discussions on the matter on at least twenty-one occasions; once he was specially summoned to Windsor.[2] As these meetings were bunched round the dates when important dispatches arrived and the answers to them were being hammered out, it is clear that the king was fully in touch with the progress of the negotiation. It is clear too that he had a conception of a middle-of-the-road policy regarding the peace which, while rejecting the high pretensions of Pitt, was by no means a policy of peace at any price; though how far this was his own opinion and not simply a reflection of Bute's is a question to which there seems no answer. In June 1762 he wrote to Bute: 'I feel at this moment more than ever the pleasure of having the D[uke] of Newcastle out of employment, he would have undoubtedly have been for yielding anything to the French, but thanks be to Heaven that is not now the case nor Mr Pitt in a situation to demand impossibilities.'[3] On the other hand, the king supported Bute, and sometimes Egremont, against other ministers, especially George Grenville, who wanted a more intransigent line; and at the end of July it may have been his personal interviews with some of them which ensured that the negotiation would not be broken off when the first statement of the Spanish terms was found to be inadmissible.[4] On occasion, however, he was involved in unpleasant wrangling with ministers in which he came off the worse. In September 1762 Grenville and Egremont, the two secretaries of state, feared that, with Bute's and the king's encouragement, the British negotiator in Paris, the Duke of Bedford,

[1] *Letters from George III to Lord Bute*, pp. 94, 106, 108, 113, 114, 115 (2), 118 (2), 120–1, 121–2 122, 124, 125 (2), 126–8, 128, 128–9, 130, 131–3, 134, 135–6, 137–8, 140–1, 142, 144, 146–7, 147, 147–8, 148–9, 150–1, 151, 158–9, 160, 171, 178.

[2] Ibid., pp. 94 (22 Apr), 106 (17 May), 108 (19 May), 116 (15 June), 118 (21June), 119 (24 June), 121 (8 July [2]), 124 (25 July), 128 (?27 July), 129 (28 July), 131–2 (5 Sept), 134 (6 Sept), 135 (19 Sept), 137 (24 Sept at Windsor), 143 (2 Oct), 147 (14 Oct), 171 (6 Dec – and mention of orders for a further interview); *Grenville Papers*, I 458 (19 June), 475 (26 Sept), 481 (9 Oct).

[3] *Letters from George III to Lord Bute*, p. 113.

[4] Ibid., pp. 124–9; Rashed, *The Peace of Paris, 1763*, pp. 157–8.

would make what they regarded as excessive concessions. An attempt by the king to put pressure on them was not successful. Egremont was determined to stand firm; and it was reported afterwards that he 'was wise enough to fly in a passion in the closet', and that 'in short the king spoke daggers to him, but to no purpose.' The arrival a day or two later of the news of a great victory, the British capture of Havana, made it impossible for the king, Bute, or anyone else to continue the pressure for concessions.[1]

These circumstances form a basis for a proper assessment of an incident which, taken out of its context, might be adduced as a remarkable display of royal authority. On 26 October 1762, in a brief pep-note to Bedford, the king told him: 'I am determined either to make the peace I now send you or to continue the war.'[2] According to Bute, the suggestion that the French be presented with a virtual ultimatum at this stage came from the king.[3] However, a full examination of Bedford's correspondence makes it clear that, whatever the king thought – and three weeks earlier Egremont had pressed this course on him only to have it rejected[4] – he was now being used to impress Bedford that altered instructions from London had full weight behind them. The need for this lay in a crisis in the personal relationship between Bedford and the secretary of state with whom he had to conduct official correspondence, the Earl of Egremont. Bedford resented the curbs put upon his discretion and freedom to bargain in Paris: Egremont suspected Bedford's pacific tendencies were leading him into concessions the ministry would not be able to defend in parliament. Each man used bitter language against the other. Bedford believed himself the victim of Egremont's hostility; and it was evidently felt in London that only the weight of the king's personal intervention would persuade him that it was the whole cabinet, and the king

[1] Egremont to Grenville, 26 Sept 1762, *Grenville Papers*, I 475; *Letters from George III to Lord Bute*, pp. 137–8; Rigby to Bedford, 30 Sept 1762, *Bedford Correspondence*, III 132–3; Rashed, *The Peace of Paris, 1763*, pp. 176–7.

[2] *Bedford Correspondence*, III 139–40.

[3] Bute to Bedford, 14 Oct 1762, ibid., p. 136.

[4] Ibid., p. 132, and *Letters from George III to Lord Bute*, pp. 137–138.

himself, whose opinions had changed under the pressure of events.[1]

The prolonged negotiations with the French over the fulfilment of the peace terms a year or two later also yield an instance of the king's involvement. In the wrangles about the length of time the French would be given to settle outstanding debts for the keep of prisoners of war, he was strongly opposed to concession. The French proposed to pay in fifteen annual instalments.[2] In Bedford's view they might be conceded five.[3] But in reply to this suggestion he was told: 'The term of years you seem to think might be allowed them . . . is more than could be justified in parliament . . . besides His Majesty seems very averse to the consenting to so long a term; I really believe the utmost he could be brought to consent to would be three years, and he told Mr Grenville not to go beyond two.'[4] In this case the king and the majority of the cabinet were at one and the French were pinned down to a period of less than four years.[5]

The next example is the mounting and the repeal of the Stamp Act. The administrative origins of this measure have been traced very fully in an article by Professor C. R. Ritcheson,[6] and a shorter passage on the repeal is to be found in Namier's Ford Lectures.[7] The whole problem of organising and financing government in North America was under discussion in the winter of 1762–3, and a stamp tax was talked of in this connection. One item among the king's letters to Bute shows that he was fully in touch with the

[1] *Bedford Correspondence*, III 114–17, 126–9, 130–1, 132–3, 137–9; Bedford to Egremont, 14 Oct 1762, Egremont to Bedford, 26 Oct 1762, Bedford MSS., letter-book 'Peace of Paris' 1763; Egremont to Grenville [26 Sept 1762], *Grenville Papers*, I 475.

[2] Grenville to Sandwich, 16 July 1764, Bedford MSS., printed in *Grenville Papers*, II 390–2.

[3] Bedford to Sandwich, 18 July 1764, copy, Bedford MSS., printed in *Additional Grenville Papers*, pp. 159–60.

[4] Sandwich to Bedford, 29 July 1764, *Bedford Correspondence*, III 263–5.

[5] By early September the French appeared to have accepted the three-year term, and a week or two later it was decided to require payment within three years and four months (Sandwich to Gower, 11 Sept 1765, Granville MSS.; cabinet minute, 21 Sept 1764, Grenville (John Murray) MSS., printed in *Additional Grenville Papers*, p. 330).

[6] 'The preparation of the Stamp Act', *William and Mary Quarterly*, 3rd series, x (1953) 543–59.

[7] *Crossroads of Power*, pp. 108–10.

subject. There is practically no other document connecting George III with the evolution of the Stamp Act, save that long afterwards Horace Walpole reported Grenville as telling him that the king had become an enthusiastic supporter of the idea.[1] On his attitude to the repeal, however, there is much more information, for he drew up a memorandum on this at the time and there seems no good reason to distrust its contents.[2]

The policy of repeal plus a declaratory act was hammered out by a special committee of the Rockingham ministry during the beginning of 1766. There is some ground for believing that the ministers were not quite decided on their course until they assessed the reactions of parliament after the Christmas recess. They were also hesitating in hopes that Pitt would give them a lead. The king had too much animus against Grenville and Bedford to feel enthusiasm in defence of their original measure: indeed, he rather gleefully anticipated that they might be discredited by parliamentary disclosures of their mishandling of it.[3] But he did not initially support repeal. So long as the ministers were still undecided he pressed for modification of the Stamp Act. If they insisted upon repeal, however, he was prepared to back them.[4] It appears as if the die was not finally cast until 7 February.[5] Rockingham then

[1] *Letters from George III to Lord Bute*, pp. 201–2; *The Last Journals of Horace Walpole*, ed. A. F. Steuart (1910) II 337–8 n.

[2] *The Correspondence of King George III*, I no. 248; and see Namier, *Additions and Corrections to Sir John Fortescue's edition . . .*, pp. 50–2.

[3] 'Duke of Grafton, Your answer on the Duke of Bedford's intended motion was perfectly right and I desire the papers may be made out fully for the Houses, and think that they should see what *great care the last* Administration took by the *wise regulations* they made for putting the Stamp Act in execution, or else they won't have the whole before them; and then I think the D. of Bedford and his friends will wish no papers had been called for.' (To Grafton, 17 Dec 1765, Grafton MSS. 482.)

[4] This conclusion can, I think, be based upon the king's message of 21 Jan 1766 to Rockingham: 'Talbot is as right as I can desire on the Stamp Act; strong for our declaring our right but willing to repeal.' (*The Correspondence of King George III* I no 212.)

[5] This view is based on the quoted sentence from the king's memorandum which follows. There is some support for it in the insinuation of Lord Coventry in the Lords' debate on the repeal bill on 11 March that the ministers had changed their minds no fewer than four times in the course of the measure (Rockingham to George III, 12 Mar 1766, *The Correspondence of King George III*, I no. 270).

went and told him, in the light of the parliamentary situation, 'that now the two parties meant to push for repeal or enforce'. In the king's view, 'enforcing could only tend to widen the breach between this country and America', and he immediately told Rockingham that if these two were the only possible courses then he was for repeal and Rockingham could say so.

This, then, is a case where the king accepted what he regarded as the second-best course, when the ministers told him that they could not or would not support his preference. He refused, however, to enable them to hold the threat of dismissal over the heads of office-holders who voted against them, a conduct which made them suspicious of him but may nevertheless have been justified by the need to avoid alienating members of parliament whose support for the government on other points was essential to its continuance.[1]

The dispute with Spain in 1770 over the Spanish destruction of the British settlement at Port Egmont in West Falkland provides an instance of the king's participation in decisions in a case where the ministers were divided.[2] The secretary of state responsible for the negotiation was Weymouth. In the earlier exchanges he took up the stand that the Spanish government must disavow the action of its local officials and provide compensation for all losses, and that the island must be 'restored unattended by any discussion on the right'. Neither he, the king, nor the rest of the cabinet were prepared to accept Spanish formulas which would entail implied acceptance of Spanish sovereignty over the islands.[3] By the end of November the negotiation had come to a standstill on this point, for the Spanish government on its part was not prepared for any

[1] Pares, *King George III and the Politicians*, p. 108. I have left out of account here the misunderstandings which arose over what people thought Lord Strange thought the king had said about preferring modification of the Stamp Act to repeal. The explanation is most probably that the king may not have been very careful with his phrasing in his talk with Strange or that Strange was not careful, or still more likely that those politicians who were opposed to repeal only heard those parts of Strange's remarks which they wanted to hear.

[2] J. Goebel, *The Struggle for the Falkland Islands: A Study in Legal and Diplomatic History* (New Haven, Conn., 1927) pp. 289–355

[3] *The Correspondence of King George III*, II nos. 838, 841; George III to Weymouth, 21 Nov 1770, Bath MSS., cited in Jesse, *Memoirs of the life and reign of King George III*, I 511.

agreement which might leave the British in regular *de facto* possession.

At this stage the unity of the cabinet began to break. Weymouth insisted upon the initial British terms and seems to have been more than ready to welcome a war with Spain.[1] North and Lord Rochford, the other secretary of state, backed by their colleagues, stood out for a peaceful settlement. Through the French secretary of embassy, who offered his services as an intermediary, North made it known to the Spanish ambassador that once Spain had given unconditional satisfaction, the British would satisfy them in return by evacuating the colony. The ministers refused to give any formal promise, or even allow the king to make it personally to Masserano, in case the opposition should bring a storm about their ears in parliament. They made it plain that Spain must rely on their good faith.[2]

At a cabinet meeting on 4 December 1770 Weymouth made his dislike of a pacific solution sufficiently clear. Remaining silent he declined to give open assent to a proposal by Rochford that all present at the meeting might be ready to accept a form of declaration from Spain if it contained simply a disavowal of the Spanish officials responsible and a restoration of the island. The next day Weymouth suggested to the king the immediate recall from Madrid of James Harris, the British chargé d'affaires. This the king refused, seeing it as a proposal 'intended with a view to prevent any accommodation'. It would entail the immediate withdrawal of Masserano and the end of negotiation. 'I own', he declared in a letter to Rochford, 'I have no expectation the Spaniards will end this affair amicably yet I do not wish they should have it to say that they would have complied provided we had not recalled the Secretary of the Embassy without giving them an opportunity to conform to our uniform demands.' He agreed the situation was such that the recall was necessary. But in order to give the Spanish court a final opportunity to satisfy British demands, Harris should be sent a statement of these and should be told to leave Madrid

[1] If William Knox is to be believed, Weymouth's under-secretary, Robert Wood, was engaged in an intrigue to precipitate war, bring Chatham in as head of a war ministry, and leave Weymouth as 'the acting minister' (H.M.C., *Knox MSS.*, p. 264).

[2] Goebel, *The Struggle for the Falkland Islands*, pp. 307–11.

only if the terms were rejected. This would furthermore give Masserano several more weeks' opportunity to reopen talks in the event of orders reaching him to offer an agreement acceptable in London.[1]

Rochford replied to George III agreeing in every particular and promising to use every possible argument in support of the king's opinion at the next 'Council'. Opposition to it, he declared, 'can only arise from a wish to see this unlucky affair terminate fatally'.[2] In a second letter later that day he commented on the fire-eating spirit of Robert Wood, Weymouth's under-secretary, and declared that Weymouth's bellicosity must be held in check so long as there was 'the least glimmering of hope' of an accommodation.[3] For Weymouth was by now talking of measures to forestall anticipated French action in support of Spain.

At the next cabinet meeting held on 7 December, Weymouth took an intransigent line. He wished to authorise the officials of the East India Company to attack Pondicherry if the French were detected in the act of fortifying it, without waiting for final notification from home of an outbreak of hostilities – a point on which he had to give way. He stubbornly declined to accept the king's proposal for the contingent recall of Harris as laid before the meeting by Rochford; and to avoid an outright breach the cabinet decided finally to send no messenger at all to Harris, reflecting that in any case Spain's final answer must be on the way. Weymouth insisted that on no account should Harris be instructed to renew the negotiation. On being 'very much pressed' by Rochford to say whether 'he would or would not accept the conditions if they came at last, his answer was that though contrary to his opinion higher demands were not made, yet as he should allwayes when he could possibly, acquiesce with the majority of the cabinet, that he certainly would recommend accepting them if they came in time'.[4] But this mood of acquiescence did not last. On 9 December, in the course of a long conversation with Rochford, Weymouth told him he could no longer go on, 'contradicted by your Majesty's servants on five occasions and where his own department was immediately

[1] *The Correspondence of King George III*, II no. 844.

[2] Ibid., no. 845.

[3] Ibid., no. 843 (misplaced by Fortescue).

[4] Ibid., no. 848.

concerned'.[1] And he again proposed the immediate recall of Harris from Madrid. His intention to retire was confirmed next day, and a week or so later he relinquished the seals.

With the remainder of the story of how the British got their way in this negotiation this study is not concerned. But the events narrated reveal the king on one hand and a minister in cabinet on the other each checking the other's proposals. Weymouth's suggestion for an immediate breach of negotiations seems to have been brushed off in the closet: it never came before the cabinet, though his personal view must have been well known. In the refusal to allow discretionary instructions to be sent to the East India officials at Madras, Rochford and his colleagues acted in the cabinet fully in accordance with the king's wishes as well as their own.[2] But the king did not get his way in the cabinet of 7 December about sending a final statement of terms to Harris, simply because of Weymouth's obstruction and the desire of the other ministers not to provoke him to resign.

The offer of Minorca to Russia as the price of an alliance was resolved upon by the British government in January 1781. This episode affords an example of the king being overborne by the cabinet.[3] The first dispatches from Sir James Harris at Petersburg indicating that this price might buy Russian support reached the northern secretary, Lord Stormont, on 31 December 1780. The Cabinet held two meetings on 3 and 7 January 1781, at which the cession was agreed in principle and a draft dispatch to Harris approved for submission to the king.[4] On the eighth George III vetoed the proposal, declaring he could never think himself authorised to make cessions of dominions, 'though an unsuccessful war might, if not supported by Parliament, oblige to yield possessions

[1] Ibid., no. 852.

[2] It seems quite clear from the letters which passed between the king and Rochford on 6 December, that on the seventh Weymouth urged action relating to Pondicherry with which the king did not agree: it must be assumed that either he brought this subject forward with the king's knowledge but without his concurrence, or (though this seems less likely) without mentioning it to the king at all (*The Correspondence of King George III*, II nos. 844, 845, 843, 846).

[3] Isabel de Madariaga, *Britain, Russia, and the Armed Neutrality of 1780* (1962) pp. 283–5.

[4] *The Correspondence of King George III*, V nos. 3230, 3233, 3237.

conquered by the enemy'. The king's letter mentioning this decision to Lord Sandwich the following day seems rather clearly to imply that the sight of the cabinet minute and draft dispatch of 7 January was the first intimation he had had of the proposal.[1] Perhaps this was the case, though it would not accord with Stormont's usually careful observance of current conventions. Within a week further dispatches from Harris led Stormont to raise the matter once more. The king responded by holding a meeting with all the cabinet ministers at the Queen's House on 19 January. The ministers spoke 'as usual' in order of age beginning with the youngest.[2] Of what was said we have only the notes of Sandwich's vehement plea in favour of the project, but it was enough to move the king from his previous sentiments and win his acceptance of it.[3]

One last case study concerns the decision about the Gelderland subsidy in 1787, the decisive move in committing Pitt's ministry to working against French influence in the United Provinces. At the beginning of 1787 the government was faced with a major policy decision regarding the United Provinces: was action to be taken to support the Orangeist party? This policy was strongly advocated by the British ambassador, Sir James Harris. It was supported by the foreign secretary, Carmarthen; and about the beginning of January Pitt, who had been lukewarm, came round to the idea, at least in principle.[4] Other ministers favourably inclined were Richmond and Sydney. The real centre of opposition in the cabinet was Thurlow, and this probably only because he was acting as mouthpiece for the king, who disliked the prospect of involvement on the Continent. At this time George III believed that, after the exhaustion of the American war, Britain needed years of peace to recover prosperity and greatness. He did not think she should play the 'Drawcansir of Europe' and considered that intermeddling there would be 'destructive at present'.[5] When Pitt, early in January,

[1] *Sandwich Papers*, IV 23.

[2] H.M.C., *Knox MSS.*, p. 272.

[3] *Sandwich Papers*, IV 23–6. Sandwich described this occasion as 'a meeting of the cabinet council . . . in the King's presence'.

[4] Cobban, *Ambassadors and Secret Agents*, pp. 121–2; Pitt to Harris, 5, 26 Dec 1786, *Malmesbury Correspondence*, II 254–5; B.M. Add. MSS., 28062, fo. 8.

[5] Cobban, *Ambassadors and Secret Agents*, p. 123, citing Carmarthen to Harris, 8 Jan 1787, B.M. Add. MSS. 28062, fo. 25 (*Malmesbury Correspondence*, II 267–8).

submitted to him Harris's estimated requirements of £12,000 a year to keep the Orangeist party going he replied with strong protests about the need for economy.[1]

By May 1787 Harris had received permission to do what he had suggested a month previously, come to England to give a first-hand account of the situation in the United Provinces and discuss the government's policy. When he arrived he also submitted a specific issue: could Britain satisfy a request from the States of Gelderland for a subsidy of 500,000 florins? This would enable the States to pay troops by which alone the pro-French Free Corps were being prevented from seizing control of the province. The States could no longer pay these forces itself. On 23 May Harris was present at a cabinet dinner at which the matter was discussed. Thurlow tried to kill the project by exaggerating the danger of possible military commitments. Pitt, however, kept the meeting to the point by posing the general question: granted the immense importance of maintaining Dutch independence, which risk was the greater, that of attempting to stop France at once or that of waiting until France was ready for an attack upon Britain? Harris pointed out that for the present all that was involved was money. He also argued that France was plainly not in a position to engage in hostilities, and he was supported in this by both Stafford, (the lord president), and Pitt.[2]

The next day Pitt prepared himself by questioning Harris closely on the details of his proposal, and he gave decisive support to it when the cabinet met again on 26 May. It was there agreed to lend a sum not exceeding £70,000 to Gelderland.[3] The minute of the meeting was sent to the king by Carmarthen, and it was accompanied by a letter from Pitt, stating that the recommendation was the product of full discussion and repeated deliberation. Pitt scouted the likelihood of France engaging in hostilities, but said if she did so he doubted if Britain could remain inactive. He met the king's financial objections by assuring him that he could get funds out of parliament to reimburse the civil

[1] Cobban, *Ambassadors and Secret Agents*, p. 124, citing George III to Pitt, draft, 8 Jan 1787, Geo. III cal. 6226, Windsor MSS.

[2] Cobban, *Ambassadors and Secret Agents*, pp. 129–30, 132–3.

[3] Cabinet minute, Geo. III cal. 6251, Windsor MSS., printed in *The Later Correspondence of George III*, I 296.

list.[1] George III grumbled but gave his reluctant consent to the measure.[2]

Here the points about the process of decision seem to be these. The concurrence of Pitt and Carmarthen determined the line of policy put before the cabinet, and the cabinet agreed to a decision which they had formulated. The king, faced with a proposal which he very much disliked, nevertheless did not overrule his ministers' desire to take it to the cabinet for discussion, and in the end he accepted the cabinet's conclusion though it was distasteful to him.

III

The evidence passed in review in the preceding section suggests some modification of the conflicting impressions of George III's relationship with the cabinet presented by Pares and Namier.[3] Namier's conclusion unduly belittles the king's role; that of Pares tends somewhat to exaggerate it. Many of the king's letters to his ministers certainly do echo their advice or signify a perfunctory agreement. But, as Lord Hillsborough said, the king was in the habit of making very sensible comments on the affairs which were coming up for discussion by the ministers; and sometimes these views received a favourable response, while at others they were ignored. From the very beginning of the reign, however timorous the king may at first have been, he was participating in the daily round of public business, keeping abreast of events, and adopting, or forming, opinions about them – doing so with increasing experience and confidence as the years passed.

This growing experience in itself probably helped to create the impression of greater activity which is gained from his correspondence from the later 1760s onwards. All the same this increase in activity can be over-stressed. The analysis of the king's very constant contact with the ministers during the course of the peace negotiations of 1762, based on his letters in the Bute papers, is a

[1] Pitt to George III, 26 May 1787, ibid., p. 297.

[2] George III to Pitt, 26 May 1787, Earl Stanhope, *Life of . . . William Pitt*, 4 vols (1861–2) I xxi. In this letter the king declared that had Pitt not supported the proposal submitted in the cabinet minute, he would not have consented to the loan.

[3] See pp. 86–7 above.

warning against assuming that in the early years he stayed in the background. In the spring of 1768 his concern with the maintenance of public order during the Wilkite riots was close and continuous. It is attested most fully in a little-known string of letters to Lord Weymouth, which supplements substantially the items on this subject in the royal archives.[1] Moreover, it must be said that some of the evidence adduced by Pares in support of his judgement cited above will not support the general inference based upon it. The sovereign was head of the armed forces, and the special concern with military affairs shown by successive members of the royal house was an embarrassment to ministers at many other periods in both the eighteenth and the nineteenth centuries. George II, for instance, placed the Newcastle ministry in difficulties about the defence of the American colonies in 1755[2]. George III's close attention to this sphere of government activity was revealed early in his reign. In September 1762 he informed Bute he had spent several days working out a new peace-time establishment with a view to economy.[3] He also kept a careful watch on the record-book of military successions, and in November 1762 even Bute was not allowed to break the rules and secure a military appointment in Ireland for one of his political connections.[4] Lord George Germain's excuses to a 'discontented general' (it was Sir Guy Carleton) do not bear the inference which Pares here placed on them;[5] for in this case Germain was sheltering himself, in a dispute with a man with whom he was particularly at odds, with all the big guns he could muster, and he quoted both the cabinet and the king as the sanction for orders which were executed in his department.[6] To describe Grafton as unequal to the dismissal of Lord Chancellor Camden is a misrepresentation of a situation in which, in fact, the cabinet was split over the questions of Wilkes and America, the removal of Camden was unacceptable to Grafton,

[1] Bath MSS., printed, with some inaccuracies, in Jesse, *Memoirs of the Life and Reign of George III*, I 426–50.

[2] I am indebted for this information to Mr D. S. Graham, who has been engaged on a detailed study of the Newcastle administration's handling of the outbreak of the Anglo-French conflict of 1754–62 in North America.

[3] *Letters from George III to Lord Bute*, p. 135

[4] Ibid., p. 154; Namier and Brooke, *History of Parliament*, II 197–8.

[5] Pares, *King George III and the Politicians*, p. 174 n. 2.

[6] H.M.C., *Knox MSS.*, p. 133.

and his own resignation followed it a fortnight or so later.[1] Rochford's 'confidential reports of cabinet discussions' and priming of the king (this was in relation to the Falkland Islands crisis) seem less significant when it is remembered that it was normal practice for the king to know about disagreements between the ministers,[2] and it was natural for him to be appealed to; here again an instance can be adduced from very early in the reign, when in 1762 the king talked with various ministers to try and compose differences which had arisen over the peace negotiations.[3] Not only are these episodes less generally significant of a trend in king–cabinet relationships than Pares supposed; but the conclusions that have been drawn also stand in need of correction in the light of the other evidence which has been presented in the preceding section.

Apart from pointing towards a more balanced assessment of George III's role, evidence now available permits certain broad trends in cabinet development in the first half of his reign to be illustrated and explained with greater precision than has hitherto been possible. The somewhat fortuitous emergence of the war committee of the Pitt–Newcastle ministry in 1757 created the essential conditions under which a new type of cabinet was to emerge. An effective cabinet came into existence large enough to replace the old cabinet council but not so large as to give birth in its turn to yet another cycle of the process. Within a very few years experience dictated that the efficient ministers and the great officers of state should form its membership, whilst the household officers who automatically enjoyed membership of the formal cabinet council should be excluded. It is possible that the long isolation of a large group of the politicians in opposition after 1766 helped at a critical stage to prevent this process from being reversed, since it reduced considerably the sorts of pressure for expansion which had been particularly noticeable under the 'coalition' condition of politics between 1742 and 1760. Finally the efficient cabinet, once in being, generated new trends of practice

[1] *Autobiography of Grafton*, pp. 229–35.

[2] Pares, *King George III and the Politicians*, pp. 157–9. Further instances of dissenting opinions being submitted after cabinet meetings could be added to those cited here.

[3] P. 95 above.

and procedure, which themselves helped to give it momentum and to consolidate its position. Although not all the experiments in minuting decisions for the king's information proved permanent a much greater formality and method were introduced, and there are indications of a greater regularity of cabinet meetings by the middle of George III's reign than there had been about the year 1760.

THREE

The Marquis of Rockingham and Lord North's Offer of a Coalition, June–July 1780 *

THE 'negotiation' between Lord North and the Marquis of Rockingham in June–July 1780 was a manœuvre preliminary to the general election of that year. I have considered it here in that aspect; but I am mainly concerned in this paper to put forward the view that the traditional interpretation of Rockingham's conduct requires modification in the light of information now available from the Fitzwilliam papers.[1] The Marquis can be given more credit for consistency of principle and for good faith towards friends and associates than has hitherto been usually conceded.

By the early summer of 1780 both George III and Lord North had reached the conclusion that an early general election was a political necessity.[2] This decision was directly due to the events of the past six months. In the course of the long parliamentary struggle over economical reform, the government had several times suffered defeats on essential points in the House of Commons. The passage of Dunning's resolutions was felt as a personal affront by the king, and the strain of the battle had severely taxed the nerves

* This originally appeared in *English Historical Review*, LXIX (1954) 388–407.

[1] I wish to acknowledge the kind permission, given by Earl Fitzwilliam and his Trustees of the Wentworth Woodhouse Estates, to publish extracts from these documents, and my thanks are also due to the librarian of the Sheffield City Library for leave to consult them, and to members of his staff for their willing assistance. I have also made use in this paper of unpublished information from the correspondence of John Robinson in the possession of the Marquis of Abergavenny; and I desire to acknowledge the permission kindly given by him to use and quote from these papers, to which I have had access under the direction of Sir Lewis Namier, in the course of preparing material for the *History of Parliament*.

[2] *The Correspondence of King George III*, V nos. 3026, 3027; B.M. Add. MSS. 37835, fo. 129.

and energies of his minister.[1] Though the government's majority recovered as the spring advanced, it seemed clear that the forces of opposition must somehow be reduced or partly neutralised. To secure this end two possible, and perhaps complementary, courses lay open. One was a dissolution. The other was a compact with some part of the opposition, and this was the object of North's bid, at the end of June, for an alliance with the Rockingham party. A coalition would immediately ease the tension in parliament, and it would, as the king understood, facilitate the general election.[2]

It seems on the face of it surprising that North should have entertained any hope of such an agreement. The political antipathies between the Rockinghams and the administration were extensive and acute. But under the growing strain of war, ministers were urgent to build up a government of national unity. They 'were very desirous and in great hopes', Sir John Lindsay reported afterwards to Admiral Keppel, 'that a strong government, pleasing to the King and the people might have been formed, that it was the time of all others that has offered and particularly now more necessary'.[3] In this mood they were ready to clutch at any straw tossed to them by vagrant eddies of the political tide: and during June, the Gordon Riots gave rise to two developments which encouraged them in this hope. One was the strong stand for the restoration of law and order taken by Rockingham and his friends. The other was an open breach in the ranks of the opposition.

In the face of the Gordon Riots the Rockinghams showed no less ardour than the ministers for the re-establishment of law and order. They pressed for the imposition of martial law. Represented by Portland and Rockingham, they – alone of the groups in opposition – took part in the full privy council summoned on 7

[1] *The Correspondence of King George III*, v nos. 2986, 2987, 3026, 3027, 3028.

[2] Ibid., p. 96.

[3] Keppel to Rockingham, 13 July 1780, Rockingham MSS. Sir John Lindsay, K.B., R.N. (1737–88), had been a partisan of Keppel during the admiral's trial in 1779, and gave up his own command after Keppel's resignation. His reports were probably well informed, since he was nephew to Lord Mansfield and first cousin to Viscount Stormont, secretary of state for the northern department (*D*[*ictionary of*] *N*[*ational*] *B*[*iography*] (1909–10) xi 1186–7).

June to deal with this question. Though bitterly critical of the hesitation displayed by ministers, and of their refusal to place the military in complete control, they appeared to be at one with them on the necessity of putting down resistance to established authority.[1] This concurrence might breed a more general co-operation. At last the eyes of the Rockinghams seemed opened to the dangers of popular movements. Might not combined resistance to the spirit of rebellion at home now be extended to the wider range of the empire? As early as 4 June, Lord Stormont was speculating along these lines in a letter to George III. 'If proper steps are taken to stem the torrent', he wrote, 'and to resist this madness, I should hope that the convulsion may bring back a love of order and legal government and awake men into a sense of that danger which threatens the whole.'[2] It remained to be seen how far this reaction would carry the Rockinghams. A month after the king's receipt of Stormont's letter, an echo of the same idea was to be traced in his own notes concerning the proposed coalition. He was then clearly nursing the hope that some of them, at least, would abandon their former, declared principles and agree to uphold 'legal government' in America.[3]

Ministerial hopes of a union with the Rockingham party might also have been encouraged by the dispute between the Marquis and the Earl of Shelburne – for an opposition deprived of some of its friends might be less self-assertive, and also more easily satisfied in a bargain for places. From early in April a divergence of view had developed between the Rockinghams and Shelburne regarding parliamentary reform and the proceedings of the county committees of association.[4] Shelburne favoured the more radical activities of the committees and sympathised with suggestions for shorter parliaments and an addition of county members to the House of Commons.[5] But neither Portland nor Burke approved of

[1] *The Last Journals of Horace Walpole*, II 311.

[2] *The Correspondence of King George III*, V no. 3043.

[3] Ibid., no. 3099.

[4] H. Butterfield, 'The Yorkshire Association and the Crisis of 1779–1780' in *Transactions of the Royal Historical Society*, 4th series, XXIX (1947) 90–1 and n.

[5] *Political Magazine*, I (1780) 238–9, Shelburne to the chairman of the Wiltshire Committee, 26 Mar 1780; Fitzmaurice, *Life of William, Earl of Shelburne*, II 51–2, Shelburne to Mahon, 7 April 1780.

constitutional change, and Shelburne especially resented Burke's attitude and his influence over Rockingham.[1]

Some time prior to the beginning of June, Shelburne had demanded Rockingham's agreement to certain terms as the price of continued co-operation.[2] This he later explained in a letter to Barré for the information of the Duke of Richmond. Though the points of dispute were not stated in this *apologia*, it may be inferred that parliamentary reform was one of them. Richmond could not, he wrote,

> be surprised at my not attending parliament: on the contrary he must have a strange opinion of my unsteadiness and irresolution, if I did: as he was present when I plainly stated the alternative to Lord Rockingham. It is plain Lord Rockingham perfectly understood it by the decided steps which he risked during the summer. As to the public proposition Lord Rockingham has certainly checked its popularity (as I have had very disagreeable experience of in this very county, through the medium of his connections) and may have made it on the whole unpopular.[3]

A month before North's approach to Rockingham, Shelburne's patience had been strained to breaking-point by the rejection of his 'alternative', and he had given every sign of an intention to secede and to abstain from attendance in parliament. On 3 June, the day after the commencement of the Gordon Riots, he spoke with particular vehemence against the government, 'tried to insinuate that the mob was raised by the ministers [and] advised an immediate repeal of the Quebec Bill'.[4] But having reiterated his belief in the need for parliamentary reform, he had ended on what seemed like a note of abdication: 'though he would not bind himself to the assertion, most probably he should not return to that House, till matters were ripe and there was a greater likelihood of speaking

[1] Albemarle, *Memoirs of the Marquis of Rockingham*, II 410–15; *Correspondence of Edmund Burke*, ed. Earl Fitzwilliam and Bourke (1844) II 340; *Political Memoranda of Francis, Fifth Duke of Leeds*, p. 30.

[2] Shelburne's ultimatum almost certainly preceded the Gordon Riots, for Rockingham dated the Earl's breach with him to his speeches of 2 and 3 June and not to any later exchange of opinions (Rockingham to Richmond, 11 July 1780, Rockingham MSS.).

[3] Fitzmaurice, *Life of William, Earl of Shelburne*, II 70–1.

[4] *Political Memoranda of Francis, Fifth Duke of Leeds*, p. 31.

there to some purpose'. With great relish the reporter in the gallery ended his notes: 'It may be said of him in scripture phrase, *that he lifted his voice like a trumpet, cried aloud and spared not*. His Lordship termed the House of Commons a venal House of Parliament, declared Lord North a guilty man, and challenged ministry to send him to the Tower.'[1] By the end of June this division within the opposition had become sharper, and its existence was common knowledge. Not only had disagreement over political radicalism become acute. The Gordon Riots, fanning religious prejudice, had raised new discord. 'Lord Shelburne and Lord Rockingham are bitter enemies', wrote Walpole on 29 June. 'Burke . . . is mad for toleration. The Duke of Richmond and Charles Fox agree with him on that point, while the Duke is as violent for annual parliaments as the Rockinghams against them. Lord Shelburne, Lord Camden and the Duke of Grafton are as strongly antipapistic.'[2] A week later, on 5 July, Lord Barrington informed the Earl of Buckinghamshire: 'Lord Huntingdon confirms the [news] that the Rockingham and Shelburne parties are entirely disunited. I cordially wish that separation may be followed by a union between the Rock[ingham] party and the Court. The Shelburnes continue sulky and take no part in public affairs.'[3] And Rockingham, on the eleventh, likewise remarked on the political self-isolation of Shelburne, 'who not only I, but also all thought had taken his own line . . . [and] . . . . had *declared off* of all unions'.[4]

In late June, therefore, it was clear to the king and his ministers that opposition leaders were at odds among themselves, and that this discord might spell advantage to the government. Less well-formed were their ideas regarding the state of opinion among the Rockinghams. Was this moving in the direction of a possible reconciliation of views? The pretensions of the Rockinghams might have been lowered by the ultimate failure of their parliamentary campaign against the ministry. The arrival of better news from America might convince them that their policies were

[1] *Political Magazine*, I 428 (this publication gives a more complete report of these debates than either Almon's *Parliamentary Register* or the *Parliamentary History* edited by Cobbett).

[2] *The Letters of Horace Walpole*, ed. Mrs Paget Toynbee (Oxford, 1903–1905) XI no. 2071.

[3] B.M. Add. MSS. 34523, fo. 191.

[4] To Richmond, Rockingham MSS.

mistaken.[1] Some such line of thought would seem to have inspired North's overtures to Rockingham, but this could be no more than a plausible speculation (the error of which was soon to be proved by events). Such were the circumstances in which North, with the king's approval, set out, ten days before the prorogation of parliament, to attempt a coalition with the Rockingham party.

Rockingham's response to these advances has been regarded with what seems undue severity. The dubious honour of setting this fashion of reprobation belongs to Horace Walpole, for when writing his *Journals* he liberally besprinkled his version of this episode with scathing comments on Rockingham's conduct. His description of the proposals outlined by Rockingham, in reply to North's request for a statement of the terms on which he would be willing to enter into a coalition, hardly does justice to the Marquis's intentions:[2]

> Accordingly, Lord Rockingham's answer was that he himself desired no place nor anything but a seat in the Cabinet. The terms he demanded (for show) were that something should be done to give some satisfaction on the Middlesex election, something likewise on the Contractors' Bill, that some part of Burke's reforming bill should be adopted, and some of the Crown's influence diminished by taking away the votes of excisemen, &c. His Lordship demanded that the King should not declare that he would never consent to the independence of America, though his Lordship, on his side, wished that his Majesty should grant independence to America. As to places, Lord Rockingham desired that the Duke of Richmond and Fox should be Secretaries of State, T. Townshend Chancellor of the Exchequer, and that Burke should have a good place, and some others; and that Admiral Keppel should be at the head of the Admiralty.
>
> Nothing could be more futile and pitiful than these demands. They were most inadequate to the language held by the Opposition and to Lord Rockingham's late remonstrance. They were far below the demands not only of the associations but of the committees, which last Lord Rockingham had subscribed; they discovered no general views, aimed at reforming no capital grievances, and still less specified complaints against anybody.

[1] Dispatches reporting the capture of Charleston by government forces reached London on 15 June (*Gentleman's Magazine*, 1780, p. 295).

[2] *The Last Journals of Horace Walpole*, II 324–6.

They were not more honourable to his party than beneficial to the nation, and were by their silence singularly disrespectful to Lord Camden, Lord Shelburne, and the Duke of Grafton. . . . The demands were so timid, so insignificant, so unmanly, that they had the appearance of being managed only to facilitate Burke's throwing himself into all the measures of the Court, and did not even preserve the dignity of a man courted to be an apostate. The Court treated the Marquis with the contempt he had so justly incurred. . . .

Lord Rockingham then first notified the transaction to the Duke of Grafton, who very properly disdained to make an answer.

It was still more indecent that Lord Rockingham had not consulted with, nor, till past, communicated the treaty to the Duke of Richmond, who was not only his intimate friend, but who, in compliment to him, had always waived . . . figuring as head of the Opposition. The Duke . . . told all these particulars to General Conway. . . .

When Doran's edition of *The Last Journals* appeared in 1859, few documents bearing on this affair had as yet been published. An isolated, somewhat reproving letter to Rockingham from Admiral Keppel, in print since 1842, could be taken as confirming Walpole's verdict, suggesting that the Marquis had let himself be drawn unwisely into negotiation.[1] The *Memoirs of the Marquis of Rockingham*, published by the Earl of Albemarle in 1852, threw no light on the episode, the only relevant document reproduced being quite the least informative out of those preserved in copy or in original in Rockingham's papers.[2] Nor is it possible to infer the incorrectness of Walpole's judgement from documents later printed in part or complete by different editors, illustrating the thoughts of George III and of Lord North upon the matter.[3] Accordingly later writers have dismissed this incident as rather discreditable to Rockingham, concluding in particular, from a

[1] T. R. Keppel, *Life of Augustus, Viscount Keppel* (1842) II 277–8.

[2] II 420.

[3] Lord John Russell, *Memorials and Correspondence of Charles James Fox* (1853–7) I 251–4; Earl Stanhope, *History of England from the Peace of Utrecht to the Peace of Versailles* (1853–4) VII app., pp. xxx–xxxi; W. B. Donne, *Correspondence of King George III with Lord North* (1867) II 327–8; *The Correspondence of King George III*, V nos. 3092, 3098–3101.

misleading observation in one of the king's letters, that the Marquis had abandoned the principles of his party by compromising on the American question, agreeing to leave American independence open to events.[1]

However, more information concerning this affair has recently become available with the opening of the Wentworth Woodhouse archives. Among Rockingham's papers are his own memorandum relating to the commencement of the Montagu conversations, explanatory letters which he wrote to Richmond and to Admiral Keppel, and the comments he received from them. From these sources a picture emerges rather different from that derived from the Walpole tradition and decidedly more favourable to Rockingham's reputation.

Rockingham's memorandum was drawn up after the conclusion of the conversations. It is probably the narrative which, in a letter of 11 July, he promised to prepare for the information of the Duke of Richmond.[2] The greater part of it, which is cited below, deals with the early stages of the affair, fixes the chronology of the first exchanges, and reveals Rockingham's own version of the terms he considered a necessary basis for joining in a coalition government:

> On Wednesday evening June the 28th 1780 – Lord North in the House of Commons came to Mr Montagu, and desired that he would come to his house on that night, expressing great desire to have some conversation with him. Mr Montagu accordingly went; Lord North then told him that the occasion of his asking to see him was, in order to talk with him, and to *sound*, in order to see whether there was any possibility of a conciliation, by which a strong and efficient Government might be formed.
>
> Lord North wished to know whether any, or what terms might bring about so desirable an event. He thought it highly necessary, and that if it could be effected it would be very happy for this country. He said that he thought that with an efficient Government *Peace* might be had. He said, Spain was much inclined to peace he desired it might be had. He said in applying to Mr Montagu to

[1] E.g. Fitzmaurice, *Life of William, Earl of Shelburne*, II 62; C. Hobhouse, *Fox* (1947) pp. 105–6; K. Feiling, *Second Tory Party* (1951) p. 137.

[2] Rockingham to Richmond, 11 July 1780, Rockingham MSS. This packet also contains the memorandum and other unpublished papers relating to this episode.

know our sentiments he did *not* actually act by the King's authority but that it was with the King's privity. He said he had much pressed this matter to the King and that his own wishes were very sincere.

He said that there was a sincere desire to conciliate with us and other parts of *opposition. Lord Shelburne was supposed separated*, and that *he* was *out of this matter*.

Lord North gave Mr Montagu to understand that he believed his Majesty would be quite averse to moving him from the Treasury and that there might also be difficulties about the Admiralty but that in efficient offices and employments *room* must be made. He recommended moderation etc.; he also gave Mr Montagu to understand that *he* was not solicitous to remain at the head of the Treasury. Mr Montagu came away well satisfied that Lord North was anxious to assist in getting a good administration formed, and that he would do what he could with His Majesty in that view; Lord North desired Mr Montagu to come immediately to me and afterwards to come to him and let him know what my ideas were.

The same Wednesday night Mr Montagu came to me about ten o'clock; he stated the business nearly as I have done in the foregoing part, he added some little circumstances which had passed in conversation with Lord North and upon the whole (according to my ideas of the awkward and calamitous state of this country) *I thought* that certain priliminary or fundamental grounds for a negotiation might be commenced.

I shall now proceed to state the essential points which occur'd in my mind in that view. I held that no separate peace with Spain could be had, or would have good effect – that peace was in every respect most desirable – that a fundamental obstacle to peace must exist if his Majesty had, or continued to have, a decisive determination against acknowledging the independency of America at any rate, or risk: I therefore desired to premise, that if any new administration was to be formed, that it should be known, whether his Majesty would put a *veto* on the acknowledgement of the independency of America; and on the *other hand* I stated that what seem'd requisite was, that it should be understood both by his Majesty and his ministers that the *ultimatum* upon that business must, and was, to depend on the circumstances of, and at, the time.

The next idea which I stated was, that it matter'd nothing changing A and B, because they did not carry public confidence along with them if C and D, who succeeded them did not act, and did not visibly shew, that they adhered in administration to the general tenor and principles on which they had conducted themselves in opposition. I stated that our friends etc. etc. in the H. of Commons had very solemnly declared that the influence of the Crown was too *big*, *encreasing*, and ought to be *diminished*. I therefore urged that *certain measures* must be assented to – I named, – Dowdeswell's, or what is now call'd Crew's Bill – the Contractors' Bill – a hint about the Middlesex question – *great parts* of Mr Burke's Bill, particularly the part relative to the 3rd Secy of State – the abolishing of the board of Trade – the curtailing the patent offices of emolument in the Exchequer, the putting a stop to the large sums of money laying in the hands of paymasters and treasurers of the Navy: – and also in general a reform in the Exchequer – and also an attention and consideration of the bill for the Duchy of Cornwall – of Lancaster – and principality of Wales.

These very latter ones were only just named by me to Mr Montagu.

I then stated to Mr Montagu for him to communicate to Lord North, that my ideas were, no efficient and good administration could be formed, without the Duke of Richmond could be prevailed upon to take a great share in that administration, that I thought it extremely essential that his Grace should be Secy of State.

That I thought Mr Fox ought to be the other Secy of State.

That it was highly essential in every consideration that Lord Sandwich should be removed, and Admiral Keppel appointed First Lord of the Admiralty.

I avoided naming anything about *the Army*, because I wish'd to converse that matter over with the D. of Richmond.

I avoided *saying anything* to be communicated by Mr Montagu to Lord North relative to the Treasury.

I open'd my ideas to Mr Montagu on *that subject*, and I stated them to the D. of Richmond on Sunday the 1st of July at Ranmer, but Mr Montagu was not to touch upon that subject to Lord North.

I understood Mr Montagu did say to Lord North, that he was not to talk upon the subject of the Treasury but that he would so far say as that he believed that I, myself, was the only person who did not wish me at the Head of the Treasury and that what are call'd our friends would be very desirous of it.

Mr Montagu return'd to Lord North either late on the Wednesday night or early on the Thursday morning, and was with

Lord North again on the Thursday night. Lord North was to have been with his Majesty after the Drawing Room on Thursday but was kept so long by some of the Directors of the E.I. Company on Thursday, that he did not get to see the King till Friday morning.

The information contained in the short remaining section of Rockingham's narrative can be briefly summarised. On Friday (30 June) North disclosed the terms conveyed to him by Montagu both to George III and to Lord Chancellor Thurlow. The same night he saw Montagu again and gave him an interim report. The king had expressed some general criticisms but would give full consideration to the propositions and would furnish North with a memorandum of his thoughts upon them. Thurlow had criticised the vagueness of the proposals relating to America: but Rockingham had independent information, from Lord Weymouth via Charles Fox, that he was 'well inclined to promote the negotiation'. After this a week passed by, whilst the king and North were framing counter-proposals, and Montagu heard nothing further from North until Friday, 7 July.

A comparison of Rockingham's own version of his proposals with the account given by Walpole (derived at third hand through General Conway, who was informed of the talks by Richmond) shows how the facts could be twisted by threefold repetition, and how Walpole's prejudices could warp his judgement. On the main outlines of the proposals the two narratives tally: the differences are in arrangement and emphasis. Rockingham pinned down the discussions to three crucial questions – American policy, economical reform, and the distribution of offices within the proposed coalition. On all of these issues he laid down definite conditions, which would in fact, if accepted, have secured the implementation of his party's programme.

The question uppermost in Rockingham's mind was America – a fact which does not emerge from Walpole's narrative. To this matter the Marquis addressed his first observations, and the demand for the abandonment of the king's veto on American independence was vital. This granted, the way would be clear to securing a peace with the former colonists. Rockingham's reservation about the 'ultimatum' was undoubtedly vague, but need not be regarded as inconsistent with his former declarations in favour of independence. Whatever the construction put upon it by Montagu, North and George III, to him it was simply a recognition of the fact that the details of a settlement in America could not be determined beforehand.

Walpole's account creates the impression that Rockingham abandoned his party's principles and made damaging compromises on the issue of economical reform. But this clearly was not the case. For according to Rockingham's own statement of his terms, Crewe's and Clerke's bills were to be accepted entire, as also 'great parts' (not 'some part') of Burke's establishment bill, whilst a string of minor, supplementary reforms were also envisaged. Belated justice must also be done to Wilkes and the electors of Middlesex. These terms were perfectly consistent with the conduct of the party during the parliamentary session now drawing to its end, and were substantially the same as those forced upon the king in March 1782.

With this insistence on Rockingham's part upon these leading issues of policy marched his claim to the key positions in the cabinet. As regards the treasury, he was impelled to silence by what seems to have been genuine diffidence and modesty. But his friends were to control the northern and southern departments – which he intended for Fox and Richmond – and Sandwich at the admiralty must be replaced by Keppel. This arrangement, if it were effected, together with the elimination of the third secretary (Germain) by the passage of Burke's establishment bill, would give them executive control of all the business concerned with the conduct of war and diplomacy, and would thus confer the facilities needed to implement their American policy. Rockingham would thus secure a radical transformation of the administration. There were nine posts in the effective cabinet in 1780. Three of these at least would thus be held by his associates – four if he took a place in it himself. Among the six remaining ministers, Thurlow was understood to be favourable; North, if he remained at the treasury, would also collaborate – for from him came the offer of a junction; and with North would go his stepbrother, Lord Dartmouth, the lord privy seal. Of the rest, neither Amherst nor Bathurst would give trouble, for neither had any political following and by temperament both were professional servants of the state rather than politicians; and Lord George Germain would be dismissed (if he did not resign) preliminary to the abolition of his office. The post intended for Fox attests the pre-eminence he had by now attained in the ranks of the opposition. And the choice of Fox and Richmond for two leading offices makes it clear that Rockingham – although he had abandoned Shelburne, and although parliamentary reform was excluded entirely from his programme – had no intention of making a general break with all those of his associates in opposition who supported the radical movement.

Montagu having delivered Rockingham's terms to North on 30 June, the next step now lay with North and George III. Three days later (3 July) the king produced his promised memorandum, sending copies to North and to Thurlow.[1] He stated first his impression of the proposals conveyed by Montagu:

> I. That as to the American War it required no discussion with Mr Montagu's friends as they did not see how the troops could at present be recalled from thence, and that the dependency of America need also not be mentioned as it could not at the present hour be necessary to be taken into consideration.
>
> II. That some public measures must be admitted that Mr Montagu's friends might coalesce with reputation such as 1° Mr Crewe's Bill for disfranchising Revenue Officers, 2° the Contractors' Bill; and 3° part if not the whole of Mr Burke's Bill.
>
> III. That Lord Rockingham did not want office, but must be empowered to offer the D. of Richmond and Mr Fox to be considered on this occasion.
>
> IV. That the Dukes of Portland and Manchester should also be employed and Mr Thos Townshend and Mr Burke; and
>
> V. That no objection would be made to any particular man remaining in office but Lord Sandwich, who ought to be succeeded by Adm. Keppel.

The comments which followed made it abundantly clear that, so far as the king was concerned, agreement on the lines proposed by Rockingham was out of the question:

> . . . there cannot be the smallest doubt but that the evasive answer on America can by no means answer my expectations, indeed on all Constitutional Points the various parts of Opposition have run so wild, that it is absolutely necessary if any

[1] *The Correspondence of King George III*, v no. 3099. A transcript of the copy sent to Thurlow is in B.M. Egerton MSS. 2232, fos. 34–5.

coalition is to be attained, that those who come into office must give assurance that they do not mean to be hampered by the tenets they have held during their opposition; . . .

The second proposition I fear shews that I am not wrong in suspecting that those gentlemen wish to bring at least part of their tenets with them, what I have said before decides my opinion on what ought to be said on this subject.

The D. of Richmond and Mr Fox have more avowedly than any others of the Rockingham Party dipped themselves for they have added shortening the duration of Parliament and the former by a strange conceit changing the whole mode and right of election and consequently altering the constitution as far as he can; this added to his unremitted personal ill conduct to me, it cannot be expected that I should express any wish of seeing him in my service, . . .

As to Mr Fox if any lucrative, not ministerial office can be pointed out for him, provided he will support the measures of Government, I shall not object to the proposition, he never having had any principle can certainly act as his interest may guide him.

The D. of Portland is a man I should with pleasure see in my service, he used to look towards Ireland if that or a great court office should please him, I should think it advantageous to my service, the D. of Manchester in a lucrative office I could not object to; Mess. Townshend and Burke would be real acquisitions.

As to Lord Sandwich whatever his private failings may be, I know no man so fit for his department, . . .

These stipulations were a bar to any further progress. On every point the conflict of opinions was complete. George III would not relinquish America: he would tolerate no mention of economical reform. The right to determine policy must be his, and policy must remain as before. 'No man of sense', he commented, 'can pretend to defend government and [yet] support the measures he employed with a view to overthrow it.' Furthermore, he would not deign to consider the appointment to high office of the men on whose employment Rockingham laid most stress. In his view the formation of a coalition meant not transforming the administration but admitting to minor office the political conservatives among the Rockingham group. Portland, Manchester, Townshend and Burke, whom he was ready to welcome into his service if economical reform were given up, were all (except possibly Manchester) indifferent to, or strongly opposed to parliamentary reform.

To North, who had genuinely hoped for an agreement which would help him out of his parliamentary difficulties, this document must have been a bitter disappointment. Jenkinson and Robinson both found him irritated and discouraged, accusing friends and subordinates of misleading him in a step the responsibility for which was his own. 'His language at first was much to the effect you describe', wrote Robinson to Jenkinson on 7 July, 'blaming the attempt to coalesce because it would be ineffectual, said that I advised him to see Mr Montagu and that he should get into a scrape by it, that it would not do.'[1] Only on the seventh, four days after receipt of the king's memorandum, did he nerve himself to see Montagu again. But in this resumed discussion, he had no real concessions to offer, and was referring back questions to which in effect the answers had already been given. Since the king for his part would not yield, would the Rockinghams insist upon giving up the attempt to recover America, upon setting Keppel in place of Sandwich, and upon enacting their programme of economical reform?[2]

But Rockingham was not prepared to bargain. He required a plain yes or no. The message and paper of questions he received through Montagu later that night (7 July) he considered as a rejection of his terms, and as putting an end to North's overture for a coalition. The explanatory letter which he wrote to Keppel on the ninth makes it clear that no idea of compromise ever entered his thoughts:[3]

My Dear Admiral

It was too late at night when Mr Montagu came to me on Friday, and as I could not write before I went to bed, and was not an early riser yesterday I could not send you an account yesterday of the final issue of the *sort* of *negotiation* which had been carrying on. It was understood I think before you left

---

[1] Abergavenny MS. 266.

[2] *The Correspondence of King George III*, v no. 3101 (a memorandum drawn up by North on 7 July for his conversation with Montagu; the date of the document is established by the reference to it in Abergavenny MS. 266).

[3] Rockingham MSS.

London that His Majesty had taken the general outlines of the proposition *ad considerandum*. In the course of the week we were told that His Majesty had drawn up some thoughts and objections upon parts, and that he had given a long paper to Lord North who was to communicate it to the Chancellor, and that the Chancellor was then to see His Majesty, and that we were to be acquainted with the result of their ideas, etc. etc. It would be too long and too diffuse for a letter to enter into the whole of the conversation which passed between Lord North and Mr Montagu on *Friday night*, but nothing could be clearer than that there seems to be a *decisive disinclination to almost every idea on which (I thought) a government either in regard to measures or persons could be formed*. Nothing by way of answer in regard to our question relative to America, but a desire of putting questions to us, upon what is *assumed* to be its *present state*.

Nothing explicit in regard to measures which were deemed by me to be necessary by way of amendment in the Constitution, and by way of satisfying men's minds: it was said that some of the propositions might be acceded to, and that *some* must as it were *originate* in *the Crown* in a future session.

Rockingham went on to report the king's views about appointments without comment, and then concluded:

. . . I believe you will naturally ask on what idea or on what sort of plan could His Majesty or his *Minister* Lord North have had a thought of opening any negotiation. The only possible way which I can account for it, is, that *ten days ago*, they thought very differently *from what they do now*: the later *intelligence* from Charles Town is perhaps the great cause. . . .

'Negotiation', indeed, is a misnomer for these *pourparlers*: there never was any negotiation, merely a statement, by either side, of terms which were very quickly realised to be irreconcilable.

The evidence of Rockingham's papers thus clears him of damaging charges against his political integrity. Contrary to the insinuations of Horace Walpole, the fact was that he had adhered to the programme of economical reform. More particularly, George III's version of the Marquis's observations regarding America – 'that it required no discussion . . . that the dependency of America need also not be mentioned' – the basis of the conclusion that Rockingham and his friends had abandoned another of their leading principles – is shown from Rockingham's own testimony to be not in accordance with fact. This requires explanation, but it is fairly clear what had probably occurred. Between Rockingham's briefing of Montagu and North's report to the king, there had been two conversations between North and Montagu. And they, in their endeavour to open the ground for a reconciliation of views, had doubtless followed the familiar method of seeking formulas on points which were not clearly defined: they had slurred over and minimised the definite question of the veto on independence, on which the talks must otherwise have broken down at once.[1] This process was probably carried further by the king himself during the three days he took to consider North's report – and so he could describe Rockingham's proposal regarding America as merely 'evasive', whereas in its original form it had been utterly uncompromising. Again, the American question, with still further glosses, was referred back on 7 July through Montagu, who then thought it 'put in such a way as it might be answered and he thought got over'.[2] But in this he was entirely mistaken. In short, Montagu, charged with the Marquis's full instructions and acting as his agent, had committed an elementary error of negotiation, that of losing sight of the essential point laid down by his principal.

Were the leaders on both sides sincere? Neither North nor Rockingham were men of intrigue. The presumption therefore is that they both acted in good faith, and there is nothing in the documents to disprove it. Furthermore, the best evidence of their sincerity is the character of the common friend, Montagu, whom they employed as intermediary. 'A man of honour, candour and integrity', Henry Dundas described him.[3] A relation of North, Montagu was intimate with the minister's family circle:[4] but he

[1] Such a proceeding also furnishes an explanation of the remarkably optimistic view expressed by Robinson and passed on by Jenkinson to the king on the morning of Friday, 30 June: 'They are content to go on with the American War, and will agree that any future resolution shall be depend[ent] on events; they talk a little of Mr Burke's Bill, but Mr Robinson thinks they will be satisfied, if the Contractors' Bill is allowed to pass.' (*The Correspondence of King George III*, v no. 3092.) But Robinson's information was unreliable, and two days later he was reporting the entirely opposite opinion: 'I think the plan has been for them to hear . . . and then to decline in general terms.' (B.M. Add. MSS. 38214, fos. 59–60.) Doubtless North did not confide in him completely.

[2] H.M.C., *Abergavenny MSS.*, no. 266.

[3] Abergavenny MS. 321.

[4] H.M.C., *Dartmouth MSS.*, III 249.

consistently opposed the American policy of North's government on grounds of conscience. Rockingham held him in such high esteem that he three times had him elected for his pocket borough of Higham Ferrers. Later in this same year, both men pressed him independently to accept office as speaker of the House of Commons – a position in which he would have commanded the respect and support of members on both sides of the House. Montagu showed the most sincere and delicate scruples in his refusal, made on the grounds that his public loyalties would be divided.[1] It is not credible that such a man should have lent himself to underhand political manœuvres.

On the government side, some doubts were soon entertained – for instance by Robinson – whether Rockingham and his friends were genuinely interested in agreement,[2] but no charges were brought against their good faith. North was at first less favoured. The most violent strictures upon his conduct were pronounced by Keppel and Richmond. Richmond declared the whole affair to be a plot to confirm the government's suspicions of the split within the opposition and to exploit it.[3] 'Am I to think Lord North a rogue or a fool', wrote Keppel, 'to attempt opening a negotiation with your Lordship upon such ideas as you have now learnt to be the King's?'[4] But four days later, when he had received an independent, trustworthy account (from Sir John Lindsay) of the minister's state of mind, the tone of the admiral's comment had softened – though he owned he found it difficult to understand a suggestion, made by North, that Richmond should pay his respects at court, the omission of this duty for several years past having given personal offence to the king. This proposal 'looked to me much like trickery', he wrote, 'and certainly could his Grace think it right to go to court, it could have no other look than a personal desire to get into office, certainly as a preparation. . . . '[5] But

[1] Montagu to Rockingham, undated, enclosing an undated letter from North; Rockingham to Montagu and Montagu to Rockingham, undated; Rockingham to Montagu, 22 October 1780, Rockingham MSS.: Abergavenny MS. 321.

[2] B.M. Add. MSS. 38214, fos. 59–60.

[3] Richmond to Rockingham, 9 July 1780, Rockingham MSS.

[4] Keppel, *Life of Augustus, Viscount Keppel*, II 277–8.

[5] *The Correspondence of King George III*, v no. 3100; Keppel to Rockingham, 13 July 1780, Rockingham MSS.

Rockingham himself, from first to last, had no doubts as to North's sincerity. It is clear from his memorandum that he placed confidence in Montagu's belief that North was 'anxious to assist in getting a good administration formed', and when the sequel proved disappointing, he sought no explanation to North's discredit but attributed it to a change of mind. The ministers, he thought, must have regained their confidence since the commencement of the talks ten days before – 'the later intelligence from Charles Town is perhaps the great cause'.[1] This was a reference to dispatches published in London on 5 July, reporting strong demonstrations of loyalty in the Carolinas, and the rallying to the colours of loyalists in North Carolina, parts of which were still in the hands of the colonists.[2] The conclusion was of course incorrect. The obstacle to agreement was not a ministerial change of front in view of this news but the refusal of the king to concede Rockingham's demands. But Rockingham's trust in North was justified, and it was greatly to his credit that he did not waver in it, despite the contrary opinions of his friends. There is no hint in the documents relating to the government side of this business of any machiavellian scheme to undermine the unity of the opposition. North's offer of a coalition arose out of a rather foolish optimism, but it was quite sincere.

Did Rockingham act a dishonourable part towards other politicians in the opposition? Walpole stigmatised his conduct towards Grafton, Richmond and Shelburne as indecent and disrespectful, on the ground that he acted without consulting them. But this charge can be shown to be without foundation.

Certainly the initial response to North's overture was made by Rockingham on his own responsibility. But according to Rockingham's own later account, Montagu was to state that the views he was reporting were solely the Marquis's, and that any agreement would depend, not only on the king's willingness to accept Richmond as a secretary of state, but also on Richmond's being willing to take this office. Rockingham was in touch with Grafton from the beginning of the affair, and went himself to Ranmore camp on Sunday, 2 July, to talk over the business with Richmond. These facts appear from his letter written to Richmond on 11 July:[3]

[1] Rockingham to Keppel, 9 July 1780, Rockingham MSS.
[2] *London Gazette*, 5 July 1780.
[3] Rockingham MSS.

. . . Your Grace will recollect what I told you on Sunday sen'night last, you will remember that it was only my *ideas* which *Mr Montagu was to communicate*, and that it was perfectly understood, that it was very doubtful whether it would be possible to persuade your Grace to take office.

It is impossible indeed in a letter to state all the circumstances but I will prepare a full narrative for your inspection . . .

. . . The D. of Grafton went out of town last *Saturday sen'-night*; Lord John Cavendish went to Brookes to give his Grace an account of the opening of the business on the *Friday night* as his Grace was to set out early on Saturday and as I could not get to him. Mr Fox was to go either to Euston or New Market last Saturday . . . to inform his Grace of the conclusion. In the origin of the transaction and during the whole of it, the system understood was a comprehensive plan in which the assent and concurrence of *all parts of opposition* was to be tried for, and to be hoped for, except Lord Shelburne, who not only I, but also all thought had taken his own line, and had declaredly separated himself by his speeches on the Friday when the mob was at the door of the House of Lords; and also still more so, on the Saturday, the general idea was that Lord Shelburne had *declared off* of all unions.

Thus neither Grafton nor Richmond were ignored by Rockingham, and his proposals were conditional and subject to their approval. Shelburne, it is true, was not consulted. The conversations with North were begun and continued on the assumption that he would not participate in any arrangement. For this reason Richmond deplored the step taken by Rockingham, for he was most anxious to keep Rockingham and Shelburne working together.[1] But in taking up this attitude, Richmond failed to allow for the fact that a clear breach had already occurred between the two men – and Walpole (whose information came indirectly from Richmond) committed the same mistake in criticising Rockingham on this ground. The later disunity and weakness of the opposition in the autumn and winter of 1780 cannot be attributed solely to the activities of Rockingham, and certainly not to his *pourparlers* with North. The causes of that weakness were manifest prior to the talks and Shelburne incurred at least equal responsibility for it by his impulsive, irritable withdrawal from public affairs. At the end of

[1] Richmond to Rockingham, 9 July 1780, Rockingham MSS.

June, Rockingham had much excuse for acting independently of Shelburne. Yet this step was perhaps unwise. It amounted to a slight upon Shelburne. And in leaving the Earl to gather what account he could of the conversations from indirect sources, Rockingham greatly increased Shelburne's suspicions of him and made a reconciliation for some time entirely impossible.

On the whole Rockingham emerged with credit from this affair, which illustrates both some of the merits and some of the defects of his personality. The evidence in his papers disposes of the greater part of Walpole's charges against him. Far from betraying his party's policies regarding peace with America and economical reform, he firmly upheld them. On all points he was consistent, he yielded nothing. Other leaders of the opposition, Shelburne excepted, were consulted and kept informed. In his attitude towards North, Rockingham compared favourably with both Richmond and Shelburne. The crux in 1780 was control of policy. But even if this were conceded, neither Shelburne nor Richmond would contemplate association in office with men whose misconduct of affairs they had been consistently denouncing. Whereas Shelburne in 1780 saw in North a 'guilty man', Rockingham, with more balance and human charity, viewed him as a fellow politician who might be led towards the light. Shelburne was a good hater, and he was the worse politician for it – so that afterwards, in 1782, when North's co-operation was necessary to him, he found it difficult to forget or to forgive. Rockingham in this business showed the moderation and the conciliatory spirit admired by all his friends, allied with a firm sense of duty, responsibility and devotion to principles. But he also displayed a less praiseworthy characteristic, ill-becoming to a political leader – a negligence which amounted at times to discourtesy. This appears in his neglect of Shelburne, and also in his failure to send a final message to North.

On parting with North on the evening of 7 July, Montagu had declared he would lay North's notes and messages before the Rockingham party and bring back an answer.[1] But this answer seems not to have been given. One possible explanation was put forward by Charles Jenkinson. North having still received no word by 22 July, Jenkinson suggested in a letter to Robinson that members

[1] Abergavenny MS. 266.

of the party were differing among themselves as to whether or not the conversations should be continued.[1] There is however no evidence to support this view in Rockingham's correspondence. This does not reveal any disagreement among his friends, or any protracted discussions, over the decision to end the talks when his full demands were not immediately conceded. Richmond, Lee and Keppel all wrote on 9 July to approve this decision as soon as they heard of it.[2] Fox and Lord John Cavendish were in touch with the Marquis in London, and neither is stated to have expressed dissent. The only complaint came from the youthful and inexperienced Earl Temple, not a close associate, who regretted the refusal to compromise and accept a foothold within the administration.[3] Rockingham's papers contain no letters concerning the conversations of later date than 13 July, and his own letters of 9 July to Keppel and to Lee both clearly convey his own feeling that the talks were at an end.[4] Jenkinson noted in his letter of the twenty-second that there had not been, in the intervening fortnight, any news of party meetings of Rockingham's friends. It appears then that Jenkinson's suggestion was wide of the mark and over-subtle: no further explanation is required than that Rockingham rather thoughtlessly considered himself under no obligation to return an answer to North.

North's first interview with Montagu had been on 28 June. While the subsequent exploratory feelers for a coalition were still in progress, he was also turning his attention to the question of the dissolution. On Saturday, 1 July, three days after first seeing Montagu, he took the decisive step of submitting this matter to the cabinet. As Thurlow was absent, he sought no immediate approval for his proposal, but referred it for further consideration at another meeting.[5] By Monday the third, 'he was full of his arrangements and the next parliament',[6] and more discussions in the cabinet were due for the following day. Two sets of plans, linked in his own mind, were now being pursued side by side but independently:

[1] Ibid., 277.

[2] Rockingham MSS.; Keppel, *Life of Augustus, Viscount Keppel*, II 277–8.

[3] Rockingham MSS.

[4] Ibid.; Albemarle, *Memoirs of the Marquis of Rockingham*, II 420–1.

[5] B.M. Egerton MSS. 2232, fo. 36.

[6] B.M. Add. MSS. 38214, fos. 66–7.

no hint of the proposed dissolution was allowed to reach the ears of the Rockinghams. Elections, he hoped, would produce a parliament more favourably inclined towards the king's government. If the hostility of the formidable Rockingham party were converted into friendship by a coalition, this object would be easily attained. But any hopes nursed by North that the one scheme might contribute to the achievement of the other were dashed on receipt of the king's memorandum. Once again, for a moment, he talked of throwing up his office.[1] Certain now was the failure of the conversations, and disheartening the consequences. He was not to escape without some damage to the uneasy harmony of the cabinet. Thurlow, bitter and contemptuous towards his colleagues, made little secret of his dissatisfaction with the existing arrangements, showed himself favourable to the idea of a coalition, and, in particular, would have been prepared to sacrifice Lord Sandwich to achieve it. This fact soon reached the ears of Sandwich, and cordial relations between these two ministers were never restored during the lifetime of this administration.[2] More serious, since a coalition was not attainable, the impending general election could not be amicably arranged between the parties. Instead of bending their efforts to restrain aspiring candidates, to negotiate electoral truces and to compromise on the representation of contestable constituencies, the leaders on either side were now committed to open conflict. The elections would be forced into the semblance of a party contest, and no effort could be spared by the government to secure a majority in the new House of Commons. Now everything possible had to be done to preserve the secrecy of North's plans for the dissolution. In August ministers dispersed into the countryside, and the treasury board was adjourned, as if normal holidays were in contemplation.[3] Rumour was countered by rumour. The *General Evening Post*, for instance, reported on 26 August: 'The Cabinet have resolved to postpone the dissolution of Parliament until after Christmas. The present Parliament will therefore meet early in November to pass the land and malt duties etc. There will be very little private business, and the dissolution will certainly take

[1] H.M.C., *Abergavenny MSS.*, no. 266.

[2] B.M. Add. MSS. 38214, fos. 66–7; 34417, fo. 102; *The Correspondence of King George III*, v 322; H.M.C., *Abergavenny MSS.*, no. 408.

[3] B.M. Add. MSS. 38307, fo. 209b; Abergavenny MS. 286.

place early in the Spring. This is the present settlement.' But that same day John Robinson's messenger was speeding down to Bath with a letter summoning Thurlow to the council for the dissolution.[1] The Rockinghams had not disarmed, so North would spring a mine beneath their feet.

[1] Acknowledged by Thurlow on the twenty-seventh (Abergavenny MS. 294.)

FOUR

*Charles James Fox**

CHARLES James Fox entered the House of Commons in 1768, while still under age. He made his mark at once as a debater; by his early thirties he was one of the leading personalities in the House, and he remained a member of it for over thirty-seven years, till his death in 1806. Yet his ministerial career is counted in months only, rather than in years: setting aside his early apprenticeship in junior posts, he held high cabinet office for three months in 1782, eight months in 1783, and seven months in 1806 – a year and a half in all. It seems at first sight extraordinary that a man of so much vitality, who commanded so much admiration from almost all who knew him, even from his opponents, possessed of dazzling parliamentary talents, and with other abilities of no mean order, should have failed to achieve positions of place and power and, through them, to leave a greater mark upon his country's history.

Between 1774 and 1782, Fox spent eight years in opposition to the North ministry, and to its attempts to recover the American colonies. But, as a close analysis of parliamentary events makes clear, it was military defeat, and not his eloquence, that eventually brought down the government. It is doubtful if the economical reform carried into law during 1782 owed much to his efforts; in any case, it was a grossly overrated policy. As secretary of state in 1783, he was responsible for concluding the Peace of Versailles, which ended the American War of Independence; but having turned out Shelburne, who had laid the foundations of the treaty, he concluded it on rather less favourable terms than Shelburne had secured, and this in part through his own negligence. The East India bill of 1783 was Burke's creation rather than Fox's: and both of them showed a remarkable political blindness in connection with it, by laying themselves open to attack for seeking to engross political patronage. After being turned out of office in consequence,

* This originally appeared in *History Today*, VIII (1958) 110–18.

Fox in his opposition to the younger Pitt was, for the most part, frankly factious. He remained in opposition for all but the last few months of his life. During this part of his career, two measures are particularly associated with his name, the Libel Act and the abolition of the slave trade. He deserves praise for taking the lead over both these issues; but it must be remembered that on the first he had the active assistance of Pitt, and on the second Pitt's posthumous support, exerted through many of his friends and associates. The student of Fox is driven to the question, not what did Fox accomplish, but why was it that he accomplished so little?

Energy and ability Fox had in full measure; about this there can be no doubt. Even his most hostile critics never denied it. His brain seemed to work at twice the ordinary speed. 'I believe,' wrote his friend Lord Carlisle about 1771, 'there never was a person yet created who had the faculty of reasoning like him. His judgements are never wrong; his decision is formed quicker than any man's I ever conversed with; and he never seems to mistake but in his own affairs.' The French traveller La Rochefoucauld, during his sojourn in England, noted that Fox amazed his contemporaries by the ease with which he mastered the intricacies of race-course betting. 'To acquire all this knowledge', he wrote, 'is so difficult, that those Englishmen who have mastered the various points regard it as quite extraordinary that Mr Fox should have been able, in five weeks of intensive study, to grasp its intricacies. In fact, they consider it to be evidence of the mastery of his genius.' Philip Francis, a hostile observer, wrote that Fox was born for litigation and would have made his mark at the bar. His gift for absorbing facts and arguments was phenomenal, as was his ingenuity in debate. Of these powers he gave early proof. Horace Walpole relates, for instance, the proceedings in 1772 on Fox's motion for a bill to amend the law regarding marriage, against which Lord North and Edmund Burke had both spoken with force and feeling: 'Charles Fox, who had been running about the House talking to different persons and scarce listening to Burke, rose with amazing spirit and memory, answered both Lord North and Burke, ridiculed the arguments of the former and confuted those of the latter with a shrewdness that, from its multiplicity of reasons, as much exceeded his father in embracing all the arguments of his antagonists, as he did in his manner and delivery.'

Fox's gift in working up a brief is evident from many of the set pieces with which he introduced a debate, notably his handling of his East India bill. His capacity for debate is evident everywhere in the reports of his speeches. Carlisle and Francis, writing after his death, confirm what Walpole noted of his early career, the aggressive assurance with which he would attack the whole body of argument put up by his opponents. Francis remarked that 'of the judicial faculty as applied to penetration and destruction in argument', he had infinitely more than a common share. Fox was not a graceful orator, nor was his matter carefully arranged. He spoke with great rapidity, the words tumbling over each other in the hurry of self-expression, and with a good deal of repetition; but his vehemence, and the facility of argument that he employed, made a powerful impression, at least until the listener had time to consider carefully what he had said. The spontaneity, that ranged from sincere emotional appeal to the broadest clowning, enabled him always to hold the attention of the House of Commons.

Another quality also might have been thought to guarantee his success. No man was a better mixer; no man ever put on less side; no man had a greater talent for making strangers feel at their ease and for winning friendships. With justice did the younger Pitt refer to 'the wand of the magician'. Charm, affability, zest, overflowing spirits – these were qualities that disarmed all-comers and captivated his friends: their strength is perhaps best seen in the reluctance with which men who had associated with him in politics for a decade or more, and who had for him the highest admiration and affection, gradually broke away when unable any longer to accept his lead on the issues raised by the French Revolution. Rarely has it been given to a man of such force of personality to stir up so few real hatreds in the course of his life.

Was he, then, unfortunate? Or was it some flaw in himself that barred him from success?

In 1783 George III admitted to William Grenville that Fox was 'a man of parts, quickness and great eloquence', but observed that he 'wanted application, and consequently the fundamental knowledge necessary for business'. One cannot simply take the king's word against Fox: their mutual dislike was notorious. But, in fact, there is a good deal of evidence to support this judgement. At times Fox displayed an enormous capacity for hard work; but he never showed himself capable of sustained effort on this scale. The will-power, the staying power, the steady, grinding application, which make for greatness, were absent. Fox relied too much upon slap-dash improvisation; his bouts of energy were too liable to be extinguished by laziness and self-indulgence. 'Slapdash improvisation' is not too harsh a phrase to describe his approach to public business. Well known is the early instance, in 1772, when he moved for, and obtained leave to introduce, a bill for the repeal of Lord Hardwicke's Marriage Act, without having taken the first step to prepare any bill on the subject: and, at a later stage, he arrived from Newmarket so late on the day that the second reading was to be taken that the bill was thrown out in his absence.

His attendance at public boards tells the same story. Ambitious young politicians would have given much to be appointed, as Fox was, to the board of admiralty, when barely twenty-one. Most of them would have made more of their chance. But for the first three months Fox was rarely there; for the next four or five he attended regularly, evidently alternating with other members under vacation arrangements; and then, for the remaining nineteen months of his appointment, there was almost complete withdrawal – during twelve of these months he made no attendance at all. Over the same period, although he intervened frequently in debate on any subject that caught his interest, there is scarcely a trace of evidence that he made any attempt to take his share as a spokesman for the admiralty in the House of Commons. A little later, the chart of his attendance after appointment to the treasury board seems to have begun following much the same course, though his tenure was too short for this evidence to be considered conclusive.

True, when Fox left the treasury he was only twenty-five. All this might be regarded as youthful peccadillo. But there are later examples of impetuosity, carelessness, inattention to detail. There was the case in 1778, when he decided to undertake an attack upon the government over the fiasco of Saratoga. 'I have business enough', he wrote to his friend Fitzpatrick, 'indeed, more than I can well manage; for though I like the House of Commons itself, I hate the preparatory business of looking at accounts, drawing motions, etc., as much as you could do.' In his haste, he launched his attack on the ministers prematurely, before the military leaders concerned had returned from America and could be called on to give information. Small wonder that his efforts misfired for lack of evidence. After his resignation in 1782, at the end of his three months' tenure of the foreign office, his successor, Grantham, remarked, 'he certainly was precipitate in many measures.' This might be discounted as mere prejudice; but then, in 1783, there was the glaring omission in the preparation of diplomatic instructions that gave away a substantial point in negotiation to the court of Spain. 'We made a concession not warranted by the preliminaries', Fox wrote to the British ambassador at Paris, and candidly owned his fault: 'The unfortunate circumstance, too, of my having left this article quite blank in my project, prevented the words coming into consideration in the same manner as those of the other articles.'[1] 'Inexcusable' would be perhaps a juster epithet. No statesman or politician is immune from mistakes, and Fox must have his allowance. But there is a consistency of evidence that seems to support the king's condemnation of him as lacking in the application necessary for public business.

An equally grave fault was his reckless lack of judgement. This was early apparent. As a schoolboy, listening to a debate in the House of Lords, he was noted by Lord Mansfield in an aside to his neighbour: 'Fox's son, Charles, with twice his parts and half his sagacity.' His impetuosity seemed to increase through the years rather than being subdued with maturity. In the opinion of George III, in 1783, he was 'totally destitute of discretion and sound judgement'. Once more, there is plenty of evidence throughout Fox's career to justify the king's view. Time and again, he seemed incapable of pausing and taking a balanced view of circumstances, and would insist upon going his own way with disastrous results. At the very outset of public life, he threw away a fair prospect of ministerial advancement, not on any question of principle, but from ungovernable pique against Lord North. During 1773 he became involved in one of the undertakings of Edmund Burke's disreputable brother, Richard – a land speculation in the Caribbean island of St Vincent. He was engaged to press Richard's claims with the treasury, and as an inducement and reward was offered a share in the profits in the event of success. Circumstances were such that North could do nothing for him; and from about the end

[1] Manchester to Fox, 15 July, Fox to Manchester, 20 July 1783, B.M. Add. MSS. 47562, fos. 90, 96.

of the year Fox, bitter with disappointment, seems to have regarded himself as cheated and treacherously deceived by him. In January 1774 he gave up all attendance at the treasury board, and in the following weeks his behaviour in the Commons is consistent with only one explanation – that, in retaliation, he intended to embarrass North as far as lay in his power; and it was for this reason that he lost his seat on the treasury board.

This circumstance explains also the vituperative personal hostility towards North that is apparent in Fox's speeches during the following years. He certainly did not break with North over American affairs. At that moment North was bringing forward his proposals for punitive legislation against the people of Massachusetts, consequent upon the news of the Boston tea-party and other incidents. Fox, for at least a fortnight after his dismissal, was still speaking in support of the proposal to close the port of Boston, though he was trying to make trouble for North over its details – notably the grant of a delegated power to the crown to reopen the port when amends had been made. It was only after some weeks that he finally went into open opposition to government policy in America. Evidence from reports of debates[1] confirms the later account by Lord Carlisle: 'If an idle quarrel had not happened between him and Lord North, we might have seen him a supporter of the American War, a champion for the prerogatives of the Crown, and a favourite in the Closet . . . the consequence was the converting a most powerful and attached friend into a bitter enemy, a driving him into the arms of a faction, the principles of which he adopted not from inclination but from resentment. Five days before that event, he was held by the opposition in execration, and in return those who composed that faction in contempt by him.'[2] These were the circumstances, and not the malice or the fear suspected by Fox's biographer, Sir George Otto Trevelyan, that led George III to condemn Fox with the observation: 'Indeed that young man has so thoroughly cast off every principle of common

[1] Speeches of 14, 25 March 1774, on the Boston port bill, Brickdale MSS., Diary, x 22; Debrett, *Parliamentary Debates, 1743–74*, VII 92–93.

[2] Character of Fox, by Lord Carlisle (1806), Carlisle MSS. My thanks are due to Professor A. Aspinall for permitting me to quote this passage from his transcripts of the Carlisle MSS.

honour and honesty that he must become as contemptible as he is odious.'

Fox thus turned to opposition to the North ministry during the American War of Independence. His attacks upon it in the Commons dwelt mainly upon the impossibility of reconquering America, and upon the incompetence of ministers in the waging of war. None of this necessarily damned his political future: the younger Pitt came into parliament in 1780, pursuing much the same conduct, and in little over three years he was prime minister. But Fox could not restrain his impulses and his passions. He developed a personal hostility towards George III which could only be assuaged by the king's complete surrender to him in political matters. This, in every way, was a mistake. It led Fox to vent his spleen in private conversation in a manner that was bound to get to the king's ear and cause exasperation; in the spring and summer of 1782, in speech and writing, he and his circle were referring to the king as 'Satan'; and on one occasion after the fall of the North ministry he was reported as saying: 'Certainly things look well, but he (meaning the king) will die soon, and that will be best of all.' It led him to attribute far too much importance to the part played by the king in prolonging the American war, and to think that it was the king alone who stood in the way of a ministry that would get rid of the war by conceding independence to America. There was a parliamentary majority in favour of the war; but Fox got over this difficulty by maintaining that it was a corrupt and hired majority, created by 'the influence of the Crown'. Nothing could have been farther from the truth. As Burke and other opposition leaders from time to time admitted, the country was behind parliament in its approval of the continued efforts to reconquer the colonies. In all this Fox sadly deceived himself about the forces that sustained a war ministry in office until after the military catastrophe of Yorktown.

Between 1780 and 1784, in the years of political crisis provoked by the loss of America, Fox's opportunism was seen at its worst. For the advantage of the moment, he snatched at constitutional conceptions that were mutually exclusive. On the one hand, he plunged headlong into the radical movement in the City of Westminster, in association with men who wished to make the House of Commons much more subordinate to opinion outside by means of electoral reform and more frequent general elections. In April 1780, he delivered himself of the view that, 'when the representative body did not speak the sense of the constituent, the voice of the latter was constitutional and conclusive'; and he even pledged himself to work for annual parliaments. On the other hand, later on in 1784, when it better suited his purpose, he upheld against outside opinion the right of a given parliamentary majority (one which he led) to have its own way and to coerce the king into restoring the coalition ministry to office.

This majority, by means of which he sought to dictate during the opening months of 1784, was that created by his junction with North in the notorious coalition government of 1783. That coalition is yet another instance of his lack of judgement. It shattered the confidence of many independent members of the Commons, who had thought that in Fox they had discovered a man of principle, and who were aghast at his joining forces with politicians whom he had previously denounced in the most forthright terms, declaring that he could never associate in office with them. Fox's words, it was clear, could not be taken on trust. Indeed, he said many things that he did not mean, and to make points in debate appealed to principles of action on which he held no real convictions. There are other instances. In 1779 he lashed out in debate at Lord Amherst, the commander-in-chief, on the ground that he was ruining the army by permitting political influence to govern military promotions; but in 1783, as secretary of state, he clashed seriously with Conway, because Conway, as commander-in-chief, resisted his and Portland's attempts to make political promotions.[1] Again in the years 1780 to 1782 no one was more vehement than Fox in denunciation of the use of patronage for political purposes. And yet, were Fox and his colleagues so entirely innocent of intention to engross patronage through his East India bill? When William Eden, one of the leading spirits in the formation of the coalition, set out to persuade John Courtenay of the merits of the measure, he 'expatiated with great zeal and party confidence on the infinite advantages of this politic expedient for infallibly securing the permanency of the present Administration for seven years at least, by

[1] Conway to Fox, 31 July, 7 Aug 1783, B.M. Add. MSS. 47568, fos. 144–151.

their possessing such an unbounded and lucrative patronage.[1]

But perhaps Fox's greatest errors in these years were to think that the king should be excluded altogether from politics – that is, that he should no longer have a voice in the selection of ministers – and to believe that the events of 1782 had made this possible: in March 1782 he even boasted that he had brought about 'a complete change in the constitution'. This was to traverse cherished conceptions about the balance of forces in the constitution, which any but party men were bound to defend. In 1784 one of the most damaging counts against him with the public was that he had denied the king his legitimate role in the system of government. Fox's actions in these years reflect an inadequate grasp of political and constitutional realities and an insensitiveness to public opinion. This, added to the personal hostility which the king, not unreasonably, had developed towards him, led to his complete undoing in 1784.

In the years immediately following 1784 Fox carried on an opposition to Pitt that was more factious than enlightened. In 1785 he and his friends conducted an unscrupulous campaign to prevent Pitt from succeeding with his proposals for a commercial agreement with Ireland, stirring up nationalist passions on both sides of the Irish Sea; and in 1786 he unsuccessfully opposed the liberal commercial treaty negotiated with France. But within five years he had again exposed himself to damaging attack – to being 'unwhigged '– by championing the Prince of Wales's claim to assume the regency during the mental illness of George III. Later, in 1792 and 1793, his resentment against Pitt and George III was such that he would not contemplate the chance of taking second place in a coalition, and persisted in an opposition which became more and more unreasonable. At the end of 1792, such was his state of mind that he 'declared with an oath, that there was no address at this moment Pitt could frame, he would not propose an amendment to, and divide the House upon'. His belief that the security precautions taken by Pitt's government against the spread of revolutionary ideas from France betokened the extinction of liberty in Britain may have been sincere; but it was certainly based on self-delusion; and his public pronouncements in debate on the subject

[1] John Courtenay, *Incidental Anecdotes and a Biographical Sketch* (1809) pp. 135–8

of France during the Revolutionary Wars attributed to French leaders an innocence of intention to damage British interests which has been imperceptible to most other observers and writers then and since. It is not surprising that he remained in the political wilderness, the leader of a tiny and ineffectual opposition, for practically the remainder of his life.

If any further explanation is to be sought for his failure, it is probable that it is to be found in an indiscipline fundamental to his nature and given full play by the defects of his upbringing, which marred all his gifts and generous impulses. The blame lies with his father, Henry Fox, who utterly spoiled and also corrupted his favourite son. Nothing that the infant Charles would do was denied him, whether it were making a blaze on the fire with state papers, or smashing a watch regardless of its cost. Nothing was done at home that might in any way inculcate in him discipline and an understanding of its advantages, or a sense of the external realities with which every human being must come to terms. Instead, the view of his father was 'Let nothing be done to break his spirit. The world will do that business fast enough.'

Nothing could have been more disastrous than such indulgence, especially when accompanied by an early introduction to the vices of fashionable society. When barely fourteen, Charles was taken for four months away from Eton, to accompany his father on a tour of the Continent. He returned so confirmed a gambler that the tone of the school suffered a long-enduring change for the worse as a result of his influence. Ever after he had the gambler's indifference to people and circumstances. This is the key to an understanding of him; and we are fully justified in dwelling upon it. There was the disregard for his father: no one ever showed less filial duty, in the way he squandered his father's fortune. There was the disregard for his friends, from whom he borrowed shamelessly, overwhelming them with storms of emotional reproaches when they showed reluctance to help him: it was pointed out to one of them, Carlisle, in 1774 that it was time Fox showed some consideration for his affairs – 'Your future friendship will then have a basis (on) which it has never yet stood, and that is reciprocity.' When the crash came, his debts amounted to £140,000. After this there was talk of his training and earning a living at the bar; and had he had the strength of character to do it, there is no doubt he would have made a brilliant and successful barrister. But it all ended in smoke; and having let others ruin him, the most constructive effort to which he eventually could rise, in the years 1781–2, was to recoup his fortunes by the ruin of others, running with three cronies a faro bank which in good times might bring in as much as £2,000 a week.

The gambler's nature was dominated by disregard for people and for facts: it was in this sense that Fox, although he gave up the card tables after 1784, remained a gambler for the rest of his life. For disregard of facts, there is his remarkable avowal in a letter to Burgoyne in 1778: 'At whist, as you very well know, it is often right in a desperate case to play upon a supposition of your partner's having a good hand, though there might be the strongest symptoms of the contrary; because if he has not the game is lost. Just so, I think of the present state of affairs. It is the duty of those who mean to act upon public motives to suppose many things which they cannot believe.' For his disregard of people, there is the testimony of two of the men who knew him well. When he was in his thirties, George Selwyn, one of his more critical admirers, wrote of him:

> Charles, I am persuaded, would have no consideration on earth but for what was useful to his own ends. You have heard me say, that I thought he had no malice or rancour; I think so still and am sure of it. But I think that he has no feeling neither, for anyone but himself; and if I could trace in any one action of his life anything that had not for its object his own gratification, I should with pleasure receive the intelligence because then I had much rather (if it were possible) think well of him than not.

Besides this we may set the observation of Philip Francis: 'The essential defect in his character and the cause of all his failures, strange as it may seem, was that he had no heart.'

The politician moves, and has his being, in a close-meshed web of human ideals and aspirations, ideas and prejudices. He must respond to the vibrations of numerous threads, each running back to some individual source. For such comprehensive and delicate perception Fox's mind was not attuned. He was constitutionally ill-adapted to come to terms with people and circumstances Consequently, his political judgement was blind and disastrous for himself and his followers. Not all his febrile energy, fertile intelligence, mental ingenuity and dexterity with words could compensate for this defect. As a politician he was his own worst enemy.

FIVE

John Robinson, M.P., 1727–1802 *

I. 'JACK ROBINSON'

John Robinson, attorney, country gentleman, member of parliament, administrator, and ancestor of the Earls of Abergavenny, was descended from a numerous and prosperous Westmorland family.[1] During the seventeenth century its leading members had risen from the rank of yeoman to that of 'gentleman'. In the early eighteenth century they became established among the gentry of the county and played their part as commissioners of the peace, while cadet branches were to be found grading downward through the professions and occasionally in trade. John Robinson's grandfather, John Robinson, J. P., of Appleby (1673–1746), inherited family properties at Winder and Appleby and seems, from his will and from the success with which he launched his numerous offspring, to have been a man if not of wealth at least of solid substance. In the next generation the family developed strong links with the legal profession and with the government service. Of the elder John Robinson's four daughters who survived infancy, two were married to 'gentlemen' and the other two to local solicitors: one of these was Richard Wordsworth, chief steward of the Lowther estates, clerk of the peace for the county from 1750 till his death in 1760, and grandfather of the future poet laureate. His two elder surviving sons, Thomas and Hugh, were sent to Cambridge, and while Hugh subsequently elected to go into the church, Thomas and a younger brother, Jeremiah, both trained at the inns of court and were called to the bar. Both briefly held posts in the Post Office before their rather early deaths, and their two youngest

* This originally appeared in part in *Bulletin of the Institute of Historical Research*, *XXIX* (1956) 108–22.

[1] The following family details are taken from Charles Best [Norcliffe], *Some Account of the Family of Robinson of the White House, Appleby, Westmorland* (1874).

brothers followed them in this arena with more success. Christopher Robinson held the office of principal surveyor from 1749 till his death in 1762. He was succeeded by his brother, Atkinson, who died in office in 1771. Christopher's daughter was married to Anthony Todd, who may have owed to Thomas Robinson his first appointment as a clerk in the foreign office of the Post Office in 1738. Todd became secretary of the Post Office in 1762, and after being briefly displaced in the later sixties, held this office till his death in 1798. Only Charles, the third of Robinson's sons to survive to manhood, failed to make a career at this social level, a circumstance which suggests the possibility of some lack of aptitude or character. He went into business, becoming a mercer and linen-draper in Appleby, probably trading also in groceries and wines. In 1726 he married Hannah, daughter of Richard Deane of Appleby, and John Robinson, the eldest of their eight children, was born little over a year later, on 15 July 1727.

Although Charles seems to have been only moderately successful, the upward social climb was resumed by his children. His only daughter married a son of the Chaytors of Croft in Yorkshire. Of his younger sons, Joseph became a solicitor and was clerk of the peace of Westmorland for about twelve years till his death in 1776; the next, Thomas, was an officer in the Royal Artillery; and the youngest, Jeremiah, was a barrister, a bencher of Gray's Inn, and for some time recorder of Appleby.[1] All this probably reflects the influence of a wide but close-knit family connection, the more prosperous members of which found openings for their young kinsmen. This was clearly the case with the eldest son. After a meritorious passage through Appleby grammar school, John Robinson was taken for training by his aunt Mary's husband, Richard Wordsworth. In due course he qualified as a solicitor and became closely associated with Wordsworth in his work as steward of the Lowther estates. The influence of his clerical uncle, Hugh Robinson, may also have been exerted in his favour. Hugh had close relations with the Lowthers. He became chaplain to Henry, 3rd Viscount Lonsdale, who presented him to the rectory of Lowther, and he was later nominated to the rectory of Bowness by Katherine Lowther, the mother of Lonsdale's heir, the famous Sir James Lowther, 5th baronet. Through one or other, or both,

[1] Three other boys died before reaching manhood.

of his uncles John Robinson also enjoyed the favour of the Lowther family. Before Lonsdale died in 1751 he had made Robinson lieutenant-colonel of the Westmorland militia and had taken him into service as joint steward with Wordsworth in charge of his estates.

As Richard Wordsworth grew older and less active, Robinson's grip on the political and economic interests of the Lowther estates became more sure. A sign of his own prosperity and consequence was the growth of his electoral interest at Appleby, where by 1754 he already had possession of eighteen burgages. In that year he managed the general election at Appleby on Lowther's behalf; and three years later, in 1757, he and Sir George Dalston managed Lowther's unopposed return at a by-election for Cumberland.[1] The careful watch he maintained over Lowther's interests caused frustration and anger among Lowther's rivals in local politics. 'If [Sir James] had consulted his cooler friends', Sir Anthony Abdy wrote to the Duke of Devonshire in 1759 concerning a proposal by Lord Thanet for a permanent agreement with Lowther to share the Appleby seats, 'he would have done it, but he is governed and directed by one Robinson, a dirty attorney of Appleby who lives with him, and I am satisfied no good can come from the company or advice of such creatures.'[2] On Wordsworth's death in 1760 Robinson succeeded him as clerk of the peace for Westmorland and became sole steward of the Lowther estates; in both cases the appointments probably formally confirmed what had been the situation in practice for some time. The same year he was chosen mayor of Appleby.

Within a year or two of these events Robinson could no longer be written off in terms of contempt as a mere attorney. In 1759 he had married Mary Crowe, the daughter of a wealthy West India merchant, who brought with her an ample dowry. At the end of 1762, on the death of his uncle Hugh, he inherited Winder Hall and other family estates in the neighbourhood of Kendal and Appleby. It seems probable that from about this date his income from landed estate was somewhere in the region of £1,000 a year, a figure in virtue of which he can be considered

[1] Robinson to Lowther, 24, 30 Apr 1757, H.M.C., *Lonsdale MSS.*, pp. 129–30.

[2] 3 June 1759, Devonshire MSS.

as comfortably placed among the lesser gentry of the county.[1]

In September 1761 Sir James Lowther married a daughter of George III's favourite, the Earl of Bute. As a consequence, despite the remoteness of Cumberland and Westmorland from London, a close connection developed between his circle and the court. This involved Robinson, who now began to enter into correspondence about his patron's affairs with Charles Jenkinson, Bute's under-secretary of state in the northern department and later his private secretary when he became first lord of the treasury. At this time Robinson is found writing about Lowther's electoral interests, forwarding for Lowther's attention congratulatory addresses to the king from the county, and negotiating about Lowther's troubles with the Customs over shipments of coal from his collieries out of Whitehaven.[2] It was a measure of Lowther's confidence in him, as well as of his own status as a gentleman of the county, that in December 1762, in the course of framing electoral rearrangements designed to preserve his political influence, Lowther contemplated having Robinson put up as candidate for Westmorland. Robinson's reputation in the Bute–Lowther circle at this time is reflected in a letter from Charles Jenkinson to Lowther about this proposal:[3]

> You act very nobly in again forgiving your brother . . . [and] making him an offer to choose him for Westmorland; I suppose if he would stand, no one would pretend to oppose him, but from his former conduct I cannot suppose that he will act so wise a part: and that being the case, you certainly act wisely in taking

---

[1] According to Norcliffe, his inheritance gave him an income well above the minimum of £600 set as a qualification for knights of the shire in parliament. In 1780 he sold most of his Westmorland estates to the Earl of Thanet for £23,000, but kept Winder Hall. At the same time he also received another £6,000 from Thanet for the burgage houses which he owned in Appleby, but much of this sum was probably in consideration of the electoral interest and bore little relation to the rents (Norcliffe, *Some Account of the Family of Robinson*, pp. 39, 42–3). G. E. C. Mingay, in *English Landed Society in the eighteenth century* (1963) pp. 21–3, places the income range of 'lesser gentry' in 1790 at 'from near £1,000 up to £3,000'; as rents had risen by about a third in the past thirty years, the comparable figures in 1760 would have been about £750 and £2, 300.

[2] *Jenkinson Papers*, pp. 12–14, 34–6.

[3] 25 Dec 1762, ibid., p. 108.

Mr Robinson in his stead; one whose excellent character is so well-known, as he is, in the county, must go down better than anyone else who is not immediately of your own family.

In the event Robert Lowther decided to stand; and Robinson successfully engaged upon the most crucial part of the canvassing on his behalf, in 'every place in the Division of the County where Lord Thanet's interest and several of the other opposite ones lay'.[1] On Robert Lowther's withdrawal from parliament some twelve months later, Robinson succeeded him as knight of the shire for Westmorland. The nomination was bitterly resented by the independent country gentlemen of the county, who were hostile to Lowther's influence but too weak to combat it. The fact that Robinson was Lowther's employee no doubt outweighed any consideration about his own status as a landed proprietor. Inquiring of the treasury whether support for Lowther's candidate would be acceptable, the bishop of Carlisle pointed out: 'Nothing can offend the gentlemen of the county equal to the setting up Robinson as their representative, consequently I should wish to have no hand in it.' However, he added (with due regard to his earthly makers), 'if a candidate arises that would be hostile to administration I would not be backward in my support of Robinson, however unpopular soever it would render me in that county. Gratitude will ever be a stronger tie to me than any other obligation.'[2] No opposition could be organised at that time, and Robinson was returned without a contest. But county feeling was such that in 1768 he and his fellow-candidate in Lowther's interest had to face a stiffly fought election, the independent candidate achieving second place on the poll.

Thus was the pattern of Robinson's career set during the sixties. His parliamentary dignity obliged him to give up the clerkship of the peace for Westmorland, in which his younger brother, Joseph, succeeded him. He continued to manage Lowther's affairs, corresponded with officials in London about his patronage matters, and organised his electoral forces at parliamentary elections.[3] Now in London during the parliamentary session, he extended his personal contacts, and a growing intimacy with Charles Jenkinson dates

[1] Ibid., p. 122. [2] *Additional Grenville Papers*, pp. 74–5.
[3] *Jenkinson Papers*, pp. 132, 182, 279, 280–1, 294–6, 315–7, 325–6.

from this time.[1] Whatever apparent anomaly there may have been in a knight of the shire still holding office as steward to the great magnate of the north-west may in practice have been blurred over by the personal relations between them. If Robinson is to be judged at this time by his later career, the loyalty he gave was, as always, more than that of a mere employee; and it is significant that when Charles Jenkinson referred to Grenville requests from Lowther received through Robinson, he described Robinson not as Lowther's agent but as his 'friend'.[2] It seems evident that these years formed a valuable apprenticeship for the next phase in Robinson's career. The stern in-fighting between Lowther, Portland and Thanet for local political advantage in the counties of Cumberland and Westmorland was an excellent education in the arts of electioneering and political management which were to be a major part of his preoccupations as secretary to the treasury.

When North's succession to the Duke of Grafton at the treasury created a vacancy for a secretary – for Grafton's friend, Thomas Bradshaw, would remain without him no longer than was necessary to hand over the business of the office – Lowther seems to have pressed strongly the merits of Robinson for the appointment: to have a client in this key position at the fount of patronage might be expected to strengthen his local influence materially.[3] Jenkinson also seems to have been involved – at this time he was one of the junior treasury lords – and Robinson's kinship with the wife of Anthony Todd of the Post Office may also have played its part in bringing him to notice. It can also be assumed that North had already become well acquainted with Robinson and had sized up his qualities, for the appointment of his highly confidential man of business was not likely to be made merely on the recommendation of others. Completion of the arrangements was delayed for some months, perhaps mainly in order that Robinson should leave all the local political affairs of his old patron in apple-pie order.[4] Towards the end of 1770 he took up his new post as the junior of the two secretaries to the treasury.

Before Robinson took up his duties, his retiring predecessor

[1] For personal contact between them, ibid., pp. 280–1.

[2] Ibid., p. 319.

[3] Robinson to Jenkinson, 4 Feb 1770, B.M. Add. MSS. 38206, fo. 207.

[4] Robinson to Jenkinson, 26 Sept 1770, ibid., fo. 285.

warned him that he was 'engaging in a sea of troubles',[1] and before he himself left office the burden was to become almost overwhelming. From the first his position involved him in two distinct though sometimes overlapping roles: those of treasury administrator and of parliamentary secretary. The first role especially brought multifarious responsibilities. It entailed regular attendance at the treasury board, and preliminary detailed preparation of business for the board by the assembly, analysis and summary of documents on which draft resolutions could be based.[2] After the meetings were over and the minutes had been recorded, it was the responsibility of the secretaries to see that decisions were put into effect: to draft commissions and instructions; to complete the work of drawing up contracts and then direct business to which they related; to frame bills to be brought into parliament by the head of the treasury; to conduct a vast correspondence with revenue officials and with opposite numbers in other departments; to carry on day-to-day financial administration; and to look after secret service funds and payments. An impression of the toil and the urgency which he faced at times is given by the following letter of 28 March 1780 to Jenkinson:[3]

> Lord North . . . is now extremely anxious to get the Bills for the Taxes and all other Bills for this Session presented on Tuesday the 5th of April or as soon after as possible. . . . I have been at work yesterday and this morning on this as much as ever I can, but find Sir Grey Cooper's gone for some days to Salt Hill and . . . has many of the Bills with him, such as he has not I have set agoing. Lord North has wished me also to undertake to analyse all our part of the Extra[ordinaries] . . . I apprehended this had been done by Sir Grey Cooper when this business was discussed in the House of Lords. . . . but I find the remarks were short and very superficial. . . . To give a detail of the Articles under proper heads, to class and digest them, to give a proper account and vouch the propriety of the proceedings and the warrants granted by the Treasury under each head and in all the cases will be a work of length.

[1] Ibid.

[2] On this subject in general see Dora Mae Clark, 'The office of secretary to the treasury in the eighteenth century', *American Historical Review*, XLII B.M. (1936–7) 31–42.

[3] B.M. Add. MSS. 38567, fos. 36–7. Cooper was the senior secretary.

In this case his plans for the Easter recess were entirely upset, including the prospect of a brief vacation at Jenkinson's country house at Addiscombe.

Business relating to contracts for the supply of the armed forces escalated beyond belief during the American War of Independence. Up till 1778 the treasury was responsible not only for directing the assembly of supplies by the contractors and trying to overcome defects in the system of supply, but also for organising the shipping to take them across the Atlantic.[1] The task involved fighting all kinds of unforeseen administrative obstruction. In 1776, for instance, Robinson was to be found urging the secretary to the admiralty to cut through red tape and give immediate clearance to provision-ships waiting to sail from Cork without sticking to rules about the submission of detailed specifications of each ship's cargo. In 1780 he had to hustle the southern department, which had neglected to give immediate approval of lists of provisions waiting to be shipped to Gibraltar.[2] As paymaster of some of the spies employed during the war, Robinson found his office becoming one of the clearing-houses for secret intelligence.[3] This engaged him in constant correspondence with his opposite numbers in other departments and sometimes in the issuing of instructions, for instance to customs officers to devise means of thwarting the exit of cargoes suspected of being intended for the enemy.[4] The rudimentary treasury department was quite inadequate to shoulder such burdens and there was a complete lack of sufficient trained and responsible administrative officials.

Still further administrative burdens fell upon Robinson. When he took office the ministry was already concerned about the control of the empire the East India Company had acquired in Bengal, but no machinery for this as yet existed at Westminster. Because attention was mainly focused upon the financial relations between

[1] The fullest survey of this sphere of administration is Norman Baker, 'The Treasury Administration of Contracts for the Supply of the British Armies in North America and the West Indies, 1775–1783' (Ph.D. thesis, University of London, 1967).

[2] F. B. Wickwire, *British Subministers and Colonial America, 1763–1783* (Princeton, N.J., 1966) pp. 159–60.

[3] Treasury secret and special service accounts, 1779–82, Windsor MSS.

[4] Wickwire, *British Subministers and Colonial America*, pp. 165–6, 167, 170.

the Company and the government, the first tasks of improvisation fell upon the treasury – mainly upon Robinson. Much of the preparation of North's Regulating Act of 1773 was done by him, and thereafter he had to give considerable time and energy to working the new arrangements. He it was who, in the first instance, imposed some sort of administrative check upon the Company, scrutinising and frequently amending the important out-letters which were regularly submitted to him. Furthermore, the anomalous state of the relations between Company and government led him to involve himself on a second political stage in Leadenhall Street, using similar techniques to those employed in the House of Commons. All the familiar methods of pressure, influence and patronage were turned to the task of controlling votes in the general court. As the date approached of the expiry both of the Regulatory Act and of the Company's charter, his growing expertise in the affairs of East India House brought new pressures upon him. In the summer of 1778 he drew up a new outline plan for the management of Indian affairs. This broke so much new ground that it formed the basis of all discussions of the subject for the next three years and parts of it eventually found a place in the India Act carried through by the younger Pitt in 1784. His scheme was notable for its elaboration and reasoned defence of the dual system ultimately adopted in 1784 – administration in the hands of the Company, general control in those of the government.[1] On top of this the Irish commercial and political crisis provoked by the American War of Independence brought further work to the treasury. In the summer of 1779, when Robinson found that masses of information about Irish trade being sent over from Dublin were being ignored in the office of the secretaries of state, he set to work to reduce it to order on his own initiative. Three months later, as a result of his urgent pleas, responsibility for this task was placed in the competent hands of Charles Jenkinson, but Robinson continued to devil under his direction, noting down observations on relevant Acts of Parliament, and securing new returns and other information from the Irish financial administrator, John Beresford, and other officials. Though he and Jenkinson both misjudged the

[1] Lucy S. Sutherland, *The East India Company in Eighteenth-Century Politics* (Oxford, 1952) esp. pp. 252 and n. 2, 272, 274–5, 337–41, 349–50, 354–6, 391–2.

political situation in Ireland and did not fix the lines of policy, they jointly prepared the ground for effective legislation.[1]

The work of parliamentary secretary involved Robinson in business relating to patronage and the House of Commons. Although, judging by the papers of other first lords of the treasury, most of the correspondence on this subject was addressed to North, whose papers have not survived to any extent, a good deal was delegated to Robinson in respect of patronage requests from other ministers. A copious correspondence in his papers from the head of the admiralty, Lord Sandwich, is full of material of this kind.[2] North's step-brother, the lord privy seal, wrote to him in 1776: 'If you have two or three jerquers or tidewaiters or other things of like value to spare, pray let me know it: I assure you I have people very ready to jump into them.'[3] Occasionally it was not places North's colleagues wanted, but emphatic refusals. 'Your refusals are too civil', Sandwich once wrote to him. 'I wanted a good set down about the prebend of Worcester, otherwise we shall return to the charge – which I mean to avoid.'[4] During the parliamentary session Robinson took his share with Grey Cooper in making notes of the proceedings, lists of the speakers, and records of votes.[5] At times of crisis he kept elaborate rolls of the voting records of members, enabling him to provide on the spot when asked tabular statements of the respective strengths of government and opposition in the House of Commons. Next to the head of the treasury there was for some years no greater expert than Robinson on the subject of the attitudes and political affiliations of members of the Commons and their connections with their constituencies. Expertise of the kind already acquired in relation to Cumberland and Westmorland was now built up for the country as a whole and provided a basis of information for action at general

[1] H. Butterfield, *George III, Lord North, and the People, 1779–1780* (1949) pp. 101–4, 148–9, 150–2, 154.

[2] Abergavenny MSS. *passim*.

[3] Lord Dartmouth to Robinson, 28 Dec 1776, Abergavenny MS. 123.

[4] 16 May 1772, Abergavenny MS. 28.

[5] Most of the notes of proceedings and lists of speakers in the House of Commons sent by North to George III are in the hand of one or other of the secretaries. On the whole Cooper seems to have been responsible for the notes and Robinson for the lists, though this division of labour was not invariable.

elections. With this special information he was the natural person to act as a whip and to round up supporters from the lobbies and coffee-rooms at times of critical divisions. On at least one occasion he was at the centre of arrangements for a conference of government spokesmen in the Commons, at which the points in defence of its naval administration were rehearsed and roles in the debate apportioned.[1]

The range of Robinson's concerns and the vast extent of his official correspondence which is encountered by all students of the history of British administrative activity during this period fully corroborate the verdict of Nathaniel Wraxall, that 'he might be considered as one of the most essential functionaries of the executive government.'[2] From 1770 till 1782 he spent himself without stint in the service. At times the tone of his correspondence during the later years of the American War of Independence suggests that he felt overwhelmed by the avalanche of business that fell upon him. In the view of his Irish friend, John Beresford, only his release from office as a result of the fall of the North ministry in March 1782 saved him from killing himself by overwork.[3]

Robinson and his colleague, Sir Grey Cooper, Philip Stephens, the secretary to the admiralty, the half-dozen under-secretaries in the various branches of the secretary of state's office, and one or two other administrative officials, such as the secretary-at-war, together made up the little group of men whose drive and initiative, under the direction of the cabinet ministers, carried through the work of the government departments. A proportion of these men, though not all of them, combined administrative roles with membership of the House of Commons and belonged, save for one or two exceptions, to that section of it which can best be described as the court and administration circle. Men of this stamp felt themselves far more the servants of the king than the clients of any great politician; and it is the purpose of the remainder of this paper to illustrate from the correspondence of one of the most articulate among them the ethos and attitude to politics of this group. In the

[1] Christie, *The End of North's Ministry*, part I *passim*, and pp. 307–16, 351–2, 356–9, 366–8, 373–5.

[2] *Historical and Posthumous Memoirs*, 5 vols (1884) I 428.

[3] *The Correspondence of the Right Hon. John Beresford*, ed. the Right Hon. William Beresford (1854) I 193.

case of Robinson the path of loyal political service was by no means clear-cut, for his parliamentary career extended through the complex party crisis of the years 1782 to 1784 and then through the regency crisis of 1788 to 1789, which threatened yet another ministerial upheaval. Furthermore, North's action in appointing him and their subsequent prolonged association at the treasury inspired in Robinson strong feelings of affection and loyalty towards his chief; and the conflict of loyalties which developed after 1782 caused him much distress of mind.

II. POLITICAL LOYALTIES, 1770–1784

An early revelation of Robinson's attitude to the public service appears in a letter written to Charles Jenkinson in 1770, a few days before he took up his appointment at the treasury. 'Seriously speaking, my friend', he wrote, 'the man who stands not forth in support of his King and the constitution of his country in times of publick difficulties and violence, without the lure of reward, is in my opinion base indeed.'[1] It is true that these were the words of a man well rewarded and content with his position. Nevertheless, Robinson's later words and actions confirm that he never thought of the public service in terms of mere careerism. His preoccupation was rather with duty to king and country. In the midst of a ticklish cabinet reshuffle in the autumn of 1775, vital to both North's and the king's peace of mind, he besought Lord Dartmouth, on whom the event depended, to be guided by his 'perfect attachment . . . to the Best of Kings and Best of Men'.[2] A similar note is sounded again, for instance, in the postscript of a letter to Lord Sandwich, at a moment in 1779 when North's indecisions seemed about to bring down the government:[3]

[1] B.M. Add. MSS. 38206, fo. 207.

[2] To Dartmouth, 8 Nov 1775, Dartmouth MSS., William Salt Library, Stafford.

[3] Robinson to Lord Sandwich, 17 Oct 1779, Sandwich MSS. My acknowledgements are due to Mr Victor Montagu for permission to make use of unpublished material in his family papers, and also to the late Marquis of Abergavenny for permitting me to use the letters and drafts to and from John Robinson in his possession, on which the remainder of this paper largely rests.

> Your Lordship [he wrote] may be assured of my utmost activity and the exertion of every ability in my power, but it is not to be described what I go through from *these indeterminations* – I carry a brown muskett however, I will obey every command and fight to the last for my sovereign and my country – office is nothing, but ruin to the state, to our country, and to ourselves disgrace, is not to be born.

On the whole he maintained a single-minded devotion to his duty to the government, and refused to be diverted into intrigues to better his lot. Indeed, place-hunters aroused his anger and contempt. He declared on many occasions, and to various friends, that he would never make demands for place or reward.[1] Financially he had little inducement to do so, for it must be admitted that he occupied one of the most lucrative offices in the government service.[2]

At one period only was Robinson drawn to act contrary to his repeated declarations. During 1780 he several times pressed North for some reward, to mark his and the king's approbation. Yet this episode reveals that he really cared little for advancement, and it makes clear his overriding sense of duty to the king. Robinson was provoked into this step by the failure of North to show any gratitude for the herculean labours he was performing. He felt humiliated and slighted. There was no real ambition behind the pretensions he then put forward. They sprang from irritation and frustration, and were stated as a way of escaping from a situation in which he felt disgraced: in the last resort, he was prepared to retire altogether and throw up his office with all its rich yield of fees. The whole affair arose simply from North's awkwardness and embarrassment when a word of appreciation to a subordinate was called for. In a conversation with North about elections and appointments at the end of January 1780, Robinson led up to the subject of himself, only to be repulsed by his chief turning tongue-tied and cold. 'Warm approbation of sentiments, not I trust improper, of my conduct if it has been right, and kind professions was all I wanted, or looked for if it was wished I was to stay', Robinson wrote later the same evening (30 January) to Jenkinson, 'but not one word is hard, and may be construed that I am better

[1] B.M. Add. MSS. 38213, fo. 102.

[2] In 1780, Robinson told North that his gross income in each of the last three years had been over £5,000 (H.M.C., *Abergavenny MSS.*, no. 266).

gone.'[1] Had North only been more affable and forthcoming in his relations with Robinson, the whole affair would probably have gone no further; but his failure in this respect hurt Robinson's pride, and made him feel that his honour and reputation were affected. 'I should deceive you . . .', Robinson went on, 'if I did not say that I did not sensibly, indeed very sensibly, feel his Lordship's coldness, and if I did not add that I was restrained for other causes than attention to Lord North from at once asking him for the Admiralty and putting him to refuse it to me.' And again, next day: 'Should it once be an established opinion, reward would tempt me to continue a lucrative appointment to my dishonour, while everyone round me were receiving promotion, marks of favor honourably holding approbation of their conduct to the world, I should be deservedly gone in the esteem of mankind; or even if it should be thought that I am useful and therefore should be kept in my situation, it is lucrative, and he will stay, never mind him, I should be disgraced and in either case, in my opinion, and to my feelings, I could not stay a day.'[2] He felt afterwards that he had gone too far in this letter, and the next day (1 February) he hastened to assure Jenkinson (being fully aware of the political reports which his friend delivered in the closet): 'Whatever happens to me, or whatever is Lord North's conduct towards me, it shall never relax my ardor, nor weaken my endeavours, for the support of His Majesty's measures and his government, in which I think is involved our constitution and our country. I feel too much duty, gratitude and attachment for that, and am ever and will remain so attached in or out of office through life.'[3] Again, in March, he wrote: 'I will go on with every exertion on my part to the utmost of my abilities or power, from duty, attachment and affection to my sovereign, and because I will not be thought to desert or flinch, in the service, and in times of difficulty, and more particularly too, at a time, when without assuming too much I at least think, I see, that I can be of use. But that situation once over I will peremptorily desire to quit, without emolument, and without asking for anything, which I prefer to serving in any station with disgrace or disregard.'[4] In

[1] B.M. Add. MSS. 38213, fo. 96.
[2] B.M. Add. MSS. 38213, fo. 103.
[3] B.M. Add. MSS. 38213, fo. 108.
[4] B.M. Add. MSS. 38567, fo. 38.

July he was once more exasperated by North's indifference.[1] The general election was looming ahead, and George III appealed to him through Jenkinson. Acknowledging the message, Robinson replied to his friend in fulsome terms that since the king wished it, he would remain in his place, whatever North's treatment of him:[2]

> Every feeling of mine shall give way to my duty to him, and that now I know his pleasure nothing on earth shall make me desert that post where he is pleased to think I may do him most service . . . to His Majesty's condescending kindness alone I shall look for my government. . . . In respect to reward, whatever His Majesty's goodness shall bestow when he shall see right will be most gratefully received as conveying a public mark of His Majesty's approbation of my duty and service, which believe me is my greatest ambition and sole wish, for with the sincere[st] truth I assure you lucrative office is not the desire of my heart. . . . If I have [a] sentiment in this respect more fixed than any other, it is . . . that I may preserve the rank in rising in His Majesty's service, which I trust I might not unreasonably expect, and not see every man . . . put over my head . . . this I will freely own to you I am ambitious [of] because my anxiety is to maintain my character, and to do my duty to the utmost of my power.

Thus, in the course of six months, Robinson's resentment had so worked upon him that a situation easily to be settled by a little personal attention and verbal assurance could now only be resolved by some more positive gesture. To preserve his self-respect, Robinson now thought in terms of a step upwards in the hierarchy of office. Yet this wish was essentially artificial, the product of emotional disturbance and overwork. So much became clear in the sequel. In September, he was once more out of patience with North, and sought an explanation with him in the full determination of resigning if satisfaction was refused him.[3] But he was willing to be content with a much more modest concession – that the office of surveyor-general of woods and forests should not be disposed of in North's election arrangements, but should remain

[1] B.M. Add. MS. 38214, fos. 66–7.

[2] Abergavenny MS. 266.

[3] Abergavenny MS. 297; B.M. Add. MS. 38567, fo. 71; B.M. Add. MSS. 38214, fo. 164.

in the hands of its existing holder, with the understanding that Robinson should eventually succeed to it.[1] This request was readily agreed to by North: 'Our explanation was not very long nor full, yet kind', wrote Robinson;[2] and no slightest trace of dissatisfaction appears thereafter in his letters. This outcome shows that what he chiefly desired was a little personal recognition; but the whole incident is of even greater interest in its demonstration how his sense of duty to the king restrained him, even when his indignation was at its height. North knew and exploited the fact, when he told Robinson that Robinson's resignation would entail his own.[3]

Apart from this one episode, Robinson appears to have nursed no envy or ambition for place and profit. To him the intrigues of party politics had no appeal, and the manœuvrings of politicians for advancement seemed to him unprincipled and filled him with dismay and disgust. His opinion of such activities can be illustrated from his comments on Alexander Wedderburn and William Eden, two men whose views on this point were as far as possible removed from his own, and for whose political methods he entertained a hearty contempt. Robinson encouraged North to resist the attempts of Eden and Wedderburn in 1779 to bully him into giving them promotion, and referred unflatteringly to their manœuvres as 'a game playing, that I am sorry to say I think has been too often practised on your Lordship with success, by alarming your fears and then soothing them by expedients to carry points'.[4] Wedderburn, he thought, writing at the end of October, bore 'rancour and malice in his heart' towards North; and though he did not, in his letters to Jenkinson, censure him openly, his disapproval was strongly implied. 'Thus on every side is the attack made', he lamented, 'I from my soul pity the poor K., my heart bleeds for him and for my country.'[5] When in 1780 Eden was pressing North to give him a seat at the treasury board as well as the Irish secretaryship, Robinson could not contain his feelings and burst out indignantly: 'What would become of this country if every man was

[1] B.M. Add. MSS. 37835, fo. 154; *The Correspondence of King George III*, v 117.

[2] B.M. Add. MSS. 38567, fo. 73.

[3] H.M.C., *Abergavenny MSS.*, no. 266.

[4] Abergavenny MS. 216.

[5] B.M. Add. MSS. 38212, fo. 204; 38567, fo. 9.

to bargain so.'[1] He had no patience either with the bludgeonlike pertinacity with which Eden would press his views and wishes: this he made clear in a letter to Jenkinson in February 1783, explaining and excusing the length of a draft letter to North: 'It is by such perpetual teazing and writing that Eden gets his influence, but which example he may trust me I will never follow but on such an occasion as the present pressing his Lordship to do what is right for himself equally with what is so for the public.'[2]

Wedderburn in 1780 became a lord chief justice. Eden, by intriguing and changing sides in the following years, obtained before long a diplomatic post and a peerage. Robinson's own colleague as secretary to the treasury, Sir Grey Cooper, secured a rise in the official hierarchy by adhering to the coalition ministry of 1783, in which he was given a place at the treasury board; and towards the end of his career, in 1795, he was hankering after a further step – promotion to the rank of privy councillor, though without post or emolument.[3] These men took the political road to advancement. But Robinson, for all his talk in 1780 of 'preserving' his 'rank', was not really interested in promotion to the higher offices contended for by the party politicians. He nursed no political ambitions, and as a government servant he could hardly rise any higher. In 1784 he waived offers of a place under Pitt, although he had most substantial claims to recognition.[4] He did not lay himself open to criticism for conduct of the kind which he himself frequently disavowed, and which, as a result of his outlook, he was prone to condemn in others. His attitude, his viewpoint, were totally different from those of the party politicians. Drawn by his interests and inclinations into the circle of the court and administration, his conduct was determined by his sense of direct attachment to the king. It remains next to be seen how this cast of mind carried him through the political turmoil of the years 1782–4.

The last stages of the American War of Independence brought fatal, irretrievable disasters to British arms, and in March 1782 the North government fell discredited. This was but the first of

[1] B.M. Add. MSS. 38567, fo. 63.

[2] B.M. Add. MSS. 38567, fos. 123–4.

[3] Sir Grey Cooper to the Duke of Portland, 10 and 29 June 1795, Portland MSS.

[4] B.M. Add. MSS. 38567, fo. 182.

four changes of ministry in the space of little more than twenty months, a period during which old party connections were strained and severed, and political alignments in parliament became confused and unpredictable.

Although Robinson's feelings towards North were tinged with exasperation at the offhand way in which North neglected to express appreciation of his services, there existed, on his side at least, a bond of close attachment, on grounds both of obligation and of personal liking and respect. In January 1780 he wrote to Jenkinson: 'Lord North, from friendship, from affection, for I realy esteem [him] with all his coldness, from attachment shall carry me to serve him in any station to my utmost, but not because I am useful and must be kept there, or for sordid motives, confidence and civility will do much, but thanks be to God not necessity.'[1] If North's appalling casualness could be overlooked, he was one of the most difficult of persons to dislike. After 1782, when he and Robinson came to differ in their politics, Robinson still tried to remain on friendly terms with him, and no one would have been happier if their personal and political association could have continued. In December 1783 he wrote to North's son: 'To show every personal friendship and attachment to your father has ever been, and, if I know myself, ever will be the leading principle of my heart.'[2] But from the moment when North's government came to an end, the possibility arose of a conflict between Robinson's obligations to North and to the king; and there was no doubt as to which his principles would lead him to put foremost.

For three months after the dismissal of the North ministry Robinson took little part in public affairs, but in July 1782, after the death of Rockingham and the secession of his friends from the ministry now headed by Shelburne, he was drawn once again into politics. In the game of parliamentary management, the knowledge gained by time and experience counted for much. Shelburne's political manager, Thomas Orde, was the merest novice, and his chief soon sought the help which only Robinson could give from his intimate knowledge of parliamentary personalities and connections and his familiarity with the technique of keeping a government majority.[3] This assistance was quickly forthcoming. Its first

[1] B.M. Add. MSS. 38213, fo. 103. [2] Abergavenny MS. 532.

[3] B.M. Add. MSS. 38567, fo. 101; Abergavenny MS. 468.

tangible result was the elaborate 'State of the House of Commons',[1] forwarded to Shelburne on 7 August. For this work Robinson received immediate commendation from George III, and it is probable that he already had had prior notice through Jenkinson that the king desired him to make his services available.[2] But in following this path of duty he was careful to observe his other obligation, for at the end of July he was in close consultation with North (to whom he hoped Shelburne might offer some acceptable office) and received North's approval for the step he was about to take.[3] He was, moreover, following a general instruction North had given him when they both left office, to give all support and assistance to the kings' government, whoever the ministers might be, 'as far as it could be done with propriety and consistent with principles'.[4] His two loyalties were not as yet in conflict. During the summer and autumn of 1782, whilst remaining out of place, he continued to act as unofficial parliamentary adviser to the government. Later in August Orde consulted him about securing a vacant seat at Gatton for a friend of Shelburne; in September he visited Shelburne at Wycombe; in October he wrote from Hampshire, advising Orde about circular letters and other arrangements for the commencement of the session, and promising to help with the work as soon as he returned from the country.[5] Meanwhile, North continued to regard him as his adjutant; in September expressed a wish to discuss with him the king's request that he (North) should support the government although without place; and in November, at the same time that Robinson was helping Orde, was arranging with him to write to those of their friends (of whom Robinson had drawn up a list) 'of whom we hear that they do not intend to come to town', and asked him to learn for him the 'state of the Address'.[6]

This happy situation did not last. North grew dissatisfied with

[1] *The Parliamentary Papers of John Robinson*, ed. W. T. Laprade, Camden Society, 3rd series, XXXIII (1922) 42–8.

[2] H.M.C., *Abergavenny MSS.*, no. 469.

[3] B.M. Add. MSS. 38567, fos. 101, 103–4; Abergavenny MS. 547.

[4] Abergavenny MS. 572.

[5] *The Parliamentary Papers of John Robinson*, p. 49; H.M.C., *Abergavenny MSS.*, no. 478; B.M. Add. MSS. 38567, fos. 117–18.

[6] *The Correspondence of King George III*, VI no. 3872; H.M.C., *Abergavenny MSS.*, no. 475; Abergavenny MS. 487.

his position out of office, and members of his circle, especially William Eden, were hard at work to stir up his resentment.[1] He was justifiably annoyed and irritated at the king's refusal to shoulder the full burden of the election debt of 1780. Also, towards the end of 1782 he developed genuine misgivings about the peace terms negotiated by Shelburne with France and America.[2] These considerations prepared the way for his coalition with Charles James Fox in February 1783. That step marked his initial rejection of the principle of supporting the sovereign's chosen ministers – which Robinson urgently exhorted him to follow – and his adherence to Fox in opposition in 1784 signified his final repudiation of it. The junction with Fox produced for the first time an open clash of opinions between North and Robinson, though the breach between them did not take place for another year.

Robinson's letters of this period reiterate his conviction that the king's government should in all events be upheld, and that engagement in political opposition was, if not disloyal, at least dishonourable. By September 1782 he was already seriously disquieted at the failure of North to make firm declarations of support in favour of Shelburne's ministry, a course which he himself was urging upon him. 'Mr Rigby tells me that he did not think Lord North was warm or decided', he reported to Jenkinson on the seventeenth. 'This circumstance . . . fixes much the suspicions which I before had . . . that Lord N. will not write and take that line which from my soul, I think is that which he should hold by every tie, and upon every principle of honour, as well as for his credit and reputation.'[3] When it became clear that North, Sandwich and others of their associates were preparing to vote against the terms of the peace negotiated by Shelburne, Robinson was even more disturbed. This step would force Shelburne out and 'storm the Closet', imposing upon the king an unwanted set of ministers and depriving him of any voice in their selection. In a letter to Lord

[1] B.M. Add. MSS. 38567, fos. 108–10; *Journal and Correspondence of William, Lord Auckland*, ed. bishop of Bath and Wells, 4 vols (1861–2) I 11, 15, 17, 28, 32–3, 36.

[2] *The Correspondence of King George III*, V 473–4; H.M.C., *Abergavenny MSS.*, nos. 475, 477, 488, 490; and see pp. 185–91.

[3] B.M. Add. MSS. 38567, fo. 108.

Sandwich, Robinson condemned such conduct in forthright terms. Not only did he consider it inexpedient: he put forward the extreme view that it was unconstitutional. 'I cannot', he wrote, 'bring my mind to a different opinion, than that *any question whatsoever* being moved and carried in the House, tending to throw a doubt about the acceptance or continuance of the Peace as it is, will be destructive of the Prerogative of the Crown, ruinous in its consequences to the public, very dangerous in its effects to the King, and to have an opposite tendency to that which your Lordship and every well wisher to the Crown desires or hopes for.'[1] The following week, in a long letter which took him the best part of two days to write, and which covers in draft seven pages of notepaper, he deployed every possible argument to convince North of the impropriety of taking any part in this manœuvre.[2] If as a result, he argued, a coalition ministry were formed, 'if I can guess at your mind and at the principles on which you have acted, I am of opinion that your heart will tell you that it could not be permanent if it could not be pleasant'. Even if Shelburne were not willing to give North a place in the government – but this he fully intended to do – North ought still to support it: to use his position as head of a 'third party' in order to force a political bargain would be a deplorable step:

> In your conversation the other day [Robinson wrote], your mind seemed to be impressed with an idea that it was endeavoured to get your assistance to carry an approbation of the peace, and that you were to be duped for this end, and treated with inattention afterwards. You will recollect that I then argued against this; that I insisted it was impossible and that I asked you if you had not had conversation with the Lord Advocate clearly contrary to every such idea. I will however for a moment's discussion suppose this even to be possible, and I will answer, with my opinion, that in such a situation and under such circumstances as I have above stated while I was acting on principles of consistency for the good of my country, I would run any risk, much more such an imaginary one, rather than permit any motive whatever to influence my mind to alter that conduct.
>
> . . . to entertain any idea of making terms now or to have any

[1] Robinson to Lord Sandwich, 25 Jan 1783, Sandwich MSS.

[2] B.M. Add. MSS. 38567, fos. 123–4; Abergavenny MS. 493.

> bargain made in my opinion (not to use harsher terms which suggest themselves to me) would surely not do you honour, and therefore I am clear ought not at present to be hinted at.

This line of argument was not a novel one. There was no question here of newfangled, unconstitutional doctrines furbished up in the councils of George III's 'king's friends'. The sound tradition which lay behind Robinson's plea may be seen by comparing it with the warning given by Lord Mansfield to the Duke of Newcastle in the previous reign. In 1757 Newcastle's situation had been somewhat similar; on that occasion Mansfield had advised him:[1]

> To mix in factious opposition, after so many years of honourable service, wou'd blast your fame and reputation for ever. Specious pretences are never wanting; but in the present distress, it is impossible for any Court, how desperate soever, to make unconstitutional attempts; if they did, every man ought to oppose such attempts. But I speak of opposition to right or indifferent measures to force a change of hands. . . .

'One time or other whatever he thinks of me now', reflected Robinson, 'I believe he will realy thank me.'[2] However his advice was ignored: in April North confirmed his junction with Fox by taking office in the coalition ministry.

In the following months, Robinson's adherence to this as yet soundly adducible constitutional doctrine was fortified by other considerations. He disliked the politicians of the Fox–Portland group, with whom North had allied himself, and he held their abilities and policies in contempt. In joining the Foxites, North had not only outraged the principles of political conduct to which Robinson paid service: furthermore, he had taken part with a set of politicians whose integrity seemed not proof against errors for which they had formerly denounced North's own ministry, and for whose amateur performance Robinson nursed the disdain of the professional administrator. He felt repelled at Jenkinson's suggestion that he should accept a place or in any way associate with them:[3]

[1] B.M. Add. MSS. 32870, fos. 427–31, cited in Sir Lewis Namier, *England in the Age of the American Revolution* (1930) p. 57.

[2] B.M. Add. MSS. 38567, fo. 125.

[3] B.M. Add. MSS. 38567, fos. 147–8.

. . . I assure you [he wrote in April 1783] I feel daily more strong impulses not to be a partaker of measures, so contrary to the dictates of my heart, and the violence of which will every day grow more disagreeable to the public. Would you believe that they yesterday parted on trivial differences not a half half quarter per cent etc. without making the loan, as Lord North stated it to me, and are to meet again on it this day. You know how dangerous this is, by giving time for operation on the stocks, and I wish that they may meet again this day at noon without the stocks, in which the loan of 12 millions is to be, having received a further depression: but would you believe further, that they have avowedly retained out of the bargain for 12 millions 3 millions for their distribution. Lord John and Mr Fox were the only people who appeared to treat with the gentlemen. Another inconvenience will arise by postponing so long the day for the first payment, by which time will be even given for any operations from abroad, should France know its power, to effectually damn the loan by depressing it to a discount.

Not only did he writhe at seeing the new ministry fumbling in amateur fashion over the loan: it was a further grievance that, after having a year or two before denounced North for arranging private distribution of government loans, they were doing the same thing themselves within a fortnight of taking office. Later on, in the autumn of 1783, it seemed to Robinson, albeit unjustly, that they were solely concerned to snatch such material benefits as they could, instead of tackling the real problems of government.[1] When this proved incorrect and the ministers produced their scheme for the government of India, Robinson found new and particular ground for disapproval: his reaction to Fox's bill was at least partly that of the professional administrator, who sees his work being botched by the amateur. Miss Sutherland has drawn attention to defects in the bill deriving largely from Burke's lack of administrative experience.[2] It seems fairly certain, from phrases in one of Robinson's letters to North, that he noted and condemned its weaknesses.[3] He was one of the few members of parliament who had expert knowledge arising from long and intimate participation

[1] B.M. Add. MSS. 38567, fos. 155–6.

[2] Sutherland, *The East India Company in eighteenth-century politics*, pp. 398–401.

[3] Abergavenny MS. 572.

in the running of East Indian affairs, and as North's assistant he had spent much time and energy in search of a solution to the problem of government control over the Company's administration. He could not with consistency support Fox's bill, which ignored the lessons he had learned in the course of his own experience; nor could he afterwards, apart from general political considerations, vote in January 1784 against Pitt's East India bill, the creation of Dundas, built up on the foundation laid by himself and Jenkinson, which was – as he pointed out to North – 'more consonant' than the proposals of Fox with the conclusions which North had previously reached on the subject.

Whilst these circumstances alone were enough to account for Robinson's abstention from active support for the coalition government, it was his attitude towards the king which led him on eventually to work against it; and here his constitutional principles were powerfully reinforced by personal feelings. Dry, legal obligation counted for much; but warm, human emotion was a stimulant to his zeal. When in February 1783 Shelburne was defeated by the votes of the coalition in the Commons, it was common knowledge that George III was furiously opposed to any parliamentary combination likely to force Charles James Fox into high office. Yet as the March days lengthened into spring, this outcome seemed inevitable; and the helpless situation of the king aroused keen sympathy among the circle of the court and administration. 'Nothing could exceed the anxiety and utmost despair which I have seen', wrote Jenkinson to Robinson on the seventeenth; and again next day: 'Everything in short is at sea, and the King in the utmost distress.'[1] 'God bless you my Dear Sir and send —— out of their distressing situation, for it is terrible', Robinson wrote to him on the eleventh; and on the twenty-fifth: 'What a terrible situation are all things in, and how greatly to be pitied and lamented is the K——.' 'Poor K——, how very much does his situation deserve pity', he wrote on 1 April, when George's surrender to the coalition was at last seen to be inevitable.[2]

In the following months, whilst George III bore with the coalition ministry only for lack of a practicable alternative, Robinson knew through Jenkinson how little he was reconciled to

[1] H.M.C., *Abergavenny MSS.*, nos. 498, 499.
[2] B.M. Add. MSS. 38567, fos. 129–30, 141–2, 145.

its members.[1] Before long he had also more direct knowledge of the king's state of mind. It was with bitter feelings towards North that the king, meeting Robinson by chance one day on the road to Westminster, praised the constant loyalty which seemed to him such a refreshing contrast to the conduct of his old minister. This was like an accolade to Robinson: pride in this vindication led him to write down and preserve among his papers a record of as much of the conversation as he could remember:[2]

> . . . On Thursday the 13th of November riding to town His Majesty overtook me about 12° at noon in the town of Kensington, on my taking off my round hat and he perceiving me, he immediately pulled up his horse and stopped for my coming up to him calling out with great heartiness 'Mr Robinson, how do you, are you come to town.' I replied that I came out of Essex on Tuesday to attend Parliament. His Majesty then said 'I hope you have recovered your health perfectly.' I answered 'Yes, Sir, I thank your Majesty, I am perfectly well.' His Majesty replied 'I am *very glad* of it (or I believe his Majesty's expression was I am heartily glad of it) for you are always the same, you do not change with the times. You are always steady.' I bowed and answered 'I hoped I should ever continue to be and act so.' His Majesty said 'Yes, you always do', and turning his head back to me as he was then riding on faster, his Majesty called out 'These are bad times indeed', and then bowed to me, and pushed on in a canter.

The preservation of this minute is a further indication of the personal element in the loyalty accorded by Robinson as a member of the court and administration circle, which helps to explain his actions in the November and December of 1783. The king's hostility to the coalition coincided with his own. Without the king's approval, however (of which he was already apprised), he would not have taken an active part against an established ministry. But the king's words were not only an implied appeal for future support, but also a commendation – indeed, the *summa laus* – and the justification for his course of action. Hence Robinson could even consider it his task to work against the coalition government, in which his old chief had been appointed a secretary of state.

[1] H.M.C., *Abergavenny MSS.*, no. 515.
[2] B.M. Add. MSS. 37835, fo. 203.

Although the final breach between North and Robinson was delayed for some nine months after the formation of the coalition ministry, Robinson's refusal to follow North in support of it was the turning-point in the relations between them. For the first time Robinson made it clear that he would reserve his future freedom of judgement and action. But two circumstances postponed the breach for a while. North was now once again a minister, and on that ground had a claim to Robinson's support; and Robinson still felt a friendship and affection for his old chief. For some time he still remained closely associated with him. During March 1783 he had continued to work on North's parliamentary business. 'By sitting up a good part of the night', he informed Jenkinson on the twenty-first, 'I have got upward of a hundred notes done and sent them . . . to town for Lord North to direct the distribution of them for his meeting tonight at 8° clock, and I have also formed and made out a list for him to guide him of friends how they voted in the divisions.'[1] In April he was employed as an intermediary in a negotiation to secure the adherence to the coalition of his friend, Lord Sandwich.[2] North continued to regard him as a party follower, sought in September to confer with him, and in November wrote to him asking him to whip up their friends to vote for Fox's East India bill on its second reading.[3] The personal relations of the two men remained as cordial as ever, although Robinson scorned to conceal his disapproval of North's political conduct, regarding it rather as a duty of friendship to make it plain. His opinions, he told one correspondent, were given to North 'with sincerity, and, as you very justly attribute to me, unshaken attachment, notwithstanding I could not bring myself to follow him throughout, and take an active part in scenes which perhaps my foolish and too weak mind could not altogether approve; I wished rather to draw into that retirement you describe. . . . I still very sincerely regard him and therefore speak my mind with freedom. But alas, what a falling off.'[4]

However, at the very moment when he wrote these words, the turn of events was leading him into a course of duplicity towards

[1] B.M. Add. MSS. 38567, fo. 135.
[2] Robinson to Lord Sandwich, 5 Apr 1783, Sandwich MSS.
[3] B.M. Add. MSS. 38567, fo. 153; H.M.C., *Abergavenny MSS.*, no. 519.
[4] *Correspondence of the Right Hon. John Beresford*, I 244–5.

his old chief, which it is not easy to defend, except on the ground of his overriding duty to the king. The same day (2 November) he sent political reports to Jenkinson with the object of countering the efforts of the coalition ministry to win over Thurlow and other members of the old Bedford party. 'I will do everything I can', he wrote, 'to perswade our friends to pause and wait for events. The great cards must be played with Lords Wey[mouth] and Thu[rlow] who if steady will keep the others so.'[1] A week later he was preparing to canvass his Essex neighbours in the House of Commons against the government, and was contemplating the shipwreck of the coalition on the 'rock' of the India bill.[2] On 13 November – the day of his meeting with the king on the road at Kensington – he told Lord North that he could not vote for the bill.[3] But he did not subsequently inform him that he was encouraging East India proprietors and urging other members of parliament to oppose it;[4] nor that on Friday, 5 December he was drawn into consultation to provide parliamentary data in support of the plot hatched by George III, Pitt and Dundas to supplant the ministry in which North was a secretary of state.[5] Indeed, this deceit was virtually forced upon him: he had to keep silence, for the secrecy of this intrigue was essential to its success.

A man of different political outlook might have felt such a course as this to be incompatible with honour. Robinson believed his own conduct to be perfectly right; but in adhering thus to his guiding principle in politics – his allegiance to the king – he was led into what can only be regarded as an act of betrayal against his old chief. North, had he known, would have had every reason to resent the way in which he had been deceived. However, it seems probable that he never did know of it, and this was not the cause of his final estrangement from Robinson. As late as 16 December 1783, after the defeat of Fox's bill in the House of Lords, he and his son still looked on Robinson as a supporter.[6] A week after the

[1] B.M. Add. MSS. 38567, fos. 158–60.
[2] B.M. Add. MSS. 38567, fos. 162–3.
[3] Abergavenny MS. 532.
[4] Sutherland, *The East India Company in eighteenth-century politics*, pp. 404–5; B.M. Add. MSS. 38567, fos. 165–6.
[5] B.M. Add. MSS. 38567, fos. 167–8, 169–70; *The Parliamentary Papers of John Robinson*, pp. 65–105.
[6] H.M.C., *Abergavenny MSS.*, no. 531.

dismissal of the coalition, when Robinson (on the twenty-sixth) at last informed North that he had been called upon by Pitt to provide such information as he could give to the new ministry, he revealed nothing regarding the massive parliamentary calculations he had put in hand on Pitt's behalf prior to Pitt's appointment to the treasury; and some days later Eden, who was acting closely with North throughout this period, expressed his conviction: 'The truth is that Robinson . . . has not (to the best of my belief and information) suffered himself to be employed further than by attending Mr Pitt once or twice on the pretext of explaining some old Treasury arrears.'[1] All North knew was that Robinson had declined to vote for Fox's East India bill (although he had refrained from voting against it), and that *since* Pitt's assumption of office he had placed information, presumably about treasury business, at Pitt's disposal. For this last step, Robinson put up a strong defence in his explanatory letter of 26 December:[2]

> In consequence of the declarations I have repeatedly made, and the conduct I have uniformly pursued since Your Lordship left the Treasury, and, with your approbation, to Lord Shelburne when he was at the head of Administration; I have been called upon for such information as it is in my power to give from the official situation I held. As it was right, on principles of duty and gratitude, before, to make such declarations, and hold such conduct, Your Lordship, I am certain, could have no doubt, but that I ought now to follow the same line, for added to what is due on those principles, there is also the rectitude of acting a consistent part.

This explanation was evidently accepted by North, for during the first week of January 1784 their relations were still perfectly cordial.[3]

The final breach between North and Robinson came, from North's side, a fortnight later. In the interim Robinson had voted against motions brought on in the Commons censuring the appointment

[1] Eden to Lord Sheffield, 4 Jan 1784, B.M. Add. MSS. 45728–30.

[2] Abergavenny MS. 547.

[3] Abergavenny MSS. 555, 558, 559; B.M. Add. MSS. 38567, fos. 181–2. These letters, of the period 5 to 10 January, refer to personal contact between Robinson and North, and Robinson's two letters to North of 6 January commence with the more intimate style of address 'My Dear Lord'.

of Pitt's ministry, culminating in Lord Charles Spencer's resolution, carried on the sixteenth, that the continuance of the ministers in office was contrary to constitutional principles; and on the twenty-third, he had divided in favour of Pitt's East India bill, which was lost on second reading by eight votes.[1] On the twenty-fifth, he found North's door closed to him;[2] and a day or two later he received a letter in which North declared he found this conduct quite incompatible with Robinson's professions of friendship made less than three weeks before:[3]

> . . . After the conversation that passed between us at Bushy [North wrote], I might possibly express a good deal of surprise at the part you have since taken, but I do not recollect having held that language which you have heard of. However I do not desire any explanation of your conduct. You are so good as to say that you felt some difficulty in making the option (which I suppose it appeared necessary to you to make) between being my friend and my enemy. Your option has necessarily determined mine.

To this letter Robinson replied on the thirty-first with a dignified vindication of his conduct:[4]

> I must draw to your recollection the line which you laid down for me, at least, to follow when you went out of office, which was to inform, to assist, and to support his Majesty's Government, in whose hands soever it was, as far as it could be done with propriety and consistent with principles. I have repeatedly explained the reasons why I could not follow the line you had taken in the East India Bill, although I did not vote against it, that I could not go along with any violent measures, and that I thought there were many in the Red Book pointing to it on your table, that also would not.
>
> Your Lordship says in the option I had made I had chosen to be your enemy – and that my option had necessarily determined yours. If my opposing quesions which are violent or voting for an East India Bill brought in with the Company's consent much less infringing parliamentary faith or the Company's rights and privileges than the first less hazardous to public credit and more consonant to every idea your Lordship had expressed to me, is to be your Lordship's enemy – it must be so.

[1] Abergavenny MS. 572.
[2] Abergavenny MS. 565.
[3] Abergavenny MS. 568.
[4] Abergavenny MS. 572.

> But my Lord, let me intreat you to read, if you have it by you, my letters wrote to you last February and at some other times (perhaps wrote with too much freedom, but however with the utmost sincerity), and then let your own breast decide, whether I have not acted in a long and very laborious service with you, and for many of the later years indeed against my repeated wishes and requests, with honest zeal and ardor, if not with the expected ability. I am so conscious of this that I trust as I shall live to see the period when your generous mind will do me justice.

Thus at the moment of his final break with North, Robinson appealed once more in justification of his conduct to the guiding principle to which he had so often declared his adherence – his overriding political loyalty to the king. His duty was to the king, not to a party: he must support the ministers of whom the king approved; and opposition to a government of the king's choice was not an honourable nor an admissable line – 'violent measures' could not command his vote.

Robinson's position in parliamentary politics was thus quite straightforward and consistent. It was determined by his bent and inclination towards administration rather than politics, and the formulas in which he defined it were simple and, in his own day, perfectly familiar. If in his bureaucratic contempt for the Foxites he struck an attitude which was, in this period, rarely found to have political implications – for professional government servants in parliament were few in number, and some of these, like Philip Stephens, the secretary to the admiralty, kept themselves entirely aloof from political disputes – in his profession of direct attachment to the crown and to its wearer, he conformed to a current practice. His view was one shared by a large proportion of his fellow members in the Commons. During the first months of 1784 the great swing over to Pitt, both of independents and of men connected with the court and government service, proved to the hilt his contention that there were 'many in the Red Book' who placed the king above party and would have nothing to do with the 'violent measures' of faction politics.

III. ROBINSON AND THE REGENCY CRISIS, 1788–1789

During the next four years Robinson gave unobtrusive support to the new administration. His active career was over; he was elderly and ailing, and probably often absent from the House of Commons; only one or two of his votes are recorded and there is no note of his participating in debate. His help in the crisis of 1783–4 was duly rewarded. Although he wanted nothing for himself, at his desire his daughter's father-in-law, George, 15th Baron Abergavenny, was advanced to the dignity of an earldom. In 1786 he at last succeeded to the office of surveyor-general of woods and forests which had been promised to him in 1780, and with unabated zeal for the public service he busied himself fostering the timber resources which formed the basis of the country's naval strength: in after years he boasted 'that he had planted above 20,000 oaks in Windsor Forest'.[1] Occasional public service was also given in other ways. In 1785 he prepared material for Pitt on the past development of the system of parliamentary representation and, at his request, sounded the opinions of members of parliament about the tentative outlines of the reforms which Pitt had in mind.[2] In 1787 he was again used as a channel of information about the state of parliamentary opinion.[3] The same year – whether voluntarily or upon request is not known – he submitted a memorandum proposing the creation of a 'marine militia' to help strengthen the country's defences.[4]

The winter of 1788–9 produced a momentary disturbance in this calm evening of political life. For much of the year George III had suffered from chronic illness, and at the beginning of November he succumbed to the full violence of a serious attack of porphyria, which reduced him to a state of intermittent delirium. His reason and his life were despaired of, and the ugliest rumours were soon astir.[5] The parliamentary opposition derived the highest hopes from the situation. Pitt had seemed impregnable; but if the king

[1] Norcliffe, *Some Account of the Family of Robinson*, p. 49. Letters from Robinson to Hawkesbury of 12 June, 18 July, 20 Sept and 9 Oct 1788 attest his preoccupations with developments in Windsor Forest, B.M. Add. MSS. 38223, fos. 86, 110, 187, 213.

[2] Abergavenny MS. 630.

[3] Abergavenny MS. 636.

[4] Chatham MSS., P.R.O. 30/8/172.

[5] Ida Macalpine and Richard Hunter, 'The "Insanity" of King George III: a Classic Case of Porphyria', *British Medical Journal*, 8 Jan 1966, pp. 65–71; Charles Chenevix-Trench, *The Royal Malady* (1964) pp. 59–62.

were to die or prove to be mentally deranged or otherwise incapacitated and the Prince of Wales became king or regent, they would undoubtedly be called into office. As Pitt's attempts to stall became clear, they bent their efforts to drawing away the vital margin of support given to him in the House of Commons.

There is very little evidence as to how Robinson was initially involved in this situation. The one firm fact revealed in his correspondence with his old friend, Charles Jenkinson (now Lord Hawkesbury) is that he was in close touch with the Prince of Wales's physician, Dr Richard Warren, an old acquaintance, who was one of the consultants in charge of the case, and was greatly impressed by his pessimistic views.[1] On 11 November he sent Hawkesbury one of Warren's reports, which was evidently of a very depressing nature, for Hawkesbury wrote robustly in reply:[2]

> I am most obliged to you for the enclosed, which I return herewith and confess I think that the physicians assume too melancholy a tone: they suppose that a King must even in illness be as wise as Solomon, and that he must not be subject to delirium like other men.

This was all very well. But on the fourteenth Robinson had a personal interview with Warren, who told him that he feared the king was affected by a 'confirmed *debility*', though he was not yet prepared to state this publicly.[3] In that case the present state of public affairs could not long continue. For the time being Robinson put a stout face on the matter in conversation with members of the opposition.[4] He was too far from the centre of affairs to know much about the government's plans. But as the days passed and the king did not mend, it was evident that there must be a regency. The Prince of Wales would take control, his friends Portland and Fox would form a ministry, and the old king's government to which Robinson had given loyal support since December 1783 would be no more.

In this situation his political compass plainly pointed the way.

[1] B.M. Add. MSS. 38223, fos. 245, 253, 255, 261, 262, 263–6.

[2] Abergavenny MS. 637.

[3] Robinson to Hawkesbury, 14 Nov 1788, B.M. Add. MSS. 38223, fos. 263–6.

[4] Walter Sichel, *Sheridan*, 2 vols (1909) II 404.

He had been the king's man, not Pitt's. No particular allegiance of any kind bound him to Pitt. He lamented the sad fate of George III, but the king's government must go on. If the old reign was effectively ending, his political loyalty must be given to the Prince, whether as regent or king; and it was natural that he should try to salvage what he could of his own personal position by aiding rather than obstructing the political forces which now seemed to be in the ascendant. A channel for this purpose was already to hand in the person of his old friend of East India Company days, Sir John Macpherson, now a member of the Prince's intimate circle. Indeed, it is likely that Macpherson had begun to try and win him over well before the date at which their surviving correspondence began. It is possible, also, that Robinson was genuinely shocked by some of the constitutional implications of Pitt's proposals for placing limitations, even if only temporary ones, on the regent's use of the royal prerogative. There is, however, no surviving evidence for his views on this point. He appears to have voted on the government side after the initial discussion of Pitt's proposals on 16 December.[1] But soon afterwards his course began to veer.

Within little over a fortnight from that date the Duke of York passed on to his brother the news that Robinson was 'inclined to treat' and advised him to employ some agent in the matter, 'it being below his dignity to speak to him himself'.[2] To the members of the old Rockingham corps this prospect was highly distasteful. A man who had been attacked as standing at the centre of governmental jobbery and corruption during the North ministry was the last sort of person with whom self-righteous whigs wished to be associated. Fox felt he would 'be a disgrace to the party and not to be tried for'.[3] But the Prince recked nothing of these scruples. He was anxious to snatch support from any quarter and was not inclined to let his dignity stand in the way. Arrangements were made through Macpherson, and some time about 4 or 5 January Robinson attended a discreetly arranged assignation in Stanhope

[1] *The Parliamentary Register*, XXV (1789) p. 91.

[2] *The Correspondence of George, Prince of Wales, 1770–1812*, ed. A. Aspinall, vol. I, *1770–1789* (1963) p. 444 n. 1, citing Sichel, *Sheridan*, II 423.

[3] Ibid. (no reference cited).

Street.[1] Here, it seems, he first discussed with Macpherson some memoranda on the situation, possibly relating to a letter which the Prince had written to Pitt on 2 January[2] regarding the proposals for a limited regency, and was asked to sound the opinions of members of the Commons. At some stage of the proceedings the Prince gave Robinson an audience, and Robinson then pledged himself to give advice and help with the House of Commons. His capacity to do so was no longer what it had been in the autumn of 1783; but a curious, shadowy repetition of his role before the dismissal of the Fox–North coalition now began, though incompletely, to unfold itself.

On 9 January Sir John Macpherson gave Robinson a reminder that his advice was awaited.[3] The urgency of the matter was stressed by a further letter to the same effect from Sir John's kinsman, James Macpherson, another old associate who had served North's ministry as a pamphleteer.[4] Robinson replied promptly and at length next day to the first of these letters.[5] He agreed that '*piano*

[1] The evidence for this meeting and its outcome is in the following passage of Abergavenny MS. 639 (Macpherson to Robinson, 9 Jan 1789): 'I have by accident seen the gentleman whom you met at Stanhope Street some days ago, twice, since I saw you. He was anxious to hear from you and to learn what you was doing. My answer was all would end well, but that *piano* and *sono* was my own idea. I am to see him tomorrow. The joint paper he has seen and approves. Whatever you may have to say you may enclose under your own seal. I will present it. Afterwards I wish you to present your own ideas. You must make allowance for anxiety in proportion to quickness and youth – and situation.' The memorandum and the action Robinson was taking are referred to in his reply dated 10 Jan: 'Conversations had on some of the points in the *minutes you had*, seem to be felt.' (*Prince of Wales Correspondence*, I 443–4. Only through the publication of this letter have the allusions in Abergavenny MS. 639 become capable of interpretation.)

[2] *Prince of Wales Correspondence*, I 436–9.

[3] Abergavenny MS. 639, partly cited above.

[4] Abergavenny MS. 638.

[5] 10 Jan 1789, *Prince of Wales Correspondence*, I 443–4. The second short letter printed on p. 444 is not in Robinson's hand, nor in Macpherson's. The docket suggests that it covered another set of suggestions forwarded at the same time by Macpherson to the Prince's secretary, John Willett Payne. The hand, which is not known to me, is the same as that of the documents printed as nos. 368 and 398, but not (as p. 463 n. 2 suggests) the same as no. 384.

and *sono*' was the right maxim for the moment. The pace should not be forced, and the Prince's own conduct should be governed by the need to attract support: 'Calmness, good temper, a conduct dignified, civil, steady and firm, and an address given by Providence when brought into action in conspicuous life, will always succeed; little prejudices and party attacks must and will fall to it, and the minds of moderate and good men will by *degrees* accede and go on to *respect* and to *revere*.' However opposed the Prince and his supporters might be to restrictions of powers in the regency, outright opposition would be tactically disastrous. 'All divisions except *those* to *mollify* the restrictions seem unwise', Robinson continued. 'They engage and *dip* men more than is necessary, make retreat more difficult, and in the state of things are of no use.' His conversations with members of parliament suggested that they might respond to moves to ensure that the restrictions were not prolonged. There were also certain detailed points regarding which an attack on the vagueness of the government's proposals might be expected to bring some support. Finally Robinson advised an immediate disclosure of 'the very proper answer given to the communication of the restrictions'.[1] The willingness to fall in with the wishes of parliament would be 'popular ground', and the knowledge that the regency was accepted and would eventuate 'would alarm some, fix the wavering, and carry others'. The whole letter breathed the tactical wisdom of an old master campaigner and was very different in tone from the hot-headed counsels which had been pressed hitherto by the main body of the Prince's supporters.

During the series of debates on the resolutions preparatory to the regency bill, which Pitt introduced in the Commons on 16 January, Robinson's advice was again sought, apparently at the Prince's desire. A party meeting was arranged for 4 p.m. before the debate on Monday, 19 January, and on the preceding evening Macpherson, assuming that Robinson would be coming up from his home at Syon to attend the House, asked him to call on him on his way to Westminster. Counsels of moderation were again required, he explained: 'Our young

[1] The Prince's letter to Pitt was published in the *St James's Chronicle* of 24–7 Jan – that is, after the debates on the resolutions were ended, and a few days before the debates on the regency bill.

friend whom we saw in Stanhope Street asked me yesterday particular questions! You may judge how some of his people may argue.' But Robinson was ill in bed with 'gout' in his head and a 'violent cold' and he asked if Macpherson could come to him; if this was not possible, he promised to send 'some minutes of my thoughts'.[1] But Macpherson was pinned down by the meeting and by a party whip to attend the debate. 'Your illness', he wrote, 'is very unfortunate. I cannot go down to see you. . . . Can you send me your ideas before [4 o'clock] and mention those whom you have or hope to set aright.' And in a reference to the headstrong opinions of some of the Foxites, he added: 'Our friend wishes arguments against those of persons who are not attached to you.'[2]

The minutes which Robinson had promised were just ready for dispatch when, at 2 p.m., Macpherson's letter arrived; and they, with a brief reply, were hastily sent off in the hands of Macpherson's servant.[3] Robinson explained that his inquiries made clear that Pitt was sure of a majority by virtue of his assurances that the restrictions on the regency were temporary and that they arose out of a concern for the feelings of the king in the event of his early recovery, which the doctors now seemed to think more hopeful. A sense of the impropriety of the restrictions would grow only after the elapse of time and after the regency itself was in being. In these circumstances the Prince's friends should proceed with caution. Objections to various restrictions should be raised in debate and a claim laid 'to *discuss* and *debate* the points in the Bill when the whole plan [was] *seen* and known'. But there should be no divisions, unless it was clear 'that the point in discussion has struck *the House* in *those* parts likely to DETACH'. The resolutions should be allowed to pass and the bill to be brought in. The right course was 'to impress on all occasions men's minds that the Bill ought to have a *short duration* and a *limited* time for its continuance, and on this *at least* take a division, for it seems the only point likely to succeed, but avoid divisions on the others'. It is possible that this wise advice carried some weight at the party meeting, at which tactics

[1] Abergavenny MS. 641, very fully docketed by Robinson.

[2] 19 Jan 1789, Abergavenny MS. 643.

[3] Robinson's docket ibid.; *Prince of Wales Correspondence*, I 447–8, where the date should be 19 Jan 1789.

for the debate later that day were planned, for North divided the House on an amendment for adding the words 'for a limited time' to the resolution before it.[1]

During the following days Robinson, still on his sickbed at Syon, received further messages from both the Macphersons. A note from James a few days later informed him: 'Your hints were conveyed and were well received.'[2] Two days later Sir John wrote what seems to have been a clear hint that North was coming round to the idea of a reconciliation with Robinson, who had been dismissed from his door in January 1784,[3] and James sent brief accounts of the parliamentary proceedings both on the twenty-sixth and the twenty-ninth.[4] In the second of these notes Robinson was also given news of a letter which the Prince was about to send to his mother, justifying the opposition to the proposed restrictions.[5] On the sixth James reassured him again that the Prince was 'perfectly convinced' of the need for moderation.[6]

By that time the crisis was nearly over. Pitt's regency bill was introduced in the Commons on 5 February and during the next fortnight it proceeded as far as the committee stage in the Lords; but by the seventeenth it was known the king was convalescent and the announcement of this in the Lords on the nineteenth brought the proceedings virtually to an end. Throughout the affair Robinson, by the good fortune of his illness, seems to have avoided committing himself publicly against the government. On 6 February he was still at Syon. 'Much inquiry is made by —— after your health – and when you will be here', James Macpherson wrote to him that day.[7] His name does not appear in the one extant division list relating to the regency bill (11 February).[8] It seems probable that his illness was genuine. There is a clear probability that he had overexerted himself at Windsor during the summer, supervising a military working-party which was being employed

[1] John W. Derry, *The Regency Crisis and the Whigs, 1788–9* (Cambridge, 1963) p. 146.

[2] 24 Jan 1789, docketed 'recd 25th', Abergavenny MS. 644.

[3] 26 Jan 1789, Abergavenny MS. 645.

[4] Abergavenny MSS. 646, 647.

[5] Printed in *Prince of Wales Correspondence*, I 459–61.

[6] Abergavenny MSS. 648.

[7] Ibid.

[8] *The Parliamentary Register*, xxv (1789) 465 ff.

in the forest.[1] At the end of February he told Hawkesbury that he was still in an extremely bad way, his face afflicted with St Anthony's fire, and that there had been symptoms reminiscent of the dangerous malady which had knocked him out of action in 1774.[2] But for this he must have committed himself irretrievably in the House. As it was, whatever the rumours which may have circulated about his desertion, evidently nothing came to light to turn Pitt against him. His surviving papers contain two cordial letters of dates in June and December 1789 about patronage and electoral matters from Pitt's secretary to the treasury, George Rose,[3] and in August Robinson was writing to Pitt himself about patronage business affecting the government interest at Harwich.[4] By this time, once again his political course lay straight before him. His loyalty was given to the king and his government, as it ever had been since his appointment to the treasury.

[1] His letters to Hawkesbury of this period all mention the pressure under which he was working: B.M. Add. MSS. 38223, fos. 86, 110, 187, 213.

[2] 23 Feb 1789, B.M. Add. MSS. 38224, fos. 16–17. Robinson's docket to Macpherson's letter of 18 Jan (Abergavenny MS. 641) suggests his illness started with a bad dose of influenza, and his invitation to Macpherson to see him showed no desire for concealment.

[3] *The Parliamentary Papers of John Robinson*, pp. 131–2.

[4] 19 Aug 1789, Chatham MSS., P.R.O. 30/8/172.

SIX

*George III and the Debt on Lord North's Election Account, 1780–1784**

THE management of the government election fund during the last years of North's ministry gave rise to a curious epsiode, in which neither George III nor North appeared at their best, and which may have been a significant factor in the course of events leading to the junction of North and Charles James Fox in the famous 'coalition' of 1783.

During the months before and after the dissolution of parliament in 1780, George III and North spent upwards of £60,000 on the general election and an appreciable extra sum on by-elections.[1] Over half of this money came out of the king's privy purse: commencing in November 1777 George III set aside and periodically handed over to North for this purpose monthly contributions of £1,000, which by February 1781 totalled £40,000.[2] Inevitably, however, their expenditure outran the funds available. Furthermore,

* This originally appeared in *English Historical Review*, LXXVIII (1963) 715–24.

[1] Christie, *The End of North's Ministry*, pp. 98–106.

[2] Windsor MSS., Geo. III cal. 4716, printed in *The Correspondence of King George III*, VI no. 3714. The draft from which John Robinson, secretary to the treasury, prepared this statement is printed in *The Parliamentary Papers of John Robinson*, pp. 55–6. Fortescue's attribution of this document to May 1782 is incorrect: the word 'May' was not in the king's original endorsement but was scrawled over part of it at a later date. The correct date is *c.* 26 Mar 1782, and it was forwarded to the king under cover of North's letter of that date (subscribed by North, 'Tuesday night, private') incorrectly attributed by Fortescue to 16 Apr 1782 (vol. V no. 3663). In both cases the date is fixed by the references to the £1,000 due from Bute, which was paid to Robinson on 30 Mar (*The Parliamentary Papers of John Robinson*, p. 60).

I have to acknowledge the gracious permission of Her Majesty to make use of information from the papers of George III in the Royal Archives at Windsor. Since this paper was prepared a number of the documents cited have been published in *The Later Correspondence of George III, 1783–1793*, ed. A. Aspinall (1962).

during the general election North acted in some cases as negotiator between candidates seeking entry into parliament and patrons willing to make seats available to friends of government. He thus pledged himself to ensure payments on behalf of clients, some of whom could not immediately refund him the prices of their seats. By December 1780 some of the debts he had incurred had become pressing. On 7 December, in order to meet them, he borrowed £30,000 on his note of hand from the king's bankers, Messrs Henry and Robert Drummond.[1] He wisely took the prior step of securing the king's approval; and indeed the Drummonds would not have made the advance to him had he not been able to add to his note of hand the signed declaration: 'Memorandum. The above-mentioned sum of money being for his Majesty's use, this note was shown to His Majesty, given by his order and approved of.'[2]

North believed at that time that the loan would be repaid within the next two or three years, partly by the belated contributions from men for whom he had found seats, and otherwise by means of the king's monthly instalments. This hope remained unfulfilled. In the months after the general election by-election expenses were heavier than expected. Several of his clients disappointed him over their contributions. The other preoccupations of the secretary to the treasury, John Robinson, who took the responsibility under North for the election account, caused the account to fall into arrears, and no steps were taken to apply further contributions from the king to the reduction of the debt.[3] Finally, the North ministry was forced out of office only eighteen months after the elections. When, in the midst of the ministerial crisis of March 1782, the election account was hastily brought up to date, no monthly instalments had been collected from George III since February 1781, and the whole of the £30,000, plus accrued interest at five per cent, was still owing to Drummonds.

[1] Geo. III cal. 4666, partly printed in *The Correspondence of King George III*, v 481, is a copy of the note (probably sent to George III on 18 Apr 1782). On the ninth North paid £18,000 out of this money to Lord Edgcumbe (Geo. III cal. 4667, printed ibid.).

[2] Henry Drummond, in a letter to the king of *c.* 22 Mar 1784, wrote of 'the sum advanced for His Majesty's *use*, which would not have been advanced but on that account' (Geo. III cal. 5792).

[3] North to George III, 20 Apr 1782, *The Correspondence of King George III*, v no. 3674 (date incorrectly transcribed by the editor).

Late on the evening of 26 March, the day before his resignation was to take effect, North sent the king the 'general state' of the election account under cover of a fairly brief letter of explanation. He remarked that there were still claims for financial assistance outstanding from government supporters in Surrey for the general election and from Richard Rigby for a recent by-election at Colchester, and he hoped that these might be satisfied by the expenditure of about £3,000 (in the event no payments were made). On the credit side there was a contribution of £1,000 promised by the Earl of Bute for the election of one of his sons. Allowing for these outstanding items, a large part, but not all, of the £13,000 due as the king's monthly contributions since February 1781 would be available to pay off part of the debt to Drummonds, but there would still remain about £22,000, which might in due course be 'rub'd off, by cheques, by the £1,000 a month, out of the Privy Purse'.[1]

The king made no comment on the subject until North, about 18 April, forwarded a final 'state of the election account', with a further, lengthy explanation of the extent of the election expenditure and the consequent outstanding debt of £32,754.[2] This letter as it now exists is incomplete. It seems probable that in the final, missing portion North repeated his remarks about paying off the whole balance (£2,754 to him personally and £30,000 to Drummonds) by means of the monthly contributions of £1,000 and made reference to enclosed copies of his note of hand to Drummond and of a memorandum about the transaction.[3]

The king, in his reply dated 18 April, took up the point about

[1] Ibid., no. 3663. In these and later figures North ignored the interest due to Drummonds.

[2] Ibid., no. 3668. The 'state' enclosed with the letter does not appear now to be in the king's papers; Robinson's draft is printed in *The Parliamentary Papers of John Robinson*, p. 57. Of the documents annexed by Fortescue to no. 3668, numbers I to V and VII concern secret service. The two which relate to the election account are both misplaced. VI was sent with North's next letter (*The Correspondence of King George III*, V no. 3674). The date of VIII is *c.* 22 Mar 1784.

[3] Geo. III cal. 4666 and 4667. The appropriate context of these documents is North's letter of [18 Apr 1782] (*The Correspondence of King George III*, V no. 3668). They would not have been appropriate accompaniments to his letter of 20 Apr to which they are annexed by Fortescue (vol. V no. 3674 n.).

repayment, and his reaction to North's suggestion was unexpected and extraordinary. While accepting his liability for £13,000, he declined to accept responsibility for the other £17,000 of the debt which had been contracted with Drummonds in his service and with his approval in December 1780. He also ignored the mounting interest charge upon £30,000 and the £2,754 which was owing to North personally. Anticipating that the newly installed Rockingham ministry would probably inflict a cut on the amount allowed for the privy purse, he declared that if that were to happen, he would have 'no means of satisfying the remainder now unexpectedly put to my account of £19,754 18*s* 2*d*'.[1]

In strict law the king had some semblance of right on his side. North, not he, had contracted for the loan with Drummonds. Moreover, it was by then clear constitutional doctrine that for whatever action a minister took in the king's service, that minister should accept responsibility. But in fairness and equity there was another side to the matter, and the most that can be said for George III was that the critical events culminating in the fall of North's ministry had rendered him incapable of seeing it clearly. His correspondence of those weeks reveals that the crisis had been emotionally shattering. In a half apology for his blunt language he pleaded: 'Lord North cannot be surprised that a mind truely tore to pieces should make me less attentive to my expressions.'[2] This is a probable explanation, but it is hardly an excuse for his stubborn insistence that North should have cleared off the debt before leaving office, even if this involved the use of practically £20,000 from the secret service money, and that having failed to do so he must take the full responsibility.[3] It had not been recent practice to draw on the secret service funds for this sort of purpose; and it would have been unwise, to say the least, for North to do this when about to be succeeded in office by political rivals who were pledged to public economy and reduction of corruption and crown influence, and who might be expected to exploit any such transaction against him if they uncovered it. Moreover, despite current

[3] *The Correspondence of King George III*, v no. 3669. Evidently the claims of Rigby and of the friends in Surrey were by now quite out of the question: there is no further reference to them in this correspondence.

[2] 21 Apr 1782, ibid., no. 3675.

[3] To North, 18 Apr 1782, ibid., no. 3669.

doctrines of ministerial responsibility, the king had a certain personal responsibility for the loan. The situation displayed, in an unusual guise, a periodically intractable problem of the eighteenth-century constitution, that of reconciling ministerial responsibility with the fact that the sovereign still had a recognised, personal role as the head of the executive government.

George III took no heed of the constitutional ambiguities. Nor did he realise (as he should have done) that he was violating the agreement which the Drummonds understood they were entering into when they took North's bond. Finally he failed to count the possible political cost of his parsimony. Blinkered by the thought of his own possible future financial difficulties (the Rockingham ministry was then busy discussing Burke's establishment bill), he left no life-lines out for North, gave no hint, for instance, that the matter might be shelved until his financial position became clearer, but brusquely unloaded the responsibility upon his ex-minister.

North's reaction was wholly in character and reflected his usual deference and weakness of will. His reply, dated the twentieth, consisted mainly of a recapitulation of the reasons for the heavy cost of the elections.[1] Reading between the lines it is evident that, after the king's past acts of generosity and protestations of friendship, North was quite unprepared for, and staggered by, the brutal assumption that he should shoulder a debt, incurred in the public service, which was equivalent to his whole private income for the next four years. It might have been better had he set himself whole-heartedly to stress the moral responsibility of his master. In particular, the obligation to the Drummonds gave him good ground and was, perhaps, the strongest card he might have played. But such a course was against his nature. 'With a heart full of the deepest concern at having incurred the displeasure of His Majesty', he immediately yielded the pass:

> Lord North does, by no means, intend by this State to propose to His Majesty to add more than £13,000 to the £40,000 already issued (which undoubtedly is a very large sum) but only to lay fairly and fully before His Majesty the principal causes of the amount of that account of which His Majesty complains.

[1] Ibid., no. 3674.

And after further explanations:

> Lord North states all these circumstances only in the hope of reinstating himself in some degree in His Majesty's good opinion. He has no other wish or desire.

These phrases were at least a tacit acceptance of North's own responsibility for the £17,000 due to Drummonds. A few weeks later he reaffirmed it more openly. On 8 May, employing Lord Brudenell as messenger, George III repaid a first instalment of £7,000 to Drummonds. He requested that the receipt might run in part of the £13,000 which he regarded as the full extent of his liability. Henry Drummond refused to agree. He knew nothing of how matters stood between George III and his ex-minister, only that a further £23,000 was due, and he asked to be allowed to give a simple receipt for £7,000.[1] Brudenell accordingly referred the matter to North. On 16 May North pointed out to the king that Drummond was reluctant to give a receipt in part of £13,000 lest it should appear he was giving quittance for the other £17,000; and he explained:[2]

> Lord North, having no money, and not being able to give Mr Drummond any security, is endeavouring to arrange his affairs in such a manner as to be able to apply the whole income of his office [Lord Warden of the Cinque Ports] to the gradual extinction of the debt, and was afraid that if he had stated the whole of the case to Mr Drummond before the necessary arrangements were settled, he might have alarmed him with respect to the safety of the debt. He therefore did not press him on that subject, especially as the note of hand is signed by Lord North, and consequently His Majesty is liable to no legal demand in whatever form the receipts are given. If His Majesty, however, should think it right to require a receipt in another form, Lord North must explain the whole of the case immediately to Mr Drummond, and trust in the generous and liberal spirit of that gentleman that he will not distress him for the payment of the money, until the note can be gradually discharged, in the manner above mentioned.

---

[1] George III to John Robinson, 19 Aug 1784, *The Parliamentary Papers of John Robinson*, p. 60.

[2] *The Correspondence of King George III*, VI no. 3753.

George III, as well he might, took this as a full admission on North's part of responsibility for repaying the £17,000; and he reasoned that he could not conveniently pay his acknowledged further debt to Drummond of £6,000 until North had discharged his portion – for when he did pay it he would require a receipt in final quittance.[1] Accordingly he let the matter lie. But he waited in vain. North was in no position to make arrangements with Drummond. This debt was not his only embarrassment. In these same weeks he also fell victim to George III's niggardliness in the course of securing quittance on the secret service account, for the king, obsessed with the need to save money, seized the opportunity to disallow a payment of £3,250 to a government journalist, the Reverend Henry Bate.[2] North had expected this sum to be available to help repay yet another loan which he had taken up from Richard Rigby; and by this disappointment his debt to Rigby was left still standing at over £6,800.[3] However generous George III had been to him in the past – granting him £20,000 in 1777 for the clearance of his debts, appointing him lord warden of the Cinque Ports and conferring this office for life upon his retirement – such treatment was not unjustifiably a cause of grievance. The wardenship for life was no more than a fair pension for over a decade of unremitting toil as head of the treasury and chief spokesman for the government in the House of Commons. And the grant of £20,000 was wiped out by the imposition upon him of the major part of the debt to Drummond.[4] In the following weeks his resentment grew. Despite the submission expressed in his letters, he seems to have expected that the king would reconsider the matter. Possibly he, or his father, Lord Guilford, dropped hints to this

[1] George III to John Robinson, 19 Aug 1784, *The Parliamentary Papers of John Robinson*, p 60.

[2] *The Correspondence of King George III*, v no. 3668, encl. vii; no. 3691; vi no. 3715.

[3] Robinson to North, 20 Sept 1784, Geo. III cal. 5888. This debt is also referred to in a letter from Rigby to North, 6 Sept 1784, ibid., 5877. There is no evidence to account for the presence of these letters in the king's papers, but presumably Robinson gave them to George III for his information. Both letters appear to be the originals, and it would have been out of character for Robinson to hand them over without North's leave.

[4] Indeed it was more than cancelled, for the interest charges were already over £2,000 and North's claim to £2,754 had also been rejected.

effect, of which no record occurs in the correspondence.[1] When, at the beginning of August, the king, using Robinson as intermediary, approached him with a request to support the Shelburne ministry,[2] his reactions were eloquent of his discontent. To the king he returned an answer which, though formally dutiful, entirely lacked the warmth expected.[3] A fortnight later, forwarding the king's letter for Robinson to read and file, he wrote:[4]

> In the meantime I wish you would prepare for me an exact copy of the note of hand which I gave some time ago to Mr D[rummond]. You will perceive by the inclosed letter that no notice is taken of it, nor a word said to relieve my mind on that subject; I wish, therefore, to have a copy of the note of hand that I may have a pretence to write again to my correspondent upon that matter.

Five days later he wrote again on the subject to Robinson: 'There is not the most distant hint of any intention to do me justice', and declared that he hoped for an early chance to reopen it, as Lord Brudenell had approached him for 'a line of explanation'.[5] But he seems to have been unable to find the opportunity he wanted.

The effect of this grievance upon North's political conduct during the following months remains a matter of surmise. In late September he outlined the problems of his situation in a letter to one of his oldest political associates, to whom he had shown the king's letter of the previous month:[6]

[1] This inference is based upon the wording of North's letter of 3 Sept 1782 to Robinson, cited below.

[2] *The Correspondence of King George III*, VI nos. 3872, 3871, 3870 (order inverted by the editor).

[3] North to George III [14 Aug 1782], ibid., no. 3873, incorrectly attributed to 10 Aug by the editor. The date is established by that of North's letter to Robinson, forwarding it to him for transmission to the king, H.M.C., *Abergavenny MSS.*, no. 471. On 22 Sept Charles Jenkinson wrote to Robinson: 'I know through a private channel that a certain person is displeased at the answer that was returned, and says that Lord N's present language is very different from the strong and repeated declarations he used to make him.' (Ibid., no. 479.)

[4] Abergavenny MS. no. 475.

[5] H.M.C., *Abergavenny MSS.*, no. 477.

[6] To Lord Bagot, 26 Sept 1782, Bagot MSS. in the possession of Mr N. E. S. Norris of Brighton, to whose kindness in giving leave to reproduce part of it I am greatly indebted.

> I do not think [he wrote] that it would satisfy my conscience or conduce to my honour to assist in running down Government in the present very critical juncture, I will go further, my opinion is, that according to my public professions, and real principles, I ought to support Government in every measure, that is necessary to carry on a vigorous war or procure an adequate peace: But I can not, as yet, with any dignity or propriety declare a general support of the present ministry, or profess any connexion with them. I know nothing of their principles, counsell, or designs. Some plans, of which they have given notice I shall most decidedly oppose, they may produce others as repugnant to my sentiments as those to which I allude.

However adverse it might be to the immediate interests of himself and his friends, he continued, he intended to stick to his political principles; and while he was prepared to 'prevent the necessary operations of Government from being baffled by any factious combination', he was determined to hold aloof from Shelburne. Finally he addressed to his correspondent the question: would the country gentlemen be disposed to continue liberal grants of men and money in order 'to support the necessary measures of Government in the conduct of the war and towards the conclusion of an adequate peace'?

This letter is particularly significant for the way in which it reveals North's determination to hold to a political course regardless of the king's desires. It also reveals his sense of isolation. But nowhere does it foreshadow the coalition of 1783. Subsequently, in speeches and writing, he revealed a number of the considerations which led him towards his eventual junction with Fox. He was critical over the peace, particularly over the failure to secure protection for the American loyalists, though it is likely that he would himself have had to defend similar terms, had his ministry remained in office to make peace with a victorious enemy.[1] He was obdurately opposed to the ideas of parliamentary reform, with which Pitt and Shelburne were particularly identified.[2] His chances of returning to office appeared far greater through Fox than through

[1] William Eden to Loughborough, 5 Oct 1782, B.M. Add. MSS. 34419, fo. 55; North in the Commons, 17 Feb 1783, Debrett, *The Parliamentary Register*, IX (1783) 241–51.

[2] North to Lisburne, 19 Nov 1782, B.M. Egerton MSS. 2136, fo. 213; *The Parliamentary Register*, IX 295, 708–14.

Shelburne, since Pitt absolutely refused to enter into any combination with him.[1] But he drifted towards the junction with Fox with no clear certainty of purpose, and his conduct during the winter of 1782–3 resembles nothing so much as that of a reed blown before the wind.[2] He had no heart for the coalition into which his friends and relatives exerted all their energies to impel him. On the morrow of its first success in the Commons he bewailed the fact to his father: 'Nobody ever was so distress'd at victory as I am; indeed I am perfectly miserable, and tremble at the vexations and troubles that are hanging over me.'[3] While evidence for a firm conclusion is lacking, it seems not unlikely that if George III had acted open-handedly towards North after his resignation, North, swayed by a more pressing sense of obligation, would have been less disposed to act against the king's wishes by assisting in the destruction of the Shelburne ministry. It was the king's generosity which had given him his hold over North during the last years of North's ministry.[4] But by the outburst of parsimony over the secret service and the election account George III cancelled out his past liberality and cast away a lever by means of which he might have exercised some degree of influence over North's conduct.

In the event George III did not even gain financially; rather he lost, for he had to shoulder the whole debt plus an increased burden of interest. North took no steps to explain the situation to the Drummonds, for his affairs were so straitened that he had no hope of discharging the debt. The affair remained in suspense until, on the eve of the general election of 1784, the king approached Henry Drummond for a further loan.[5] The amount he sought was £24,000 on his bond, 'with assurance of repaying three thousand pounds every three months and of paying five per cent for the money'. The arrangements were put in hand during the last week

[1] Stanhope, *Life of . . . William Pitt*, I 87–8.

[2] From Aug 1782 onwards complaints of North's indecision were constant on both sides ,e.g. B.M. Add. MSS. 34418, fo. 513; 34419, fos. 24, 37–8; 38567, fos. 107–12, 117–18; 38309, fo. 75; 38218, fo. 154.

[3] [18 Feb 1783], Waldershare MSS., Kent Record Office. The date is suggested by the endorsement on an accompanying note of congratulations from Guilford: 'My answer to Ld N. Feb 18, 1783', ibid.

[4] Butterfield, *George III, Lord North, and the People*, pp. 17–19.

[5] Draft, 22 Mar 1784, Geo. III cal. 5791.

of March (only £10,000 was actually borrowed).[1] He could hardly broach this subject without some reference to the £6,000 he had not yet repaid, under what he regarded as his settlement with North in 1782; and accordingly he proposed to Drummond the merging of this debt into the new one:[2]

> By the account I settled with Lord North when he quitted the Treasury, he stated that I owed thirteen thousand pounds to Mr Drummond, of which I have paid through the hands of Lord Brudenell seven thousand pounds. The other six is still owing, and was kept back at the desire of Lord North, he having a personal account to settle with Mr Drummond on which subject I fear he has not acted very explicitly. He has never explained this as yet; this indeed has the more made me on the present occasion not wish to employ a middle person. Consequently the bond must be for thirty thousand pounds at five per cent.

This was the first that the Drummonds had heard about any arrangement with North, and the king's description of the transaction differed profoundly from their understanding of it. Accordingly Henry Drummond, in a letter agreeing to raise £24,000 for a new loan, pointed out that the original advance would not have been made had it not been understood that it was for the king's use, and that payment of the £6,000 referred to by George III would still leave '£17,000 of the principal remaining undischarged besides the interest'. He enclosed a copy of North's note of hand, bearing North's certification that the money had been borrowed for the king's use by the king's order, and showing the £7,000 written off as a part-repayment out of £30,000, leaving a balance due of £23,000. To make matters quite clear he added 'that the partnership are entire strangers to the transaction between His Majesty and Lord North, further than that it was to be discharged by installments'.[3]

[1] Drummond to George III [*c.* 22 Mar], 31 Mar, George III to Drummond, draft, 28 Mar 1784, ibid., 5792, 5798, 5803. On 23 Sept George III explained to Robinson that he owed Drummond £10,000 in addition to previous debts, draft, ibid., 5891, and in Robinson's copy of the final bond settling the whole matter there is a calculation of interest due on £10,000 from 3 Apr to 25 Oct 1784, B.M. Add. MSS. 37836, fos. 172–3.

[2] Geo. III cal. 5791.

[3] [*c.* 22 Mar 1784], Geo. III cal. 5792. The note of hand enclosed is the document printed by Fortescue as if of Apr 1782 (*The Correspondence of King George III*, V no. 3668, encl. VIII).

The king promised to make an immediate investigation of North's conduct.[1] But there is no indication of any action in his correspondence. Perhaps he found the matter too delicate to commit to paper. In the end he fell back upon the expedient of sending Drummond (through the agency of Robinson) North's letter of 16 May 1782,[2] in which North acknowledged his 'having nothing further to pay than the £13,000', of which £7,000 had already been returned. He indicated that Drummond should show the letter to North and seek an arrangement with him for the repayment of the outstanding £17,000.[3] After North had repaid this, he would himself pay Drummonds the final £6,000 'and any interest due finally to close the transaction'.[4]

This suggestion came to nothing owing to the disordered state of North's finances. On 10 September Henry Drummond returned North's letter to the king[5] and enclosed a separate memorandum of North's verbal answer to his request for a settlement:[6]

> Lord North perfectly recollected the letter, but informed Mr Drummond that the whole of his income does not exceed £2,500 nett per annum, the larger part of which he holds for the life of Lady North, the rest for his own; and that the office which His Majesty had been so kind as to confer upon him does not produce £3,000 a year. It is therefore absolutely out of his power to make any arrangement to discharge the debt to Messrs Drummond.

This answer greatly shocked the king. To Robinson he wrote: 'This crowns the rest of that lord's ill behaviour to me and shows that in every line I have equal reason to complain of him.'[7] A little later he described North's conduct as 'the most barefaced fraud'.[8]

[1] To Drummond, draft, 28 Mar 1784, Geo. III cal. 5798.

[2] *The Correspondence of King George III*, VI no. 3753.

[3] George III to Robinson, 19 Aug 1784, *The Parliamentary Papers of John Robinson*, pp. 60–1. Robinson acknowledged these instructions on the twenty-first and reported that he had carried them out on the twenty-fourth, B.M. Add. MSS. 37835, fo. 205 (copy), fo. 206 (draft).

[4] George III to Robinson, 2 Sept 1784, ibid., fo. 209.

[5] Geo. III cal. 5880.

[6] Ibid., 5892; filed beside the draft of George III's letter to Robinson of 23 Sept 1784 (ibid., 5891), informing Robinson of its contents.

[7] Draft, 23 Sept 1784, ibid.

[8] To Henry Drummond, draft, 24 Oct 1784, ibid., 5909.

There is no sign that he recognised any fault on his own side. But he agreed that in the circumstances Drummond must not be allowed to be a loser, and that if North could not discharge the debt he must assume the obligation for the whole £23,000 and the interest due. Robinson was accordingly instructed to have a new bond prepared covering both the old debt and the £10,000 borrowed from Drummond the previous April.[1] This business was completed during the latter part of October; George III repaid £6,000 immediately and undertook to discharge the remainder of the debt in six instalments by payments in March and October during the next three years.[2]

[1] To Robinson, draft, 23 Sept 1784, ibid., 5891; acknowledged by Robinson, 30 Sept 1784, ibid., 5896. Robinson reported Drummond's agreement to the proposal on 6 Oct 1784, draft, B.M. Add. MSS. 37835 fo. 215.

[2] Robinson to George III, 23 Oct 1784, Geo. III cal. 5903; George III to Drummond, draft, 24 Oct 1784, ibid., 5905, to Robinson, same date, *The Parliamentary Papers of John Robinson*, p 61; Drummond to George III, 25 Oct, Robinson to George III, 26 Oct, Geo. III cal. 5906, 5907; Robinson's copy of the bond, B.M. Add. MSS. 37836, fos. 172–3. George III's note of the proposed schedule of payments sent in his instructions to Robinson is printed with a line omitted in *The Parliamentary Papers of John Robinson*, p. 62 – the king's draft is in his papers, Geo. III cal. 5910.

SEVEN

*Was there a 'New Toryism' in the Earlier Part of George III's Reign?**

THE reissue after twenty years of G. H. Guttridges's study, *English Whiggism and the American Revolution*, is very welcome.[1] In many of its judgements this lucid, aseptic dissection of the ideas, attitudes and policies of the opposition groups in British politics during the period of the Revolution bids fair to stand the test of a much longer period of time than has elapsed since its first appearance in 1942. The virile political traditions (some still traceable in modern British practice) which Hanoverian England inherited from the whiggism of the seventeenth century contained not one but several potentially competing principles; and the great strength of this study lies in the author's exposition of the ways in which these divergent principles were taken up by different political groups, with the effect of determining the stand taken by each, both on the American question and on concurrent issues of domestic politics. In Locke's writings radicals found justification for the creed of personality as the basis of political rights. All groups drew from them a belief that parliament had an essential role in maintaining 'the contractual obligation of monarchy to preserve certain fundamental rights',[2] but more than one principle followed from this premise. In the minds of William Pitt, Earl of Chatham, and his friends, it was combined with pre-Lockian concepts of fundamental law as an element in the constitution beyond the power of parliament to alter. For the leaders and members of the Rockingham connection, parliament's role was seen in, and secured by, its supremacy. The inability of Rockinghams and Chathamites to combine in dealing with the American question was in part the outcome of these basic differences in opinion. The rounded exposition

* This originally appeared in *Journal of British Studies*, v (1965–6) 60–76.

[1] G. H. Guttridge, *English Whiggism and the American Revolution* (Berkeley and Los Angeles, 1963).

[2] Ibid., p. 11.

of this theme throughout the course of Guttridge's essay is a fine intellectual achievement and one which is of the greatest service to an understanding of the period.

It may perhaps be permitted, however, to ask if on one point the author does not push his intellectual constructions beyond what the evidence will bear. He believes in the emergence after 1760 of a 'new toryism', the antithesis of the whig politics represented in one mode by Chatham and in another by Rockingham. This toryism, in his view, stood for the principle of unity and authority, as against the whig assertion of particular rights.[1] It was anti-party, 'the creed of the non-partisan state',[2] and as such opposed to the Rockinghams' stress on the importance of party. He concludes that an interpretation of the politics of the period in terms of a conflict between whigs and tories is viable:[3]

> Once more, as under the Stuarts, the advocates of authority and the non-partisan state were challenged by the champions of individual and corporate rights, organised in some degree as a party. This new antithesis is sufficiently near the old to justify the transference of the old terms, and they were actually so transferred.

The practical manifestations of this new toryism were the active participation of the new king in politics and the association by his chosen ministers of his government with 'an illiberal and authoritarian policy which made John Wilkes and the American colonies the centres of violent controversy'.[4]

Many historians, as Guttridge notes, 'have denied all validity to the names of whig and tory' in the period after 1760.[5] The writer of this article confesses himself to be of their number. The reappearance of a monograph asserting the thesis of a whig–tory conflict in British politics in these years seems to invite a reappraisal of considerations making for the opposite view.

To what extent were the old terms in fact transferred to the new political alignments? This was done at the level of anti-ministerial propaganda, both in parliamentary speeches and in public prints, more particularly during the later years of the American war. There is no question but that Rockingham, Charles Fox and others

[1] Ibid., p. 1. [2] Ibid., pp. 13–14. [3] Ibid., p. 16.
[4] Ibid. [5] Ibid., p. 15.

began to think of themselves as the true representatives of the whig tradition, and the aura of whiggism was regarded as a political advantage to be exploited. Spokesmen on the government side, however, did not concede them this claim and, as Guttridge mentions, represented themselves as upholding whig principles against tory tendencies in the colonies.[1] Granted this, the extent to which these terms were used should not be exaggerated. It is relevant here to quote the conclusion of a scholar who has recently made a detailed examination of the printed and manuscript sources for debates in the parliament of 1768–74:[2]

> Collective references or designations of political alignments were usually made with regard to the respective sides of the House, to administration and opposition, and, less frequently, to the majority and the minority. Little use was made of the terms whig and tory. On infrequent occasions a member might assert he was expounding whig doctrines: never did any claim to be a tory, but the term was sometimes used as a method of reproach.

This conclusion could almost equally apply to debates during the last two years of the North administration which the present writer has examined in detail. One or two backbench country gentlemen then laid claim to the name of tory, but they were tories only in the vestigial, pre-1760 sense, by virtue of family tradition.

But in any case propaganda labels must be regarded by the historian with the greatest of caution. It is necessary to look behind the propaganda. When politicians were jotting down their thoughts for private, not public, consumption, they found it better to avoid the cant terms of politics or admitted their emptiness. It was John Wilkes who in 1767 observed: 'You never can trust any ministers in our country. The Whigs in power turn Tories; tho' alas the Tories do not turn Whigs!'[3] – the real distinction he sensed being that between oppositionists and those whose conduct was influenced by the pressures and responsibilities of office. And it was Burke who in 1782 considered that there were only five or six real tories in Lord North's following – he was evidently thinking of survivors of the early eighteenth-century tory tradition and did not

[1] Ibid., pp. 62, 105.

[2] P. D. G. Thomas, 'The Debates of the House of Commons, 1768–1774' (Ph.D. thesis, University of London, 1958) p. 166.

[3] John Almon, *Memoirs of an Eminent Bookseller* (1790) p. 45.

regard this as a meaningful term to use of North's party.[1] Events after 1782 seem to bear out his judgement. Had North, previously a tory, become a whig when early in 1783 he told Fox that 'the appearance of power is all that a king in this country can have'?[2] And was Fox a whig or a tory when he set on foot a major modification by parliamentary authority of the chartered privileges of the East India Company?

Guttridge picks out a number of episodes in domestic politics as evidence of the advance of the new toryism, and he refers to the opposition whigs as championing 'the waning cause of liberty'. These episodes are: the use of a general warrant against Wilkes and others involved in the *North Briton* in 1763 and the prosecution of Wilkes for seditious libel; the alteration of the return to the Middlesex election in 1769, when the candidate defeated by Wilkes, Henry Lawes Luttrell, was declared duly elected; the declaration of Lord Mansfield in the Woodfall case in 1770 that juries in cases of libel could not decide the vital question whether the matter complained of was libellous or not; and the dispute over the London printers and the publication of parliamentary debates in 1771.[3]

There is, however, a difficulty in this thesis. Ministerial action in all these cases had a more or less respectable backing of precedent, running back into, or through, the whig ascendancy of the half-century before 1760; and some of the people who raised the clamour against ministerial action had done the same sort of things while in power under George II.

The use of general warrants in the eighteenth century was an adaptation of a practice which had developed under the Licensing Acts of later Stuart times and which was continued, without anyone's thinking of challenging its legality, when the Acts finally lapsed in 1693.[4] In 1764, when the legality of the warrants was debated in parliament, a mass of evidence was produced in support of the current practice. This included 'a series of warrants from

[1] E. B. de Fonblanque, *Political and Military Episodes . . . from the Life and Correspondence of . . . John Burgoyne* (1876) p. 421.

[2] Russell, *Memorials and Correspondence of Charles James Fox* II 38.

[3] Guttridge, *English Whiggism*, pp. 16, 28, 45.

[4] Lord Camden, 1765, cited in W. C. Costin and J. Steven Watson, *The Law and Working of the Constitution: Documents, 1660–1914* (1952) I 307.

the [year] 1662 quite down to the present time', and an observer reported:[1]

> Among the warrants produced there were some of every secretary of state since the Revolution. Vast numbers of the Duke of Newcastle, and among them some general as to the crime (which had in the case of Justice Scroggs been the ground of impeachment). Among Mr Pitt's were two which mentioned no cause of commitment and were therefore a violation of the Petition of Right.

The prosecution of Wilkes for seditious libel in consequence of his comments on the Peace of Paris in the *North Briton* was in conformity with a definition of this term which had been current throughout the eighteenth century. Legal doctrine on this point had remained virtually unchanged since the reigns of Charles II and James II. Public criticism of the activities of government was regarded as tantamount to stirring up the people against it and was accordingly treated as a crime. The lawyers of the eighteenth century had no conception of what the nineteenth century was to accept as 'fair political comment'. Lest there should be thought to be a gulf between the thinking of whig and tory lawyers on this subject in the years after 1760, it is as well to recall the concluding passages of the judgement in which Pitt's ally, Lord Camden, finally established the illegality of general warrants:[2]

> Before I conclude, I desire not to be understood as an advocate for libels. All civilized governments have punished calumny with severity; and with reason; for these compositions debauch the manners of the people; they excite a spirit of disobedience, and enervate the authority of government; they provoke and excite the passions of the people against their rulers, and the rulers oftentimes against the people. . . . I will always set my

---

[1] Gilbert Elliot to his father, 18 Feb 1764, in G. F. S. Elliot, *The Border Elliots* (1897) p. 391. For much illustrative detail supporting this and other points which follow regarding the position of the press, see H. R. F. Bourne, *English Newspapers: Chapters in the History of Journalism*, 2 vols. (1887); D. H. Stevens, *Party Politics and English Journalism, 1702–1742* (Menasha, Wisc., 1916); L. Hanson, *Government and the Press, 1695–1763* (1936); and F. S. Siebert, *Freedom of the Press in England, 1476–1776* (Urbana, Ill., 1952).

[2] Costin and Watson, *Documents, 1660–1914*, I 310.

face against them, when they come before me; and shall recommend it most warmly to the jury always to convict when the proof is clear. . . . When licentiousness is tolerated, liberty is in the utmost danger; because tyranny, bad as it is, is better than anarchy, and the worst of governments is more tolerable than no government at all.

The decision of a majority of the House of Commons, on a government motion, not to accept Wilkes as the choice of the Middlesex electors in 1769 was another action for which undoubted precedent might be found. The Commons had long enjoyed an unquestioned right to the sole decision of disputed returns in parliamentary elections, and throughout the eighteenth century up to 1770 this privilege was exploited in the interests of the governing politicians, often with little or no regard to the rights or wrongs of the parliamentary electors. By comparison with the sort of partisan decisions which had been common in Walpole's time, the exclusion of a convicted criminal after the amount of warning which had been given to the electors seems almost respectable.[1]

Much the same point can be made about the attempt in 1771 to ban the publication of parliamentary debates. This course had been followed by the House of Commons consistently ever since the Revolution. The *Journals* from 1694 till 1722 recorded a series of resolutions against authors of newsletters, and from 1722 onwards the ban was extended to newspapers and magazines. The position the House was attempting to defend in 1771 had been in substance established by a resolution passed in 1738 with the concurrence of all parts of the House, including the opposition whigs, and was reaffirmed in 1762.[2]

The remaining count – the denial to juries of the right to judge of the libellous nature of publications – also rested on a firm body of legal precedent. Mansfield, by his ruling on procedure in the Woodfall case, was making no alteration in the law. He was merely

[1] 'We have for a long time beheld the suffrages of the people wantonly sported with, not only by ministers, but by the avowed defenders of public liberty.' (George Grenville, 7 Mar 1770, cited in *The Parliamentary History*, ed. Cobbett and Wright, XVI 905.) Cf. John, Lord Hervey, *Some Materials towards Memoirs of the Reign of King George II*, ed. R. Sedgwick (1931) I 75–6, on the election of 1727.

[2] E. and A. G. Porritt, *The Unreformed House of Commons* (Cambridge, 1903–9) I 589–93.

confirming a long-established practice.[1] Its origins went back to the heyday of Stuart monarchy. There was no positive change in the law at the Revolution to release the courts from the string of precedents which had bound them before 1689. For over forty years thereafter the practice continued to be followed without question. Not till the case of Rex *v.* Francklin in 1731 was it seriously challenged. The challenge was certainly necessary, for long before then it had become out-of-date. As reformers were to argue, the Revolution had effected a fundamental change in the theoretical relationship between sovereign and people. In doing so it had implicitly, if not explicitly, confirmed as a principle of public law the subject's right of open, peaceful discussion of public affairs. The objections to the old rule, first raised in 1731, were to be repeated regularly by liberal-minded lawyers during the next sixty years, among them Camden during his years as a king's counsel; but judges unanimously insisted upon its observance, and Mansfield in the case of the Dean of St Asaph in 1783 paraded very fully the evidence that it had been uniformly followed. The most eminent scholar in this field has concluded that 'the view . . . held by Lord Mansfield and the other judges was the historically correct view of the law.'[2] It was those who pressed for change who were the innovators. They were correct in their assertions that this branch of the law needed to be brought into conformity with the needs of the eighteenth-century political system and the principles of the constitution as it had developed since 1689; but such a change required legislation and time was needed to achieve this.

The same general conclusion can be drawn about all these incidents. To interpret them as manifestations of a new toryism, to think of liberty waning in face of an authoritarian trend in politics, is to stand the evidence on its head. What is significant about these incidents is not any development of arbitrary tendencies on the part of George III's governments (for there was none), but

[1] Rockingham himself admitted this. 'However disagreeable these doctrines may be', he wrote to Dowdeswell on 11 Feb 1771, 'yet it must be acknowledged that they can be defended and supported by the opinion of the generality of the present judges etc., and upon old authorities from good constitutional lawyers.' (Rockingham MSS., printed in *Sir Henry Cavendish's Debates*, II 354.)

[2] Sir William Holdsworth, *A History of English Law* (1903–52) x 680; and see his illuminating discussion of the whole subject, pp. 672–96.

the novelty of the opposition raised against long-standing governmental practices which had not, before 1760, been regarded as exceptionable by a number of the politicians who thereafter began to criticise them. Moreover, it is also significant that quite quickly, or in the not-so-long run, alterations were made in law or practice to meet all but one of these complaints. Once the use of general warrants was challenged and submitted to expert legal analysis, it was quickly condemned as illegal, a decision with which the supposedly tory Lord Chief Justice Mansfield was as fully in agreement as Camden.[1] In response to parliamentary pressure Grenville himself, then first minister, agreed in 1764, while the issue was still *sub judice*, that if court decisions did not curtail this procedure to the general satisfaction, he would not oppose a bill to amend the law.[2] Over the trial of disputed elections, the independent members of the House of Commons once again bolted, accepting the proposal of Grenville, at this time in opposition, to take such matters out of the House itself and place them in the hands of small committees where political bias would be less exercised and less effective. This decision was later confirmed and made perpetual, once again in spite of ministerial opinion.[3] The attempt in 1771 to check the publication of parliamentary debates failed ignominiously when, for the first time, the magistrates of the City of London opposed their jurisdiction to the privileges of the House of Commons. The complaints about the status of juries in trials for libel took longer to obtain satisfaction, but this was secured, in the teeth of orthodox legal opinion, by Fox's Libel Act of 1792. Liberty was not waning but broadening in the years after 1760. This would have happened less quickly had not powerful subjects of George III been jockeyed into opposition in the early years of his reign. As Camden remarked about general warrants in 1765, up till then there had been 'a submission of guilt and poverty to power and the terror of punishment'.[4] The situation was very

[1] See Mansfield's *dicta* in the case of Dryden Leach, cited in Costin and Watson, *Documents, 1660–1914*, I 296.

[2] *Additional Grenville Papers*, pp. 90–1. This parliamentary episode is fully discussed in J. R. G. Tomlinson, 'The Grenville Papers, 1763–1765' (M.A. thesis, University of Manchester, 1956) pp. 77–101.

[3] *Correspondence of William Pitt, Earl of Chatham*, III 439; *Grenville Papers*, IV 515–16; *The Correspondence of King George III*, III nos. 1403–5.

[4] Cited in Costin and Watson, *Documents, 1660–1914*, I 307.

different when criticism of government came to be backed by men like Temple, Newcastle or Rockingham. Had an aristocratic opposition not developed, the bounds of liberty might have stood still, but there is no ground for believing that they would have suffered diminution. More probably they would have been broadened in any case, under the pressures of various other factors which a closer analysis would reveal at work in the years after 1760 – factors both social and intellectual, the expansion of the urban middle classes and the rationalising, proto-utilitarian spirit of the later eighteenth century, factors linked, that is, with the Enlightenment or with 'The Age of the Democratic Revolution'.[1]

Guttridge sees 'the reappearance of the King as a personal force in politics' after 1760 as an essential element in his picture of the new toryism confronted by the new whiggism which was represented most completely by the Rockinghams.[2] 'When', he says, 'under George III a group began to call itself the "king's friends", that in itself is enough to indicate that the king might be regarded as a political leader within the accepted system of personal groups.'[3] He 'became an active participant in politics. He attempted to dissolve parties, and his chosen ministers associated his government with an illiberal and authoritarian policy.' 'He was no Stuart tyrant. He preferred to govern as a parliamentary leader.'[4] By 1770 Lord North was 'leading the king's friends to a more united and triumphant course'.[5] The basis of the system was patronage: 'The vulnerable financial structure . . . was also the key to ministerial control of parliament.'[6] In sum: 'The king, using the great resources of the monarchy, succeeded in building his own parliamentary majority by absorbing the strongest features of both [whig and tory] creeds.'[7] And the keynote of this new toryism was 'unity and authority'.[8]

This approach to the question, however, raises a number of debatable issues. Was the idea of unity and authority in politics emphasised only after 1760, as distinct from the years immediately

[1] For some pointers to this, see Ian R. Christie, *Wilkes, Wyvill and Reform: The Parliamentary Reform Movement in British Politics, 1760–1785* (1962) ch. 1.

[2] Guttridge, *English Whiggism*, p. 15.

[3] Ibid., p. 13.

[4] Ibid., pp. 16, 32.

[5] Ibid., p. 42.

[6] Ibid., p. 117.

[7] Ibid., p. 138.

[8] Ibid., p. 1

before? Does what is known about the structure of politics and the behaviour of politicians, especially in the House of Commons, leave room for a party of 'king's friends' of the type postulated, or justify the degree of emphasis placed on patronage as a cement holding such a party together? What part did George III play in the conduct of affairs? Did he 'govern'? And to what extent did his role differ from that of George II?

The spirit of authority in politics before 1760 is reflected in the general, unthinking acceptance of the various practices discussed in the preceding paragraphs. A sense of the desirability of unity in politics also seems to be clearly discernible. Comprehensiveness was certainly the keynote of government under the Pelhams, who gradually drew in virtually all the politicians, whether lapsed tories or dissident whigs. In 1746 they won their duel for power with Granville, but within six years he was accommodated as lord president of the council. By that date, and in some cases well before it, such former tories as the Foxes, Winningtons, Gowers, Finches and Legges had become absorbed in the main body of active whig politicians and had secured a share of office.[1] In the last years of George II's reign, the Duke of Newcastle maintained the system of comprehensiveness by the assiduity with which he courted support or smoothed the ruffled feelings of discontented politicians. Another indication of the concern for unity is the distaste with which Newcastle and his close friends regarded the possibility of involvement in opposition during the ministerial crisis of 1757.[2]

Did George III govern in a sense in which George II did not? Such a view has undergone successive modifications, particularly in the work of Richard Pares, who restated it with an emphasis on differences arising out of personal factors.[3] Further research may whittle down even more the contrasts between the two kings. But even in the present state of knowledge, the differences between them were hardly of the nature and extent to support Guttridge's thesis.

There is certainly no question but that George III enjoyed a

[1] J. B. Owen, *The Rise of the Pelhams* (1957) p. 69.

[2] Namier, *England in the Age of the American Revolution*, 2nd ed. (1961) pp. 48–51.

[3] See his *King George III and the Politicians*.

greater freedom of manœuvre in the recruiting of cabinets than his grandfather. There were various reasons for this, both personal and political, but it is probable that the most important single factor was the changed attitude of the sovereign to Hanover. Hanover was the vulnerable point for George II and for his ministers. The greatest cause of George II's frustration in the 1740s over the selection of ministers was that he found most personally acceptable two men, Granville and Bath, who were 'the two most notoriously unpopular politicians of the day'.[1] To this unpopularity Granville's willingness to consult Hanoverian interests probably contributed. His rivals, the Pelhams, were uneasily aware how careful they too had to be, for the sake of their parliamentary standing, to avoid falling under suspicion of the same tendency. The anti-Hanoverian sentiment of Parliament was a powerful weapon to be used in arguments with the king. But after 1760 George III, by his identification of himself with Britain and his disregard for Hanover, made himself immune from it, and there was no comparable lever which the Rockingham party (or any other party) could find to use against him. This circumstance helps to account for the frequency of ministerial changes in the 1760s. They were changes which in general arose out of matters of personality or of personal politics rather than questions of policy, and they were at times the despair of the king himself, who on one occasion burst out in front of General Irwin: 'Ce métier de politique est un très vilain métier; c'est le métier d'un faquin; ce n'est pas le métier d'un gentilhomme.'[2]

More pertinent to the problem under consideration is the question of the extent of the sovereign's participation in the making of policy and in the direction of administration. The assessment of the degree, if any, to which there was a break in this respect in 1760 cannot be more than provisional until much more detailed work has been done on the reign of George II. Nevertheless, there are already available pointers to the conclusion that George II's participation in affairs was greater than has sometimes been allowed by authors writing on George III, and that no real break in royal practice is marked by the succession of the grandson in 1760.

[1] Owen, *The Rise of the Pelhams*, p. 36.

[2] *The Correspondence of King George III*, I no. 179; *Grenville Papers*, IV 184.

Passages in Hervey's memoirs indicate the tiresome and exhausting task which at times confronted Walpole in arguing over policy matters with George II. Walpole once told Hervey:

> You, my Lord, are enough acquainted with this Court to know that nothing can be done in it but by degrees; should I tell either the King or the Queen what I propose to bring them to six months hence, I could never succeed. Step by step I can carry them perhaps the road I wish.

And again: 'Though he will hear nobody but me, you do not know how often he refuses to hear me when it is on a subject he does not like.'[1] In 1743, in a long letter of advice to Henry Pelham, Walpole stressed the need for 'address and management' in dealing with the king; and upon this the just comment has been made by a recent scholar:[2]

> Coming from one who had been the king's chief counsellor for fourteen years, it fully explodes the myth that George II was a 'king in toils', the helpless captive of scheming ministers who dictated his every move. The independence of the sovereign was no less marked than that of the House of Commons, and he who would win the confidence of both, and act as an intermediary between them, must be a diplomat of the first order.

After the fall of Walpole, Newcastle and his brother encountered similar difficulties, and in the forties, in the view of one expert on the diplomatic history of the period, 'the King, though he might on some great occasion be overruled, was still normally the dictator of foreign policy, and the Secretaries of State carried out his orders.'[3] In his later years he was described as having 'more knowledge of foreign affairs than most of his ministers';[4] and his

[1] Hervey, *Memoirs*, II 361; III 904; and cf. I 100–1; II 341, 375, 378, 445–6, 456.

[2] Owen, *The Rise of the Pelhams*, pp. 188–9.

[3] *Private Correspondence of Chesterfield and Newcastle, 1744–1746*, ed. Sir Richard Lodge (1930) p. XXXVII. See also Sir Richard Lodge, *Studies in Eighteenth-Century Diplomacy, 1740–1748* (1930) pp. 370–4. Lodge's statement, although an exaggeration, is indicative of George II's active participation in policy-making.

[4] Earl Waldegrave, *Memoirs from 1754 to 1758* (1821) p. 5.

insistence that Philip Stanhope's dispatches should be clearly written so as not to be difficult for his failing sight is evidence of his determination to the last to retain his grasp of public business.[1]

The king's involvement in government business was, then, no novelty of the years after 1760; and it seems open to argument, despite all that has been urged to the contrary, that George III was no more, and perhaps less, concerned in policy-making than his grandfather. One outstanding motive for royal interference was extinguished by his own inclination: he did not think, as George II had constantly thought, of the repercussions of British policy on Hanoverian interests. In 1769 Henry Seymour Conway gave Horace Walpole to understand that George III 'never interfered with his ministers', but 'seemed to resign himself entirely to their conduct for the time',[2] and it has been observed that this was 'a statement borne out by the king's voluminous correspondence wherein, as a rule, he repeats with approval advice tendered by his ministers',[3] Confirmation of this comes from no less an expert witness than Lord North. According to one report, when the first steps towards the coalition of 1783 were being taken, Fox urged that the king should not be suffered to be his own minister. North denied, first implicitly and then directly, that this had been the case. He told Fox:[4]

> If you mean there should not be a government by departments, I agree with you. . . . There should be one man, or a cabinet, to govern the whole and direct every measure. Government by departments was not brought in by me. I found it so, and had not vigour and resolution to put an end to it. . . . *Though the government in my time was a government by departments, the whole was done by the ministers, except in a few instances.*

Like George II, George III kept his finger on the pulse by perusal of dispatches and by regular discussions with his ministers, but it would be an error to think that this placed him in the position of

[1] *The Letters of Philip Dormer Stanhope, 4th Earl of Chesterfield*, ed. B. Dobrée (1932), cited below as *Chesterfield Letters*, IV no. 2019.

[2] Horace Walpole, *Memoirs of the Reign of King George III*, III 66.

[3] Namier, 'Monarchy and the Party System', in his *Crossroads of Power*, p. 215.

[4] Russell, *Memorials and Correspondence of Charles James Fox*, II 38: my italics.

his own chief minister – and the truth was that for large stretches of the period 1760–82 no such minister existed. This conclusion has begun during the last few years to be buttressed by a different sort of evidence. Monographs dealing in detail with major policy issues of the reign give George III very little place in the stories which they tell. They present narratives in which policy-making is traceable in close detail, from the first stages of the arrival of information in the departments, through the discussions which took place in cabinet or in private between cabinet ministers, sometimes with the specialist advice of under-secretaries and of the law officers, to the result in terms of diplomatic or administrative instructions.[1] Exactly the same business formalities were observed after as before 1760: the king's pleasure was taken before a matter was referred to the cabinet, and the cabinet reported its recommendation in the form of advice, which was almost invariably accepted. The king would pass observations and encouraging comments. Occasionally, if the ministers were divided in opinion, his own view might tip the balance.[2] Sometimes he might be obstructive, whereupon, if the ministers were sufficiently agreed among themselves, a steady pressure would be exerted to wear him down.[3]

[1] Some examples, in chronological order of subject, are: Rashed, *The Peace of Paris, 1763*; J. M. Sosin, *Whitehall and the Wilderness: The Middle West in British Colonial Policy, 1760–1775* (Lincoln, Neb. 1961); Sutherland, *The East India Company in Eighteenth-Century Politics*; Donoughue, *British Politics and the American Revolution*; Mackesy, *The War for America*; de Madariaga, *Britain, Russia, and the Armed Neutrality of 1780*; Cobban, *Ambassadors and Secret Agents*; J. Ehrman, *The British Government and Commercial Negotiations with Europe, 1783–1793* (1962). It is not inappropriate to include the last two works, for in the view of the whig opposition after 1783, Pitt was merely carrying on the bad old system of government by influence where North had let it drop, whereas, in fact, a continuity of a different kind can readily be traced. For a general survey of the procedures by which business was conducted, see Pares, *King George III and the Politicians*, pp. 148–63 and pp. 70–8 above.

[2] This seems to have happened at one stage in the diplomatic crisis over the Falkland Islands at the end of 1770: *The Correspondence of King George III*, II nos. 838–52; Goebel, *The Struggle for the Falkland Islands*, pp. 289–325. See pp. 99–102 above.

[3] E.g. over the proposed cession of Minorca to Russia in 1781 (de Madariaga, *Armed Neutrality*, pp. 283–85); and over the Gelderland subsidy in 1787 (Cobban, *Ambassadors and Secret Agents*, pp. 123–4, 132–4). See pp. 102–5 above.

But there are few occasions when he seems to have made any positive contribution to decisions. There is yet another sort of evidence which can be called in to support this view. The correspondence of ministers and officials, especially their semi-official and private letters, often contain observations which imply that the real momentum of government lay in the departments and in the cabinet, and that it was what was decided at these points in the political structure that really mattered.[1] This evidence bears out the remark of Hillsborough to Thomas Hutchinson during a conversation early in 1775 about American affairs:

> The K[ing] himself thinks as you do; but will always leave his own sentiments and conform to his Ministers, though he will argue with them and very sensibly; but if they adhere to their own opinion he will say – 'Well: do you chuse it should be so? Then let it be.'

And sometimes Hillsborough had known him to add 'You must take the blame upon yourself.'[2]

Similarly, historians have sometimes been tempted to draw too strong a contrast between the two kings with regard to parliamentary and administrative business. In his concern with parliamentary elections George III was no innovator. The study of Newcastle's correspondence as first lord of the treasury has led to the conclusion:[3]

> Numerous entries and letters prove that George II, so far from being uninterested in elections, actively concerned himself in them, that the names of government candidates were submitted to him, and that his approval was required for the disbursement of government money in elections. Contemporaries had no doubt as to the king's share in the business.

It has been observed that 'George III claimed and exercised the

[1] See pp. 88–91 above. [2] *Hutchinson Diary*, I 480.

[3] Namier, *England in the Age of the American Revolution*, pp. 109, 110–13. See also Sir Lewis Namier, *The Structure of Politics at the Accession of George III*, (1957) pp. 306 and n. 2, 391; and B. Bonsall, *Sir James Lowther and Cumberland and Westmorland Elections, 1754–1775* (Manchester, 1960) pp. 20–30. Lord Hervey attests the king's (and the queen's) concern about elections earlier in his reign: Hervey, *Memoirs*, II 417–20, 434–5.

right to make appointments of his own mere motion, but mainly in certain departments – the Church, the army, the royal household, and, to a rather less degree, the peerage.'[1] On some of these matters also he was acting in a way similar to his grandfather. George II kept a firm grip on army appointments and promotions.[2] There were occasions when he set his face against requests for peerages, and in general he seems to have desired to keep the number down.[3] He could be obstructive about appointments, and not merely those about the household, and on occasion he took an initiative about dismissals.[4] When George III wrangled with Grenville about the keepership of the privy purse, he was taking the same sort of ground that George II had done nearly twenty years before during one of his rows with the Pelhams.[5]

The remaining problem posed by Guttridge's thesis is that of a party of 'king's friends', organised by the king acting as a leader and led, after 1770, by Lord North.

It may be presumed that Guttridge is here referring, not to the more or less permanent 'court and administration' party, the existence of which has been traced back well before 1760, but to the parties or factions which made up the more positively 'political' portion of the majorities supporting North's ministry in the House of Commons. Between 1767 and 1775 the long-lived and, at first, somewhat chameleon-like ministry, of which Chatham, Grafton and North were successively the titular heads, recruited various groups to the mosaic fragments originally assembled by Chatham – the Bedford party, subsequently led by Earl Gower, the followers of George Grenville (was this group tory on its performance over Wilkes in 1763–4 or whig on its attitude towards him in 1769–70?),

[1] Pares, *King George III and the Politicians*, p. 144.

[2] Hervey, *Memoirs*, I 153; III 771–2; Owen, *The Rise of the Pelhams*, pp. 58–9; Namier, *England in the Age of the American Revolution*, p. 253.

[3] Hervey, *Memoirs*, II 496, 668; Namier, *England in the Age of the American Revolution*, p. 23 and n.

[4] W. Coxe, *Memoirs of the Life and Administration of Sir Robert Walpole, Earl of Orford* (1798) II 630–1; III 532–3; Owen, *The Rise of the Pelhams*, pp. 100–1, 244, 248–9; Earl of Ilchester, *Henry Fox, First Lord Holland, His Family and Relations* (1920) I 246–7; *Chesterfield Letters*, I 191; III no. 1480; V no. 1893; H.M.C., *Egmont MSS.*, I 374–5.

[5] *Grenville Papers*, II 209–11; *Private Correspondence of Chesterfield and Newcastle*, p. 111.

and dissident politicians from the party of Lord Rockingham, notably Lord George Germain. There was some shifting among these factions subsequently, and in addition North, like every eighteenth-century head of the treasury, acquired his own following; but this section of the government majority always remained a coalition of factions,[1] and under the stress of the events of 1782–4 these once again drifted apart, Lord North and his friends into the coalition with Charles Fox, the much smaller Bedford group into an alliance with the younger Pitt. To call this short-lived coalition of factions attached to North's ministry the king's party is a misnomer – had it really been such, North and his friends would have bowed to the king's wishes and supported Shelburne's ministry in the winter of 1782–3.[2]

The story of British colonial policy between 1763 and 1783 makes perfect sense if it is considered apart from the domestic issues concerning Wilkes and the press, which were connected with the rise of an opposition of a more formal and formidable type than had been seen in British politics before and which reflected an entirely separate political development. True, Burke and the rest of Rockingham's followers linked these issues with America. This was to follow the correct political tactics of hitting their opponents in every possible way; and the story of how they did it is an important part of the history of their party. It was also expedient to represent the claims to greater liberty of discussion which they championed as being merely the defence of what was already enjoyed before 1760 – a system of tactics which radical reformers of the time adopted with equally little historical justification, and which is probably as old as politics itself. They believed in their propaganda. But this does not mean that they were necessarily right in their analysis of contemporary developments. It is the onlooker (in this case the historian), not the player, who sees most

[1] Christie, *The End of North's Ministry*, pp.197–210.

[2] North's conduct at this time is discussed in paper 6. See too Pares, *King George III and the Politicians*, pp. 81–2. Members of a political group attached to Bute up to 1766 called themselves 'king's friends', and the term has sometimes been used by writers as synonymous with the 'court and administration party' (ibid., pp. 107–8, 117 n.), but neither of these corresponds with the postulated party created by the king and led by North. Unless clearly defined, the term 'king's friends' is better avoided.

of the game; and the partial and limited views of the opposition politicians cannot be allowed to obscure the fact that America and Wilkes were two entirely different affairs. On the American question, most British politicians were thinking 'imperially' after 1763, and it is closer to the facts to analyse British colonial policy in terms of an imperialism which failed to find a way through the problem of freedom versus authority than to connect it with any general concept of toryism. Here the pressure for change came from the government. By contrast, on the issues connected with Wilkes, the impulse for innovation came from the other side, from the forces ranged against the government. The early stages of the evolution of a regular parliamentary opposition involved a quite different process, a broadening of liberty, its progress being signalled by a series of incidents in which the traditional assumptions of the political world about 'subordination' were challenged and overcome. The genius of government through free public discussion was astir, cracking the bonds of its chrysalis, groping towards the sunshine maturity of the 1820s.[1] Whatever the image of themselves the opposition were attempting to present, they were in fact fighting the battles of a more liberal future against the past, not defending existing liberties against a tory reaction. If any term be appropriate to describe those politicians who, remaining on the government side in politics, had an interest in resisting rather than welcoming the new developments, and who opposed them on the basis of the assumption that familiar, traditional positions were legally and constitutionally right and proper, that term is 'conservative', not 'tory'. In sum, the domestic political events which after 1762 divided Newcastle and the Rockinghams from the government do not give ground for belief in the emergence of a new toryism in terms of trends of policy; the degree of continuity in the character of the kingship before and after 1760 gives no ground for tracing it in the activities of George III; and the relatively ephemeral political groupings which provided the 'party' section of the majorities for Lord North's ministry give no ground for adducing the emergence of such an entity in terms of men.

[1] For the growth of the London press and the development of political and parliamentary reporting up to 1774, see P. D. G. Thomas, 'The Beginning of Parliamentary Reporting in Newspapers, 1768–1774', *English Historical Review*, LXXIV (1959) 623–36.

EIGHT

*Veitch's 'The Genesis of Parliamentary Reform'**

RAMSAY Muir, in his introduction to the first impression of this book, marked as its great distinction the attention given to political movements outside the circle of court and parliament. In this break with the dominant trend of writing British history almost exclusively from the viewpoint of Westminster and Whitehall, Veitch was not quite a lone pioneer in his treatment of his theme. It was also taken up by the American scholar Walter Phelps Hall, whose *British Radicalism, 1791–1797* appeared a year earlier, in 1912, and again by the Englishman Philip Anthony Brown, whose book *The French Revolution in English History* had been completed by 1914 although not published till four years later. But of these three works Veitch's is in almost all respects the most valuable. In particular he gave proportionately as much attention to the earlier reform movements associated with Wilkes in London and with Wyvill in Yorkshire as to the radical outbursts which followed the French Revolution. The fullest and most satisfactory treatment of the whole subject from 1760 to 1800, his book has long maintained its position as a standard work. For twenty years after 1918 the subject was left practically untouched. More recently a few scholars have begun to explore aspects of it with which he was not concerned and to challenge some of his conclusions, but his book is far from being superseded.

To some extent the interpretation of the story of parliamentary reform in this period has been modified since Veitch's day in consequence of the displacements in eighteenth-century historical studies arising out of the work of Sir Lewis Namier. Namier's studies have deepened our understanding of the way in which the old representative system, despite its illogical absurdities, had an effective functional role in a society in which politics was the virtually

* Introduction to the second impression (1964) of G. S. Veitch, *The Genesis of Parliamentary Reform*.

unchallenged preserve of a landed oligarchy. The continuance of such a system depended upon the maintenance of a stable and homogeneous society, homogeneous in the sense that people were for the most part conscious of the direct or not very indirect connection of their fortunes with the 'landed interest' and were, despite diversities of rank and fortune, on the whole satisfied with their niches in society. By the later years of the eighteenth century, when Paley (and others) called attention to the way in which the House of Commons represented the important interests in the nation,[1] the situation was in fact changing (it is usually when systems are breaking down that they evoke methodical definition and defence). Increase of population and industrialisation were both disturbing the *status quo*, giving rise to a fair amount of individual hardship – though this was much less in the aggregate than was to be encountered in the years after 1815, and for large sections of the population the standard of living was rising.[2] But in the present state of our knowledge it is in the harmony of the system of representation with the social structure, rather than in other reasons adduced by Veitch,[3] that we find the ground for the complacency with which Englishmen regarded it in the early years of George III's reign.

Apart from this, greater understanding of the unreformed parliamentary system has pointed to the need to make a clearer distinction between the reformers' conceptions of the system and the system as it really was. This level of interpretation was not methodically developed by Veitch. The explanation of his neglect of it is perhaps to be found in the intellectual climate in which his work was done. The assumption that the reform movements in the reign of George III were the first steps on the road towards the more rational democratic system of his own time seems implicit in his treatment. In one sense this belief was true. But it may have deflected his attention from what now seem important aspects of the subject: the degree to which reformers were misled in their suspicions about the working of the parliamentary system of their day, and the extent to which a good deal (though not all) of their

[1] Veitch, *Genesis of Parliamentary Reform*, pp. 19–20.

[2] T. S. Ashton, *An Economic History of England: The Eighteenth Century* (1955) pp. 46, 215, 233.

[3] Veitch, *Genesis of Parliamentary Reform*, pp. 18–22.

agitation was backward-looking rather than intelligent anticipation of the nineteenth-century rationalisation of institutions.

Caroline Robbins, in *The Eighteenth-Century Commonwealthman*, published in 1959, has emphasised the continuity of an intellectual tradition current among parliamentary reformers of the late eighteenth century which runs back to Locke and Sydney and beyond. In this tradition the machinery of representation was seen as the barrier against authoritarianism on the part of the executive – separation of powers was an inherent part of the concept – and its spokesmen were concerned with reforms that would subserve this end. It was in fact the whig political theory. It spurred its votaries on to the defence of 'Liberty', the rallying cry which Wilkes found so potent, a concept re-echoed in the writings of Major John Cartwright and other reformers through and beyond the period of the great French wars. It gave birth, in a watered-down version, to the economical reform programme of the Rockingham party. But the fullest expression of it in political action was the county association movement of the years 1780–5. The two distinctive demands of the county movement – shorter parliaments and an increase in the number of knights of the shire – were both directed towards the establishment of a greater degree of separation between parliament and the executive. There was no conception here of making parliament more representative in the modern democratic sense. The difference between Wyvill and Burke was one of 'more' or 'less', not a reflection of fundamental disagreements about the basis of state organisation; and Wyvill, far from being a pioneer of a 'democratic revolution' might more plausibly be represented as a doctrinaire whig reactionary. The movement led by Wyvill had a definition of its own, and this is merely obscured by labelling him as on the right wing of the reformers.[1]

Movements with other definitions are also to be distinguished in this early period of George III's reign, before the onset of the French Revolution. There were at least two tributary head-waters of the liberal democracy of the late nineteenth century the immanence of which insensibly shaped Veitch's treatment of his subject. One was the re-emergence, a hundred years after its earlier airing in a somewhat different guise by the Levellers, of the idea of personality as the basis of political rights. This concept

[1] Veitch, *Genesis of Parliamentary Reform*, p. 280.

appeared in various writings in the 1770s, and it captured the minds of the little band of intellectuals who came together in 1780 to form the Society for Constitutional Information, but there is little evidence to show that it had any influence on popular political agitation. The other, more material, was the demand of a minority of the commercial community in the metropolis for a larger share of the parliamentary representation, based on the conviction that, as an 'interest' whose stake in the country could be measured in terms of tax burdens, they should have a proportionate strength in spokesmen and voting power. It is impossible however to say to what extent this idea took precedence over whig political theory in the minds of those who supported reform in the metropolis in those years. It may be observed of this demand for political power on the part of a class or group distinct from the landowners, that the social-economic development which gave rise to it had preceded the 'Industrial Revolution'. And it is significant that it attracted little support in the northern and midland areas where industrialisation was already crowding people into the towns.

As Veitch did not see clearly the extent to which parliamentary reform movements before 1789 displayed diversities and a certain degree of constitutional atavism, it is to be expected that his treatment of British radicalism in the period of the French Revolution should show similar limitations. He tended to stress the continuity from the earlier period of the pressures tending towards democratic reform and to give less emphasis than it deserves to the 'commonwealthman' tradition which continued to colour the utterances of many of the reformers. As a result, although he constructed a very full and valuable narrative of the growth, proceedings and collapse of the corresponding societies of the 1790s, in which for the first time men of the 'working class' engaged in organised political activity, he paid little attention to certain features on which a writer of the present day would perhaps lay more stress, in particular their novelty, the degree to which they represented a change, a discontinuity, in the character of reform agitation in comparison with the years before 1789. The idea of associations had indeed had wide circulation in reform literature during the years of the American Revolution, but it is extremely difficult to find any evidence for 'mechanics' engaging in political activity of this kind before 1791. The sense of discontinuity is heightened by the reflection that in the period before 1789 practically all those who engaged in reforming activity were already within the pale of the constitution, at least having the parliamentary franchise if not (as in many cases) some wider opportunity for political self-expression; whereas the most characteristic section of the reform movement after 1789 drew its strength from men who were not of the 'political nation'. Also Veitch did not probe far into the problem of what kind of men enrolled themselves in the corresponding societies and he showed even less concern with the reasons which led them to do so. It is a weakness in his handling of this part of his theme that he paid practically no attention to reflections upon social and economic discontent which some pamphleteers of the time clearly linked up with the demand for parliamentary reform – a feature of the movement to which attention had already just been drawn in the work of W. P. Hall. It is true that the corresponding societies never formulated programmes of social change and confined themselves to demands for constitutional reform; for were they not being told in effect by these writers, 'Seek ye first the political kingdom'? But it can hardly be doubted that part of their popular appeal can be traced to the outpourings of hostility towards the material privileges of the propertied classes and to various unsystematised pleas for greater attention to the interests of the poor, which are to be culled from the writings not only (as Veitch mentions) of Mary Wollstonecraft, but also of Paine, Thelwall, Catharine Phillips and other pamphleteers.[1] It was this note, perhaps, as much as the purely political demands of the societies, that aroused a fear of 'levelling' tendencies in the minds of anti-reformers.

Veitch devoted much attention to the relationships between French revolutionaries and British reformers. On this subject he drew together material from both the British and the French archives, and it may fairly be claimed that his treatment is authoritative and also definitive. The two other most detailed scholarly studies give no ground for questioning his judgements.[2] He

[1] Veitch, *Genesis of Parliamentary Reform*, p. 169; Hall, *British Radicalism*, pp. 139–56.

[2] Brown, *The French Revolution in English History*; W. A. L. Seaman, 'British Democratic Societies in the period of the French Revolution' (Ph.D. thesis, University of London, 1954).

concluded that in general the British reformers were both pacific and loyal. The outbreak of the French Revolution undoubtedly stimulated a great deal of interest in Britain and gave a powerful impetus to the movement for reform. There were numerous exchanges of fraternal greetings between British and French societies and between British societies and the French assemblies. These gestures of mutual admiration, however, were not inevitably evidence of a desire on the part of the British to emulate the French. The British attitude was often rather one of somewhat condescending pleasure that Frenchmen were at last securing political liberties which had long been enjoyed north of the Channel. As for reform, their own problems were different, their own modes of thinking about them were firmly established, and there was no need for them to borrow from French example. To the extent that Paine's *Rights of Man* overlaid the negative attributes of the universal suffrage preached by John Cartwright with a more positive concept of popular sovereignty derived from revolutionary France which was incompatible with individual right, it probably lost far more support for the reformers than it attracted, especially among the middle class.[1] Their gladness at the French achievement of 'Liberty' developed naturally and readily into sympathy with the French when the eastern monarchies appeared to league against them to restore Bourbon despotism. But with the onset of republicanism and violence in Paris, the contacts made by the societies were soon broken off, the wave of British enthusiasm for the Revolution lost much of its force, and the few individual Britons who remained in contact with France cannot be regarded as representative of any general body of opinion. Members of the corresponding societies were opposed to the policy of war with France and identified Pitt with the whig bogy of executive tyranny, just as the North administration had been so identified during the American War of Independence. But very few of them were prepared to go beyond the legitimate bounds of peaceful protest.

On the basis of a thorough examination of Home Office papers, Veitch set in proper perspective a few treasonable incidents which were unduly exaggerated in the work of W. P. Hall,[2] rejected the

[1] *The Debate on the French Revolution 1789–1800*, ed. Alfred Cobban (1960) pp. 14–16.

[2] *British Radicalism*, pp. 197–224.

view that there was widespread revolutionary disaffection in the country either before or after the outbreak of war with France in 1793, and presented much evidence to indicate the peaceful intentions of the corresponding societies and their concern to seek reform only by constitutional means. Although Talleyrand assured his principals in 1792 that there was not the slightest likelihood of a revolution in England,[1] successive leaders of revolutionary France did not accept this view, and it would appear as if some Continental historians, to the present day, still hesitate to do so. The problems posed by their interpretation merge with those raised by proponents of the view that from about 1770 onwards the western world, including Great Britain, was going through a general phase of 'democratic revolution'.[2] The assumptions underlying these interpretations, so far as Britain is concerned, seem to some extent to beg two questions: the nature of the British reformers' intentions, and the extent of their numbers.

The work of Veitch and Brown reveals clearly enough that, save for a few exceptions, the British reformers were not revolutionaries. They were themselves fully conscious of the difference between a revolutionary and a reformer. In December 1791 the Sheffield Constitutional Society – a 'working-class' organisation – prescribed the following declaration for new recruits:[3]

> I solemnly declare myself an enemy of all conspiracies, tumults, and riotous proceedings, or maliciously surmising any attempt that tends to overturn, or anywise injure or disturb the peace of the people; or the laws of this realm; and that my only wish and design is, to concur in sentiment with every peaceable and good citizen of this nation, in giving my voice for application to be made to parliament, praying for a speedy reformation, and an equal representation in the House of Commons.

In so doing its members were evidently determined to make clear to which category they belonged. Plenty of similar evidence has

[1] Veitch, *Genesis of Parliamentary Reform*, pp. 209–11.

[2] Jules Dechamps, *Entre la guerre et la paix: Les Iles Britanniques et la Révolution Française (1789–1803)* (Brussels, 1949); R. R. Palmer, *The Age of the Democratic Revolution: A Political History of Europe and America, 1760–1800*, vol. I, *The Challenge* (1960); Jacques Godechot, *Les Révolutions (1770–1799)* (Paris, 1963).

[3] Cited in Seaman, 'British Democratic Societies in the period of the French Revolution', p. 59.

been adduced by Veitch and Brown to support this instance. It is therefore confusing the issue when a French historian, to take the most recent example, Jacques Godechot, writes of 'l'opposition révolutionnaire en Grande-Bretagne'.[1] In their own eyes, as in the eyes of British historians since, these reformers were not revolutionaries: their object was to build up a sufficient body of public opinion to secure a peaceful and generally accepted change achieved through the existing legislative instruments (as was to be effected to a limited extent in 1832).

There is much more ground for placing some sections of the British reform agitation within a general picture of a western trend towards democracy, provided a *caveat* is observed over the term 'revolution', and provided also that the definition 'democratic' is applied with strictness. Little of the reform agitation in Britain before 1789 falls within the definition. After 1789 the outlook of some reformers, Wyvill for instance, was not 'democratic', and the thinking of others, even of Cartwright, was coloured by concepts of 'constitutional balance' not necessarily identical with democracy in the modern sense of the term.

There remains the problem of the numbers of the British reformers. This subject is a quagmire in which it is all too easy to sink. The evidence appears to be so inadequate that it is unlikely that any very firm estimates will ever be reached. But figures of two quite different levels of magnitude have emerged in the discussions. Those of the larger magnitude derive from pamphlet literature, scares and rumours. A well-known example is Burke's estimate that out of a 'political nation' of about 400,000 a fifth (80,000) were 'Jacobins',[2] a figure which in any case had little relevance to the corresponding societies which drew most of their membership from lower social strata. But information of this kind (and there seems to be a certain tendency on the part of Continental writers to rely on it)[3] cannot be regarded as so valuable as the information to be culled from government investigations at the

[1] *Les Révolutions (1770–1799)*, p. 304. Godechot relies on a limited number of secondary works for his treatment of this subject. It is odd that Veitch's book is not among them.

[2] Edmund Burke, *Works*, v 5, 189–90.

[3] Dechamps, *Entre la guerre et la paix*, pp. 43–4. This work is cited as fundamental' by Godechot, *Les Révolutions (1770–1799)*, p. 305.

time and from the records of the societies themselves. Pamphlets were written to create an effect, either confidence among reformers, or on the other side fear and a stronger reaction. Veitch judiciously ignored the propaganda and made what tentative deductions he thought possible from the records. His estimates point to the conclusion that a number of thousands, but still only a small minority, of the British people were involved in the corresponding societies.[1]

The Genesis of Parliamentary Reform remains an admirable one-volume survey of the parliamentary reform movement during the first forty years of George III's reign. Veitch's scholarship was exact, and in the pursuit of those questions which he considered important he ranged broadly and deeply in the manuscript and the printed evidence. At the level of political action – the activities of societies, manifestos, petitions, parliamentary discussions, and the development of the government's policy of repression – his narrative is full and at many points seems likely to be proved exhaustive. For historians turning their attention to aspects of the subject which he did not examine his book is a rock on which they can safely build.

[1] Veitch, *Genesis of Parliamentary Reform*, pp. 217–18, 321. Cf. Brown, *The French Revolution in English History*, p. 59 and Seaman, 'British Democratic Societies in the period of the French Revolution', pp. 49, 52, 54.

NINE

Private Patronage versus Government Influence: John Buller and the Contest for Control of Parliamentary Elections at Saltash, 1780–1790 *

THE downfall of ministerial control in a government borough, the exploitation for personal ends of the tangled anomalies of the franchise, contested elections conducted without the remotest reference to great questions of national politics – all these features of the eighteenth-century electoral system were exhibited in connection with Saltash in the seventeen-eighties, as a result of the breezy irruption of John Buller of Morval into the peaceful routine of the borough's election affairs. In that age there was nothing very novel about either Buller's activities or their consequences. Among the leading politicians of Cornwall the extension of their electoral influence was almost a regular occupation – such infrequent contested elections as did occur were often simply the outcome of their rivalries – and in pursuing his designs to control the borough of Saltash, John Buller was following familiar and successful examples set elsewhere by the Boscawens, the Edgecumbes and the Eliots, and by earlier generations of his own family. One way to attain success in public life was to acquire a borough interest; the patron able to place three or four seats at a minister's disposal might gain advantage in many ways – places, favours, even promotion to the peerage, were not beyond his grasp – and before Buller's first intervention at Saltash in the summer of 1780, he had already attempted elsewhere to establish claims of this kind to advancement.

As landed gentry and as members of parliament, the Bullers had long enjoyed a position of some prominence in Cornwall. In Queen Anne's time they had provided a member for the county. For many years before the Hanoverian succession they had exercised a considerable electoral influence at Saltash, but they had later allowed this interest to lapse. In the mid-eighteenth century they

* This originally appeared in *English Historical Review*, LXXI (1956) 249–55.

possessed – apart from properties in Devon – estates at Morval and Shillingham lying near to Saltash and the Looes; and in the course of acting as election managers for the Pelhams, they had acquired a controlling influence over both the boroughs of East and West Looe. A little later the inheritance became divided. John Buller – born in 1744, second son of James Buller but the eldest by his second wife, Jane, daughter of the first Earl Bathurst – succeeded to the Morval and Shillingham estates, and by a family arrangement obtained control from his uncle, another John Buller, over the borough of West Looe.[1] There also passed to him properties still owned by the family at Saltash, which included a number of houses variously described as burgages or ancient freeholds.[2]

A seat in the House of Commons was the first step in Buller's pursuit of his ambitions, and in 1768, at the first general election after his coming of age, he entered parliament as one of the members for Exeter. Six years later, at the general election of 1774, he made his first bid to extend his electoral influence in Cornwall by intervening at Launceston which, with its neighbour, Newport, had long been under the control of the Morices of Werrington. Success in this contest gave him a foothold in the borough,[3] and enabled him to offer the treasury both seats at West Looe for other friends of the administration. In the House of Commons he continued regularly to vote, and occasionally to speak, in support of the government. By 1780 he had begun to press for some reward for these parliamentary services and joined the roll of those importunate politicians whose names recurred in the provisional lists of arrangements drawn up from time to time by Lord North. In 1779, in one such paper, he was proposed for housekeeper of Whitehall.[4] But North had many promises to keep. The Buller connection was already well provided, John's uncle and namesake being a lord of the admiralty and his maternal uncle, Lord Bathurst, lord president of the council; and there were other politicians with greater claims

[1] Sir Lewis Namier, *The Structure of Politics at the Accession of George III* (1929) II 413.

[2] Alexander Luders, *Reports of the Proceedings in Committees of the House of Commons upon Controverted Elections*, 3 vols. (1785–90) II 147.

[3] *The Parliamentary Papers of John Robinson*, p. 22; *The Correspondence of King George III*, v no. 3013 – the enclosure can be dated from its third paragraph to the year 1775.

[4] *The Correspondence of King George III*, IV no. 2651.

to consideration. In January 1780, when plans for broadening the basis of the ministry were under discussion, John Robinson, secretary to the treasury, wrote to his friend, Charles Jenkinson: 'The arrangements to be made may now be large, but I fear Lord North will still be entangled and embarrassed by his engagements to young Buller, A. Paulet, and Mr Combe, which except the first is not gaining any strength, and even that but little.'[1] Nothing came of these arrangements; and when, eight months later, North drew up new lists of promotions before the general election of 1780, Buller was still a disappointed man. North had no place to give him, and he now faced the unpleasant prospect of a reduction in the parliamentary assets which he held for bargaining purposes. There was little chance of his consolidating his success at Launceston, for in 1775 Humphrey Morice had sold his interests in that borough to the Duke of Northumberland, a magnate whose wealth was not lightly to be challenged in an election contest.[2] Buller was thus obliged to arrange in 1780 for his own return for West Looe, and so could command only one other seat instead of two as formerly.

From the sequel, we may well imagine Buller as now casting about for some means of offsetting these reverses, and of increasing his parliamentary consequence to such a degree that the head of the treasury would no longer dare to ignore his claims to preferment. An opportunity seemed to present itself at Saltash, where he already had property and influence, and he resolved to revive there the old electoral interest his family had formerly enjoyed.

In 1780 Saltash ranked as a 'government borough', and had been considered as such for at least a generation. By a charter of 1774, which repeated the provisions of an earlier grant of 1683, the parliamentary franchise was restricted to the members of the corporation – the mayor, six aldermen and an unspecified number of burgesses. Saltash lies just across the Tamar estuary from Plymouth, and 'the members named in this charter were most of them placemen in the dockyard at Plymouth or persons holding office under government.' In practice the number of burgesses was kept

[1] B.M. Add. MSS. 38567, fo. 24.

[2] Conveyance of the Werrington estates to the Duke of Northumberland, dated 21 to 22 April 1775, Northumberland MSS. (information kindly furnished by my colleague, Dr F. M. L. Thompson).

low, and the crown reserved the right to displace corporators at pleasure.[1] About 1782 the corporation was composed of the following persons:[2]

Caleb Colton, mayor – lieut in the sea service.
Edward Hawkins, justice – master of a man-of-war, superannuated.
Aldermen: Robert Hickes – commissioner of appeals; Nicholas Mill – solicitor for the admiralty at Plymouth Dock and town clerk; John Clevland; Richard Thomas.
Lord North – recorder.
Non-resident free burgesses: Lord North; Lord Sandwich; Lord Mount Edgecumbe and Valletort; William Masterman; John Lloyd – clerk of the check, Plymouth Dock, deputy recorder; Rev. John Lyne; Digory Tomkins – Built a house in Saltash, but never inhabited it – the agent victualler at Plymouth; Admiral Thomas Graves; Admiral Nicholas Vincent; Charles Thomas – carpenter of the Artois; John Blight – custom house officer; John Scot – store keeper at Plymouth Dock, and has kept a house at Saltash which they say is a colourable inhabitancy only; Rev. Robert Hughes – chaplain to Plymouth Dock; Rev. John Coles; Earl of Seaforth; Sir Hugh Palliser, Bart; Sir Richard Bickerton, Bart; Rev. Jerome Decallis.
Resident free burgesses out of whom an alderman must be chosen: Nicholas Napean – custom house officer; James Guborian – lieut on the press service in Ireland; John Webb – carpenter of a man-of-war in the West Indies; Thomas Luar – carpenter of a man-of-war at Saltash; John Taylor; John Trehearne – lieut in the navy.

The borough was regarded as one requiring no trouble and little expense at election time,[3] and it was accordingly used to provide easy entry into the House of Commons for members or assured supporters of the ministry of the day.

So long as the right of voting remained the monopoly of the

[1] T. H. B. Oldfield, *The Representative History of Great Britain and Ireland*, 6 vols. (1816) III 139.

[2] List of the Corporation of Saltash, Bolton MSS., Hants Record Office.

[3] Sir Grey Cooper to [Thomas Orde], 26 Dec 1782, Bolton MSS., Hants Record Office. Cf. Robinson's classification in 1784, *The Parliamentary Papers of John Robinson*, p. 127.

narrow clique which composed the corporation of Saltash, direct control of the borough by the government was completely assured. Buller's interest in the town was useless to him unless he could secure a widening of the franchise which would admit the inhabitants occupying ancient freeholds to the right of voting at parliamentary elections. If this change were made, his interest would become predominant. Some of the freeholds were in the hands of his friends and dependents: others which he owned himself could be used to create more votes in his favour. Since the House of Commons exercised the right to determine disputed elections, the restrictive provisions of the charter of 1774 presented no obstacle, for these could be set aside by the decision of an election committee of the House. To secure such a decision now became Buller's primary object. At the general election of 1780 his resolve brought a rude shock to the Government nominees, Sir Grey Cooper, secretary to the treasury, and Charles Jenkinson, secretary-at-war, who were expecting to be quietly elected *in absentia*. Receiving the unwelcome news by express, Cooper reported post-haste to Jenkinson: 'The Buller family brought a Trojan horse into the borough on the day of election, and a multitude of freeholders sallied out of it and polled for Mr Buller the younger and Sir William James. The Mayor never having heard of any such right of voting, has returned you and your humble servant.' Soon afterwards he hazarded the shrewd conclusion that Buller was seeking to capture the borough 'merely to have the merit of surrendering it in order to obtain possession of the Wardenship of the Stannaries'.[1]

Buller, who, with James, sat in the new parliament for West Looe, lost no time in petitioning against the return of Cooper and Jenkinson. In support of this move he also arranged for a second petition to be presented in the name of his brother-in-law, Sir William Lemon, and other freeholders of Saltash, claiming recognition of their right to vote, which the mayor had refused to acknowledge.[2] On 4 February 1782, after over a year's delay, an election committee declared it had found the sitting members duly elected and so pronounced against Buller's claims: but his *coup* had nearly succeeded, for his opponents won the case in an equally balanced

[1] 14 Sept, 1 Oct 1780, B.M. Add. MSS. 38214, fos. 172–3, 198–9.
[2] *Commons Journals*, 38, 27^{b}, 49^{b}.

committee only by the casting vote of the chairman.[1] In putting members of the ministry to trouble and expense, Buller had not improved his standing with either the king or Lord North. 'I am glad to find Saltash has concluded so well', was George III's comment. 'It does not make the conduct of the Bullers less reprehensible.'[2] Applications to Robinson showed Buller that he could expect no sympathy from the treasury. In all directions his schemes and ambitions were frustrated. If his parliamentary services were to bring no return he might, so it seemed, as well discontinue them. About a fortnight after the decision against him was announced, he appeared in the House of Commons and voted with the government against Fox's motion of 20 February attacking Lord Sandwich's naval administration. But on the twenty-second and twenty-seventh he abstained from further critical divisions, although this was a time when North and Robinson were scraping up every vote they could muster to keep the ministry's majority in being.[3] There was no political motive behind this manœuvre: Buller did not intend going into opposition to the government – a course which was not in accordance with the usually accepted proprieties of eighteenth-century politics. But if North would not serve him, neither would he exert himself to support North in the Commons. A week later, at the beginning of March, he decided to withdraw entirely and relinquish his seat in the House. To Bathurst fell the distasteful task of asking the king to give his nephew the Chiltern Hundreds, with long explanations about 'repeated ill-usage' and the breach of 'solemn promises and assurances'.[4] But Buller did not allow his disappointment and irritation at the conduct of the minister to deflect him from his traditional political line. His successor in the House was no member of opposition but his relation, John Sommers Cocks, the son of Sir Charles Cocks, the clerk of the ordnance.

When Cooper vacated his seat and sought re-election on taking

[1] Luders, *Reports upon Controverted Elections*, II 114; Cooper to Jenkinson, 20 May 1783, B.M. Add. MSS. 38218, fo. 186.

[2] *The Correspondence of King George III*, V no. 3513.

[3] B.M. Add. MSS. 30895, fo. 136v; Abergavenny MSS., '22 February 1782, Minutes of Division', B.M. facsimiles 340, IV, fos. 141–7; Debrett, *The Parliamentary Register*, XXIII (1782) 330–41.

[4] Bathurst to John Robinson, 7 Mar 1782, Abergavenny MSS. 443, B.M. fascimiles 340, II, fos. 280–1.

a post in the coalition government of April 1783, Buller stood a second time for Saltash, on the same ground as before. Again the returning officer refused to count the votes of the freeholders, and Buller promptly petitioned against Cooper's return.[1] This time, perhaps finding the legal expense of election disputes too heavy a burden, he allied himself in his enterprise with the young and wealthy William Beckford of Fonthill[2] – thus began an election partnership of many years' duration. The election committee's decision was again a disappointment to him, and Cooper was able once more to rejoice that the chairman had given the casting vote in his favour.[3] But two such narrow triumphs, in different committees, were hardly reassuring to the parliamentary managers. Although towards the end of 1783 John Robinson, now at work for William Pitt, was still confident of controlling Saltash, Jenkinson complained to him that if it was intended to give him a place in the new government, 'some attention should be paid to the difficulty of my re-election, and Lord Bathurst should be applied to that he may prevent his nephew from opposing on this occasion'.[4]

As for Buller, defeat by so slight a margin did nothing to damp his hopes, and with Beckford's assistance he was back in the field at the general election of 1784. As before, personal interest, not political motives, directed his actions. Between December 1783 and April 1784 he co-operated with the government by keeping a seat open at West Looe for Warren Hastings's agent, Major John Scott – occupying it himself as a sort of locum tenens[5] – and at the general election Scott was returned for West Looe in company with Buller's brother-in-law, John Lemon, a mere stop-gap who soon withdrew in favour of another government supporter. But at Saltash, in April 1784, he and Beckford put up against the

[1] *Commons Journals*, 39, 385^{b}.

[2] Since Beckford in his journals described the by-election of 1786 as his third intervention at Saltash, this must have been the first. (*The Journal of William Beckford in Portugal and Spain, 1787–1788*, ed. Boyd Alexander (1954) pp. 58–9).

[3] To Jenkinson, 20 May 1783, B.M. Add. MSS. 38218, fo. 186.

[4] *The Parliamentary Papers of John Robinson*, p. 83; Abergavenny MSS. 544, B.M. facsimiles 340, 11, fo. 336.

[5] Scott to Hastings, 22 Dec 1783, 11 Jan 1784, B.M. Add. MSS. 29161, fos. 241, 222.

government nominees other candidates who were both supporters of Pitt's ministry.[1] To Buller, giving facilities to the government in one constituency was perfectly compatible with fighting it in another, and he did not let himself be deflected by his friendliness towards the administration from his purpose of extending his electoral influence to Saltash.

With wearisome repetition an election committee a year later disappointed Buller and Beckford by declaring the government candidates to have beeen duly elected.[2] Less stubborn men might well have now accepted defeat, but Buller had at least the virtue of tenacity, and his persistence was soon to reap its reward. In 1786 on the elevation of Charles Jenkinson to the peerage, John Lemon was put up at Saltash in opposition to the government candidate, Lord Mornington, and in support of the subsequent petition fresh evidence was presented as proof of the electoral rights of the freeholders. After the hearing the committee gave its ruling that Lemon ought to have been returned as burgess for Saltash, and that he was the duly elected member.[3] No direct pronouncement was made regarding the franchise, but the committee's decision was a tacit affirmation of the freeholders' right of election and therefore as effective for Buller's purposes as an outright declaration in their favour. The seats at Saltash were henceforth a perquisite of his family, although the prize had to be defended and recovered again in 1806 and 1807.[4]

[1] In 1784 Beckford took the place, as member for Wells of one of these candidates, John Curtis, but his papers yield no evidence confirming this indication of an arrangement between them.

[2] *Commons Journals*, 40, 19[a], 888[b].

[3] *Commons Journals*, 42, 306[b], 727; Luders, *Reports upon Controverted Elections*, II 207–25.

[4] Oldfield, *Representative History of Great Britain and Ireland*, III 144; Lord Buckingham to Lord Grenville, 14, 15 Oct, 2 Dec 1806, 19 Feb 1807, H.M.C., *Dropmore MSS.*, VIII 384–6, 455; IX 56; Fremantle, 4 Apr Grenville, 26 Apr 1807, to Lord Buckingham, in Richard, Duke of Buckingham and Chandos, *Memoirs of the Court and Cabinets of George III* . . . , 4 vols (1853–5) IV 157, 171; Beckford to his secretary, Franchi, 1 Nov 1807, Hamilton MSS. (Lennoxlove) – I wish to acknowledge the kind assistance of Mr Boyd Alexander in letting me see manuscripts and providing information from the Beckford papers at present in his custody: I have also to acknowledge the permission of the Hamilton and Kenneil Estates Limited and of his Grace the Duke of Hamilton, to make use of this material.

Saltash was thus the scene of four contested elections in six years, in none of which was any of the voters or participants in the least concerned with national politics – whichever party won, the members returned to parliament would vote on the side of the administration. As a result, on the one hand the government lost control of what Cooper complacently described in 1782 as 'one of the very few remaining jewels of the crown'.[1] On the other, Beckford and Buller extended their spheres of electoral influence. By a written agreement between them, Beckford was to have the disposal of one seat for his lifetime, and he had the satisfaction of nominating members until he relinquished his rights for hard cash in 1809.[2] Buller, in the few years left before his death in 1793, was in a position to make demands upon the government with far more confidence than in the days when North had rebuffed him. It can hardly be regarded as coincidence that, three months before the general election of 1790, he was appointed by Pitt to one of the most coveted posts in the revenue services, a place on the commission of excise.

[1] To [Thomas Orde], 26 Dec 1782, Bolton MSS., Hants Record Office.

[2] *The Journal of William Beckford in Portugal and Spain*, pp. 58–9; Richard Samuel White to Beckford, 11 Apr 1809, Hamilton MSS. (Lennoxlove) – White's letter refers to the 'original agreement', but no copy of this document has been found among Beckford's papers or among the surviving fragments of the Buller family's eighteenth-century correspondence. Other letters in Beckford's papers establish the connection with Beckford of the following members who sat for Saltash for the periods indicated: Edward Bearcroft, 1790–6; Robert Deverell, 1802–6; John Pedley, 1808–9.

TEN

William Masterman (1722–1786), Political Agent and Member of Parliament

WILLIAM Masterman was not a political figure of any great importance in his day. He represented Bodmin in parliament only for the short span of three and a half years; no speech by him was ever reported; he came into the House of Commons too late in life to make his mark in it. Nevertheless, his career presents several points of interest. It was a 'success story' typical of the eighteenth century, perhaps the more typical because not particularly dramatic. Here was the son of a Yorkshire craftsman, who moved up into the class of the professional men, raised himself into the ranks of the country's legislators, and achieved a place in county society – his daughters finally marrying into the Cornish gentry. It illustrates the importance in the eighteenth century of 'connections' – essential for advancement equally in professional and in public life. In Masterman's case the establishment of such connections and the shaping of his subsequent career hinged upon two events – his entry into partnership, and then his marriage. Not least, it is interesting because it adds one more facet to the now established and fascinating picture of the eighteenth-century Cornish political scene, with its emphasis on the close interconnection between Cornwall and London. Generally speaking, the counties on the northern and western periphery of England were areas where local interests predominated at parliamentary elections, and where the constituencies more often than not returned to Westminster independent men of local standing. By contrast, the peculiar electoral structure of the Cornish boroughs was such as to ensure the presence always of a high proportion of 'foreigners' among their representatives.[1] Among these 'foreigners' William Masterman

[1] For the general character of Cornish parliamentary politics in the mid-eighteenth century, see Namier, *The structure of Politics at the Accession of George III*, 2nd ed. (1957) pp. 299–357, and on the proportion of strangers among the Cornish members, ibid., pp. 355–6. In 1780 the

may well be included. Until his entry into partnership he had no connection whatsoever with the county: he did not own property in it prior to 1764; and his acquisition of the Trinity and Restormel estates on which he partly based his interest at Bodmin dated back only six years before his election to parliament. Bodmin is further from London as the roads run than is York, but, politically, in that age it was far nearer; and it was in Cornwall, and by way of London, that Masterman of Yorkshire achieved the summit of his social and political career.

William Masterman, the only surviving son of Thomas and Catherine Masterman, of Little Ayton in Cleveland, Yorkshire, was born in 1722.[1] His father, a properous tanner, died in 1727, bequeathing him lands in Little Ayton and neighbouring parishes. In 1743 Masterman, then living at Stokesley, attained his majority, and was granted double or cessate probate as executor of his father's will. It must be assumed that at this time he was serving his articles as apprentice to a local solicitor and learning his profession. Now London beckoned him, with prospects of wider opportunities for an ambitious young man than were to be found in his native Tees-dale. In London he appeared two years later; and having by this time completed his legal studies, he was, on 4 July 1745, admitted a solicitor, his address being given as Old Southampton Buildings.

Before 1750 Masterman had been taken into partnership by a London solicitor with west-country connections, William Luke

---

number of strangers was about the same as in 1761 – 13 out of the 44 elected in 1780 were Cornishmen; two were connected with the county through their mothers; and two by marriage, of whom Masterman was one.

[1] C. Masterman and C. R. Everett, *The Pedigree of the Masterman Family* (Newcastle, 1914) pp. 15–21, gives a sketch of Masterman's personal and family history. Information for which no other source is cited is drawn from this work. A few deeds and other business papers relating to Masterman exist in the Gregor MSS. now in Cornwall Record Office but none of his correspondence appears to have survived in his descendants' papers. Some notes about him, mainly anecdotes about his irascibility, are recorded in a memoir of the Gregor family by his grand-daughter, Loveday Sarah Glanville, preserved in this collection (item 1952) and also available in typescript; but as she was born six years after his death, as her mother died immediately after her arrival, and as she was writing nearly sixty years afterwards, her recollections about the grand-father she never knew were slight.

whose death in that year left him in sole control of the practice. This partnership brought him into contact with the Edgecumbe family, and eventually opened to him the prospect of lucrative office. Lord Edgecumbe was a leading 'professional' borough-monger in Cornwall and had thereby secured places both for himself and for his second son, George Edgecumbe, in the duchy court of Lancaster. An unconfirmed report states that through his patronage William Luke held the duchy office of surveyor of the woods and lands in the south part.[1] Be that as it may, nevertheless a link existed between Luke and the Edgecumbes, for Luke's brother-in-law, Thomas Jones, of Trinity, near Lostwithiel, a solicitor formerly in practice in St Austell, was Lord Edgecumbe's election agent in the various Cornish boroughs under his control.[2] In view of later events it is likely that Jones referred to the firm of Luke and Masterman legal business requiring attention in London which arose out of Lord Edgecumbe's election affairs in Cornwall. Masterman's appointment as high bailiff of the Savoy in December 1756 may have been a first instance of Edgecumbe's favour.[3] A year or two later, there is no doubt that wider prospects were opened to him through the Edgecumbes either by his connection with Jones or by his own merit as their legal agent in the capital. In 1758 he succeeded Richard Wolfe as secretary to the chancellor of the duchy of Cornwall and as deputy clerk to George Edgecumbe, who was holder under a patent for three lives of the place of clerk of the council of the duchy. When Edgecumbe resigned in 1762, after succeeding his brother as third Baron Edgecumbe, Masterman took his place as clerk of the council, a grant of the office in succession for two lives being made to him.[4] He later added to this appointment the other duchy offices of register and secretary to the council, axe-bearer and surveyor of Tutbury, and surveyor of woods north of Trent. Apart from the business connections between Jones and Masterman, after Luke's death they had a common interest in looking after the affairs of his two children. In Luke's

[1] Masterman and Everett, *The Pedigree of the Masterman Family*, p. 18. This is not supported by the contemporary directories.

[2] Namier, *The Structure of Politics at the Accession of George III*, p. 300, n. 4.

[3] *Gentleman's Magazine*, 1756, p. 596.

[4] *Court and City Registers*, 1758 and 1759; *Gentleman's Magazine*, 1762, p. 295.

will Jones was named as executor and as trustee until they should come of age, and Masterman gave him assistance in discharging these duties. In time the association between the two men was drawn closer by Masterman's marriage to Loveday Sarah, Luke's daughter and Jones's niece.[1]

In 1764 Masterman's wife succeeded to the small fortune left by her brother, William Luke, of Lostwithiel, and from this time dates his closer connection with Cornwall and with Cornish affairs. Later, in 1771, he purchased a further estate in the county, the manor of Bridge-end and Polmorgan. By 1764, too, he was being inducted by Thomas Jones into Cornish politics. Steps in his collaboration with Jones in the electoral management of Cornish boroughs included his election in 1764 as mayor of Lostwithiel and his appointment in 1771 as deputy town clerk of Tintagel (Bossiney) – of which he later became town clerk in 1781.[2] Both places were under the patronage of the Edgecumbe family. In 1768 he handled election arrangements for Lord Edgecumbe at Bossiney.[3] When Jones died in July 1774, Masterman fell heir both to his estates and to his employment as election agent to Lord Edgecumbe. He thus came into possession of the beautiful park of Restormel, 'with the adjoining mansion of Trinity, and an estate of somewhat about £150 per annum', the lease of which was bequeathed to him with remainder to his elder daughter and her heirs.[4] At the general election in the following October, he was instrumental in securing £3,000 apiece for Lord Edgecumbe's five borough seats instead of the £2,500 for which Lord North, then first lord of the treasury, had hoped to gain them.[5] By 1780 he had probably retired from this employment, for the papers of John

[1] The date of this marriage has not been ascertained. About 1762 seems likeliest, though it might have been earlier, since Loveday Sarah Luke, born 23 Nov 1737, had been of marriageable age for some years. Delicate in health – a weakness which she passed on to her daughters – she died at Hampstead on 3 May 1773, and was buried on the tenth at St Andrews, Holborn.

[2] H.M.C., *MSS. of Lostwithiel Corporation, Various Collections*, v 337; Sir John Maclean, *Parochial and Family History of the Deanery of Trigg Minor* (1872) III 211.

[3] Namier and Brooke, *History of Parliament*, I 224.

[4] John Nichols, *Literary Illustrations* (1817–58) v 861–2.

[5] *The Parliamentary Papers of John Robinson*, p. 26.

Robinson, secretary to the treasury, who had all the management of election business for the government under Lord North, contain no reference to his acting again for Lord Edgecumbe in the general election of that year.

Masterman continued his London practice as a solicitor for several years after his inheritance of Trinity. He had taken a partner, John Lloyd, and carried on business in offices in Holborn Court, Grays Inn.[1] It is probable that he specialised to some extent in business involving electoral law, for a compilation by him upon this subject is listed as among the papers of the first Marquis of Lansdowne.[2] Meanwhile, in addition to his activities on behalf of Lord Edgecumbe, he had also established a direct professional connection in Cornwall with the treasury. In 1774 he drew up the new charter granted to Saltash, and thereafter he continued to act as government agent for the borough.[3] Expenditure by government in nursing constituencies of this type was mainly indirect, by way of places and favours – 'the price of this system of indirect subsidies was enormous, but incalculable'[4] – but they usually gave rise to a small steady drain of incidental expenses, and occasional payments out of secret service funds were made to Masterman on account of Saltash.[5] The government also found his services of value elsewhere. His expert knowledge of corporation law seems to have been called into play during the campaign which the ministers and their friends carried on during the mid-seventies against the nonconformist radical faction at Portsmouth. On 7 January 1777 Thomas Binstead of Portsmouth wrote to the head of the admiralty, the

[1] Both partners appear in the list of attorneys in *Browne's General Law List*, 1779. In 1782 and 1787 John Lloyd appears there alone.

[2] H.M.C., *Fifth Report*, p. 257. It is described as a folio volume in red morocco, labelled 'Rights of Burroughs. Mr W. Masterman's compendium of the rights and privileges or mode of election of Members to serve in Parliament, drawn alphabetically in tabular form with an abstract of the gradual alterations in representation'.

[3] On the new charter, see above pp. 225–6.

[4] Namier, *The Structure of Politics at the Accession of George III*, p. 205.

[5] Windsor MSS., Secret and Special Service Accounts of George III, 1779–82. These incomplete accounts show payments to Masterman by Sir Grey Cooper, secretary to the treasury and M.P. for Saltash, of £300 in the first quarter of 1779, of £489 1*s* 10*d* in the last quarter of 1780, and of £60 in the first quarter of 1781. I have to acknowledge the gracious permission of Her Majesty the Queen to make use of these documents.

fourth Earl of Sandwich, supporting a request for command of a sloop by a near relation of 'Mr Masterman, who has so judiciously and zealously conducted our Portsmouth law matters'.[1] This new business brought him by 1780 a certain reputation among his friends as a borough manager. When the East India nabob Richard Barwell – the member of council in Bengal, and colleague of Warren Hastings – was about to leave India for home, his friend, Sir Elijah Impey, chief justice of Bengal, wrote: 'Dear Masterman . . . I shall give him a letter to you . . . the purport of my letter is to procure him your assistance in his parliamentary views'; and he later requested help of the same nature from Masterman for himself and Hastings.[2]

Solicitation and flattery are gratifying. But Masterman was soon to sample the irksome side of election management. At first he and John Robinson appeared to have every excuse for complacency regarding the political state of Saltash. Government control seemed to be safely established. During the first six years after the grant of the new charter affairs went smoothly: three by-elections passed without disputes over the corporation's monopoly of the parliamentary franchise. So far all was well. But at the general election of 1780, the peace of the borough was rudely broken when John Buller of Morval opened his campaign to establish his own controlling interest.[3]

The government candidates at Saltash in September 1780 were Sir Grey Cooper, secretary to the treasury, and Charles Jenkinson, the secretary-at-war. Neither considered it necessary to attend in person. Recuperating at his country retreat near Newmarket, Cooper first learnt by express letter from Robert Speke, the mayor, of the unwelcome intervention of Buller. He wrote immediately to Masterman for advice and help,[4] and summed up the situation in a letter of explanation to Jenkinson (14th September):[5]

> I send by the messenger which will deliver this to you, a dispatch to Mr Robinson with a letter from the Mayor of Saltash which

[1] Sandwich MSS.; Namier and Brooke, *History of Parliament*, I 298.

[2] B.M. Add. MSS. 16260, fos. 13 and 43. A vacant seat was found for Barwell at Helston in March 1781, but I have not so far come across proof that Masterman had any part in this arrangement.

[3] For Buller's campaign, see the previous essay, pp. 223–31 above.

[4] See Cooper's letter to Jenkinson of 1 Oct, below.

[5] B.M. Add. MSS. 38214, fos. 172–3.

has given me some surprise but not much apprehension. . . . I am utterly at a loss to conjecture upon what ground this sudden attack has been made: I recollect that the present Earl of Radnor made some motion when he was in the House of Commons, respecting the last charter for Saltash, and a copy of it was laid before the House. But the squib consisted, I think, of some weak objections to the mode of the charter being granted, and a doubt of the legal revocation of the old charter. Whether Mr Buller's enterprise goes on this ground, I cannot say, but certainly if the charter was not null and void ab initio our return must be a good one. We shall soon hear more of the business from Mr Masterman, who was the fabricator of the charter, and has been the agent for the borough ever since it passed the Great Seal.

Masterman proceeded at once to Saltash on a tour of investigation. It was to be expected that Buller would claim rightful election by means of a petition to the House of Commons: if so, witnesses would have to be ready and sworn copies of documents prepared, in order to contest his allegations. Little imagination is required to picture the astute and experienced election agent going about his business, searching the borough records, and interviewing the older inhabitants, who might have to be brought up to Westminster to give evidence about the franchise. His report was reassuring, as Cooper informed Jenkinson at length in his further letter of 1 October:[1]

I have received a letter from Mr Masterman since I saw you at St James, on the subject of the late attack on the borough of Saltash. I had written to him immediately on the receipt of the express from the Mayor and Justice which was communicated to you by Mr Robinson; and desired him to consult the charters, to examine all the old papers and documents of the Corporation and to make enquiry of the oldest people in or near the borough respecting the right of voting for members of parliament: and

[1] Ibid., fos. 198–9. The mayor and justice were Robert Speke and Nicholas Mill. Mill was also town clerk. The following January Jenkinson solicited for him from the judge of the admiralty court (Sir James Marriott) the place of commissioner and actuary for naval prizes sent into Plymouth, a post he had formerly held during the Seven Years War (ibid., 38308, fo. 60).

you will see by his answer which I have by this post sent to Lord North that the charters (as well that granted to the borough by King Charles II as the late charter) are full and clear to the point where you with your usual judgement thought the stress would lie, and the gist of the case must be found. *The right and power of electing members ot serve in parliament are by both those charters expressly placed and vested in the Mayor and Free Burgesses therein named and in their successors to be elected under the powers thereby given, respectively*, and all the old people in the borough amongst the rest the late Mayor, Mr Hickes, who is an intelligent man, and has known the borough upwards of 40 years can attest that the usage has run with and accompanied the grants. There were however it seems two attempts of a similar nature to Mr Buller's made in 1721 and 1739, and Mr Howell one of the freeholders who tendered his vote against us, pretends that his vote for a freehold was received in 1721.

The anticipated petition of Buller and his colleague was presented in the House of Commons a few days after the meeting of the new parliament. The sitting members, however, had ample time to prepare their defence, for the committee on this election dispute was not appointed until the beginning of 1782. Once again Masterman's services were in demand. On 11 January 1782 Robert Hickes notified Cooper that a Mr Hewes had arrived, sent down from London to make further inquiries in preparation for the impending trial of the petition. Hewes had first called at Trinity to consult Masterman and had stayed there two days; and Hickes expected to see Masterman himself in Saltash on the following Monday.[1] Eleven days later, on the twenty-second, Jenkinson attended a conference on the business in London, at which Masterman may have been present.[2] The trial of the petition came on in the following week, and was concluded on 4 February – to the satisfaction of Cooper, of Jenkinson, of the treasury, and of the king himself.[3] By the resolution of the election committee the sitting members were declared duly elected. This was not the end of Buller's

[1] Ibid., 38217, fo. 244.

[2] *The Correspondence of King George III*, v no. 3508.

[3] *Commons Journals*, XXXVIII 633, where it is stated in error that the second petitioner with Buller was Sir William Lemon, Bart; *The Correspondence of King George III*, v no. 3513.

eventually successful campaign to establish his interest at Saltash,[1] but evidence of Masterman's further involvement in this struggle has not survived.

Meanwhile, from the stage of borough agent, William Masterman had pursued his upward career: 'As it so often happened in the second generation of borough managers, he finished by being himself returned to Parliament.'[2] At the same general election which saw the commencement of all his troubles at Saltash, Masterman secured election as member for Bodmin. He did not, however, as was more usual with men of this type, arrive by the sort of usurpation which consisted of converting a managerial into a controlling interest.[3] About this time he gave up active work in the London practice. A journalist's description of him shortly after his election runs '. . . formerly an attorney in London, in partnership with Mr Lloyd, in Holborn Court Gray's Inn, in the honourable line of which he acquired a very independent fortune'.[4] Doubtless on the strength of this 'very independent fortune' as well as the influence he enjoyed through his control of the Trinity and Restormel estates, he managed to secure the favour of a majority of the thirty-six electors of Bodmin, and was chosen without the trouble of a contest. Probably his close links (as a political agent) with the treasury, the fount of patronage, also weighed heavily with the corporation. Lord Edgecumbe, his patron, had little influence at

[1] See pp. 228–31 above.

[2] Namier, *The Structure of Politics at the Accession of George III*, p. 300, n. 4.

[3] Examples of the more normal method of advancement are furnished by the Bullers at East and West Looe (ibid., pp. 323–4 and 334–5), by the Phillipses at Camelford (ibid., pp. 335 and 343–4), and by the Pentons at Chichester. Henry Penton the younger (*c.* 1737–1812) succeeded his father as a political agent and acted at Chichester for the Duke of Bolton, and later for the Duke of Chandos. It was noted of him, however, about 1780 that: 'He has recently . . . contrived so to improve his connections in this borough, which consists of the corporation only, that he now stands upon his own interest, independent of any superior authority, and has acquired the power of introducing himself. This increase of parliamentary influence has been attended with the further advantage of procuring Mr Penton a seat at the Admiralty Board.' ('Parliamentary Characters 1779–1781', p. 44: a scrap-book of contemporary newspaper cuttings, formerly in the possession of Sir Lewis Namier.)

[4] 'Parliamentary Characters', p. 38.

Bodmin, and Masterman came in on his own interest there, displacing another supporter of the government, Sir James Laroche, 1st Bart.[1] And here is a perfect illustration of the way in which, during the eighteenth century – even when controversy in parliament over national policy was acute, and even in areas which felt the tug of London politics – local interests and personal aspirations so often dominated parliamentary elections, to the exclusion of any thought about men's political alignment on national issues. Laroche, like Masterman, was a friend of the government. The other member for Bodmin, George Hunt of Lanhydrock, was an independent in politics and a steady opponent of North's administration. Yet it was typical that Masterman should push his candidature at Bodmin, where he was able to cultivate his own electoral interest, and not elsewhere, although it was known (not only to himself but also to John Robinson at the treasury) that he was more likely to throw out Laroche than Hunt by his intervention.

Thus Masterman had attained his place in the select circle of the House of Commons. He was now fifty-eight. A small oil painting of him in later life, commissioned perhaps to commemorate this success, displays a face with a long, prominent nose and wide, firmly set mouth, suggestive of a tenacious and thrusting personality.[2] However, he came to the House too old to make his mark in it. His political connections were already firmly established, and he joined the silent ranks of the 'party of administration', appearing classed as a supporter in a 'State' of the Commons drawn up by John Robinson in February 1781.[3] No speech by him was ever reported; but his name can be traced through various lists of divisions. He was absent from the division of 12 December 1781, when the administration secured the rejection of Sir James Lowther's motion for the ending of the war against the American colonists: but he voted for North's government in all but one of the

[1] *The Parliamentary Papers of John Robinson*, pp. 22, 47. By this time Laroche had become a bankrupt and had no funds available for election purposes (Namier and Brooke, *History of Parliament*, III 21–2).

[2] A reproduction is printed in Masterman and Everett, *The Pedigree of the Masterman Family*. The original was at Trewarthenick at the time when this work was written.

[3] Abergavenny MSS., parliamentary list dated November 1781 (but drawn up in February of that year).

five critical divisons of February and March 1782 which preceded its collapse.[1] In August 1782, after the formation of the short-lived administration of the Earl of Shelburne, John Robinson considered that he would probably support it,[2] and in the following February he voted for Shelburne's peace preliminaries. In common with the rest of the 'party of administration' he voted for Fox's East India bill in November 1783, but he went over to Pitt, as did most of the men in this political group, by the time of the general election the following year.[3] At this general election he stood again for Bodmin, but was beaten in a contest by a local wealthy Foxite candidate, Sir John Morshead, 1st Bart.

This election defeat of 1784 brought to a close Masterman's career in parliament, but it did not end his active engagement in Cornish politics. Saltash still claimed his attention, and he continued to nurse the government's interest with the members of the corporation. In July he was intermediary for the payment of a quarter's allowance or pension of £50 to Edward Hawkins of Saltash.[4] A week later he was in correspondence with Charles Jenkinson about the provision of favours for the electors; and Jenkinson wrote to him on 1 August 1784 (in reply to a letter which has not been preserved in the Liverpool Papers):[5]

> I have very seriously pressed Mr Rose to tell Lord Howe, that some of the favours which we ask for our naval friends at Saltash must be complied with; which he has promised me to do. When I hear of what Mr Rose has done, I will then apply to Lord Howe myself in favour of Mr Scott's son. This I take to be the most prudent mode of proceeding and the most likely to succeed.

---

[1] Abergavenny MSS., parliamentary lists; Debrett, *The Parliamentary Register*, V 150, VI 331 and 476; B.M. Add. MSS. 30895, fo. 136. (Illness caused his absence from the last but one of these divisions.)

[2] *The Parliamentary Papers of John Robinson*, p. 47.

[3] *Political Magazine*, VII (1784) 4; *The Parliamentary Papers of John Robinson*, p. 124.

[4] *The Later Correspondence of George III*, I no. 158; P.R.O. 30/8/229. The payment is included on a sheet of election expenses among the king's papers, and Masterman's receipt is in the Chatham MSS.

[5] B.M. Add. MSS. 38309, fo. 94. Lord Howe (1726–99) had now become first lord of the admiralty, and George Rose (1744–1818) had succeeded to the office of secretary to the treasury formerly held by Robinson.

He seems also, by this time, to have extended the range of his contacts in the West Country, for during the preparations for the general election of 1784, John Robinson listed him as able to give information regarding Plymouth and also various boroughs in the west of Cornwall – Helston, Penryn and Truro.[1] And in the June and July following, he received from George Rose sums of £3,000 and £4,000, for purposes not specified on his receipts but probably in connection with Cornish elections.[2]

Masterman did not live to see the downfall of the government interest at Saltash, an event which followed swiftly after his death. He died at Restormel House about the end of July 1786. His adopted county had the last claim upon him, and on 4 August his remains were laid to rest at Lostwithiel church. The career was ended that had led from small beginnings in the austere dales of north Yorkshire to professional advancement in London, and so to political and social success, honour and ease, among the lush, fertile valleys of east Cornwall. To his inheritance in Yorkshire and the Cornish lands of his wife's family he had added, by 1784, estates scattered over six other counties.[3] After his death his properties were valued at £125,000.[4] Wealth had come to him and with it recognition. Nor was one final triumph denied him – for he died after having witnessed the marriage of his elder daughter to Francis Gregor of Trewarthenick, one of the leading gentlemen of the county of Cornwall, and later one of its members in three parliaments.[5]

[1] *The Parliamentary Papers of John Robinson*, pp. 114–5.

[2] P.R.O. 30/8/229 (Chatham MSS.).

[3] Masterman's will, Somerset House, P.C.C. 482 Norfolk.

[4] Memoir by Loveday Sarah Glanville [Gregor MSS., 1952], Cornwall Record Office, typescript copy, p. 197. His fortune was divided between his two daughters.

[5] Francis Gregor (1760–1815), sheriff of Cornwall, 1788, M.P. for the county, 1790–1806. His wife, Catherine Luke Masterman, died in 1794. Her younger sister, Loveday Sarah Masterman, married in 1790 Francis Glanville (1762–1846) of Catchfrench, St Germans, sometime M.P. for Malmesbury and, later, Plymouth: she died in 1792, when not yet twenty-one, of an overdose of laudanum immediately after the birth of her daughter, Loveday Sarah Glanville, the compiler of the Gregor family memoir, and the ultimate inheritrix of the whole Masterman estate.

ELEVEN

*The Wilkites and the General Election of 1774**

ON 11 June 1771, at the London Tavern in the City of London, the Society of the Supporters of the Bill of Rights assembled for a crucial meeting, from which were to flow important consequences. More than two years before, this select political club had come into existence to uphold the fortunes of John Wilkes and the cause of 'Liberty'. The occasion had been the rejection by the House of Commons of Wilkes as a duly elected member for Middlesex, a move to uphold the dignity of the House and of government against a demagogue whom the great William Pitt himself had described as 'a blasphemer of his God and a libeller of his King', but a move which gave critics ground to cry out against a breach of the constitution – for if the House could thus tamper with its own membership, what safeguard was there for the independence of the legislature which guaranteed English liberties from executive tyranny?[1] For Wilkes, a disreputable adventurer, many of the members of the Society had little respect, but they believed his cause to be of the greatest constitutional importance, more particularly since for several years past antiministerial propaganda and a fortuitous string of incidents had fixed upon the groups in power in the government a reputation for tyrannous designs (of which they were in fact wholly innocent). The original aims of the Society – financial support for Wilkes and the reversal by the Commons of the resolutions on the Middlesex election – were objects too limited and undefined to satisfy for long a considerable proportion of its adherents. By early 1771 their discontent and desire for stronger measures were avowed; and now, in June, for the first time they proceeded to adopt a comprehensive pro-

* This originally appeared in *Guildhall Miscellany*, II iv (1962) 155–64.

[1] For the details of this incident, see H. Bleackley, *Life of John Wilkes* (1917) pp. 204–24, and for a recent brief scholarly discussion of the circumstances, Watson, *The Reign of George III*, pp. 132–9.

gramme of parliamentary reform, as a plan of political action to be pursued both in London and throughout the country. The meeting came to a close with a resolution 'that it be recommended . . . to every county, city, and borough in this kingdom, that every person, who shall henceforth be a candidate to serve as a member in this or any future parliament, shall be required to sign a declaration and confirm it upon oath, that in case he is elected he will vote for and use his best endeavours to obtain a Bill to limit the duration of parliaments, and to reduce the number of placemen and pensioners in the House of Commons and also endeavour to obtain a more fair and equal representation of the people'. All current political grievances (especially the Middlesex election question) should also be examined in parliament. A further resolution referred the whole subject to a committee, which included several present and future members of parliament. Within a few weeks this committee produced an elaborate declaration of radical policy, which was published and distributed to radical sympathisers throughout the country.[1]

During the next three years this plan was occasionally adopted in by-elections,[2] but its real test came with the general election of 1774. Despite the curious anomalies of the eighteenth-century system of representation, the idea of such an appeal to public opinion was not quite meaningless. True, there were well over one hundred borough constituencies where tiny electorates and the influence of patrons took all political reality in the modern sense out of elections. But although the representation had evolved as the expression of a predominantly oligarchical political system, it was by no means unresponsive to public feeling. In the forty English counties the voters were numerous; and if the gentry and professional classes, who formed the educated, dominant minority, became convinced that certain lines of action were desirable, they could make this plain, even with decisive effect. Fully as numerous,

[1] *The Public Advertiser*, 13 June, 25 July 1771. The twelve persons named upon the committee were: Brass Crosby (lord mayor), Sir Joseph Mawbey, Frederick Bull, John Wilkes, Edmund Dayrell, William Bullock, William Ellis, Charles Hitch, James Adair, George Grieve, John Reynolds and the Rev. Thomas Wilson, 'together with such other members as choose to attend'.

[2] E.g. London 1773, Worcester 1773 and 1774.

and even more free from the dominance of a social minority, were the great urban electorates of London and Westminster; and there were about another eighteen large cities and towns, with electorates ranging from one to three thousand, where a strong movement of public opinion might find expression. Nor were all the smaller boroughs to be ruled out of consideration. Thirty-six had electorates of intermediate size, from about 500 to about 1,000. There were also twenty or so others, with electorates of less than 500, where demonstrations of public opinion could occur, these including, on the one hand, a few large centres, particularly Plymouth, Portsmouth and Southampton, where a resticted corporation electorate was ludicrously small in comparison with population and, on the other, a number of quite small country towns, such as Cambridge, Lewes, Bury St Edmunds and Peterborough.

The Supporters of the Bill of Rights knew, and the general election proved, that in the metropolis their strength was formidable. The less disillusioned among them hoped also for some response in the country at large. The propagation of their cause, their ideas, their programmes, by means of agents and corresponding committees had been continuous, though from the small extent of surviving evidence it seems clear that these efforts were very limited in scale and effect, depending often upon the proselytising zeal of one or two individuals in particular districts. However, the members of the Society believed it worth while in 1774 to launch a national campaign, and the onset of the general election drove them into a flurry of action. The *Middlesex Journal*, a newspaper especially associated with the movement, reported in its issue of 1–4 October that 'circular letters' were 'preparing by the society . . . to be sent off with all proper expedition to the several counties and boroughs in the kingdom', exhorting constituents to bind their candidates with pledges to the radical programme. By this time a still longer list of complaints had been accumulated. With some effect, the Wilkites added the American question to their own grievances and posed as champions against tyrannous government on both sides of the Atlantic.

What justification was there for their optimism? And what was the effect of the radical campaign?

In the metropolitan area the general election resolved itself almost entirely into conflicts between those candidates who were prepared to subscribe to the programme of the Bill of Rights Society and those who would not, whether or not they were supporters of the court. John Wilkes himself, encouraged by the progress of his campaign to win election as lord mayor, took a prominent part in the management of the contests, and the men he supported were, for the most part, his close connections in city politics.[1]

In London the tone of the election was set from the beginning at the meeting of Common Hall for the nomination of candidates on 3 October, attended by some two thousand people. The chairman expressed the hope 'that the choice would fall on men who might counterwork the machinations of an administration which would, if it should be in their power, abrogate the government in England, as they had done in America'.[2] A declaration for candidates was then adopted on the lines advocated by the Bill of Rights Society. Among the points which candidates were to subscribe were: shorter parliaments; exclusion of placemen; a fair and equal representation; imposition of oaths against bribery upon candidates; redress for the Middlesex election; renunciation of attempts to tax the American colonists otherwise than in their own freely elected assemblies; repeal of all recent punitive legislation against the colonists; and repeal of the Quebec Act. Candidates were also required to promise to accept no place of profit under the crown, and to follow such instructions as their constituents assembled in Common Hall might prescribe.[3]

[1] Wilkes's diary for this period states that on 13 and 20 Sept, before the dissolution was known, but when it was probably suspected, he twice dined with the Bill of Rights Society at the London Tavern. On 7 Oct he dined in Colman Street with Thomas Scott, a wealthy and prominent resident of Westminister, about whose career at this time I have no information, but who became active in the Association Movement after 1779. On 14 and 15 Oct he dined with the 'committee for the city election of members' at the Paul's Head in Cateaton Street, and on one or two occasions during these weeks he dined in the company of Wilkite aldermen at the Corporation Club. B.M. Add. MSS. 30866, fos. 47 ff.

[2] The reference was to the recent passage of the Quebec Act, establishing non-representative government with recognition for the Roman Catholic church in that province and to the 'intolerable Acts' passed in answer to the Boston tea party, closing the port of Boston and modifying the Massachusetts Charter.

[3] *Middlesex Journal*, 1–4 Oct 1774, 3a–c; *Public Advertiser*, 4 Oct 1774, 3d; *London Chronicle*, 1–4 Oct 1774, 7b.

This pledge was promptly subscribed by John Sawbridge, who had now reconciled himself with Wilkes after their quarrel of three years before – cynics declared it was a mere political bargain to secure his seat for the City – and by Wilkes's three faithful followers, his brother-in-law, George Hayley, Brass Crosby and Frederick Bull, the retiring lord mayor. Of the other three candidates, who all declined it, Richard Oliver, a follower of Chatham and Shelburne, accepted all the planks of policy which it contained, but refused to subscribe a test which, as he afterwards explained, would bind him to accept instructions regardless of what faction might come to control the livery in the future.[1] Another, William Baker, declined on similar grounds to be bound by a promise to accept instructions under future circumstances which he could not foresee, and in view of his association with Edmund Burke he may well also have had undisclosed reservations about some of the more radical demands which the undertaking contained.[2] These two, and also John Roberts, an East India Company director, connected with the court, organised their separate election campaigns. The only one of these three to win a seat was Oliver, whose political views accorded most closely with those of the Wilkites: his success excluded Crosby, one of Wilkes's adherents. During the course of the election there was a short-lived attempt, proved useless almost from the start, to organise an anti-Wilkite front. The *Public Advertiser* of 6 October carried an announcement that 'the worthy liverymen of London who wish to support Mr alderman Hopkins and John Roberts Esq. as candidates . . . are requested to meet at the Kings Arms Tavern, Corn Hill, this evening, the 6th instant, at 6 o'clock, in order to consider of the expediency of putting two other gentlemen in nomination with them.' It was found that Hopkins, after all, would not face a contest, but the meeting resolved that Roberts's candidature should be joined with those of Baker and Oliver.[3] Hints in George III's correspondence seem to indicate that these manœuvres were probably inspired by the court; Roberts, if elected, was expected to be a ministerial supporter, and though

[1] *Middlesex Journal*, 6–8 Oct 1774, 4a.
[2] *Middlesex Journal*, 4–6 Oct 1774, 4b.
[3] *Middlesex Journal*, 6–8 Oct 1774, 1d.

Oliver and Baker were connected with parties in opposition, they were preferable to Wilkites.[1] However, neither Baker nor Oliver was likely to accept any association with a man whose court connections were believed to be strong, and nothing came of this attempt. In London Wilkes thus carried three of his candidates, while the fourth member, Oliver, if a personal antagonist, was nevertheless equally a supporter of radical reform.

Across the river in Southwark, two Wilkites contested the borough and won one seat. At the nomination meeting at the Town Hall on 4 October those present 'unanimously' approved a proposal to require a political test from candidates similar to that approved by the Londoners. This was immediately signed by Nathaniel Polhill, a tobacco merchant in the borough, and by the American-born William Lee, a merchant engaged in the North American trade, an ardent supporter of Wilkes in Middlesex and one of the retiring sheriffs of London.[2] Lee, in a speech denouncing another candidate for refusing the test, laid stress on the delegate character of a member of parliament. 'Promises are vague: but when a person has signed his name to articles, they are always to be produced against him; and no man need enter into service if he don't like his Master's proposal – Masters, I say, Gentlemen, for so you are: every person who becomes your representative becomes your servant, and consequently ought to do as you direct.'[3] At the election one seat was won for the reformers by Polhill, a success which probably reflected a combination of general anti-government feeling, support for reform which was thought to be in the interests of the metropolis, and prejudice against one of Polhill's opponents for having reinsured by purchase of a seat in a rotten borough.[4]

In Middlesex Wilkes triumphed out of hand. Having subscribed the Bill of Rights programme, he and Serjeant Glynn were returned without opposition. Strenuous efforts by the ministers to

[1] *The Correspondence of King George III*, III nos. 1523, 1520 (3 Oct, incorrectly dated by the editor), 1526, 1534, 1535.

[2] William Lee (1739–95), a member of the prominent Virginian family, later served the Continental Congress as a diplomat during the American War of Independence.

[3] *London Chronicle*, 4–6 Oct 1774; *Public Advertiser*, 5 Oct 1774.

[4] This last reason for Sir Abraham Hume's failure at Southwark was stressed by North to George III, 11 Oct 1774, *The Correspondence of King George III*, III no. 1534.

find two court candidates ended in ignominious failure.[1] The one check to Wilkes in the metropolis occurred in Westminster. The strength of his position was such that his support was thought essential by anti-ministerial candidates – for lack of it Edmund Burke immediately gave up his hopes in that direction. His choice fell on two young aristocrats, Lord Mountmorres and Lord Mahon, both enthusiastic radicals who accepted the Bill of Rights programme. But these were themselves the candidates of rival connections, Grenvilles, Pitts and Stanhopes and the Earl of Shelburne backing Mahon, while the interests of the Duke of Portland and the Marquis of Rockingham, after some initial hesitation, were given to Mountmorres; and in the end victory fell to a well-conducted campaign by the joint forces of the administration and its aristocratic allies, the Dukes of Northumberland and Newcastle, and the managers of the Duke of Bedford's interest.[2]

Outside the metropolis, and apart from Middlesex, the only county contested by a Wilkite was Surrey. Even in the eighteenth century, the spill-over of greater London into the North-eastern districts of Surrey introduced a strong metropolitan element into county politics, and in 1774 the traditional landed interests were challenged by Sir Joseph Mawbey, a rich distiller of Vauxhall, M.P. for Southwark since 1761, and a strenuous supporter of Wilkes and reform. Mawbey, in his election address, publicly pledged himself to 'continue to vote for shortening the duration of parliaments; for a bill for the exclusion of placemen and pensioners from the House of Commons; and for repealing the Quebec Bill, by which popery and French law are established, not tolerated, in that extensive country'. At the county meeting for nomination of candidates, he 'spoke largely of his having embraced the solicitation of the friends of freedom . . . dwelt long on the necessity of resisting the measures of administration, which apparently led to

[1] *Middlesex Journal*, 27–9 Sept, 8–11, 11–13 Oct 1774; *The Correspondence of King George III*, III nos. 1513, 1528–31, 1518 (10 Oct, misdated by the editor), 1532.

[2] This account is based on *Middlesex Journal*, 1–4 Oct, 1c, 4b–c; *Public Advertiser*, 30 Sept, 7, 12 Oct 1774; election correspondence, Sept–Oct 1774, Newcastle MSS., Nottingham University Library; *The Correspondence of King George III*, III nos. 1510, 1511, 1515, 1516, 1522, 1520, 1523, 1524, 1529, 1518; *Burke Correspondence*, III 28–35, 49–52, 58–60.

despotism, talked of the establishment of popery in Canada, and declared nothing was safe while the right of election remained violated . . . declared, as he had always voted for shortening the duration of parliaments, he hoped if he was elected, he should meet them three years hence . . . he would never accept of any place, pension or emolument whatever from any minister'.[1] It is noticeable, however, that on these occasions Mawbey, although a founder-member of the Bill of Rights Society, and a zealous reformer, seems to have omitted references to 'a fair and equal representation': this is perhaps some indication of the indifference of the county to the question. Mawbey's ministerial opponents rejoiced that virtually none of the gentry of the county supported him[2] – here also, it seems, the strained relations between Wilkes and the aristocratic opposition had some effect[3] – and Mawbey lost his election by 1656 votes to 1390: a check to the new political forces which proved only temporary, for he was triumphant at the county by-election in the following year.

In one other county, Essex, the ground was tested by an independent candidate, Lord Waltham, whom the Wilkites regarded as a sympathiser,[4] but two other anti-ministerial candidates, the late members, were already in the field, and nothing came of his inquiries.

Followers of Wilkes also attempted a small numbei of open boroughs, where there appeared to be a nucleus of support for the radical cause, and where they, as individuals, had particular connections. The metropolitan press provides occasional tantalising hints of the role that was played in these proceedings by non-resident freemen of certain boroughs who lived in London. Such men, drawn into the vigorous political life of the capital, might provide instruments for infiltration into quiet, conservative provincial centres, and it appears that attempts were made to use them in this way by the Wilkites in 1774. The *London Chronicle* of 4–6 October reported that on the evening of the third,

[1] *Public Advertiser*, 6 Oct 1774, 2a; *Middlesex Journal*, 13–15 Oct 1774.

[2] George Onslow to Newcastle, [13 Oct 1774], Newcastle MSS., Nottingham University Library.

[3] Sir Robert Clayton to Rockingham, 3 June 1775, Rockingham MSS., provides an instance of the feeling against Mawbey as an upstart, and in a man himself only three generations removed from business.

[4] *Middlesex Journal*, 8–11 Oct, 3b, 13–15 Oct, 1c.

> a meeting was held at the Griffin in Holborn by the freemen of Worcester who favour Sir Watkin Lewes. The numbers were between two and three hundred. At half-past nine o'clock, the present Lord Mayor of London [Bull] paid Sir Watkin and his friends a visit. His Lordship staid some time, drank success to the freemen of Worcester who dare be free, and to their then present candidate. Immediately after the meeting was over Sir Watkin set off for Worcester to recanvass that city.

Lewes was a staunch Wilkite and a founder-member of the Bill of Rights Society. Similarly, the *Public Advertiser* of 6 October reported:

> At a very numerous and respectable meeting of the freemen of Bedford,[1] resident in and near London, assembled by general advertisement at the King's Arms in Cornhill, it was unanimously agreed to support the election of Sir William Wake Baronet and Robert Sparrow Esquire . . . on condition of their signing a previous engagement (which was then fixed on) to suggest certain public measures in favour of the people. Several gentlemen having declared that they knew the substance of the engagement to be agreeable to the principles of both these candidates, Sir Robert Bernard was desired to transmit the same to them by express.

How did the elections go in these two boroughs?

Lewes's candidature at Worcester was his third attempt. He had already lost two by-elections during the past eleven months. There seems to be little doubt that some of the men who invited him to intermeddle in the city were concerned simply with financial profit: so much is clear from his later complaints about turncoats. But it also appears that there was a strong core of support for him among both the inhabitants of Worcester and the non-resident freemen living in London, inspired by a mixture of nonconformist dislike of the bishop and the cathedral chapter, resentment at the dominance of the corporation, which created additional freemen in its interest, and to some extent attraction to the radical programme of the Wilkites. At the commencement of the poll the candidates were tendered, and Lewes subscribed, a political test similar to that signed by Wilkes and Glynn in

[1] According to the *London Chronicle* of 4–6 Oct, the meeting numbered about 150.

Middlesex. On this third attempt, as before, Lewes was able to poll about 700 votes, and failed by little more than 100 to secure his election.[1]

At Bedford the radical leadership came not from the Wilkites, but from the group round parson John Horne, who in 1771 had broken with Wilkes and founded the rival Constitutional Society. It was, indeed, pointed out by a contributor to the *Public Advertiser* of 14 October that these two bodies might cause confusion by issuing different sets of instructions to be presented to candidates; but though their leaders were not on speaking terms, they were working for similar ends. Bedford was at this time split between a corporation and an inhabitant interest. In 1769 the corporation had withdrawn from its dependence on the Duke of Bedford and had adopted as its patron the wealthy Huntingdonshire squire, Sir Robert Bernard, a founder-member of the original Bill of Rights Society, and M.P. for Westminster in the radical interest from 1770 to 1774. The corporation's influence was sustained by the creation of non-resident freemen, numbers being admitted after 1769 in Bernard's interest, including Huntingdonshire dependents and supporters in greater London, among them Wilkes's enemies, James Townsend and Horne. Of the two men approved, largely as a result of Horne's efforts,[2] at the meeting of London freemen, Wake was a Northamptonshire squire of radical leanings and Robert Sparrow was Bernard's brother-in-law.[3] Both, having already been formally adopted as the corporation's candidates, agreed to subscribe the declaration proposed at the London meeting;[4] and they carried their election mainly on the vote of the non-resident freemen, after the votes of a great number of the inhabitants cast for their opponents had been struck off by the returning officer, on the dubious ground that participation in

[1] *A circumstantial and impartial account of the grand contest for . . . the city of Worcester . . . also particulars of the second election* (1773, 1774) (Worcester City Library, M. 246); *Berrow's Worcester Journal*, Aug–Oct 1774, *passim*; S. Douglas, *History of the cases of controverted elections* (1777) III 243 ff.

[2] Horne to Bernard, [2 Apr. 1784], Manchester MSS., Hunts. Record Office.

[3] Rev. Hadley Cox to Hardwicke, 10 Oct 1774, B.M. Add. MSS. 35693, fo. 234.

[4] *Public Advertiser*, 6, 8 Oct 1774.

a local bounty constituted a disqualifying acceptance of charity.[1] Sparrow's election was later set aside on petition, but the corporation's connection with the Constitutional Society resulted in Bedford being represented for the next few years by one Wilkite sympathiser. Comparison of the circumstances at Bedford with those at Worcester reveals some of the many political oddities produced by the anomalies of the eighteenth-century electoral system. In Worcester the corporation was clearly the symbol of reaction and privilege, the target of jealousy and reforming zeal. In Bedford, on the other hand, the corporation was drawn into support for the reform movement; and yet, how reformist in character are those men to be regarded, who dominated the representation by their use of non-resident votes?

It seems probable that other meetings similar to those of the London freemen of Bedford and Worcester were used to assist the attempts of Wilkes's supporters to secure election for other boroughs, mainly in the vicinity of greater London. At Dover the general election brought a successful end to a Wilkite campaign which had commenced in support of John Trevanion as far back as the summer of 1769. Although Trevanion was defeated at the by-election of 1770, Wilkite sympathy in Dover was so strong that at another by-election in 1773, his refusal to stand was followed by attempts to get other London radicals, William Colhoun or Sir Watkin Lewes, to take his place. By 1774 Trevanion was able to secure his election without opposition, for the government preferred to abandon one seat to the Wilkites rather than undertake the risk and expense of a contest.[2] But this was almost the full extent of the Wilkite successes. The American-born Stephen Sayre, the other retiring Wilkite sheriff of Middlesex, in company with a fellow-candidate, polled a majority of the votes of the inhabitants of Seaford, but they were kept out on petition and were unable to make good their claim that as their supporters had been wrongfully prevented from paying scot and lot but were fully

[1] *London Chronicle*, 18–20 Oct 1774, 6.

[2] Stephen Sayre to Wilkes, 29 Aug 1769, B.M. Add. MSS. 30870 fo. 185; *Kentish Post and Canterbury Journal*, 21 Nov 1769, 9, 30 Jan 1770; *Canterbury Journal*, 27 Sept–4 Oct, 11–18 Oct 1774; Sir Joseph Yorke to Hardwicke, 18 Oct [1774], B.M. Add. MSS. 35370, fo. 286.

qualified to do so, these votes should be regarded as valid. There was much Wilkite enthusiasm at Cambridge, where two candidates, Thomas Plumer Byde, of Ware Park, Herts., and Samuel Meeke, a London merchant, stood against the ministerial candidates returned on the Hardwicke interest. The excitement and animosity engendered by the contest were such that at the close, so Lord Hardwicke was informed one of his correspondents, 'if we had attempted to chair the members . . . murder would have been the consequence';[1] but the Wilkites were easily defeated. There is less clear evidence of Wilkite contests in other constituencies. At Southampton, apparently at the instigation of one of the king's brothers, the Duke of Cumberland, Lord Charles Montagu, brother of the Duke of Manchester, put up against the two candidates favoured by the government, and tried to exploit feeling in favour of the Wilkite programme.[2] At Portsmouth Joshua Iremonger was the unsuccessful candidate of 'the Patriotic Party', but the Wilkite press seems to have ignored this contest, which may have been entirely inspired by the feud existing between factions within the corporation.[3] At Peterborough the defeated candidate, James Farrel Phipps, and his supporters to the number of about a hundred, drowned their sorrows at a roistering party, at which numerous Wilkite toasts were given.[4]

Further afield, a Wilkite element is discernible in the election politics of the two provincial centres, Bristol and Newcastle, but in neither place does it seem to have played a decisive part.

Five years before, the beginnings of the London radical agitation had evoked a clear reponse in Bristol. On 8 March 1769 a public meeting of the citizens passed resolutions to instruct the representatives to support a comprehensive reform programme, including examination of public expenditure, shorter parliaments, exclusion of placemen from the Commons, freedom of election; and an 'Independent Society' was founded to carry on the campaign. Early in 1772 another meeting voted instructions in favour of shorter parliaments, and discussion of the subject continued for

[1] James Day to Hardwicke, 11 Oct 1774, B.M. Add. MSS. 35680, fo. 355.

[2] *London Chronicle*, 11–13 Oct 1774.

[3] Lake Allen, *The History of Portsmouth* (1817) p. 107.

[4] *Middlesex Journal*, 8–11 Oct 1774, 4c.

several weeks in the local press.[1] Ringleaders of the movement included the future member, Henry Cruger, his father-in-law, Samuel Peach, and Thomas Mullett, a friend and correspondent of John Wilkes. Undoubtedly there was a nucleus of radical leaders of respectable commercial standing in Bristol in 1774, but continuous organised radical club activity has not been traced; and as the detailed study of the Bristol general election of 1774 makes plain, many personal vendettas and cross-currents of local politics were involved.[2] In the very full description of the Bristol political scene with which Richard Champion furnished Edmund Burke at the time of the election, there is no mention of a radical party connected with Cruger.[3] On the hustings Cruger upheld the contention that members should accept instructions from their constituents, and he called for shorter parliaments and a place bill (but not 'equal representation').[4] In government circles he was regarded as a 'hot Wilkite'.[5] Yet at Westminster, though voting for reform, Cruger, far from joining with the Wilkites, took pains to dissociate himself from them. 'I shall not', he told his brother-in-law, 'oppose government for *the sake* of opposition, but will join Lord North whenever I think him right. . . . You may rely upon it, I will connect myself with none of the violent parties, but endeavor to temper my fire with prudence. I go into the House with a good character, except in the opinion of Lord North, whom somebody, no friend of mine, has made believe I am all gunpowder. Before the month is out, he and the whole House shall be undeceived, if a moderate and a modest speech can effect it.'[6]

A somewhat similar situation existed at Newcastle. Here also the Middlesex election crisis of 1769 had evoked a lively response.

[1] *London Chronicle*, 11–14 Mar 1769; *Sarah Farley's Bristol Journal*, 11, 18 Mar 1769; *Bristol Gazette*, 17–27 Feb 1772. I am indebted to Dr P. T. Underdown for information about this episode.

[2] P. T. Underdown, 'Henry Cruger and Edmund Burke, Colleagues and Rivals at the Bristol Election of 1774', *William and Mary Quarterly*, XV (1958) 14–34.

[3] 1 Oct 1774, *Burke Correspondence*, III 42–7.

[4] Underdown, in *William and Mary Quarterly*, XV 24–5, 31.

[5] *The Correspondence of King George III*, III no. 1518.

[6] To Peter Van Schaack, 6 Dec 1774, Henry Cruger Van Schaack, *The Life of Peter Van Schaack* (New York, 1842) pp. 30–1.

A Constitutional Society had come into being, and was kept alive by a band of active reformers who embraced the Wilkite radical programme. Moreover, in June 1774 two new radical societies with similar programmes were founded, the 'Independents' and the 'Sydney Club'.[1] The clubs maintained by each of the incorporated companies in the town provided further centres for political agitation. In the early summer of 1774, well ahead of the general election, an active radical propaganda campaign was set on foot in the local press, and a group known as 'the select committee of free burgesses' set about finding candidates and making preparations in their support.[2] The contacts between these men and the radical agitator, George Grieve, an Alnwick solicitor who in June 1773 secured admission as a freeman of London, provided a direct link with the Wilkites. At the beginning of July two representatives of local landed families, Captain Constantine John Phipps, R.N., and Thomas Delaval, were found to stand in the 'patriot interest', and during the following weeks many of the younger burgesses in the incorporated companies entered into formal associations to support them. With faithful adherence to metropolitan example, a test was drawn up for parliamentary candidates, requiring them to pledge themselves to four points: reversal of the Middlesex election decision, shorter parliaments, reduction of the number of placemen in the Commons, and a more equal representation, to which was added a special complaint at the denial of the franchise to freeholders in the town. Phipps and Delaval ostentatiously gave their adherence to this programme on the hustings, while it was rejected by the other candidates, Sir Walter Blackett and Sir Matthew White Ridley, who stood on the corporation interest.[3]

[1] [John Sykes], *Local Records of Durham and Northumberland* (1824) pp. 122–3; *Newcastle Chronicle*, 4, 11 June 1774. Almost all the information about Newcastle politics in the following section is based on the issues of the *Newcastle Chronicle* of June to October 1774.

[2] The members of this committee were: Alexander Adams, Benjamin Brunton, William Adison, Henry Gibbons, Matthew Hunter, Matthew Laidler, Thomas Madison, Thomas Maude, William Smith and Nicholas Tyzack. The last-named chaired the meeting of freemen at which Phipps and Delaval were adopted as candidates.

[3] *A Complete Collection of the papers which appeared from the different parties in the contest for members for the county of Northumberland in the year 1774* (Newcastle, 1774) pp. 29–30.

Radical elements indeed existed at Newcastle. But other, more local issues dominated the election. The initial purpose of the 'select committee' had been to pursue the townsmen's quarrel with the corporation about the use of the Town Moor,[1] and the columns of the *Newcastle Chronicle* during the period of the election leave no doubt that the vendetta against the town magistrates was their main concern. Evidence for or against the sincerity of Delaval's professions is lacking. But Phipps's signature of the radical declaration meant nothing more to him than a contract of convenience. An able naval and political careerist, at this time he was raising his political stock by vehement opposition. Within three years he accepted first a parliamentary seat and then a government post from the head of the admiralty, the Earl of Sandwich, and his name does not appear in any of the lists of the minorities voting for parliamentary reform between 1780 and 1785.

The part played by George Grieve in the Northumberland county election provided a link there also, though a tenuous one, with the London radicals, and the election literature produced during the contest included a certain number of radical broadsheets.[2] Grieve took an active part in support of candidates standing against the Percy interest; but in this contest the issue was the local one of resistance to aristocratic predominance, and one report in the *Middlesex Journal* seems to indicate that the Wilkites felt they had been misled into sympathising with 'pretended patriots' in Northumberland.[3]

In greater London Wilkes and five of his friends had been returned; in popular constituencies outside London two more. At the end of the elections, including one or two other friends and sympathisers like Crisp Molineux, M.P. for King's Lynn, and Temple Luttrell, M.P. for Milbourne Port, he could count out of the 558 members of the House of Commons at the most about a dozen who were of his party, and whom he dubbed, with characteristic profanity, his 'twelve apostles'. The elections made it clear that as a political force radicalism had some significance in the metropolis, but elsewhere it counted for little. Apart from the

[1] Namier, *The Structure of Politics at the Accession of George III*, pp. 96–7.

[2] *The Contest* (Newcastle, 1774).

[3] *Middlesex Journal*, 8–11 Oct 1774, 4d.

instances cited above, it is difficult to find any indication of organised Wilkite groups in the provincial constituencies. Many of these constituencies were not contested, and in those that were the candidates appear to have had no connection with the movement.[1] The following year, in *An Address to the People of England, Scotland, and Ireland*, Mrs Macaulay fulminated against the indifference of the provinces to the radical cause:

> The electors of this kingdom . . . have shown themselves incorrigible, by recently abusing what the author of *The Patriot* calls a high dignity, and an important trust; and this after a ruinous experience of the effects of a former ill-placed confidence.
>
> It is not to be supposed, that either the beauty of justice, the interests of liberty, or the welfare of individuals as united to the common good, can have any avail with men, who, at this important crisis of British affairs, could reject the wise example set them by the city of London, in requiring a test from those they elected into the representative office; a test which, had it been generally taken, and religiously observed, would have dispersed the dark cloud which hangs over the empire, restored the former splendour of the nation, and given a renewed strength, vigour, and purity, to the British constitution.

In 1774 there was as yet no evidence of any widely felt desire for reform which might lead the House of Commons to consider seriously any change in the way in which it was constituted.

The plan of the Bill of Rights Society had failed. There were indeed insuperable obstacles. Parliamentary electorates, even if relatively free from aristocratic domination, could only be seed-plots for radical ideas if they had attained a certain level of political education and awareness. The gentry who dominated the county electorates fell within this category, but they had no social grievance and in general displayed a conservative dislike of the constitutional changes proposed in the radical programmes. In the towns outside greater London the voters, however numerous and independent they might sometimes be, were, except for small

[1] In the *Middlesex Journal* and other metropolitan newspapers connected with the Wilkite movement, there occur references to the good prospects of three or four of the candidates mentioned in the foregoing survey, but no others – a negative indication of the limited impact of the reformers' campaign.

educated minorities, indifferent to questions of national policy and were concerned only with local issues or with the personal benefits they might exact from competing candidates. Even the primary vehicle to create awareness among them was lacking. In the metropolis newspapers were beginning to be a stimulus to political thought and action, but outside it the circulation of journals printed in London or Westminster was very limited. There could not as yet be said to be a national press. There was nothing to overcome the traditional provincialism of the countryside. And so elections in eighteenth-century England were rarely fought over national political issues. Local questions and personal rivalries were of more account. Indeed, many seats were not contested at all. In 1774 there were election contests in eleven only of the forty English counties and in 64 of the 203 city and borough constituencies.[1] Members of the Society misjudged the extent of support in the country for their convictions. It seems also that they misjudged conditions. Based in London, they fell, perhaps, into the error of thinking conditions in the provinces to be less unlike those in the metropolis than in fact they were.

[1] Scottish and Welsh constituencies are left out of account, as they were not affected by the reform movement at this time.

TWELVE

*The Yorkshire Association, 1780–4: A Study in Political Organisation**

THE Yorkshire Association of the early 1780s marked the first effective extension of modern political radicalism in Great Britain from the metropolitan region into the provinces. During what may for convenience be described as the first – the Wilkite – phase of British radicalism, in the early 1770s, the focus of the radical movement had lain in and around London. Attempts to stir up the country provoked only a brief response in a very few constituencies. There was little trace anywhere of sustained radical activity.[1] Provincial apathy at the general election of 1774 caused acute disappointment to the metropolitan radicals.[2] Six years later the situation had changed remarkably, and from 1780 till 1784 politics in Yorkshire were dominated, and in the rest of England considerably affected, by that remarkable political phenomenon, the Yorkshire Association. Starting in December 1779, an extraordinary, widespread upsurge of discontent among the members of the 'upper class' in the county, provoked by the North ministry's inept handling of the American crisis, first produced the well-supported petition of 1780 for economical reform, and was then channelled and organised into an instrument of agitation for reform of the parliamentary system. The association proper came into being between its adoption at a county meeting on 28 March 1780 and the middle of the following August, when the parchment copies which had been circulated for signature were gathered in and the roll of some 5,800 names was compiled from them.[3] An impressive proportion of the gentry, clergy and freeholders of the

* This originally appeared in *Historical Journal* III (1960) 144–61.

[1] Lucy S. Sutherland, *The City of London and the Opposition to Government, 1768–1774* (1959) *passim*.

[2] Catherine Macaulay, *An Address to the People of England, Scotland, and Ireland . . .* (1775) pp. 3–4.

[3] The Roll of the Association, York City Library.

county, by the act of signature, pledged themselves to work for parliamentary reform by legal and constitutional means; signified their assent to the threefold programme, economical reform, triennial parliaments and the addition of a hundred county representatives to the House of Commons; and undertook in particular to vote only for such parliamentary candidates as would support these propositions. The ultimate aim of these reformers was a 'free parliament'. They believed ministerial control over the House of Commons to be excessive. Of the three heads of reformation which they adopted, economical reform was designed to reduce, by abolition of government posts and sinecures, the number of members whose employments led them to adopt an 'administration' point of view; increased county representation to introduce a counterbalance of independent members reflecting general opinion in the provinces; and shorter parliaments to make members more responsive to the views of their constituents. Ovei the whole period, including the early months before the association had formally come into being, the movement had a considerable record of achievement. Within Yorkshire two petitions were promoted, the association was created (no mean feat in itself), and at two general elections a potentially strong opposition to its approved candidates was defeated without resort to a poll. Beyond the borders of the county a great deal of effort was poured forth (most of it to no avail) in the endeavour to promote the cause of reform on a national scale.

This paper is concerned mainly with the form taken by the association movement in Yorkshire, with the men who were involved in it, and with the way in which they went about their business. It is based partly upon a collection of some eight hundred documents very recently discovered among the York City archives.[1] Very few of these papers have appeared in print. They seem to have been left aside as unimportant by Christopher Wyvill, the leader of the movement, when he was preparing for publication his edition of the correspondence relating to the association.[2] It is not

[1] York City Library MSS., M. 25 and M. 32. I am grateful to the York City Council for permission to make use of this material, and to the librarian and staff of the York City Library for their helpfulness when I was reading this and other material in their custody.

[2] C. Wyvill, *Political Papers, chiefly respecting the Attempt of the County of York and other Considerable Districts . . . to effect a Reformation of the Parliament of Great Britain*, 6 vols (1794–1808).

known how they came to be separated from his main collection. It may be that they had been, and were left, in the hands of the clerk of the association, William Gray. The collection includes the original parchment rolls of the association. Other documents illustrate particularly the work of the active nucleus of the reformers in collecting signatures to petitions, and to the association, and the preoccupation of Wyvill with press publicity and propaganda. With the help of this material it has been possible to illustrate some aspects of organisation and method within the Yorkshire Association not discussed by the Master of Peterhouse in his published work touching on this subject.[1]

By 1780 a good deal had been written and widely circulated in print regarding associations to secure reform;[2] but in the sphere of practical application, it was to Wyvill that the association movement in Yorkshire owed its inception and its inspiration.[3] The correspondence now in York City Library confirms the evidence in his published papers of the central part he played in the direction of its affairs. Wyvill's family background linked him with the gentry and with the closely allied class of professional government servants. His father, minor scion of a Yorkshire gentry family, had been a senior excise official at Edinburgh. His maternal grandfather, William Clifton, a member of a Nottinghamshire landed family, was for many years solicitor to the Scottish board of excise. Early life in the stimulating *milieu* of Edinburgh may have helped to foster the restless, tireless energy he displayed and his critical attitude to the established order. At Queens' College, Cambridge, he was exposed to broadening and liberal influences: the recent election to the presidency of Robert Plumptre, progressive and broad-minded, 'a very enlightened man',[4] presumably reflected the general spirit of the fellows. Wyvill's ordination in 1763, before he had taken his degree, and his immediate establishment in a good living as rector of Black Notley in Essex, have the appearance of a family arrangement for him rather than a call to a vocation; and, indeed,

[1] Butterfield, *George III, Lord North, and the People*; 'The Yorkshire Association and the Crisis of 1779–80', *Transactions of the Royal Historical Society*, 4th series, XXIX 69–91.

[2] Butterfield, *George III, Lord North, and the People*, pp. 259–68.

[3] Wyvill, *Political Papers*, I 49–50; III 159, 181–2.

[4] D. A. Winstanley, *Unreformed Cambridge* (Cambridge, 1935) p. 300.

he showed little interest in his clerical duties, leaving them entirely to a curate's care. More congenial were the pursuits of a country gentleman and politician, opened to him by his marriage in 1773 to his cousin, Elizabeth Wyvill, heiress of the elder branch of the family, and by her inheritance the next year of the Constable Burton estates. With a rent roll, according to one estimate, of some £4,000 a year,[1] Wyvill could now claim standing among the leading gentry of the North Riding.

In 1772 Wyvill acted with the small but influential group of Church of England clergy who approached parliament by the so-called Feathers Tavern Petition, seeking abolition of the clerical obligation to subscribe to the Thirty-nine Articles. His participation may have reflected the continuing liberal influences of Cambridge, for the petition was strongly supported by members of the university, including the president and every fellow of Queens'.[2] Thus early he gained notoriety, at least in Yorkshire.[3] After 1779 his leadership of the association movement made him for some time a national figure. Responsive to the new ideas about constitutional reform which were gaining ground among the discontented politicians of the metropolis, and which were spread by the writings of a small but influential intelligentsia, he adapted and shaped them with an assurance and firmness of purpose which gave a characteristic stamp to the Yorkshire movement. In energy and in fertility of resource he was a host in himself. To his combination of ardour and caution, his grasp of the practical, his dexterity in argument and supple firmness in negotiation, his understanding of the importance of propaganda (of which more below), was due much of the limited success of the reformers. The story of the association is very largely the story of Wyvill's activities. There were, however, certain leading men in the county whom he had to carry with him, and one or two at least whose advice he valued. At the beginning he leaned heavily on the support and encouragement of William Chaloner of Gisborough, another leading landowner of the North Riding who, as chairman, gave dignity to public meetings of the freeholders. Members of the family of

[1] *Leeds Intelligencer*, 4 Apr 1780.

[2] N. Sykes, *Church and State in England in the Eighteenth Century* (Cambridge, 1934) p. 381; Winstanley, *Unreformed Cambridge*, p. 300.

[3] *Leeds Intelligencer*, 4 Apr 1780.

Croft of Stillington were active supporters who provided a line of contact with the Marquis of Rockingham, the leader of the nobility in Yorkshire. William Mason, the poet and biographer of Gray, and Samuel Tooker of Moorgate, were other zealous partisans of the association on whom he later largely depended for help and counsel.

Wyvill and the few enthusiastic friends who first encouraged him would have achieved little but for the wide response to their initiative from Yorkshiremen of similar social rank, many of whom took at least some effective, active part in support of reform through the county committee, later the committee of association. As Professor Butterfield has observed, there is 'clear evidence' that at the outset 'there was a higher class of landowner . . . well-educated, and skilled directors of an agitation – who consciously gave the lead to a mass of smaller freeholders, summoning them to an interest in politics.'[1] In answer to Wyvill's initial circulars, over two hundred men authorised the attachment of their names to the public advertisement summoning the county meeting of 30 December 1779 at which the movement was launched. Those to whom Wyvill sent circulars he regarded as the gentry and leading men of the county, 'gentlemen of weight and character' as he described them in more than one letter about this time.[2] In May 1780 a Leeds businessman, Gamaliel Lloyd, remarked that one of the considerations which particularly recommended the association among his friends was that it had been promoted 'by so many gentlemen of large independent fortunes, who from education and other circumstances, have had much better opportunities of being rightly informed in politics than ourselves'.[3] A paragraph inserted, almost certainly by Wyvill, in the *York Chronicle* of 9 November 1781 reported, for the benefit of readers outside Yorkshire, the circumstance, already known to Yorkshiremen, that the sixty-two members who had attended the last meeting of the committee of association were together worth little less than £100,000 per annum. Those who from 1780 onwards carried the main burden of the association's activities were in many cases already prominent in the public life of the county. They served on the commission of the peace, took their turns as sheriff, acted on the committees of

[1] *Transactions of the Royal Historical Society*, XXIX 79.

[2] Wyvill, *Political Papers*, III 115–16, 150–1.

[3] Ibid., 260.

hospital and charity trusts, of the Yorkshire Agricultural Society, and other such bodies. When the grand jury of nineteen was empanelled for the opening of the assizes at York in March 1781, there were only eight of its members who appear to have played no part in the association between 1780 and 1783, and six of the jurors were then members of the committee. As the movement progressed, more and more of those engaged in industry and commerce, men who, like Gamaliel Lloyd, stood somewhere on the fringe of political life, were drawn, at least for a time, into the main current of political activity. In eighteenth-century parlance, as used for instance twenty years before by William Beckford of London, these landed and commercial men were the leading elements of the 'middling people' of the county,[1] distinct on the one hand from the thin upper crust of the aristocracy, and on the other from the mass of workers in field, cottage and factory.

Throughout the years 1780–4 the movement launched by Wyvill continued to command a solid core of support among these 'middling people' in Yorkshire. About half the two hundred or so individuals who in December 1779 had given their approval to Wyvill's plan for a county meeting continued to be active promoters of the association and the reform petitions; and fifty or so others drawn in during these years, as active canvassers or as members of the committee of association, belonged to the same stratum of county society. At the end of 1783 the committee numbered rather over 150.[2] Not all these members were active participants. The main burden of the committee's work was carried by about fifty members. But there were another forty or so who, although their attendances were less frequent, did yeoman service in gathering signatures for the association and for the petitions. Even the remaining sixty or so members of the committee were at least sufficiently interested in the cause of reform to have accepted nomination and to have placed themselves under obligation to subscribe a pound or two each year towards its expenses. And outside the committee there were at least another twenty or so country gentlemen and professional men who were

[1] Cited in Lucy S. Sutherland, 'The City of London in Eighteenth-century Politics', in *Essays Presented to Sir Lewis Namier*, ed. R. Pares and A. J. P. Taylor (1956) p. 66.

[2] Wyvill, *Political Papers*, II 322–4.

prepared to help in canvassing and forwarding the aims of the association.[1] Only much detailed research would give a really clear idea exactly what proportion this active body of reformers bore to the whole group of their class in Yorkshire. There seems enough evidence to conclude that it was substantial and influential. When opponents of the movement began to take its measure at the end of 1779, although an opinion was expressed that outright opposition by a small, determined group of leading men (twenty or so were thought of) might check its progress by clever argument and moral example, there does not seem to have been any idea that weight of numbers could be employed to stop it;[2] and Yorkshire was not one of the counties where, later, opponents of the petitions for economical reform thought it worth while to organise a counter-address. The ability of the reformers in 1783 to secure over ten thousand signatures for the petition for parliamentary reform, despite the disapproval of most of the leaders of the Rockingham party as well as of the former connections of North's ministry, was a most remarkable evidence of their strength in the county.

By long-established custom the community of an English shire stated views on matters of particular political concern at a county meeting, a gathering of the gentry and yeomen in numbers sufficient to be regarded as genuinely representative of county opinion. This opinion would be stated by resolution, followed sometimes by petition, protestation, or address to the throne. During the period of the Yorkshire Association Wyvill and his friends accordingly looked to county meetings as the ultimate spring of authority for

[1] The rolls of the petitions of 1780 and 1783 in the York City Library contain lists of the canvassers and their returns from each district. That for 1783 was printed by Wyvill (*Political Papers*, II 249–51). There were at least a few omissions, as one or two more names can be added from the surviving correspondence. The names of the leading canvassers for the association itself during the spring and summer of 1780 are recorded on the parchment returns of signatures (York City Library MSS., M. 32). The known canvassers numbered in January 1780 sixty-seven, in the spring and summer fifty-six, and in January 1783 eighty-five. A few of the most active members of the committee did not engage in canvassing. These men were mostly resident in York and presumably lacked the necessary local 'interest' and contacts.

[2] Alexander Wedderburn to William Eden, n.d. [mid-Dec 1779], John Robinson to Eden, 23 Dec 1779 (B.M. Add. MSS. 34416, fos. 510, 489).

their activities. From the six hundred or so nobility, gentry, clergy and yeomen who assembled at York on 30 December 1779 came approval for the petition for economical reform; and by its vote was established the county committee, with a membership of sixty-one named persons, 'to carry on the necessary correspondence' for promoting the petition and to engage in 'such other measures' as might 'conduce to restore the freedom of parliament'. When the committee and its leaders, in accordance with the resolutions of 30 December, had thrashed out the project of a county association, this in turn was submitted, on 28 March 1780, to the approval of another county meeting. Yet another attended by at least three hundred people was convened on 19 December 1782 to adopt formally the petition for parliamentary reform which the committee of association had prepared.[1]

The main formal organisation of the reform movement was provided by the committee, originally the county committee of 30 December 1779, later the same members confirmed in office, with some additions, as the committee of association on 28 March 1780. Originally sixty-one in number, on 28 March the committee was increased by an undisclosed number to somewhere between seventy and eighty.[2] At the same time it was given powers to co-opt, which it used with some freedom: between the end of March and the end of August over forty members were co-opted, a fair number of them extremely active supporters, either as committee men or as canvassers for the association. Recruitment at this stage seems to have been mainly with a view to drawing as many willing helpers as possible into the organisation. Later on Wyvill, at any rate, regarded the enrolment of more members as a means of impressing the government with the strength of reformist feeling in the county.[3] The committee discussed, amended and approved plans of action before they were put into effect. Attendance as measured only by the more important meetings was fairly high, around fifty or sixty.

For so large a body, including men from all over the county, and

[1] Wyvill, *Political Papers*, I 4–6, 148; II 38–9; *Leeds Intelligencer*, 31 Dec 1782.

[2] Wyvill, *Political Papers*, II 148.

[3] Wyvill to William Gray, 14 Sept 1781, encl., York City Library MSS., M. 25. All documents cited below without further reference are in this collection.

with a quorum of twenty-one, frequent meetings were out of the question. It proved necessary almost immediately, in January 1780, to establish a small sub-committee for routine business. This consisted of such committee members as lived in or near York and, after March 1780, any other members who might happen to be there from time to time. Its terms of reference were limited to sending formal acknowledgements and preparing answers to correspondence, and, when the occasion required, looking after canvassing.[1] At times small *ad hoc* subcommittees were appointed to discharge particular limited tasks.[2]

One other element of organisation helped to give coherence and effectiveness to the activities of the association. Among the first steps taken by the county committee in January 1780 was the appointment of a salaried clerk. The committee contracted for this service with the firm of Graves and Gray, solicitors of York, and it was in this way that the William Gray who makes an occasional fleeting appearance in Wyvill's printed correspondence came to be intimately associated with the activities of the Yorkshire reformers. Gray proved a most able, diligent, and whole-hearted servant. The son of a minor customs official at Hull, he had served his articles with one of Yorkshire's well-known political attorneys, William Iveson of Hedon, and in 1772 had become assistant to Graves at York at the modest stipend of £60 per annum. The firm then was, and for some time continued to be, in low water. Graves was elderly and inactive. In 1774 Gray hesitated before accepting a partnership, suspecting that his share might bring him less than his salary as assistant. The firm suffered further embarrassments during the following years through a rascally nephew of Graves, who in 1782 finally absconded with most of his uncle's assets. In such circumstances even the unusual line of business offered by the committee would be acceptable. But it was not merely this situation which brought Gray into the service of the reform movement. Wyvill and his friends were good judges of their man. Gray was by temperament an idealist and a reformer. The connections he began to form from 1780 onwards with such leading Yorkshire personalities as Wyvill, Henry Duncombe, Wilberforce and Sir

[1] Wyvill, *Political Papers*, I 50–1, 52–6, 61–2.

[2] E.g. in August 1780 a subcommittee was set up to receive and report upon the enrolment of members of the association (ibid., I 262).

Robert D'Arcy Hildyard soon opened to him ample opportunities for profit and advancement in the county, but he never coveted a great fortune. From an early date he devoted at least a twentieth, and before long a tenth, of his income to charity, he became a minor associate of Wilberforce in the promotion of the evangelical movement in Yorkshire, and he was a supporter of good causes in the county throughout his life. On receiving in 1790 the post of distributor of stamps in the West Riding, he protested that the emolument ought to be reduced. In later days he was so determined not to profit unduly from the government service that in 1815 and 1816 he anonymously returned over £2,000 to the treasury as conscience money.[1] Hard-working, conscientious and devoted, he was in every respect well fitted for the role now offered him, and he laboured diligently in the reformers' cause. The unprinted correspondence of the association, at the same time as it stresses further the importance of Wyvill's leadership shows that Gray played no less essential a part as its chief executive officer, receiving instructions from the committee, the business subcommittee and from Wyvill himself, translating them into action, disseminating propaganda according to Wyvill's direction, maintaining constant contact with the printers of the York newspapers, whose facilities were continually in demand, and helping to set in motion the mass of mainly voluntary effort by means of which support for the association and for the county petitions was obtained. In 1780 and in 1784 he took an equally important role in the organisation of the association's successful county election campaigns. Wyvill's many unprinted letters to Gray give ample evidence of his reliance upon him. In June 1784 Wyvill wrote to him: 'I am with great esteem for your firm and conscientious adherence . . . and the great assistance I have all along had from your industry and exactness in executing the office you had undertaking [*sic*].' Six years later, when Gray was offered the distributorship of stamps, Wyvill stood as one of his sureties.

During the years 1780–3 the Yorkshire committee organised three mass demonstrations of opinion in the county: the petition of 1780 for economical reform, the association itself, and the petition for parliamentary reform of 1783. County petitions and addresses

[1] Almyra Gray, *Papers and Diaries of a York Family, 1764–1839* (1923), especially pp. 30–7.

might be raised in either of two ways. One – the least troublesome – was to get a well-attended county meeting, secure the signatures of as many as possible of the freeholders who were present, and represent this as the act of the county. The later petitions for parliamentary reform submitted from Yorkshire in 1784 and 1785 were of this kind. But an instrument signed in this fashion was open to the objection that it was the work of merely a few enthusiasts, not really representative of county opinion; and in preparing the petitions of 1780 and 1783 Wyvill and his associates set out to secure the expressed views, by signature, of as many as possible of the electors in the county. The enrolment of members of the association imposed a labour of a similar nature. In addition the associators carried out successful preliminary campaigns for two general elections. All these enterprises presented various problems of method, and in the course of surmounting them the reformers built up an organisation of increasing scope and efficiency.

Canvassing and collection of signatures was carried out mainly by the voluntary efforts of enthusiastic supporters. The unprinted correspondence of the association contains more than one suggestion for the employment of paid agents,[1] but resort to this expedient remained exceptional. On 28 January 1783 William Gray told Pemberton Milnes: 'The circulation of duplicates of the petition for signature is, in general, by means of gentlemen friendly to it, free of expence to the committee'; though in his view the committee would agree to the payment of agents where this was thought necessary. In the manuscript roll of the 1783 petition there is only one record of the use of agents, though others were employed by individual associators.[2] To cover the whole county by voluntary assistance was difficult, though with experience, and with a growing body of support, considerable improvement was achieved after the spring of 1780. In December 1779 the county committee made no formal arrangement about the first petition beyond the allocation of so many parchments to each riding.[3] The assignment of personal responsibility for forwarding the collection of signatures may in part have been arranged informally, before

[1] William Baines to Gray, 23 Jan, James Stovin to Gray, 28 Jan 1780, Pemberton Milnes to Gray, 26 Jan 1783.

[2] Ibid.; Wyvill, *Political Papers*, II 250.

[3] Wyvill, *Political Papers*, I 51.

committee members dispersed. Otherwise it depended upon requests sent in the committee's name to likely individuals. This method of allocation was bound to be haphazard, some districts were left ill-served through lack of helpers, and in two cases at least parchments were sent to people who were away from home or unwilling to act.[1] Even when these matters were reported, further delay in providing remedies arose from the lack, until 21 January, of a business subcommittee able to meet in frequent session. The newly appointed clerk of the committee had not then the standing, which he acquired later, to take the initiative. Three months later, when the association came be to circulated for signature, the business subcommittee was detailed to take such measures as were necessary.[2] But there were still complaints about lack of assistance, especially in the industrial districts of the West Riding. 'No gentleman in the neighbourhood of Halifax has undertaken a parchment except Mr Buck', John Milnes reported to Gray on 1 June; and he also noted the difficulties he faced working alone in the Wakefield area: 'Had I more time don't doubt getting a great majority of the freeholders in this part, but in this manufacturing country the houses lie wide from each other so makes it very tedious.' About six weeks later, on 10 July, he reported: 'Many and indeed the greater part of my neighbours are very sanguine in the cause but will not put themselves out of the way to forward the signing. . . . I must acknowledge myself obliged to Mr Richard Milnes who went with me twice upon this business, but now that I am going from home I fear not one of the gentlemen will give themselves the pains they ought to do.' On this occasion again, in one or two instances, the committee placed reliance upon individuals who failed, for lack of wish or will, to give proper assistance.[3]

At the end of 1782, when the committee came to launch the second petition, the response at the county meeting gave it justifiable hopes of enlarging the little army of canvassers. It was resolved 'that engrossed copies of the petition be sent to the gentlemen who circulated the former county petition, and that these

[1] Richard Wilson to the committee, 6 Jan 1780; Wyvill, *Political Papers*, I 52, 53–4, 70; James Stovin to Graves and Gray, 19 Jan 1780.

[2] Wyvill, *Political Papers*, I 167.

[3] Thomas Weddell to Gray, 27 July, Sir James Ibbetson to Gray, 30 July 1780.

gentlemen be requested to apply particularly to any other gentlemen, who are friendly to the measure, for their assistance, in tendering the petition to the freeholders in their respective neighbourhoods for their signatures'.[1] Despite the continued opposition from the high nobility of the county, many people gave support to the petition who had hitherto stood aloof from the reformers,[2] and more than twenty new canvassers were drawn into service. There were still gaps. Complaints came in about neglect in Holderness and, once more, about the difficulty of covering the clothing districts round Wakefield.[3] In the north, so Sheldon Cradock of Hartforth reported to Gray on 5 January: 'It is between thirty and forty miles along the Tees banks from this place into Mr Chaloner's neighbourhood, and not one active friend the whole way, rather the contrary, nor does Mr Cradock hear of a petition in circulation.' The action taken in this case is not known, but other instances show that the committee had by this time achieved an added effectiveness through the expertise acquired by its clerk, William Gray, and his willingness to shoulder responsibility. When John Milnes warned Gray on 8 January that there was no associator in charge of the districts round Keighley and Bradford, where adverse Cavendish influence would be encountered, and suggested the names of two possible helpers, Gray wrote to both next day.[4] On receipt of a letter from Pemberton Milnes stressing the need to employ paid agents in the Wakefield area, he did not hesitate an instant: 'As there will not be a sub-committee meeting of some days, and the time is short, I take the earliest opportunity of answering.' Normal practice, he explained, was to depend on voluntary canvassers: 'Yet where the employment of agents cannot be dispensed with, I have no doubt but the committee would wish it without regarding the expence. If therefore you would have the goodness to procure such assistance as you may think necessary of I will reimburse the expence out of the first committee money that comes to my hands.'[5]

[1] Wyvill, *Political Papers*, II 235.

[2] *York Chronicle*, 27 Dec 1782; William Chaloner to Gray, 5 Jan 1783.

[3] William Battle to Gray, 8 Jan, Pemberton Milnes to Gray, 26 Jan 1783.

[4] Gray's endorsement on Milnes's letter.

[5] Gray to Milnes, 28 Jan 1783, draft on the blank sheet of Milnes's letter of 26 Jan.

Members of the county committee did not realise at first how much personal effort would be necessary to secure really effective subscription to petitions or to the association. The easiest way to get signatures, but also quite the most unsatisfactory, was to lodge duplicates in various alehouses or other places of resort in each parish or township and advertise this arrangement for the information of the freeholders. Those who took responsibility for the first petition in 1780 soon became aware that this method was little better than useless, and that more active steps to secure signatures would have to be taken. On 26 January Pemberton Milnes reported from Leeds: 'I am obliged to send a person with it from from house to house, not the least regard was paid to the printed advertisement of its laying at such and such places for signing, I have since also sent persons with it into all the villages many miles round this neighbourhood.' And about the same time William Baines (who eventually collected 331 signatures) reported from the Skipton district: 'I have sent a person round the country to the distance of near about 20 miles every way, who has been out day and night since I sent off the petition from York, and I shall take the liberty to recommend the same practice in every part of the county; being sensible that had I suffered it to lie at the public house, for such people only as might chuse to come in and sign it, I would not at this day have got above 30 or 40 names to it.' 'I am now well satisfied', James Stovin wrote on 28 January to William Chaloner, 'that the mode of lodging it on particular days at the market towns will not do, and that the only way to have it well filled, is to tender it to every freeholder at his own house, and I hope the committee will immediately take proper measures for this purpose.' The expense, he thought, would not be very great, and a subscription might be raised to meet it. One or two at least of the canvassers felt that the petition would have been much more successful if this circumstance had been realised and acted upon in time.[1] The measure of success with the association during the spring and summer, and still more with the second petition in 1783, was due at least in part to the more general adoption of this practice.

What of the relations between canvassers and subscribers? On at least one occasion during the canvassing of the first petition the assertion was openly made that the lesser freeholders were being

[1] Richard Wilson to Graves and Gray, 3 Feb 1780.

dragooned into signing by their social superiors. The *York Chronicle* of 4 February and the *Leeds Intelligencer* of the eighth both carried the report that one gentleman active in promoting the petition had given all his tenants possessing forty-shilling freeholds orders to sign. 'May it not be fairly inferred from this one instance', was the comment, 'that similar methods are used by most of the leaders of opposition? . . . With what face can they condemn ministerial influence, when they are acting the same part in respect to their own dependents?' Similarly, the *Leeds Intelligencer* of 14 January 1783 reported that leading merchants of the town were putting pressure upon men dependent upon them to sign the petition for parliamentary reform. That such individual cases occurred is not unlikely. That the general inference should be drawn is much less certain. There are scattered pieces of evidence throughout the correspondence of the Yorkshire association which indicate an extremely scrupulous attitude on this point among its members. Gamaliel Lloyd of Leeds, writing on 17 April 1780 to the committee about the circulation of duplicates of the association, observed:

> I must own . . . I do not like to see men subscribe to any opinions that they either do not understand, or of the truth of which they are not thoroughly convinced: now I found that if I read the association paper half a dozen times over to some of them they were no wiser than at the first; to obviate this inconvenience I have taken with me a person that speaks the Leeds dialect in great perfection and who in a concise and intelligible manner explained the nature of the three propositions, so that I trust that those who sign the duplicate I hand about, do it from conviction, and not merely because their neighbours have signed it before them.

On 28 July Gray was informed by William Raines of Wyton:

> When Sir Robert Hildyard came down from London he signed the association himself, but desired me not to press any of the freeholders to sign, as he thought if they were not inclined to do it voluntarily we were better without their names. I have followed his instructions and those whose signatures are annexed were none of them pressed but only asked if they chose to sign, there are many others who desired to consider of it which I have not had their answers.

Quite apart from the moral obligation which the reformers thus recognised, they soon came to realise that it was absolutely necessary to give full explanations of their objects if they were to get the best results on their canvass – and unlimited patience was essential. On 25 January 1780 John Matthews reported to the committee from Whitby: 'The people in general in this neighbourhood were very averse to it [the petition] at the first, but by degrees their prejudices subside, and we hope several will sign it.' '[I] wish a little more time had been allowed me, as the freeholders have signed with greater spirit since the association business was explained', St Andrew Ward wrote to Gray on 2 February.[1] During the next phase of the reformers' activities, in some places, if not in all, application for signatures to the association was preceded by the circulation of printed copies of it for the information of the freeholders. 'I am waiting', Sir Robert Hildyard told Gray on 2 April, 'for some of the printed copies of the association etc. that I may disperse them in the country before I can get any hands to the parchment.' Three years later, in a letter reporting progress with the petition of 1783 at Beverley, John Courtney declared: 'Many people would not have signed had we not explained the nature of the petition to them, which shows the usefulness of *tendering* it.'

Coercion was thus eschewed by the reformers, and it was in any case often out of the question. They sought to enrol support based upon conviction. In the process the influence and prestige of social superiority was bound, of course, to have some effect. This sort of influence the reformers did not think improper. They were prepared to exercise such leadership as lay naturally with them in virtue of their position in county society. When the association was launched the advisability of making public the names of the gentry who had signed it at the adoption meeting at York was strongly urged upon Wyvill by one of his well-wishers: 'Such an example would greatly encourage the inferior freeholders and even others who were not at the meeting yesterday.' And one of his chief colleagues on the committee hoped that the names of all the committee would appear on the printed copies of the association which were being circulated for information, as this would 'give a sanction

[1] The point alluded to in Ward's letter is explained on p. 280 below.

to the cause in the county'.[1] The associators also realised, or soon discovered, that during canvassing local class relationships had to be taken into account. The situation varied greatly from district to district. In some parts of the county the attitude taken up by the local squires was paramount. 'I agree with you', William Raines wrote to Gray, discussing the circulation of the petition of 1783, 'that if it was made known amongst the Holderness freeholders of Mr Constable's intention of signing the petition it would have great weight to induce them to sign it. When I return home [I] will have a little conversation with Mr Raines of Burton and if I find it will not be disagreeable to Mr Constable to communicate his intention of signing the petition will endeavour to make it known to them as much as in my power.'[2] Pocklington, the Reverend John Bourne reported, was not worth canvassing, unless the approval of the Anderson family were obtained: 'I have written to Lady Anderson, to desire she will allow her youngest son to meet me there. . . . Under the influence of that name, I trust we may be able to do something.' With the aid of a letter from one of the Andersons he was able to secure about a dozen signatures.[3] Canvassers who moved into districts not their own without some local recommendation might find their efforts entirely in vain. In January 1780 James Stovin reported to Gray: 'Mr P[richard] had it [the petition] at Howden last Saturday and Selby on Monday and returned with nine more names, but not one from Howden. . . . Why he was not more successful I cannot tell – only I have since been told, that he was a stranger at Howden, and was so warm on the subject, that nobody would come near him.'[4]

But not all the canvassers faced this sort of situation. Scarborough, for instance, was a case peculiar to itself, in that the animosities between the corporation and the leading gentry of the neighbourhood meant that applications to the latter might do more harm than good.[5] In parts of the West Riding the gentry had little influence, or such as they had needed backing by the interest of

[1] Francis Peirson to Wyvill, 29 Mar, Sir Robert Hildyard to Gray, 2 Apr 1780.

[2] 9 Jan 1783.

[3] To Gray, 21 Jan, 2 Feb 1783.

[4] 19 Jan 1780.

[5] Col Barnard Foord to William Withers, 24 Jan 1783.

the leading clothiers; and in some districts it was the clothiers alone who had the interest. In the Skipton district the gentry on the whole disapproved of the petition for economical reform. Nevertheless, William Baines informed the committee, 'the middling branch of freeholders are so little influenced by the refusals of their superiors, that I have got about two hundred and fifty names.'[1] In the Huddersfield area John Milnes thought a letter of support from Sir John Ramsden would be desirable; with that, he concluded, 'as we purchase at least one half of the white cloths, don't doubt getting all of them to a man'. But round Wakefield he declared there were no gentry with whom to reckon: 'The freeholders in the district of Morley and Agbridge are chiefly clothiers or in the stuff way of business, so that none but merchants have much interest in that country.'[2] The approach of the associators had to be varied according to the characteristics of each district. There was no simple formula to success.

The progress of the associating movement inevitably depended to some extent upon these influences of a traditional kind. But Wyvill placed great reliance on reasoned argument aimed at a wide public: in this, perhaps, more than in anything, the movement took shape and character from his hand. He believed that the campaign for reform must and would stand by its own merits. Men's minds and hearts must and would be won by the rational nature of the appeal made by the association. Counter-argument was welcome, for the resulting debate, whether in speech or on paper, could not fail to bring out the advantages of reform. It was as part of his deliberate policy that in 1780 and in 1782 long accounts of the discussions at the county meetings, with reports of speeches on both sides of the question, were inserted in the local press. In November 1782 Blanchard, the printer of the *York Chronicle*, referred to Gray a contribution criticising the association, which he was ready to reject if Wyvill desired. Gray in turn consulted Wyvill. On 28 November Wyvill replied that he felt much obliged to Blanchard; but 'you may assure him, I have not so poor an opinion of the solidity of the ground we have taken to have the smallest desire to stop any publication against it; neither, indeed, should I think it right; unless it were some piece containing gross

[1] 23 Jan 1780.
[2] To Gray, n.d. [rec. 10 Apr] and 10 July 1780.

abuse, or calumny, evidently injurious to the character of the association or individuals.' With this answer he forwarded a paragraph to be printed in refutation of the hostile argument. Attacks upon himself, provided they were not scurrilous, he treated with the same bland equanimity. 'I am obliged to Mr Blanchard for his attention to me personally', he wrote to Gray on 7 January 1785, in a similar connection, 'but I do not desire any publication in which my character may be treated freely or even harshly to be suppressed. I have no manner of objection to the thing in question appearing in the next paper.'

His awareness of the importance of the press was outstanding. Two newspapers were being published in York during this period. The *York Courant*, owned by Mrs Ann Ward, and managed and printed for her by D. A. Russell, tended to eschew politics. On the whole it accepted less matter about the Yorkshire Association than the *York Chronicle*, owned and produced by W. Blanchard and Co. Wyvill's references to the *York Chronicle* show that he regarded it as the more important mouthpiece for the reformers;[1] and from Blanchard's offers to suppress material hostile to them it would appear that the publicity he gave them was due not merely to business considerations but to genuine political sympathy. These two journals were the mainstay of Wyvill's press campaigns, though he was always ready to plant material elsewhere if the occasion demanded. He had insertions placed in the *Leeds Mercury* through the associators in that town[2] – the other Leeds paper, the *Leeds Intelligencer*, was blatantly hostile and rarely accepted advertisements or favourable comment – and at times in the Newcastle *Hue and Cry*.[3] On a few occasions at least he made use of the *London Courant* and one or two other metropolitan journals which favoured the reformers.[4]

From the start Wyvill used the press as an instrument of persuasion and propaganda. Professor Butterfield long ago drew attention to the fact that, at the end of 1779, 'the local newspapers which in the preceding months had given no evidence of general hardship in the country or particular grievances in Yorkshire, now

[1] Wyvill to Gray, 6, 12 Mar, and n.d. [June] 1783.
[2] Wyvill to Gray, 6 Dec 1783, 13 Dec 1784.
[3] Wyvill to Gray, 12, 14, 19, 24 Nov 1782, 13 Dec 1784, 7 Jan 1785.
[4] Wyvill to Gray, 30 Oct. 1781, 10 Jan 1783, 13 Feb 1785.

began to print paragraphs illustrating the extravagance of the government, the decline of commerce, and the decay of the landed interest.' Paragraphs and anonymous letters were contributed to stimulate interest in the petitioning movement.[1] A great part of this material almost certainly came from Wyvill himself. Once or twice his hand was openly seen. For instance, early in 1780, when the experience of canvassers circulating the first Yorkshire petition had shown the need to state publicly that nothing illegal was intended by the plan of association mentioned at the county meeting of 30 December,[2] and a paragraph had been inserted in the *York Chronicle* for this purpose,[3] a published exchange of letters between Wyvill and Dr A. Hunter was designed to provide repetitions of the explanation and so ensure as wide a circulation for it as possible. The public was assured that the action contemplated by the reformers would be 'conformable to law and the constitution', and that the object of the proposed association was simply to withhold support at future elections from parliamentary candidates who declined promising to promote the reforms requested in the petition for economical reform.[4] Other pro-reform material in the York press in these early months of the movement cannot be traced directly to Wyvill, but from the numerous later instances when this can be done it may justifiably be inferred that he provided most of it. In April 1780, after the project of the association had been fairly launched, he stressed the necessity of keeping the York newspapers 'constantly well supplied with paragraphs relative to the association'. The printers were to be persuaded that it was in their interest to maintain an open press on the subject and not to insist upon charging for insertions. Paragraphs taken from the London papers were to be reproduced and supplemented with short letters 'adapted to the state of sentiments, objections, etc., at the time'.[5] From the beginning of 1781 the unprinted correspondence of the association contains an increasingly frequent, though irregular, series of letters from Wyvill to Gray with in-

[1] *Transactions of the Royal Historical Society*, XXIX 77.

[2] Wyvill, *Political Papers*, I 54; cf. St Andrew Ward to Gray, 2 Feb 1780, cited on p. 276 above.

[3] Ibid.

[4] *York Chronicle*, 18 Feb; reprinted in Wyvill, *Political Papers*, III 173–8.

[5] To [?] Gray, 25 Apr 1780.

structions for the insertion of items, some of them printed cuttings from the London papers, others short manuscript paragraphs, or letters to the printer, or items of association correspondence. In connection with the preparation of the petition of 1783, there were eight such letters in November 1782, two in December, and six in January 1783. Much similar correspondence survives for 1784 and 1785. The material published was designed, depending upon circumstances, to keep up interest in the association and the movements for petitions, to encourage supporters, to present and explain from time to time the policy of the associators, and to answer criticisms and expose misrepresentations. It was deliberately intended to stimulate interest in politics among a wider public, if only for the very practical reason that by this means alone did it seem possible to budge the forces of conservatism in the House of Commons. As many as possible of the people who already had the vote should be provoked into using it with genuine political considerations in mind. A paragraph in the *York Chronicle* of 14 February 1783 – one of many probably contributed by Wyvill – declared: 'The freeholders in general are now much better informed than they were . . . in consequence of their frequent meeting and communicating their sentiments . . . and also of perusing the different tracts, and weighing the several arguments which have been produced on each side concerning this important question.' The reformers probably exaggerated the extent to which a wider public had become conscious of political questions, but there was doubtless some truth in this report. Although the pace of the movement was not sustained after 1783, and those achievements with which it could be credited were due mainly to the labours of a devoted minority of influential men, the political education of the lesser freeholders cannot have been negligible.

What, finally, can be said, without an immense detailed social analysis, of the numbers and the quality of the freeholders who were thus drawn into the weft of politics, and who gave support to the reformers by signing the petitions and the association? The numerical proportion of them within the county as a whole is uncertain. Yorkshire had so long been without a contested parliamentary election that the number of its electors could only be roughly estimated. The associators, using the last poll, of 1741, as their basis, reckoned the electorate at about 16,000.[1] They claimed accordingly that the totals of about 8,000 and about 10,000 subscriptions to the petitions of 1780 and 1783 showed that more than half the voters were on their side.[2] According to a hostile report in the *Leeds Intelligencer* of 31 December 1782, only 300 out of 30,000 freeholders had attended the last county meeting, but these figures are too obviously propagandist to be accepted. Still, in view of the upward trend of population, the associators' estimate of 16,000 may have been too low, and their claims to the support of a strict numerical majority unfounded: Sir George Savile, the veteran parliamentary representative of the county, in 1780 referred to his 'twenty thousand' constituents.[3] Even so, the reformers may have been in the right, in the sense of having the majority of the more substantial freeholders behind them. In an exchange of letters with Wyvill early in 1780 Savile gave the reformers some important advice:[4]

> You say you judge that 6,000 will have signed in a fortnight . . . if among this 6,000 there is a strong proportion of property, I should reckon it a very respectable petition: because the grievance complained of is such as must be supposed to be best known to persons of some rank in the world. If 10,000 persons of more retired lives (from their situations) were to speak of the abuses of office, everybody would see that they went upon a weaker degree of evidence than those whose situations put them more in the way of knowing those abuses, as well as of feeling, in common with the rest, the effects of them; and you would be tauntingly asked, *how John and Thomas came to know of these abuses*? and the great number of signatures would be ascribed to diligent canvassing and telling stories in ale-houses.

Here was fair warning that it was not only the numbers but the respectable standing of the petitioners that mattered. Savile's views were regarded with great respect by the leading associators, and there are at least one or two indications that his advice was followed. From reports about the West Riding cited above, it would seem that many of the subscribers there belonged to a pretty indepen-

[1] *York Chronicle*, 29 Sept 1780.
[2] Wyvill, *Political Papers*, I 106–7.
[3] Ibid., 281.
[4] Ibid., III 201.

dent set of men. For instance, it was the 'middling freeholders' of the Skipton district, not the humble Johns and Thomases, who made up William Baines's collection of over 300 names to the first petition. Ralph Jackson of Normanby, returning on 25 July 1780 the copy of the association which he had been circulating in the neighbourhood of Northallerton, remarked that he had secured the signatures of 125 freeholders, 'many of whom have considerable property in freehold estates in this county'. From the almost complete set of the parchments of the association it appears that practically all the subscribers were at least sufficiently literate to sign their own names: the number whose marks had to be attested was less than 2 per cent. In early September 1780 Savile considered that 'the number and respectability' of the 5,800 or so signatures were such 'as to stand in his judgment for a declaration of the sense of his constituents'.[1] In the extent and the character of the support which the reformers attracted, the situation in Yorkshire stood in marked contrast with that in most counties, where the associating movement died of inanition or could command only a derisory measure of support.[2]

[1] *York Chronicle*, 8 Sept 1780. Cf. Savile's election address, Wyvill, I 282.

[2] By late 1781 only six other counties had associations on the Yorkshire model, and two others had associations pledged to economical reform only (Wyvill, *Political Papers*, I 381–3). In Cambridgeshire subscription to an association was begun but produced only forty names (B.M. Add. MSS. 35681, fo. 413). Lack of support for the movement in the country as a whole is also evident from comments by Savile in the autumn of 1780 (Wyvill, *Political Papers*, III 236–9, 270–1).

THIRTEEN

*Great Yarmouth and the Yorkshire Reform Movement, 1782–1784**

DURING the period of the Yorkshire reform movement in the early 1780s, citizens of Great Yarmouth twice joined in the presentation of petitions for parliamentary reform to the House of Commons.[1] Their petitions were drawn up in what was more or less the standard form, adopted everywhere on the suggestion of the Yorkshire committee of association,[2] and they give little indication of particular Yarmouth grievances. However, a full statement of those grievances is available elsewhere. One of the circumstances which in many places sharpened the demand for reform during the fifty years preceding the passage of the great reform bill of 1832 was jealousy of the privileges enjoyed, and abused, by the old borough corporations. In the papers of the Marquis of Rockingham, now in Sheffield Central Library, there are two documents showing that as early as 1782 discontent at the activities of the corporation was a driving force behind local radicalism. Arising from this was a secondary grievance, the interference of local families whose political fortunes in the borough were linked with the corporation.

For many years before 1782 the family interests of the Townshends and Walpoles, in alliance with the corporation and with each other, had dominated parliamentary elections in Great Yarmouth, and much else besides. During the earlier part of George III's reign, an increasing opposition developed against this combination of groups. The nonconformists played a prominent part in this borough opposition, and among its leaders were members of the family of Hurry, 'then a numerous family of wealth and influence in the town'.[3] In the decade before 1782 the animus

* This first appeared in *Norfolk Archaeology*, XXXII (2) (1959) 104–10.

[1] *Commons Journals*, 3 Feb 1783, 16 Mar 1785.

[2] Wyvill, *Political Papers*, II 36, 237.

[3] C. J. Palmer, *The History of Great Yarmouth* (1856) pp. 233–4; Palmer and E. A. Hurry, *Memorials of the Family of Hurry* . . . . (1873) pp. 10–14.

against the corporation and the allied aristocratic interests was stimulated by dislike of the North administration and by disapproval of its policies, which had brought Great Britain into disastrous armed conflict with the American colonies. But while Charles Townshend,[1] one of the members of parliament for Great Yarmouth at this time, was a place-holder, and a supporter of the North ministry and its policies, his colleague, Richard Walpole,[2] was connected with the great political clan of Cavendish, belonged to the parliamentary group led by the Marquis of Rockingham, and voted constantly in opposition. Walpole's position in Great Yarmouth was, nevertheless, as much as Townshend's, the butt of attack by the local radicals. Radicalism in the borough was inspired primarily by local, not national, issues.

In April 1782 Lord Rockingham received an address from the 'citizens of Great Yarmouth,' signed by ten of their number.[3] Barely a month before, Rockingham had become head of a new administration. The war in the American colonies had come to final disaster at Yorktown, North, after some delay, had been forced to resign by the threat of defeat in the House of Commons, and the Rockinghams and their political allies had taken over the task of government. The new ministers were publicly committed to a policy of 'economical reform', intended in part to cut government expenditure and the weight of taxation but even more to reduce the influence of the executive in the House of Commons. Three legislative measures, in train since 1780 but blocked in the past two sessions by North's parliamentary majorities, now seemed certain of passage. These were Edmund Burke's establishment bill, for reducing the number of government posts tenable with a seat in the House of Commons, Clerke's bill for exclusion of government contractors from the House, and Crewe's bill for disfranchising all persons holding posts in the revenue services. Crewe's bill was of some interest to the inhabitants of Great Yarmouth, for

[1] Charles Townshend of Honingham (1728–1810): See *D.N.B.*

[2] Richard Walpole (1728–98), a banker in London, third son of Horatio, 1st Baron Walpole of Wolterton.

[3] The subscribers were: W. Manning, Will. Pettingill, Will. Urquhart, Geo. Hurry, John Fowler, Thos Dade Thos Scratton, Jas Walker, John Drake, Edmond Cobb.

the borough voters included a fair number of customs and excise officers and employees. But it did not really solve their problem.[1] Their object of attack was the 'spoils system' in local appointments, a practice as universal in English eighteenth-century political life as it still is in that of the United States. The root of the trouble lay in the fact that the spoils system, especially in conjunction with the rights of the unreformed corporation, and the legal debarment of nonconformists from local office by the Corporation Acts, had divided the inhabitants into a privileged and an unprivileged class. The unprivileged were becoming increasingly aware and resentful of the extent to which they might be exploited and their rights to political self-expression be rendered ineffectual; and they saw the privileged gaining greatly from practices which were in themselves scandalous and pernicious.

Rockingham was given a very full explanation of what were felt to be the chief grievances and of the way in which the Yarmouth radicals hoped that they might be overcome:[2]

> Those who now do themselves the honour of addressing you, firmly rely on the representation of Lord Chedworth to convince you, that that line of conduct which they conceive to be the duty of every subject of a free state, has hitherto on all occasions . . . been observed by them, and will continue to be so, in an adherence to the true principles of the English constitution, and an opposition to every future violation of them, which they may have the opportunity to notice, and the ability to prevent. They have seen the strength of this country almost exhausted, and the spirits of their countrymen nearly reduced to a state of despair from the abuses that have been silently creeping into every department of the state, and the gradual progress of vices – from prodigality, to dependence, through all degrees of society. We, my Lord, have had the misfortune to be fixed in a place, where the purchase of consciences has been an open traffic; and where, as every honest trade has been checked by the fury of war,

[1] In general this measure was greatly overrated, and its effects were very disappointing to its sponsors. Betty Kemp, 'Crewe's Act, 1782', *English Historical Review*, LXVIII (1953) 258–63.

[2] 20 Apr 1782, Rockingham MSS. My thanks are due to the Earl Fitzwilliam and the Trustees of the Wentworth Woodhouse Estates, and the City Librarian of Sheffield, for permission to quote this and the following document.

freedom has been the most marketable commodity – the price of it exactly ascertained, and the sale of it encouraged, by frequent ministerial bounties.

As you, my Lord, and the other great characters that compose the present ministry, have uniformly opposed the pernicious influence which has wasted our internal strength and sullied our national glory, it is not doubted, but that the uprightness of your intentions will now be evinced, by the immediate exertion of that power which alone can give them efficacy. And although it be requisite, that the great work of general reformation should be performed by principle, rather than by detail; yet, your Lordship well knows that it is absolutely necessary to stop those foul, though latent streams, which join to swell the tides of national corruption. From the want of freedom in elections many important evils have arisen, and although we cannot flatter ourselves with being able to proceed far towards restoring it; yet, conscious that by the exertions of individuals, of which the community is composed, the best endeavours of the best statesmen can alone be rendered effectual; we will not hesitate to point out to your Lordship, certain grievances which the independent part of a large borough have long complained of, and are eager to see redressed.

Every attempt of this nature has hitherto been successfully opposed by those who have caused them, and it is to implore, in the most earnest terms, your Lordship's patronage in this salutary labour, that we have ventured to represent to you the slavery with which we have for many years been oppressed; and over which, we trust, your assistance will soon enable us to triumph. Your Lordship will doubtless require no apology for the warmth of these expressions. As they spring from the heart, declamation becomes argument; and feeling all the ardour, which good citizens feel for the welfare of their country, and all the pleasure of hope, from the prospect of its returning greatness; we cannot but loudly express our sorrow, at being disgraced by a representative, who has ever yielded patriotism to private interest; and received the emoluments of office, which ought to be the reward of useful and honourable service, as the wages of servility and the means of corruption.

Not to detain your Lordship's attention to observations of a general nature, we beg to represent to you, that *Mr Charles Townshend, by his interest with the late ministry, has given places to above one hundred and thirty revenue officers in this town.* A list of these persons, with their respective employments, is herein inclosed.[1] All those, therefore, who owe their public existence, and are indebted for the preservation of it to his pleasure, dare on no occasion run the hazard of losing it, by disobeying his commands, or opposing his interest.

But the influence, arising to this bestower of every political good, does not end with those who are the immediate objects of his favour; it extends to a long train of family connections, who are fearful of disobliging the patron of a relative; and it actuates every humble dependent on these placemen, and every eager expectant of some reversionary advantage.

Your Lordship will therefore clearly see, how far those who possess – those who solicit, and those who have been promised some employments, have the power of deciding an election; when the number of voters does not amount to six hundred at most. Yet, in spite of this deadweight, which has baffled every attempt to remove it, you may perceive, how ardently the independent part of this town panted for freedom, when you are informed, that at the general election before the last, the sanction of a great and worthy name (Sir Charles Saunders, who was not present) went so far, that, at the close of the poll, Mr Charles Townshend had not the majority of a hundred votes.

Your Lordship will observe, a long list of names opposite the place of coal-meters; and in the appointment, there is a glaring and remarkable species of abuse made use of by the corporation; who faithfully execute all the schemes of their representative. Every coalmeter is to be nominated by government. But the corporation first sells the place to him (for which they receive the sum of one hundred and fifty pounds, and upwards) and place the money to their own uses; and then recommend the person with whom they have dealt, to the appointment of government. Mr Townshend takes care, that he and no other, shall obtain the appointment. Here, your Lordship will observe iniquity through the whole transaction: they take money for places, they have not legally the disposal of, under pretence of receiving it as a reward for the interest they intend to make for the purchaser; the money arising from the sale returns to strengthen undue influence in some other channel; from corruption it came, and to corruption it invariably returns. It may at first sight appear strange, that no session of parliament has escaped, without Mr Charles Townshend's returning the trust of representation, into the hands of his constituents, secure

[1] Missing.

of meeting with all the proofs of increased affection he could desire. Your Lordship's memory may trace him through all the subordinate, yet lucrative offices of government: from the Admiralty to the Treasury, and from that to the vice-treasurership of Ireland.

That his interest in the corporation might be immoveably fixed, he appointed one of the aldermen to be receiver general of the county of Norfolk, and the power which property always carries with it, and above all others pecuniary property in a commercial town has enabled that gentleman to introduce into that body a long train of relations and dependents, whom gratitude and interest prompt to the support of Mr Charles Townshend, their common benefactor.

A curious instance of inconsistency and intrigue lately presented itself. It was the desire of the receiver general, to obtain the freedom of the town for a relation, who had not obtained it by the regular mode of servitude, and who was not at that time, an inhabitant of the place. To prevent much opposition to the proposal, it was thought expedient to accompany it with a measure that should be popular: it was therefore voted, that all those who had heretofore, or should hereafter marry, the daughters of freemen, should be entitled to their freedom. The temporary purpose, for which this specious popularity was courted being answered by the admission of the aforesaid gentleman to his freedom, it was no longer necessary to abide by their vote. Within the space of a week therefore another corporation meeting was called, in which it was determined, to rescind the order respecting those who had, or should, marry the daughters of freemen, and accordingly applications from four gentlemen, who wished to avail themselves of the first order, were immediately rejected.

From such instances, your Lordship will perceive, how much the attempt to restore a free election is impeded by the power resident in corporations, to increase at pleasure, the number of votes, as the spur of occasion may require; to make choice of their favourites, and to refuse all others. We, therefore, beg leave to refer it, as an object worthy of your Lordship's consideration, whether to *the great advantages likely to result to the cause of freedom from the success of Mr Crewe's Bill*, an additional and important one might not be added, by obliging those corporators (who now have the choice of those who shall be admitted to their freedom) to admit all persons, under certain descriptions; such, we mean, as are by their property most interested in the establishment of a free and honest representation.

This, my Lord, is a short sketch of the slavery, to which this town, for many years, has been subject; and from which they most earnestly implore your Lordship's assistance, to set them free. It will clearly appear to your Lordship, that there is but one possible mode of doing this; and that is, by taking from Mr Charles Townshend the power of conferring the large emoluments, arising from the number of places in the gift of government, upon his creatures; who are from that circumstance the most decided enemies to the present administration.

To give encouragement to the well deserving, and check the friends of corruption in their future career, is, we are assured, not the vaunt, but the firm determination, of the new ministry. And as we think it the duty of every private person to aid, as far as in him lies, this virtuous resolve, we shall be happy to have the liberty of giving your Lordship frequent information of the interior management of the borough of Great Yarmouth, that you may be enabled to pursue such measures as your judgement and integrity may suggest for our emancipation.

From the whole of this representation, we assure your Lordship, we have but one wish, that one indeed, is nearest our hearts: it is, that our ability may equal our desires, to strengthen the hands of government under your Lordship's administration.

This address apparently produced no reaction from Rockingham. Indeed, in view of his political alliance with the Walpoles and Cavendishes, it must have been an embarrassment to receive it. It was true that, since the change of ministry, Charles Townshend no longer had a friend at the treasury. Local patronage recommendations now came up through Rockingham's supporter, Richard Walpole. But they still buttressed the same joint interests in the borough. From the point of view of the independent citizens the situation was not one whit better than before North's fall. Accordingly, at the beginning of June, the Yarmouth radicals took up the matter with Sir Edward Astley and Thomas William Coke, the members of parliament for the county:[1]

Gentlemen, we had the pleasure of drinking long life and

[1] 6 June 1782, Rockingham MSS. The subscribers this time were: W. Manning, Samuel Hurry, Will. Hurry, Will. Urquhart, Edm. Laron, Thos Scratton, George Hurry, John Drake, John Fowler, Edmond Cobb, Jas Walker, Thos Dade.

health to Sir Edward Astley and Mr Coke at dinner given on Tuesday last by Captain Hurry to his independent company and to his friends and indeed to have had the opportunity of saying that in person which is now the subject of this letter.

That you may the more readily perceive our intention we beg to refer to the address to the Marquis of Rockingham, presented some time since, of which we sent you a copy, and also to some private conversation that passed between us at Norwich. That address informed you of the present state of this town, and pointed out a mode by which we apprehended it might be materially altered for the better, and in our interviews with you, you will recollect that we explained matters more fully than can be drawn in the compass of a letter. The grand object we have ever had in view is the restoration of a free election and the diminution of every interest that obstructs the attainment of it. As long as the disposal of the local places shall continue with either of our present members in parliament, so long is their seat secure, and the system of corruption will continue, and no longer. The object of this letter therefore is to entreat you to use your interest that it may henceforth be with the friends of the present ministry, and not with their enemies. Amongst the long list of placemen there are several at this moment far advanced in years, and some likely to make vacancies any day; we know that when any vacancy is made, it will be too late to make an application in behalf of a successor, unless the precautions we wish to use be found of avail.

Immediately upon the death of any person of this description, or perhaps before that period, Mr R. Walpole will have intimation of the event certain or probable, and immediately apply to Lord Rockingham for a friend, which friend will be a steady supporter of Mr C. Townshend and a creature of the corporation of Yarmouth. Mr R. Walpole will doubtless endeavour to enforce his petition by the whole weight of the Cavendish interest, and if he succeeds all one's hopes are frustrated. The friends of Mr C. Townshend still give out that his power in the disposal of places remains as great as ever; by these means people, however disaffected to him, do not think it prudent to declare openly against him, but keep a fixed eye on the political barometer, and will guide their future conduct as they shall perceive that to fall or to rise. We know no other method of attaining the leading object of an unbiased choice of representatives than by its being found that the disposal of the places here shall henceforth rest with our county members, and be given as they fall to the friends of the ministry, whom we will carefully represent to you, not fixing places merely as they may suit the exigencies of men, but their capacity to fill them with credit and their honesty to execute them with diligence.

We shall therefore be very happy if it prove agreeable to you gentlemen to act conjointly with Mr Windham in this borough, and we will not allow ourselves to doubt that a joint application made by you to Lord Rockingham to permit you to recommend his Lordship such persons as you shall think best qualified to fill the several offices in the port of Great Yarmouth as they become vacant will meet his Lordship's approbation and consent.

We have written on this subject to Mr Windham with whom we request the favor of you to have a conference, and if it be agreeable to you and him to meet our wishes, we shall wait with anxious expectation to hear the result of your application to the Marquis of Rockingham.

The cause once removed, the effect would immediately cease, and when Mr C. Townshend shall have lost the means of corruption, his interest here from that moment expires for ever. . . .

Coke and Astley evidently turned the letter and the problem over to Rockingham, but there is no indication that the Marquis took any action. Within a few days his fatal illness was upon him. Within a month he was dead, his administration broke up, and a new one was formed by the Earl of Shelburne. At the end of September, after Shelburne had had time to settle into office, his help in turn was solicited by the men of Yarmouth. Their case was supported in a series of letters from the well-known Presbyterian minister, the Rev. George Walker; possibly Walker was known personally to Shelburne, who had many contacts among the nonconformists.[1]

The question was no less embarrassing to Shelburne than to Rockingham. In the autumn of 1782 the last thing he wished to do was to offend any member of parliament, and in particular any friend of North. His administration had no assured parliamentary majority, and its fate would depend upon the goodwill of the North party in the House of Commons. Shelburne accordingly continued to accept recommendations to offices in Great Yarmouth from Townshend (not from Walpole, who had gone into opposition with

[1] Walker to Shelburne, 26 Sept, 9 Oct. 2 Nov 1782, Lansdowne MSS.

Charles Fox). To Walker he replied that this was the customary procedure and that he saw no reason to change it. The game was lost for the moment, but Walker directed one parting shot:

> The condescension with which your Lordship has urged in stating the reason why you could not attend to the petition from Yarmouth is worthy of your Lordship, and the reason must receive the approbation of everyone, as a general rule of action. Those who are interested therein, and see things only in a partial view may perhaps complain, that a revolution in politics brings not to them a revolution in favours, and that men who have been no friends to their country, and never can be steady friends to your Lordship, still possess the dispensation of rewards, and strengthen their provincial interest.

Four months later Townshend followed his leader, when North joined forces with Charles Fox, helped to turn out Shelburne, and took part in the formation of the coalition ministry. The two borough representatives were now on the same side in politics, and the links binding administration, members and corporation seemed stronger than ever. But the existing dominant system of politics in the borough was preserved only for one more year.

What in 1784 destroyed it, at least temporarily, was not a reform, but a new revolution in politics. When, at the end of 1783, George III dismissed the coalition and called upon William Pitt to form a ministry, both members of parliament for the borough found themselves, for the first time, together in opposition to the government. It was no longer possible, as before, for one at least of them to negotiate with a friendly treasury over the appointments, promotions and favours required to maintain the joint interests of their families and of the corporation. By the time of the general election of April 1784, not only had the coalition been overwhelmed almost everywhere by a storm of obloquy, not only had Lord Orford, the head of the Walpole family, turned against his relative and promised his support to Pittite candidates,[1] but the government interest also was directed against the retiring members and their friends in the corporation. Although, as a result of Crewe's Act, the revenue officers themselves could no longer vote, all their relatives and dependants among the electors knew that the right thing to do was

[1] Palmer, *History of Great Yarmouth*, pp. 223–4.

to vote for candidates who stood as friends of Pitt.[1] Richard Walpole declined to stand. Townshend tried the ground with another colleague, but gave up, realising that in a contest he would have no chance of success. The new members, returned amid the ruin of the old interests in the borough, were Sir John Jervis, one of Shelburne's political connections,[2] and another opponent of the coalition, Henry Beaufoy, a prominent dissenter, who owed his introduction into Yarmouth to the Hurry family.[3] On 1 April the triumph of the radicals was gloatingly reported in the sympathetic columns of the *Bury Post*:

> Never sure was a more glorious victory gained over intrigue and corruption! The triumph of Sir John Jervis and Mr Beaufoy, in this instance, may be considered as the demolition of a monstrous system, which has grown for years, under the venal influence of the exchequer and its creatures. A spirit of disgust, detestation, and determined resistance had long prevailed, amongst those who were constant witnesses and frequent victims to the evils of that local tyranny, which owed its extent and continuance, to the more dreadful tyranny of North and his minions. Many vain struggles have been made to emancipate the town; but the present moment is that in which the interest of popularity is strengthened by advantages never known before.

Radical agitation in Great Yarmouth did not immediately cease after this local victory. In 1785 the citizens, again following the lead of Yorkshire, petitioned for reform in support of William Pitt's reform bill, and their two representatives voted for the bill in the House of Commons. But the political revolution of 1784 gave them what they chiefly desired. The corporation could now be denied any share in political spoils, and the patronage recommendations of the radicals could be passed direct to the treasury by Jervis and Beaufoy: a corporation complaint about this being done in one

[1] Townshend, in his notice of his withdrawal, referred to 'the full exertion of ministerial influence' against him – a case of the biter bitten! (*Bury Post*, 8 Apr 1784.)

[2] Captain Sir John Jervis, K.B., R.N. (1735–1823), the future Earl St Vincent: see *D.N.B.*

[3] Henry Beaufoy of Claverley, Salop (d. 1795): see *D.N.B.*, Palmer, works cited, and Gwendoline Beaufoy, *Leaves from a Beech Tree* (1932) pp. 134–44.

instance survives in Pitt's papers.[1] Throughout, the Yarmouth reformers had not proposed any radical change in the spoils system. Indeed, this was hardly conceivable until the possibilities of competitive recruitment to the government service were explored under the different conditions of the mid-nineteenth century. Their object was to capture the system for themselves, to seize from the corporation the springs of power and influence in the borough. Thanks to the election triumph of Jervis and Beaufoy, they were able to succeed. But it was a fragile achievement. On the one hand, the treasury, in alliance with a great local patron, might easily rebuild the old structure of patronage. On the other, while the leaders of the Yarmouth radicals were, perhaps, men of greater probity than most of the members of the corporation, it might well be doubted whether they or their successors would long remain so, under the influence of what was inevitably a corrupting system.

[1] Mr Stiles to Joseph Smith, 22 Oct 1786, Chatham MSS., bundle 181 P.R.O.

FOURTEEN

*Economical Reform and 'The Influence of the Crown', 1780**

IN 1780 the champions of economical reform openly admitted that their principal aim was not economy but the reduction of the influence of the executive in the House of Commons. In pursuit of this object the Rockingham party rallied other opposition groups in parliament in support of its elaborate programme of constitutional purification – a programme embracing Crewe's bill for the disfranchisement of revenue officers, Clerke's bill for the exclusion of contractors from the House of Commons, and Burke's establishment bill, which provided for the abolition of numerous offices and sinecures, and for a strict limitation of the grant of royal pensions at pleasure. 'The saving of money', declared Dunning on 21 February, 'is but a secondary object. The reduction of the influence of the Crown is the first.' And on 8 March Thomas Townshend similarly asserted that 'the first great consideration was the lessening of the influence of the Crown, which in the opinion of the people, and he believed, a majority of that House, had enormously increased of late years, and particularly so since the accession of his Majesty.'[1]

Townshend's appeal to 'opinion' was typical of the controversy about 'the influence of the Crown'. It was a marked feature of the debates on this question that neither the reformers nor their ministerial opponents produced much specific information in support of their charges and counter-assertions. The opposition was insistent that this influence had increased, the government as insistent that it had not. But both sides relied upon arguments of a general kind. Opposition leaders were apt to appeal to 'the notoriety of the fact':[2] on the rare occasions when they ventured to cite

* This originally appeared in *Cambridge Historical Journal*, XII (1956) 144–54.

[1] Almon, *The Parliamentary Register*, XVII 133, 257.

[2] The phrase was used by Burke on 2 March (ibid., p. 199). See also the general tenor of his speech on the clause for abolishing the third secretary ship of state, on 8 March (ibid., pp. 265–8).

figures, they indulged in mere guesswork, and took little heed of what we should now regard as essential statistical data. Miss Kemp has shown, in a recent short essay, that spokesmen of the opposition supporting Crewe's bill made the wildest guesses about the numbers of revenue officers and the proportion of these entitled to vote at parliamentary elections: their estimates were absurdly in excess of the true figures.[1] Other instances may be found. In the debate of 21 February on Sir George Savile's motion for a return of all pensions, Dunning spoke in terms implying that there might be as many as forty pensioned retainers of the ministry in the Commons[2] – an assumption which the secret service accounts for the period show to have been greatly exaggerated.[3] Scholars dealing with the episode of economical reform find themselves from the outset in a morass of unproven assertions; and the object of this essay is to establish one or two patches of firm ground by posing two specific questions regarding the period 1761 to 1780. First, had the number of placemen in the Commons increased? Secondly, had the executive power added to the number of constituencies under its direct control?

Admittedly the leaders of the opposition did not contend that the number of actual place-holders in the House of Commons had increased. Indeed, the proportion of placemen in the Commons was of only secondary concern to the campaign for economical reform – for that campaign was aimed against the aggregate distribution of government money in all the ways that might, directly or indirectly, affect the composition of the House or the voting of members. Fox, for instance, employed the argument that since the American war had caused an unavoidable increase in the patronage wielded through the armed forces and their ancillary

[1] In *English Historical Review*, LXVIII 258–63.

[2] Almon, *The Parliamentary Register*, XVII 133.

[3] Both secretaries to the treasury kept secret service accounts. John Robinson's copy of his accounts for the years 1779–82 is in B.M. Add. MSS. 37836, fos. 58–140. A fair copy of these accounts for most of the same period, combined in one statement of account with the accounts of Sir Grey Cooper, exists among the papers of George III in the Royal Archives at Windsor. I have to acknowledge the gracious permission of Her Majesty the Queen to make use of this material and also of the 'State [of the Parliament] 1780', drawn up by Robinson for George III in preparation for the general election of 1780.

services, the only recourse was to reduce the patronage distributed through the civil list.[1] This was why the main plank of the economical reform programme took the shape of Burke's establishment bill, instead of a place bill. Only after the defeat of the main clauses of Burke's measure, at the end of March, was an attempt made by Dunning to introduce a place bill, as a second best, in pursuance of his famous resolution.[2] Nevertheless, on various occasions opposition leaders denounced placemen, pensioners, and contractors in the House as agents of a corrupting executive influence; their publicists campaigned against them;[3] and, on the other side, the secretary to the treasury, John Robinson, was himself inclined to view places at pleasure as a means of fixing political loyalties (and those granted for life as inviting disloyalty).[4] Knowledge about the number of placemen in the Commons between 1761 and 1780 contributes to our understanding of the nature of the economical reform programme.

The approximate numbers of placemen in the House of Commons elected in 1761 have been investigated by Sir Lewis Namier.[5] The numbers for 1780 are ascertainable from the contemporary directories, from the secret service accounts, and from the information about government contracts to be found in the minutes of the boards of treasury and ordnance.[6] A comparison of the figures for these two years shows that in the intervening period the number of placemen in the Commons had declined by over a fifth. This reduction was most sharply marked in certain categories, while in others there was virtually no alteration. As might be expected, there was least change in the number of members of the administration – that is, the leaders of the government, junior ministers, and civil servants. In 1780, as in 1761, these numbered between forty and fifty. But the numbers of sinecure-holders and of court officials dropped by over a third. In 1761 there were about fifty

[1] Almon, *The Parliamentary Register*, XVII 272.

[2] Ibid., p. 488.

[3] E.g. the broadsheet issued after the dissolution of 1780, showing how members had voted in recent divisions, with notes of the offices or relationship to office-holders of those who had voted with the government (B.M. Add. MSS. 27837, between fos. 7–8).

[4] B.M. Add. MSS. 38210, fo. 325.

[5] *England in the Age of the American Revolution*, pp. 257–62.

[6] T. 29/48–50; W.O. 47/93–6; P.R.O.

members holding sinecures and between forty and fifty court officials. By 1780 the numbers in these categories were respectively about thirty and twenty-five. A reduction on this scale is remarkable, but it appears that the numbers of these placemen reached a peak in 1761 which was never again to be approached. This was due partly to the amalgamation of the old and the new courts on the accession of George III, but probably still more to the strenuous efforts of the Duke of Newcastle to find pasture for all the beasts he had to feed. After 1761 the number steadily declined. To take one example – in 1762 the Commons included two lords and thirteen grooms of the bedchamber and one gentleman of the privy chamber, but by 1780 the numbers were respectively one, six and one. If the numbers of holders of these offices in each year after 1762 are plotted on a graph, the result is a gradually descending curve, flattening out after 1770 into an almost horizontal line. Among the reasons for this reduction during the 1760s were the retirement from office of Newcastle and the destruction of the Pelham connection,[1] the king's concern for economy, virtue and aristocracy in the making of household appointments,[2] and his refusal, from a sense of justice and obligation, to deprive old servants of their places whenever they fell out of the ranks in the Commons. In 1780 there were still a number of officials about the court who in 1762 had held their places with a seat in the House, but who had since withdrawn from it. Here, it would seem, was an opportunity which a king and a minister whose primary concern was to pack the House would have seized upon without delay. Members of North's personal following were quick to point out this same opportunity at the time of the coalition, and among his papers relating to its formation in 1783 is a memorandum headed 'To restore the influence taken away by Burke's Bill, the following places may be given to members of parliament',[3] containing a list of forty-three places including 'nine grooms of the bedchamber'. But in fact between 1770 and 1782 George III and North did not take such opportunities to increase the number of placemen. The lists of office-holders are themselves sufficient indication of the

[1] Namier, *England in the Age of the American Revolution*, pp. 447–9, 468–83.

[2] Pares, *King George III and the Politicians*, pp.57–8.

[3] Waldershare MSS., Kent Record Office.

fact that such posts as bedchamber appointments were normally secure till the occupant died, or resigned, or obtained another office.

The officers in the armed forces in the House in 1780, not included in previous categories of place-holders, numbered sixty-four, somewhat above the figure of fifty-seven for 1761. Holders of bare secret service pensions numbered eleven, as against ten. In neither case can the increase be described as significant. And on the other hand, by 1780 the number of government contractors serving the forces was considerably reduced. Whereas Newcastle had found employment for thirty-seven out of fifty merchants returned to the House in 1761, in the House which debated Dunning's resolution there were only eleven merchants connected by contracts with North's ministry.[1] War, so it was frequently presumed, enlarged the business ties between the administration and the House of Commons. Yet in 1780 there was much less justification for the passage of Clerke's bill for the exclusion of contractors from the House than there had been in the days of Newcastle – when only old-fashioned tories had troubled their heads about the matter.

In round figures, the House of Commons in the early months of 1780 contained about fifty government officials, thirty sinecurists, twenty-five court officials, sixty-five military and naval officers not included in these previous categories, eleven contractors and eleven holders of bare secret service pensions. The total was a little under two hundred placemen,[2] as compared with the two hundred and fifty of 1761. If Burke, Dunning and Fox had merely alleged that their measures were to counter an increase in the number of placemen in the Commons, their case could quickly have been shown to be without foundation. By choosing the broader ground of complaint for their attack, they avoided this difficulty, but they thus exposed themselves to damaging counter-arguments of a general kind. In effect, they tried to equate patronage in the country as a whole with political influence, and they argued that

[1] This number was abormally low. There were about fifteen contractors in the House in 1778 and again in 1781. But these slightly higher figures do not invalidate the argument.

[2] This number remained practically unchanged after the general election of 1780.

because patronage in general had increased so too had the influence of the crown. Indisputably government patronage was increasing. War – and especially the American war – caused an unprecedented expansion of naval and military establishments, and war taxation required more revenue officers. But against this it might well be maintained that the wealth of the people had more than kept pace with the income of the crown. This argument was ably stated in debate by William Adam:

> The increase of the influence of the Crown without doors, or anywhere [he declared] was to be estimated by the proportion the revenue of the Crown bore to the revenue of the subject, that if the first had encreased more than the last, that revenue had rendered influence greater: but the direct reverse was true; the revenue of the Crown remained stationary, or nearly so, while that of the people had encreased tenfold since the revolution, and consequently rendered the people more independent.[1]

Despite Adam's rhetorical exaggeration, his basic assumption – that the people, especially the upper class which mattered politically, enjoyed increasing wealth relative to the level of government expenditure – was probably correct. But in the absence of statistics this is incapable of proof.

'Government boroughs' furnish another instance where we can apply a fairly precise test to the assumption stated in Dunning's resolution. Some government interest existed in many, indeed in most, constituencies, but the few 'government boroughs' were a fairly clearly defined class. In such constituencies one or more government departments – chiefly the treasury and the admiralty – acting through local political managers or agents, distributed favours directly to the voters and could carry the election of nominees at parliamentary elections. Although sometimes more or less material assistance might be derived from the personal influence of a leading minister, these were, by definition, boroughs where the governmental interest predominated.

In 1761 the administration had about thirty seats under its own more or less immediate patronage. Nineteen were under the direct management of the treasury. Of these, two seats at Harwich and

[1] Almon, *The Parliamentary Register*, XVII 314.

two at Orford were the most secure. One could be obtained at Dover and two at Dartmouth. One seat at Totnes was precariously held with the assistance of local interests. Five seats in the three Isle of Wight boroughs were at the treasury's disposal, 'with a first lien on them for the family of Lord Holmes, the Government manager'. Seaford, Hastings and Rye were controlled by a combination of treasury influence and the Duke of Newcastle's personal interest. The admiralty could dispose of ten seats in six constituencies – two each at Saltash, Plymouth, Portsmouth and Rochester, one each at Queenborough and Sandwich. At Queenborough the second seat was controlled by the board of ordnance independently, and often in competition with the admiralty.[1]

Not all these government seats could be counted as safe in 1761, and this buttress of the ministerial interest in the House of Commons had undergone appreciable erosion by the time of Dunning's resolution. Although, in the intervening nineteen years, one or two other seats fell under government influence, the losses in the same period more than counterbalanced the gains. The maintenance of ministerial interest was beset with hazards. Among the politicians a parliamentary borough was a highly coveted prize; and during George III's reign, as the result of a *coup de main*, or even of sheer negligence on the part of the administration, several government seats became the property of private patrons. It was difficult to check the pretentions of government managers, who were apt to turn the techniques of management to their own advantage, pack electorates with their own relatives and connections, and so usurp the controlling influence in the borough entrusted to their care. There were electorates so corrupt and covetous that not even the lures of ministerial patronage could avail to keep them faithful in the face of passing temptation, and others where indignant radical purists exploited popular interests and prejudices to destroy governmental control.

By 1780 the treasury had lost eight of the nineteen seats it had

[1] Namier, *The Structure of Politics at the accession of George III* (1929) I 171–4. Thirty-two seats are referred to in this passage, but Sir Lewis Namier has told me that he now considers Hedon to have been under Anson's personal influence and not a government borough. [Further note, 1969: More recent work has shown that the admiralty is to be credited with influence over both seats at Sandwich throughout the period (Namier and Brooke, *History of Parliament*, I 453–4).]

controlled in 1761. Orford had passed in 1766 into the hands of the Earl of Hertford, by a curious political arrangement which extinguished government influence in one of the two places where it had formerly been most secure: this episode certainly exculpates George III from any charge of seeking to extend the electoral influence of the crown in the early years of his reign.[1] At Dartmouth the governor of the castle, Arthur Holdsworth, had risen from the rank of borough manager to that of patron and member of parliament by making himself the sole channel for the distribution of patronage and by careful attention to the recruitment of freemen.[2] John Robinson's minutes in preparation for the general election of 1780 reflect the decline of ministerial influence. 'This borough', he wrote, 'although generally esteemed a government borough, is only canvassed as hopeful because Mr Holdsworth has not yet been seen and some reports go as if the present members again look up to it. Further enquiries are making.' Holdsworth proved sufficiently sure of his ground to decline any treasury nominee in place of his friend, Lord Howe, although Howe at this time was on the worst possible terms with the ministers; on 30 July Robinson added to his notes a confession of impotence: 'Mr Holdsworth is much attached to Lord Howe. His Lordship will therefore have his support. Mr Hopkins will not. Perhaps Mr Holdsworth will offer himself: it is now settling.'[3] At the general election, Holdsworth returned himself as Howe's colleague and thereafter acted an independent part in the Commons. Government influence over one seat at Totnes was giving way to private interests, and the treasury depended upon the support of Chief Justice Francis Buller to secure the election of a friend. In 1780 Robinson still had doubts about Buller's influence, but by 1784 his control of the seat was firmly established.[4] By 1780 private patrons, rather than the treasury, dominated the constituencies in the Isle of Wight. Only Newport still ranked as a ministerial

[1] Ibid., II 471–85, where this episode is narrated in detail.

[2] Oldfield, *Representative History of Great Britain and Ireland*, III 341–2; P. Russell, *Dartmouth, a History of the Port and Town* (1950) p. 145.

[3] 'State, 1780', p. 12, Windsor MSS.

[4] 'State, 1780', p. 37, Windsor MSS.; *The Parliamentary Papers of John Robinson*, pp. 72, 115. Cf. T. H. B. Oldfield, *An Entire and Complete History, Political and Personal of the Boroughs of Great Britain*, 3 vols (1792) I 242–3.

borough.[1] Newton was the object of a tripartite bargain beween Sir Richard Worsley, Sir Fitzwilliam Barrington and the Rev. Leonard Troughear Holmes, and it was then the turn of the two first-named patrons to nominate the members.[2] Yarmouth had been entirely captured by the families of Holmes and Clark Jervoise (the process had begun at least as early as 1762), and government nominations were rejected in 1780.[3]

After all these defections, the treasury interest was confined in 1780 to two seats at Harwich, two at Newport, and nine in the Cinque Ports. Its control of Hastings had remained unbroken. A seat at Rye and one at Seaford were temporarily relinquished or lost in 1768 to the Duke of Newcastle, but were soon recovered after Newcastle's death.[4] At Hythe the treasury had gained a rather precarious and expensive influence, about equivalent to one seat, joining forces with the lord warden and with neighbouring country gentlemen. A few years later, influence in the borough was regarded as almost equally divided between William Evelyn of St Clere and the treasury, but Robinson in 1780 noted Evelyn's re-election as certain, whilst he was by no means so confident about the other seat, classing it merely as 'hopeful'.[5] A more certain, if temporary, hold had been gained over one seat at Winchelsea, owing to the financial embarrassments of the Nesbitt family. Albert Nesbitt having died in 1779 heavily in debt – owing the crown, it was said, about £100,000 – the treasury was in a strong position to strike a bargain with his nephew and heir, John Nesbitt, who returned himself and a ministerialist in 1780.[6] At Dover the government

[1] *The Parliamentary Papers of John Robinson*, p. 89.

[2] 'Parliamentary Characters', (scrap-book formerly in the possession of Sir Lewis Namier) p. 62. Cf. *The Parliamentary Papers of John Robinson*, p. 89, and Oldfield, *History of the Boroughs*, II 88–9.

[3] *Jenkinson Papers*, pp. 126–8; Lord North to Robinson, 7 Sept 1780, Abergavenny MS. 301, cf. *The Parliamentary Papers of John Robinson*, p. 89; Edward Morant's diary, entries of 8 Sept, 3 Nov 1780, Morant MSS. I wish to acknowledge the kind permission of the late Marquis of Abergavenny, and of Mr J. Morant of Brokenhurst Park, Hants, to use information from the manuscripts in their possession.

[4] *The Structure of Politics at the accession of George III*, I 170.

[5] Oldfield, *History of the Boroughs*, III 63; 'State, 1780', p. 20, Windsor MSS. Cf. *The Parliamentary Papers of John Robinson*, pp. 81, 108, 111.

[6] Oldfield, *History of the Boroughs*, III 89; *The Parliamentary Papers of John Robinson*, p. 81.

continued to command one seat, but had to admit the claim of the independents in the town to choose the second member; after two bitterly disputed by-elections in 1770 and 1773, the two factions at Dover agreed in 1774 to divide the representation.[1] In 1783 not one of these thirteen treasury seats was classed by Robinson as under 'decisive influence'.[2]

At Queenborough, the ordnance and the admiralty each continued to return one member. These were regarded by Robinson in 1783 as two of the four 'safe' government seats.[3] Between 1761 and 1780, the admiralty retained unbroken control over Saltash and Plymouth – though in 1780 its nominees were confronted by an opposition in both places – and over one seat at Sandwich. In and after 1774 it was forced into hazardous expedients to secure a temporary extension of its hold upon Portsmouth.[4] For a time, in collaboration with the treasury, it even increased its interest by gaining one seat at Scarborough: this development began with the candidature of Sir Hugh Palliser in 1774 and was confirmed by the return of another naval candidate, Captain Charles Phipps, in 1780.[5] But by 1780 only one seat at Rochester remained at its disposal. At Rochester a body of independents joined forces with the London radicals soon after the commencement of the Middlesex election crisis, apparently encouraged thereto by one of their members, John Calcraft, who had been returned in 1768 with ministerial support but shortly afterwards 'turned Patriot'.[6] On Calcraft's death his seat was recaptured without a contest by the government.[7] But by 1774 the independent party was sufficiently strong to prevent the election of two ministerial candidates and

[1] *Canterbury Journal*, 9, 30 Jan 1770, 23, 30 Mar, 6 Apr 1773, 4 Oct 1774. Sir Joseph Yorke to Hardwicke, 18 Oct 1774, B.M. Add. MSS. 35370, fo 286.

[2] *The Parliamentary Papers of John Robinson*, p. 106.

[3] Ibid.

[4] Oldfield, *History of the Boroughs*, II 61–4; R. J. Murrell and R. East, *Extracts from Records . . . of the . . . Borough of Portsmouth . . .* (Portsmouth, 1884) pp. 297–321.

[5] *The Parliamentary Papers of John Robinson*, p. 73.

[6] William Gordon to Lord Sandwich, 16 Oct 1771, Abergavenny MS. 19A; Calcraft's obituary, *Canterbury Journal*, 8 Sept 1772.

[7] North to George III, George III to North, 24 Aug 1772, *The Correspondence of King George III*, II nos. 1118, 1119; *Canterbury Journal*, 22 Sept 1772.

to return Robert Gregory of the East India House, a friend of Rockingham. Robinson hoped to reverse this verdict in 1780, 'with management and attention, and a sudden declaration at the moment all being prepared',[1] but in the event the government could again only carry one seat. Though faced with increasing opposition the admiralty still controlled ten[2] seats in 1780. The great crash of the admiralty interest only occurred in the next few years, when both seats at Portsmouth, both at Saltash, and the newly acquired one at Scarborough were successively lost.

Altogether the number of government seats dropped from thirty to twenty-four between 1761 and 1780. Moreover, this reduction was a continuing process: both treasury and admiralty lost control of still further seats in the following decade.

At Portsmouth an important section of the corporation – which was 'principally composed of men of independent fortune' – disapproved after 1770 of the government's American policy and of North's ministry in general, and rebelled against the continuance of admiralty control over elections. Early in 1774 they tried their strength at a by-election and the government nominee only secured his return by three votes. To try and purge the electorate, the government moved for information in the nature of *quo warranto* against the mayor, several of the aldermen, and over sixty of the burgesses, all of whom were consequently displaced. But this was a game at which two could play. The independents similarly attacked supporters of the ministerial party and secured the dismissal of twenty-nine of them. By the general election of 1774 the government was left with a majority in the rump of the corporation and the body of burgesses. But this hold was exceedingly precarious. The survival in office after the *quo warranto* proceedings of only four aldermen, two independents and two ministerialists, produced a deadlock which prevented all regeneration of the corporation: no mayor could be elected, for nominations had to be made by the court of aldermen, and no new aldermen could be created or new burgesses elected until the mayoralty was once again filled.[3] The admiralty's control depended upon the survival of its aldermanic champions, and it was clear by 1780 that this could not be relied

[1] 'State, 1780', p. 32, Windsor MSS.
[2] [Additional note, 1969: For 'ten' read 'eleven'. See p. 302, n. 1 above.]
[3] Oldfield, *History of the Boroughs*, II 61–2.

upon for long. Robinson noted in his minutes preparatory to the general election: 'the same [members] for this time, but not again without a compromise'.[1] In September 1781 Lord Sandwich felt it necessary to treat for a compromise: 'We must trust to their promise', he told Robinson, 'for we are not in a situation to insist on a share of power in the borough.' But the independents insisted that they should have full control.[2] On the death of the ministerial aldermen Linzee and Varloe, they had the game in their hands.[3] The two independent aldermen, Carter and White, nominated Carter as mayor, and proceeded to pack the corporation and the body of burgesses with their own supporters.[4] 'This borough is now in the family of the Carters', Robinson minuted in 1783.[5] Pitt's ministry was able to obtain one seat for a friend, William Cornwallis, in 1784, but could not keep it for him at the next general election. 'You and Phillipson are to be chosen at Eye', Cornwallis's uncle informed him in April 1790, 'Erskine will be returned for Portsmouth, government having quite lost it.'[6]

In 1784 Robinson classed Saltash as one of the two safest government boroughs.[7] Yet little more than three years later this place also had passed out of admiralty control. In the two previous years it had already been twice contested before election committees of the House of Commons and only saved for the government by the casting vote of the chairman.[8] Whilst the franchise remained restricted to the members of a corporation packed with government officials and employees, the admiralty could dispose of the seats without difficulty. But in 1780, and again in 1783, John

[1] 'State, 1780', p. 31, Windsor MSS.

[2] Sandwich to Robinson, 7 Sept, 21, 25 Nov 1781, Abergavenny MSS. 385, 396, 397.

[3] Edward Linzee died in May 1782, at the age of eighty-four, *Gentleman's Magazine*, 1782 p. 263.

[4] Oldfield, *History of the Boroughs*, II 63–4; Murrell and East, *Records of the Borough of Portsmouth*, pp. 321–2.

[5] *The Parliamentary Papers of John Robinson*, p. 88.

[6] Frederick, bishop of Lichfield, to William Cornwallis, 29 Apr 1790, H.M.C., *Various Collections*, VI, *Cornwallis-Wykeham-Martin MSS.*, p. 353.

[7] *The Parliamentary Papers of John Robinson*, p. 106.

[8] Luders, *Reports upon Controverted Elections*, II 108, 114; Sir Grey Cooper to Charles Jenkinson, 20 May 1783, B.M. Add. MSS. 38218, fo. 186.

Buller of Morval stood as a candidate, claiming that the right of election should be in the inhabitant freeholders of ancient burgages: as he himself owned most of the burgages, this was tantamount to asserting his own mastery of the borough.[1] With the aid of William Beckford of Fonthill, Buller supported candidates on the same ground in 1784 and at a by-election in 1786, and on the fourth occasion his cause was successful – his brother-in-law, John Lemon, was declared duly elected.[2] After 1787 the management of the borough was firmly in Buller's hands, though his sons and Beckford had to defend it again in 1806 and 1807.[3]

By 1790 the admiralty had also lost its short-lived hold over Scarborough. From 1780 the government seat in this borough was coveted by a neighbouring landowner, Admiral Lord Mulgrave, who exploited his influence with Lord Sandwich to insist upon his brother, Captain Charles Phipps, being adopted as the government candidate.[4] Up to 1784 his scheme made little progress.[5] But thereafter he was successful in ensuring that patronage for the electors of Scarborough should flow through his hands, took credit with them also for what the Duke of Rutland obtained for them,[6] and by 1790 was able to divide the borough interest with Rutland. Direct government influence was eclipsed, and the two families of Manners and Phipps dominated the constituency until the Reform Act.

The treasury interest likewise underwent a further decline after 1780. Newport in the Isle of Wight was regarded by 1784 rather as under private patronage than as a government constituency, and Troughear Holmes brought in his son-in-law, Edward Rushworth, who voted more often against than with the ministry, and

[1] List of the Corporation of Saltash, Bolton MSS., Hants Record Office; Oldfield, *History of the Boroughs*, I 86–9, 96.

[2] *Commons Journals*, 42, 727 a–b; Luders, *Reports upon Controverted Elections*, II 107–225; *The Journal of William Beckford in Portugal and Spain*, pp. 58–9. On Buller's activities at Saltash see above, pp. 223–31.

[3] Oldfield, *Representative History of Great Britain and Ireland*, III 143–5; H.M.C., *Dropmore MSS.*, VIII 384–6, 455; IX 56; John Pedley to Beckford, 8 Jan 1808, Lewis Melville, *Life and Letters of William Beckford of Fonthill* (1910) pp. 269–70.

[4] On this see Sir Hugh Palliser to Sandwich, 7 Mar 1784, Sandwich MSS.

[5] *The Parliamentary Papers of John Robinson*, p. 132.

[6] H.M.C., *Rutland MSS.*, III 298, 302, 428.

Hugh Seymour Conway, a follower of Lord North then in opposition.[1] Opposition men were again returned in 1790. Seaford, after 1784, was captured by Lord Pelham in alliance with the 'independent' interest, after a campaign in which T. H. B. Oldfield himself played an active part. The right of election at Seaford was vested in the inhabitants paying scot and lot. Government managers had long maintained their control by ensuring that rates were levied only upon those residents who held some place of profit in the public service. Now, after a series of petitions, the independent electors established their status as persons from whom rates ought to have been collected and whose votes must be accepted at parliamentary elections.[2] Seaford was thus freed from ministerial control, to become a prize of contention between Lord Pelham, the Duke of Richmond and various local patrons. Finally, before 1790, John Nesbitt had sold his interest at Winchelsea to Richard Barwell and the Earl of Darlington, and the seats were no longer available to the treasury without the grace and favour of the new patrons.[3] Thus, in the single decade following Dunning's resolution, the administration lost a further ten seats in six constituencies formerly under its direct control – and by processes which had no connection whatever with the enactments of economical reform.

The view has long been gaining ground that the legislative programme of the economical reformers was in many respects singularly ill adapted to achieve the ends they had in mind. It is also evident that the reformers stirred up a great deal of fuss about nothing. 'Influence' in the sense of corruption was of little account in the House of Commons of the later eighteenth century. In fact, that House was a far more unruly and independent body than its twentieth-century successor. The distribution of patronage doubtless helped to cement support for the government, but with most of its supporters political opinions and the commonly current attitude of respect and loyalty towards the king's administration counted for more than the mere enjoyment of place. Often place was clearly a consequence, not a cause, of political behaviour. This

[1] *The Parliamentary Papers of John Robinson*, p. 108. Cf. Oldfield, *History of the Boroughs*, II 83, 90–1.

[2] Oldfield, *History of the Boroughs*, 115–25, 145. See also Luders *Reports upon Controverted Elections*, III 1–138.

[3] Oldfield, *History of the Boroughs*, III 88–90.

was more particularly the case after 1765, when Wilkes and America had brought great controversial questions back into politics. The more we come to know about individual members of the Commons in that period, the more we find them acting in accordance with their own judgement and conviction – and the placemen formed no exception to this general rule. To explode the opposition story of the corruption and sordidness of politics in parliament in the time of Lord North, it is hardly necessary to examine the minutiae of placemen and of government influence over parliamentary elections. But such an examination is justified as providing a background to the story of the movement for economical reform. It is worth knowing that the champions of the movement argued their case – as politicians very often will – with a sublime and beautiful disregard of easily ascertainable facts and trends. Neither in the number of placemen nor in the number of ministerial constituencies had government 'influence' been increased in the nineteen years before Dunning's resolution.

FIFTEEN

British Newspapers in the Later Georgian Age

THE role of newspapers in the general development of British society during the reigns of George III and George IV still requires considerable investigation. Even the growth of the newspaper press itself in this period is a story which remains largely untold. The last general history, by H. R. Fox Bourne, was published as far back as 1887 and though good in its day is manifestly inadequate now.[1] As yet we are far from ready to replace it. Far too much ground work still remains to be done. First-class histories of individual newspapers are rare: the only volumes relating to this period which can be put into this class are Dr R. L. Haig's study of the *Gazetteer*, a model of its kind,[2] and the magisterial *History of the Times*.[3] A number of particular questions have been dealt with in monographs. Legal restraints on the press at the beginning of the period have been ably elucidated by Fredrick Siebert,[4] and the older study by Wickwar provides much useful material on the decades during and after the French wars.[5] American scholars have provided valuable studies of the British press in relation to the crisis of the American Revolution.[6] For the period after assumption of power by the younger Pitt, Professor Aspinall's monograph, *Politics and the Press c. 1780–1850* (1949), is a mine of information. It is, however, oriented in certain directions; and – inevitably, in

[1] *English Newspapers: Chapters in the History of Journalism.*

[2] Robert L. Haig, *The Gazetteer, 1735–1797: A Study in the Eighteenth-Century English Newspaper* (Carbondale, Ill., 1960).

[3] [S. Morison], *The History of The Times*, vol. I, '*The Thunderer' in the making, 1785–1841* (1935).

[4] *Freedom of the Press in England, 1476–1776.*

[5] W. H. Wickwar, *The Struggle for the Freedom of the Press, 1819–32* (1928).

[6] Dora Mae Clark, *British Opinion and the American Revolution* (New Haven, Conn., 1930); Solomon Lutnick, *The American Revolution and the British Press, 1775–1783* (Columbia, Mo., 1967).

view of the lack of previous detailed studies – it relies more on 'outside' evidence than on knowledge of what the newsmen were about as evinced in their own productions. The technical evolution of newspapers is dealt with excellently in Stanley Morison's *The English Newspaper*, and in his short but valuable sketches of Edward Topham and John Bell.[1] One or two monographs and unpublished theses throw light on the press in provincial areas during the first half of the nineteenth century.[2] Much remains to be done. A number of the major newspapers of the later Georgian age deserve thorough 'biographical' investigation. Other questions, too, deserve examination: for instance, over thirty years ago, the authors of volume I of the *History of The Times* pointed to the lack of any proper study of the change in the character of journalism which developed markedly in the first decade of the nineteenth century.[3]

A thorough understanding of how the newspaper press developed during the later Georgian age has an importance far transcending the history of the press itself. The free interplay of opinion and the dissemination and exchange of information by means of public prints are hall-marks of the 'open society', of which western, and especially British and American, civilisation provide the exemplars. In Great Britain the progress of the press towards the role of

[1] *The English Newspaper: Some Account of the Physical Development of Journals printed in London between 1622 and the Present Day* (Cambridge, 1932); *Edward Topham, 1751–1820* (1933); *John Bell, 1745–1831* [1930].

[2] For the provincial press on the eve of George III's reign, G. A. Cranfield, *The Development of the English Provincial Newspaper, 1700–1760* (1962) is invaluable. Nothing similar exists for the second half of the eighteenth century. There is a useful general survey of the position about 1829 in *Westminster Review*, XII (1830) 69–103. See Donald Read, *Press and People, 1790–1850: Opinion in three English Cities* (1961) for newspapers at Leeds, Sheffield and Manchester; Donald Clare, 'The local newspaper press and local politics in Manchester and Liverpool, 1780–1800', *Transactions of the Lancashire and Cheshire Antiquarian Society*, LXXIII–LXXIV (1963) 101–23; Derek Fraser, 'The Nottingham Press, 1800–1850', Transactions of the Thoroton Society of Nottinghamshire, LXVII (1963) 46–66; Asa Briggs, 'Press and Public in early nineteenth-century Birmingham', *Dugdale Society Occasional Papers*, no. 8 (Oxford, 1949); K. G. Burton, *The Early Newspaper Press in Berkshire (1723–1855)* (privately printed, Reading, 1954); J. Money, 'Public Opinion in the West Midlands, 1760–1793' (Ph.D. thesis, Cambridge, 1967) ch. II.

[3] P. 87.

'fourth estate', which it achieved by the middle of the nineteenth century, was intimately interconnected with the broadening of political liberty, which led onward to the political democracy eventually achieved some half a century later. How far the growth of the press was cause, and how far effect, is a question which it is difficult, perhaps impossible, to answer. One might as well ask, did the hen or the egg come first? However, it appears that before the end of the Georgian period the press had matured and established itself to the point where its reactions upon politics were significant. At any rate, it is easy enough to show that people thought this;[1] though the truth of the fact is less easy to demonstrate, at least at the present state of our knowledge of the subject. But by the 1830s something significant had happened; and the more we can come to know about the process that led to this situation, the better will be our understanding of one of the crucial phases of British political evolution and of some of the basic principles and traditions which still govern political conduct in this island. A large and complex field of investigation presents itself; and the following outline of certain salient features of newspaper development between about 1760 and 1830 is offered less for purposes of explanation than as a framework of reference for future inquiry.

The sheer expansion of the newspaper press in the years between the accession of George III and the death of his eldest son is, despite its limitations, a fact deserving emphasis, one which may be illustrated in a number of ways.

The number of stamps on sheets of newsprint issued by the stamp office was 9,464,790 in 1760, rose to 12,680,000 by 1775, and exceeded 16,000,000 by 1801. In 1816 it rose to just over 22,000,000, and by 1837 it was over 39,000,000.[2] The correlation between these figures and the increasing numbers of newspapers being produced is not direct: certain types of newspaper – dailies and weeklies – multiplied more rapidly than the tri-weeklies, and in the early nineteenth century the distribution of stamps was also affected by the growth of one or two newspapers with rather large

[1] Aspinall, *Politics and the Press*, pp. 1–5.

[2] Bourne, *English Newspapers*, I 225, 371–2; II 67. Aspinall, 'The circulation of newspapers in the early nineteenth century', *Review of English Studies*, XXII (1946) 29 n.; *Politics and the Press*, p. 6 n.

daily issues, notably the *Courier* and *The Times*. The proportion of provincial to metropolitan circulation seems to have increased somewhat during the period. It has been calculated that in 1760 the English provincial newspapers, numbering between forty and fifty, together with the one or two Scottish journals then in existence, took about one fifth of the stamps issued by the stamp office.[1] By 1821 the proportion had reached one third.[2] About 1830 over a hundred and fifty English provincial newspapers were being published, and another thirty-seven in Scotland.[3] But the expansion in the metropolis was probably the more significant; it was here that new trends in development began and that a real impact could be made on a very numerous reading public. About 1760 the metropolis had four daily newspapers and five or six evening newspapers published three times a week.[4] Thirty years later the number had increased to thirteen morning dailies, one evening daily, and nine tri-weeklies, most of them appearing in the evening.[5] Thirty years on again, in 1821, a contemporary count showed fourteen morning and evening dailies, four tri-weeklies, nineteen bi-weeklies, and a further eighteen appearing weekly, of which some were Sunday journals.[6] By 1790 the number of daily newspapers supported by the metropolitan public had almost reached saturation point: newcomers rose only on the ruins of the old. Henceforth the most striking expansion was among those which appeared once or twice a week, including those published on Sunday. It seems not unlikely that the principal factor causing this change in the pattern was the increasing burden of stamp duties. This was raised from 1½*d* to 2*d* in 1789, increased to 3½*d* in 1797, and in 1815 to 4*d*, and restriction of circulation was undoubtedly one of the government's motives. The stamp duty also was the main factor restricting newspapers to a single large sheet, usually folded once to make four pages each of four columns. Slight concessions regarding size in later Stamp Acts enabled early-nineteenth-

[1] Cranfield, *The Development of the English Provincial Newspaper*, pp. 172–3, 176.

[2] *Annual Register*, 1822, appendix to chronicle, p. 351.

[3] *Westminster Review*, XII 71–2.

[4] Thomas, 'The beginning of parliamentary reporting in newspapers, 1768–1774', *English Historical Review*, LXXIV 624.

[5] Morison, *The English Newspaper*, p. 197.

[6] *Annual Register*, 1822, appendix to chronicle, p. 351.

century newspapers to appear in slightly larger format with five-column pages.[1]

The evolution of the press can also be traced in terms of its business organisation, and here the last quarter of the eighteenth century brought decisive developments. Early newspapers had been small-scale ventures by individual master printers, partly for the purpose of keeping presses and workmen occupied at times when they might otherwise have been idle. London newspapers had passed beyond this stage early in the eighteenth century (though this was still the pattern at its close for many provincial papers). The physical growth of the newspaper, which was in part bound up with the development of advertising, carried this type of enterprise to the stage where it was beyond the resources of single individuals. In mid-century the typical newspaper was founded and run on behalf of a syndicate, usually of twelve to twenty businessmen, each of whom held a single share in the property. Only in this way could the necessary capital be raised.[2] By the late eighteenth century two or three thousand pounds were required to launch a newspaper, and before long the figure was substantially higher.[3] Most of the investment was provided by the leading booksellers in the metropolis. Even if they did not run a press themselves – and some did – they had intimate connections with the printing houses. Their demands for assured space for advertisements complemented newspaper needs for an assured revenue from advertising – an understanding that a proprietor would give advertising support was often a part of the bargain under which he took a share in a newspaper.[4] Interest in advertising also attracted businessmen in other fields: the early proprietors of the *Morning*

[1] For the most reliable references to changes in the stamp and also the advertisement duties, see A. Aspinall, 'Statistical Account of the London Newspapers in the Eighteenth Century', *English Historical Review*, LXIII (1948) 201–32, and 'The Circulation of Newspapers in the Early Nineteenth Century', *Review of English Studies*, XXII (1946) 29–43. The statutory restriction on the size of stamped sheets of newsprint was abolished only in 1825, and this made possible the issue of 'double' eight-page newspapers at a reasonable cost (*History of The Times*, I 324–5).

[2] Morison, *The English Newspaper*, pp. 143–4.

[3] Aspinall, *Politics and the Press*, p. 69 n. 1; Bourne, *English Newspapers*, I 371–2.

[4] Morison, *The English Newspaper*, p. 144.

Post, founded in 1772, included the horse-dealer, Richar Tattersall, and the founder of the great London auctioneering firm James Christie.[1] Except where this was excluded by the terms o partnership, proprietor seem habitually to have spread thei investments among a number of newspapers.[2]

In the early part of George III's reign the actual production o the newspaper was often still in the hands of the printer, himsel normally required to be one of the partners. He provided much o the non-advertisement copy and depended otherwise on casua contributions in the form of letters, essays, miscellaneous shor paragraphs and verse.[3] But before long the more enterprisin syndicates came to realise that the successful conduct of a news paper demanded qualities of education and literary capacity rathe higher than those normally displayed by master printers – henc such appointments as that of the Rev. Henry Bate as editor of th *Morning Post* in 1775, and those of John Henley Wall and Jame Perry as editors of the *Gazetteer* in 1780 and 1783. Appointment of this kind marked the first stage in separating the two activitie of conducting (or editing) and of printing the newspaper. To thi point can be traced the beginnings of an editorial and reportin staff. But this was slow to emerge. Till the end of the century, sta writers and reporters were still rarities. James Perry took a nev and exceptional step when he employed two other people to hel him report parliamentary debates for the *Gazetteer* during th 1780s.[4]

A new phase in the organisational development of the Londor press corresponded roughly with the period of the French Revolu tion: this was marked by the rise of the early newspaper tycoons Over many years the old system of proprietorial syndicates ha

[1] Bourne, *English Newspapers*, I 206 n., 271.

[2] According to articles of agreement drawn up in 1748, no proprietor the *Gazetteer* should possess a holding of shares in any other newspape (Haig, *The Gazetteer*, pp. 22–3). When the prominent London publishe John Newbery, died in 1763, his will disclosed possession of interests no fewer than six newspapers, five in London and one in the province (Morison, *The English Newspaper*, p. 114 and n.).

[3] E.g. Haig, *The Gazetteer*, pp. 33–9, 120–5. Henry Sampson Woodfall the *Public Advertiser*, and William Woodfall of the *Morning Chronicle* are ou standing examples of the craftsman-reporter-conductor during this perio

[4] Ibid., p. 191–2.

served the press well and helped to carry it through an important phase of its growth. Nor was its usefulness at an end, for many newspapers continued to be run in this way.[1] But it tended towards conservatism and lack of enterprise. Excessive concern about the advertisement-reading public dulled appreciation of changing public demands for other fare: this seems, for instance, to have been the downfall of the once highly successful *Gazetteer*.[2] During the second half of George III's reign the most striking advances in journalism were associated with a swing back to individual control. The changes reflect the greater facility with which the go-ahead individual venturer in journalism could raise capital and even acquire, by good management, a small fortune. Not every individual entrepreneur was equally successful: there was little distinction about *The Times* under its first owner-manager, John Walter I, nor did it produce much profit. But it was at the hands of a small number of talented individuals that the most exciting and significant advances were made.

The first notable development of this kind was the launching at the beginning of 1787 of the *World and Fashionable Advertiser* by the partners Edward Topham and John Bell.[3] Edward Topham, a captain in the guards and a man of fashion, having fallen in love with Mrs Wells, a beautiful actress whose husband had deserted her, engaged in this enterprise expressly to forward Mrs Wells's theatrical reputation and ambitions – as he afterwards jested: 'Love first made the World.' She herself took an active part in the affairs of the paper, keeping in contact with the various theatre managers and writers and attending at Westminster Hall in order to provide reports of the early, dramatic stages of the trial of Warren Hastings. Topham's influence gave a new twist to journalism by the production of a newspaper slanted to the tastes of 'West End' society, and he seems to have been the first to make a distinct feature of witty paragraphs and jokes, a practice soon copied by his competitors. John Bell, a leading London bookseller and publisher, seems to have begun his ventures in journalism as one of the original proprietors, and business manager, of the *Morning Post*.

[1] Aspinall, *Politics and the Press*, p. 202, n. 1.

[2] Haig, *The Gazetteer*, p. 231.

[3] See the biographical sketches by Stanley Morison, *Edward Topham* and *John Bell*.

By 1786 he was ripe for the greater freedom of initiative provided by the dual partnership in the *World*, in which he furnished the business and technical expertise. In 1789, hankering after still more independence and unable to buy out Topham, he sold out to him for £4,000 – a sum indicative of the paper's remarkable and rapid success – and went on to establish further newspapers of his own: the *Oracle*, started in 1789, which failed and was sold a few years later, and then the successful Sunday journal, *Bell's Weekly Messenger*. Although Bell's personal affairs seem never to have recovered from embarrassments leading to bankruptcy, occasioned by his offering an entertainment to the Prince of Wales, professionally he was highly successful: Leigh Hunt remarked on his newspaper being 'profitable to everybody but himself'.[1] Bell's greatest contribution to newspaper development lay in the brilliant artistry with which he dealt with the problems of visual presentation, and the experiments with new types and layouts which he carried on in the *World* and the *Oracle* set fashions perforce copied by the rest of the London press.

James Perry presents a formative influence of a very different type.[2] Employed for about seven years as editor of the *Gazetteer*, he became joint owner-editor of the *Morning Chronicle* in 1790 and obtained complete control on the death of his partner in 1796. Perry was a truly dedicated journalist: although illness obliged him to relinquish detailed control of the paper during the last years of his life, he could not bear to sell out and retire. Furthermore, as a journalist he was guided by strong political principles and convictions. A devotee of Charles James Fox, he made the *Morning Chronicle* the unofficial but constant press organ of the party led by Fox and his political heirs, and in doing so he turned it into the most influential of the London dailies during the period of the French wars.

During much the same time the entrepreneur, Daniel Stuart, developed a remarkable talent for converting derelict newspaper properties into gold-mines. Originally a printer by trade, and enjoying the contract for printing the *Morning Post*, he seized the chance to buy the paper when it was in a moribund state in 1795; subsequently amalgamated it with two other dying journals cheaply acquired, the *Telegraph* and the *Gazetteer*; and in seven

[1] Leigh Hunt, *Autobiography*, ed. Roger Ingpen, 2 vols (1903) I 170.

[2] See the biographical sketch in paper 16.

years nursed it to the position of being first in circulation among the London morning papers, when he finally sold out at about forty times the price he had paid. In 1799, in partnership with T. G. Street, he also purchased the evening daily newspaper, the *Courier*, and soon pushed it into a leading position among the London dailies. By 1817 Stuart had amassed a sufficient fortune to retire from active journalism, buy an Oxfordshire estate, and settle into the life of a country gentleman: in 1823 he served as sheriff for the county.[1]

In a style more akin to that of Perry than to Stuart's, John Walter II, after 1803, rescued his father's newspaper, *The Times*, from imminent decease and by 1819 had brought it to the foremost place in circulation among the London morning dailies and made it the successful rival in influence of the *Morning Chronicle*. Walter's achievements have been described elsewhere in detail, and here will only be briefly analysed in a broader context below.[2] It may be noted that another side of his journalistic activities remains wholly unexplored – the running of the *Evening Mail*, of which he was one of the proprietors, and which by 1811 had achieved the highest circulation among the six or seven tri-weeklies then published in London.[3]

Some of the impact of these men on metropolitan journalism will be considered later in a wider context. At this point it is to be noted how, so far as their own papers were concerned, they were transforming the scale and character of the newspaper business in the years from about 1790 to 1820. In general the capital value of

[1] On Stuart see the article in *D.N.B.* For a government estimate of the circulation of the *Courier* in 1811 (about 5,800), see Denis Gray, *Spencer Perceval: The Evangelical Prime Minister, 1762–1812* (Manchester, 1963) p. 132; and for the next figure, *Gentleman's Magazine*, 1847, II 323.

[2] *History of The Times*, I, VI–X.

[3] The *Evening Mail* had been started by John Walter I as a ministerial journal in 1789 (Aspinall, *Politics and the Press*, pp. 270–1). His son once described it as 'the handmaid' of *The Times* and it is a pity that the authors of the *History of The Times* did not try to evaluate it, merely remarking that it summarised the news and leading articles of *The Times* (I 180 n.). In 1806 Walter put its circulation as equal to the *Morning Chronicle* (ibid., p. 102) and in 1811 it was selling about 5,000 copies (Gray, *Spencer Perceval*, p. 133). It was a separate enterprise from *The Times* with a separate board of proprietors, of whom John Walter II was chief in the early nineteenth century (*History of The Times*, I 180 n.).

newspaper enterprises was getting larger. In 1798 Sheridan estimated that £2,000–£3,000 was sufficient capital to launch a newspaper; and the careers of Perry and Stuart show that a fortunate speculator able to pick up a derelict property might start from far less.[1] But even ten years earlier than this Bell's third share in the very successful *World* was valued at £4,000, and even earlier, in 1785, the proprietors of the *Morning Post* had valued it at £8,400[2] However, this was small beer by comparison with the leading journals nursed by the tycoons of the day. In 1803 Stuart sold the *Morning Post* for £25,000. Perry's property in the *Morning Chronicle* was sold in 1822 by his executors for £40,000 (or perhaps slightly more), and there is an indication that the capital value of the shares in its chief rival, *The Times*, was about the same figure in 1819.[3] Similarly, the scale of profits was changing. In 1774 the total profits of the *Public Advertiser* were £1,740.[4] In 1785 the proprietors of the *Morning Post* shared out £1,500, and in 1786 they reckoned an annual payment of £1,370 a suitable consideration for a seven-year lease of the paper to two of their number.[5] The *Gazetteer*, then going downhill, was yielding about that time a total annual profit of less than £400.[6] A generation later the figures for the chief newspapers are in another dimension. James Perry's *Morning Chronicle* was said to be bringing him in £12,000 a year during the last two or three years of his life.[7] There are reports that at about the same time (1820) the *Morning Herald* was

[1] Aspinall, *Politics and the Press*, p. 69 n. 1. According to the recollection of James Gray's close friend, Pryse Lockhart Gordon (which was not, however, always reliable), Perry and Gray were able to acquire the *Morning Chronicle* for about £210 at auction in 1790 and seem to have laid out about £1,000 on the undertaking (see p. 341). Daniel Stuart spent only £600 in acquiring the *Morning Post* complete with the business house and the plant in 1795 (*Gentleman's Magazine*, 1838, II 241).

[2] Aspinall, *Politics and the Press*, p. 72; Wilfrid Hindle, *The Morning Post, 1772–1937: Portrait of a newspaper* [1937] p. 44.

[3] Aspinall, *Politics and the Press*, p. 85, n. 3; p. 358 below; *History of The Times*, I 174.

[4] Bourne, *English Newspapers*, I 195–6.

[5] Aspinall, *Politics and the Press*, pp. 72, 274.

[6] In the 1780s the capital value of the *Gazetteer* was put at £3,200, and the average total annual dividend during Perry's editorship was about £360 (Haig, *The Gazetteer*, pp. 210–11).

[7] See p. 357.

making an annual profit of £8,000 and the *Star* £6,000.[1] At that time *The Times* seems to have been making little if any profit, but the situation is obscured by the fact that John Walter also owned the press as a separate business and was probably taking a substantial profit at that stage; also he was ploughing back money lavishly in generous payments to writers and staff. A decade later the annual profit was rumoured to be about £20,000 and there is one piece of evidence indicating that it was at least half this figure in the late 1830s.[2]

Similarly the financial rewards for a salaried journalistic career changed remarkably between the beginning and the end of George III's reign. In the early 1770s, when an abortive proposal was made to Roger Thompson to take over the printing and conducting of the *Middlesex Journal*, he was assured he might expect a profit of between £100 and £150 a year. In the same decade Thompson's successor as conductor of the *Gazetteer* was paid a salary of one and a half guineas a week. However, the *Morning Post* set new standards with an editorial salary (to a man with university training) of four guineas a week, and the proprietors of the *Gazetteer* followed this example when Perry was appointed editor in 1783.[3] The first reporters and writers who made their appearance in the 1770s received similar modest stipends for regular engagements, though an able and active writer might well make a comfortable competence by writing for more than one journal. James Perry began his career in 1777 as an article-writer for the *General Advertiser* at a guinea a week, with an additional half-guinea for assisting on the *London Evening Post*.[4] As a young law student in the early 1780s, James Stephen was paid two guineas a week as parliamentary reporter, doing duty sometimes for twenty-four hours at a stretch.[5] By the end of the century, despite the increased burden of taxation carried by the press, the rewards were rising. Around 1800 a regular writer and reporter could

[1] Bourne, *English Newspapers*, I 371–2.

[2] Aspinall, *Politics and the Press*, p. 380, quoting the MS. journal of Le Marchant. However, the figures for dividends in 1837 and 1838 on half shares indicate a total annual dividend of only £10,000 (*History of The Times*, I 174, n. 1).

[3] Haig, *The Gazetteer*, pp. 125, 135, 189; Aspinall, *Politics and the Press*, p. 71.

[4] See p. 356 below.

[5] Hindle, *The Morning Post*, pp. 53–4.

expect four guineas a week from the better journals: This was what John Campbell received from Perry in 1800; Thomas Campbell from the *Star* in 1804; John Dyer Collier as a law reporter for *The Times* between 1804 and 1808, and his son, John Payne Collier, as a reporter about 1809.[1] Owing to the inflation of the late 1790s purchasing power had not doubled in twenty years as the rate had done, but it had probably increased considerably. Fewer figures for editorial salaries are available; but the appointment of William Jerdan as editor of the *Sun* in 1813 at an annual salary of over £500[2] shows a comparable increase when set beside the rates of editorial pay about 1780. In the early nineteenth century the scale of emolument for senior literary appointments offered by *The Times* seems to have been unique. The first John Walter, making final testamentary dispositions just before his death in 1812, valued John Walter II's services as conductor of the paper at £1,000 per annum. This was the salary fixed in turn by Walter when the great editor, Thomas Barnes, took over full control in 1819, and for a brief period before this he had even been paying £1,500. From 1812 he was paying £300 a year to the columnist, Edward Sterling, for one or two articles a month on current topics.[3] It was only in the decade or two after 1810 that the increasing financial resources of the great newspapers began to be used for a significant expansion of the regular reporting staffs. About 1781 no printing house employed more than one parliamentary reporter, and there must have been a number of cases of a man's services being shared between two or three papers.[4] Even in the next thirty years staffs grew only slowly. Around 1808 *The Times* seems to have been employing four reporters, or perhaps one or two more, exclusive of Henry Crabb Robinson, who was being used partly as an assistant editor and partly as a foreign correspondent on European assignments.[5] In 1811 the *Morning Chronicle* seems to

[1] Mrs Hardcastle, *Life of John, Lord Campbell*, 2 vols (1881) I 56; Bourne, *English Newspapers*, I 288; *History of The Times*, I 135–6.

[2] Aspinall, *Politics and the Press*, p. 81.

[3] *History of The Times*, I, 81–2, 154–5, 158, 177.

[4] *Memoirs of James Stephen*, ed. M. M. Bevington (1954) p. 291, cited in A. Aspinall, 'The Reporting and Publishing of the House of Commons Debates, 1771–1834', *Essays Presented to Sir Lewis Namier*, ed. Pares and Taylor, p. 237.

[5] *History of The Times*, I 136–9, 142–5.

have had only three regular parliamentary reporters.[1] However, by the 1820s *The Times*' staff of parliamentary reporters numbered about a dozen, and the *Morning Chronicle*, its chief rival, probably employed almost as many. The numbers for these two papers seem to have been still about the same in the 1830s.[2] At that time the total number of parliamentary reporters was stated to be between forty and fifty,[3] and the large proportion of this total attached to the two leading daily papers indicates both their primacy and the limited expansion of the profession so far as other newspapers were concerned.

According to the stamp office figures, the number of copies of newspapers in circulation increased by about four times between 1760 and 1837.[4] In London the increase was rather less than this; and it was achieved by a multiplication of the number of newspapers rather than by the emergence of journals with relatively large circulations. Indeed, there is some indication that about the turn of the century, as a result of this fierce competition, the circulations of individual London newspapers were in general lower than they had been twenty years before. In a list of estimates of circulation for eighteen journals in 1782, ten appear with daily issues of 2,500 or over.[5] Another for 1801, covering twenty-two journals, places only two, and possibly a third, as having daily sales of over 2,000.[6] The next two decades were a time of gradually increasing circulations among the better-conducted newspapers. According to government estimates in 1811, seven papers then had a daily sale of nearly 3,000 or upwards, and three were well out in front – the *Courier* (about 5,800), *The Times* (5,000) and its subsidiary, the *Evening Mail*, with about the same circulation three days a week.[7] There was little difference in the pattern ten years later,

[1] Gray, *Spencer Perceval*, p. 132, n. 5.

[2] Aspinall, in *Essays Presented to Namier*, p. 251 and n. 1. In 1833 a published remonstrance against O'Connell was signed by the full *Times* staff of eleven parliamentary reporters and another by the ten reporters of the *Morning Chronicle* (*History of The Times*, I 314–5 and n.).

[3] Aspinall, in *Essays Presented to Namier*, p. 251, n. 2.

[4] See p. 313 above.

[5] Lutnick, *The American Revolution and the British Press*, appendix.

[6] *Annual Register*, 1822, appendix to chronicle, p. 350.

[7] Gray, *Spencer Perceval*, pp. 132–3.

but more of the journals not in the front rank had climbed back to a daily issue of over 2,000.[1] It seems evident that financial stringency and heavier taxation in the later 1790s caused a distinct setback to London journalism, but that, despite the renewal of war in 1803, the press shared in a growing national prosperity during the following decades. The excitement of the last years of the war against Napoleon was a powerful stimulus to sales: the *Courier* was then said to have a daily issue of 8,000, but this was exceptional.[2] The introduction of steam printing by John Walter II in 1814 made no spectacular difference to the circulation of *The Times*. The capacity to print the day's edition in six or seven hours gave Walter an important lead over his rivals in printing late news, but there was no public demand to support a large increase in the daily issue so long as *The Times* (and other newspapers) retailed at 7*d*. At the beginning of 1817 the daily circulation of *The Times* was just approaching 7,000, and it remained at that figure until mid-1820 when it was temporarily boosted to 15,000 by Barnes's popular decision to support the cause of Queen Caroline. But it was back at about 7,000 the following year, though even at that level well ahead of its chief rivals, the *Courier* (about 5,100) and the *Morning Chronicle* (about 3,100). By 1830 it had crept up to almost 11,000.[3]

By modern standards, and also in relation to the population of Great Britain in the early nineteenth century, these figures were small. Nevertheless the newspapers were widely read. London coffee-houses were places of popular resort, where merchants and factors of all kinds met to do their business, and provision of newspapers was a regular service. A Continental visitor to London about the turn of the century considered that the principal reason why Englishmen went to coffee-houses was to read the papers, and he noted that 'the most frequented houses take in ten or

[1] *Annual Register*, 1822, appendix to chronicle, p. 351. By this date a small number of weekly newspapers were attaining large circulations, though the number of copies each week was less than for the leading dailies – the *News*, and *Bell's Weekly Messenger* about 10,000, *John Bull* slightly less, the *Observer* about 14,000.

[2] *Gentleman's Magazine*, 1847, II 323.

[3] *History of The Times*, I 163, 245; Aspinall, *Politics and the Press*, pp. 129 and n. 3, 313; *Annual Register*, 1822, appendix to chronicle, p. 351.

twelve copies of the same paper not to make people wait.'[1] In 1841, in evidence before a parliamentary committee, one coffee-house keeper, whose house received four or five hundred customers daily, declared that before the reduction of the stamp duty in 1836, he had paid £400 a year for newspapers and magazines and for binding back numbers.[2] The number of coffee-houses in London in the second half of the eighteenth century was about two hundred. By 1820 the number had risen to nearly three hundred.[3] Although doubtless few fell into the category described above, the potential reading public they served must have been considerable. To these must be added the clientele of an unknown but certainly large number of inns, ale-houses and gin-shops, where the provision of newspapers was also customary. The early nineteenth century saw the rise of further facilities in the subscription reading-rooms. Friends clubbed together to share the cost of a paper; and although the practice of hiring out newspapers was illegal, it was virtually impossible to suppress it. Radical newspapers were often read aloud at meetings of societies and political clubs in ale-houses.[4] In the years after Waterloo the average daily circulation of newspapers in the metropolis was around 40,000.[5] About 1829 it was estimated that every London newspaper was read by about thirty people.[6] The product of these figures is roughly equal to the total population of the metropolitan area at that time. There is no doubt, therefore, that most men who wanted to get information about public affairs from the newspapers could do so, and that the papers reached down to groups fairly low in the social scale. The habit of

[1] J. W. Archenholtz, *A Picture of England* (1797) p. 311, cited in Dorothy Marshall, *Dr Johnson's London* (1968) p. 207.

[2] Aspinall, in *Review of English Studies*, XXII 36–7. As *The Times* cost 7*d* in the years before 1836, a year's subscription (unless discount were given) was about £16 12*s* 0*d*.

[3] Bryant Lillywhite, *London Coffeehouses* (1963), from which these figures are abstracted.

[4] Aspinall, in *Review of English Studies*, XXII 29–43.

[5] The *Westminster Review* (XII (1830) 99) put the figure at 35,000, but the total of stamps issued in respect of London newspapers in 1821 noted in the *Annual Register* for 1822 (appendix to chronicle, p. 351) gives an average daily figure of over 40,000 and it seems unlikely that it declined in the years following.

[6] *Westminster Review*, X (1829) 478, cited in Aspinall, *Politics and the Press*, pp. 24–5.

reading newspapers in public places may have meant that proportionately more people than nowadays took stock of a variety of different opinions presented in different journals. In some areas of the provinces a comparable process was at work. By the 1790s the Manchester area was supporting four local journals, with circulations ranging from about 1,000 to well over 4,000. By the 1820s their number had increased to seven.[1] The West Riding, Liverpool, York and Nottingham were centres for a similar proliferation of local newspapers, and in all these areas there was a vigorous presentation of political opinions. The *Leeds Mercury*, purchased by Edward Baines in 1801, is perhaps the outstanding example of a successful provincial newspaper with a strong political slant. Baines developed it as an organ of moderate radical opinion in the district as a counterblast to the reactionary *Leeds Intelligencer*. In the early years the circulation of this weekly newspaper was about 2,000 and by 1829 it had risen to over 5,000, rivalling all but the most successful of the metropolitan journals.[2] In rural areas, however, political comment in local newspapers continued to be muted till well on into the nineteenth century. The reading public was smaller, and to alienate any large section of it could be financially fatal.

After this survey of the growth of the newspaper press during the later Georgian age, we may consider briefly some wider questions concerning its role in British society. From one viewpoint a newspaper was simply a business run for profit. There is no indication that anything other than financial gain motivated John Walter I in his establishment of *The Times* and the *Evening Mail*, and in his attempts to exploit the advantages of a pro-ministerial line of conduct. Many of the late-eighteenth-century editors and owners were venal and corrupt and despised by the politicians.[3] Profit dictated a careful concern for advertisements, a point stressed in the titles of many newspapers, and in this respect the press performed a

[1] Clare, in *Transactions of the Lancashire and Cheshire Antiquarian Society*, LXXIII–LXXIV 106–8; *Westminster Review*, XII 73.

[2] E. Baines, jun., *The Life of Edward Baines*, 2nd ed. (1859); Read, *Press and People*, pp. 74–8.

[3] A. Aspinall, 'The Social Status of Journalists at the beginning of the Nineteenth Century', *Review of English Studies*, XXI (1945) 216–25.

considerable and important commercial service to the community. The expansion of the newspaper industry, however limited it was by modern standards, was a significant element in the accumulation of capital and the extension of services which accompanied the economic growth of Great Britain at this time. It was buoyed up by both the economic and the social effects of that growth. Particularly significant for the history of the press was the concentration in the City of London and its urban environs of great numbers of relatively well-to-do people, to many of whom, engaged as they were in the day-by-day pursuits of buying and selling, advertising and other commercial intelligence was a service of considerable immediate importance. During the period under discussion 'greater London' contained roughly one-tenth of the total population of Great Britain. Such a community was uniquely placed to demand, and sustain, a press development of the kind which took place during this period.

However, the significance of the press was far more than merely commercial. The public which it served wanted information on all kinds of subjects, particularly public affairs, both domestic and foreign; and woe betide the newspaper conductor or editor who fell behind in the business of satisfying this demand! In relation to the development of British political institutions this concern was paramount; and in consequence of it, as often unwittingly as consciously, the owners and editors of the later Georgian newspaper press were creating an institution of vital importance. In doing so they built on foundations already securely laid. It was crucial that for over half a century before the accession of George III it had become a firmly-established principle of English public law that there should be no pre-publication censorship, and that an Englishman had the right to print what he pleased subject only to the *post facto* deterrents of the law. It was also crucial that the Revolution of 1689 had established that England (and hence Great Britain) would in essence be no longer a monarchy but a monarchical republic, in which monarch, government and the law were all alike understood to be the servants of the public interest. Therefore neither the letter of the law nor the interpretation of it were static but were open to change in accordance with public demand. The importance of these circumstances to the growth of the press is evident. They lay behind the significant extensions of the freedom of the press wrung from public authorities in the early years of the reign of George III; the successful limitation of the secretary of state's power to harass journalists with general warrants; removal of the secrecy surrounding the proceedings of parliament; the curbing of judicial interpretation of what constituted seditious libel. Each of these advances gave further impetus to the growth of the newspaper press, and it is almost impossible to err in exaggerating the importance of the second. It was true that the weapon of prosecution for seditious libel could still be used against journalists; but Fox's Libel Act of 1792 ensured that the criterion of seditious libel would conform not to the opinions of authority expressed by the judges but to those of the public from whom the juries came. Some newspapers fell foul of the law and suffered frequently from prosecutions; but these instances did not amount to such sustained persecution as the piling up of examples in the study by Wickwar would suggest. In many instances such prosecutions arose over outrageous perpetrations in print, which reflect the continued low tone of much of the press. Outspoken criticism of government did not necessarily involve risks of legal action. James Perry's conduct of the *Morning Chronicle* for thirty years with only two (unsuccessful) prosecutions and one unpleasant brush with the House of Lords illustrates how a journal of probity vigorously opposed to the government could be carried on without difficulty at that time.[1]

During the period of the French wars, the press as a whole was by no means so independent as Perry's *Morning Chronicle*. Professor Aspinall has shown in exhaustive detail how many journals were willingly, or reluctantly, harnessed to the government by means of money subsidies, advertising contracts, preferential mailing facilities, advance disclosure of information, the supplying of articles and puffs by hired writers, and the threat of withholding favours and facilities.[2] But the degree of control enjoyed by the government was always limited, and very early in the new century a trend towards emancipation was under way. A stamp-office survey in 1811, already cited, disclosed that out of 53 London papers, '17 were pro-government, 18 hostile, 15 neutral, and 3 wavering. But the opposition had a majority of 8 to 5 among the dailies (excluding *The Times*) and could also rely on the higher

[1] See below, p. 342. [2] *Politics and the Press, passim.*

standard and greater prestige of its press.'[1] The historians of *The Times* have suggested that a new spirit of independence was developing in journalism from about 1802, its pioneers being Cobbett with the *Weekly Political Register* (1802), John Hunt with the *News* (1805), followed by his brother Leigh's *Examiner* (1809), and John Walter II with *The Times* from about 1805.[2] There is a question here which requires a good deal more probing and analysis than can be given in a paper of this scope. The nature of the change should not be exaggerated. In the long view independence was inherent in British journalism and the struggle to secure it reached far back into the history of the newspapers. Conspicuous successes had been attained in the early years of George III's reign. Even in a much shorter perspective, it is necessary to keep in mind the examples of James Perry and Daniel Stuart. So far as politics were concerned, Perry had hardily asserted his independence of any government or self-interested group from the very beginning of his editorial career in 1783; his partisanship for the party led by Charles James Fox sprang entirely from political conviction and owed nothing to material considerations.[3] Similarly, so long as Daniel Stuart exercised active control over the *Courier*, from 1799 till about 1807, though supporting the government he preferred to remain unconnected with it and disapproved of his partner's later reversal of this policy.[4] Before John Walter II took control of *The Times* in 1803, it was already evident that the public was distrustful of hireling newspapers and that independence could reap a golden reward. However, bearing in mind these antecedents of developments after 1803, it remains true that thereafter editors and proprietors of leading journals pressed for independence with increasing vigour; and in pursuit of it Walter pushed certain developments further than they had hitherto gone – notably in his refusal to receive any favours from theatre managers, in his use of foreign correspondents, and in the elaborate stratagems he employed to prevent the government from inter-

[1] Gray, *Spencer Perceval*, p. 133.

[2] *History of The Times*, I 87 ff.

[3] See p. 338 below.

[4] Aspinall, *Politics and the Press*, pp. 206–7. It was only after Stuart had yielded control to his partner, Street, about 1807, that the *Courier* became subsidised and closely associated with the government.

fering with his prior receipt of foreign news.[1] By abandoning the state of clientage to government with which his father had been content,[2] he immeasurably raised the reputation of his paper and gave it an independence comparable to that of Perry's *Morning Chronicle*, which it was in due course able to surpass.

The lure of bigger circulations was thus one factor changing the character of the newspaper press in the early nineteenth century. So was a growing resentment of government interference: this proved particularly embarrassing during the period of rapid changes of administration from 1801 to 1807. What other causes may have been at work? One question that arises is: was it that because the newspaper press was increasingly prosperous it could command a higher level of intellectual talent? Among the leading proprietors, James Perry and his early partner, James Gray, and John Walter II were all men of culture who had attended universities. Perry, Walter and Daniel Stuart were conspicuous for the galaxies of talent which they attracted to their newspapers. Perry's chief assistant after the death of Gray was a graduate of St Andrews who eventually made a distinguished career at the bar and in the service of the East India Company.[3] Contributors to the *Morning Chronicle* included at different times the poets, Thomas Campbell and Thomas Moore, the barristers, Sir James Mackintosh and Joseph Jekyll; and leading whig politicians such as Brougham and Holland. John Campbell, a future lord chancellor, at one time served him as reporter and theatre critic,[4] and later many brilliant theatrical reviews were contributed by Hazlitt. The team of writers which Daniel Stuart attracted to the *Morning Post* and afterwards carried with him to the *Courier* included Wordsworth, Coleridge and Southey, Sir James Mackintosh, who was his brother-in-law, and Charles Lamb, who for a time supplied his witty paragraphs. To the *Morning Post* Coleridge contributed some of the most brilliant and biting anti-Napoleonic material ever to appear in the British press.[5] Similarly John Walter II, during the decade or so of his active management of *The Times*, brought into its service the abilities of Henry Crabb Robinson, John Payne Collier, Peter Lovatt Fraser, and above all Thomas Barnes and

[1] *History of The Times*, I chs. VI, VII, X.
[2] Ibid., ch. IV.
[3] On Robert Spankie, see p. 348 below.
[4] Pp. 349–50 below.
[5] Bourne, *English Newspapers*, I 292–314.

Edward Sterling, who were to transform the paper into 'the Thunderer' during the 1820s.[1] One or two of these men were fellows of Oxford or Cambridge colleges, a notable proportion of them were university graduates or men trained or training for the bar, and a number of them had distinguished careers. The appearance of men of this calibre as writers for the leading newspapers is part of a wider development in British literary history and is linked with the rise of the great reviews and magazines. That the rewards were such as to tempt men like this into journalism was of no small significance for the development of the press. It was not only that in general more intelligent and ingenious efforts were made to exploit its potentialities. But the quality of discussion of public issues was eventually transformed into a new dimension. As early as 1783 the impact of a trained mind was immediately evident when James Perry took control of the *Gazetteer*.[2] It was no coincidence that as more men of this type came to the fore, the leading article gradually evolved to the point where the chief newspapers became forums for high-level debate about great public issues. The quality of press society in the Strand and Fleet Street about the first decade after 1800 reached in some respects a level which was not sustained later in the nineteenth century.[3] Even in the lower echelons the quality was improving. It was noted in the House of Commons in 1810 that of the twenty-three persons then employed in parliamentary reporting for the newspapers, no fewer than eighteen were men with a university education.[4] By the eighteen-twenties editors of newspapers were becoming respectable, especially if they enjoyed the independence conferred by ownership of their journals; and what their newspapers said commanded attention.

It is tempting to speculate how far a quality of youth also had something to do with the decisive phase of evolution which overtook the press during this period. If one considers editors, writers and reporters connected with the formative papers in the period from about 1775 to 1820, it seems clear that the expansion of an increasingly prosperous profession gave young men of real ability

[1] *History of The Times*, I ch. X.

[2] Haig, *The Gazetteer*, pp. 187–8.

[3] See the nostalgic reflections in Cyrus Redding, *Fifty Years' Recollections*, 3 vols (1858) I 71, 225.

[4] Aspinall, in *Review of English Studies*, XXI 230.

every opportunity to make their mark. It is striking how young a number of the outstanding journalists were when they first reached the editorial chair or as owner-editors launched their own journals: Henry Bate, editor of the *Morning Post* at thirty; James Perry, editor of the *Gazetteer* at twenty-five, and owner of the *Morning Chronicle* at thirty-three in partnership with Gray, who was then twenty-eight. Daniel Stuart was twenty-eight when he became owner of the *Morning Post*, and had added the *Courier* to his property by the time he was thirty-two. John Walter II was made joint-manager of *The Times* by his father as soon as he came of age, and at twenty-six took over the sole management. John and Leigh Hunt were in their mid-twenties when they started the *News* and the *Examiner*. These men, and many of the galaxy of writers who surrounded them in the early years of the nineteenth century, made their impact on the press during the most vital years of their lives, when they were able to bring a fresh, critical approach to all the problems of newspaper work and to the discussions of public affairs which formed one of the chief selling-points of the newspaper press. A thorough examination of the intellectual development of these editors and writers, and of the individual and the collective influence of their newspaper activities, could throw considerable light on a crucial phase of the early-nineteenth-century history of the British press.

John Walter I and James Perry present an instructive contrast. Walter came to journalism relatively late, after a career as a coal-merchant, and he was interested less in newspapers than in the hoped-for potentialities of the logographic press. His approach to journalism was frankly commercial: the customer must be pleased. 'A newspaper', he wrote in 1785, ' . . . ought not to be engrossed by any particular subject, but, like a well-covered table, it should contain something suited to every palate.'[1] In the following years his maladroit, but on the whole submissive, relations with Pitt's government are reminiscent of politics in the age of Newcastle.[2] Two years earlier James Perry had been appointed editor of the *Gazetteer*, and opened his editorship with a forceful statement of its independence of any administration and of the role of its staff as 'servants to the people of England'.[3] The phrase was hackneyed

[1] *History of The Times*, I 26
[2] Ibid., ch. IV.
[3] Haig, *The Gazetteer*, p. 188.

enough; but in the general context of Perry's pronouncements, it clearly meant what it said. From his pen the phrase pointed away from the age of Newcastle to the age of Gray and Peel. A new type of editor had arrived, and in the next thirty or forty years Perry and his peers were to carry the press across the divide. In the new world to which their activities led, there was still room for more than one kind of editor. Indeed, there would be two styles in particular – on the one hand, editors like Perry and Black of the *Morning Chronicle*, who championed a particular party and set of political principles; and on the other, those like Thomas Barnes of *The Times*, who held that the highest (as well as the most profitable) duty of the newspapers was to discover and then express the prevailing public opinion upon contentious public issues. What was dying by the 1820s was the type of editor held in slavish dependence upon the government or some other great interest. The demands of the public and the response to it of the magnates of the newspaper world were forcing him out of business. Whatever the factors, and they were many and complicated, that had brought about this transformation, they had worked an irrevocable change in the nature of British politics. Even in the eighteenth century governments had not been wholly immune from storms of public opinion. Now they were open to all the gales that blew, and the operations of ministries and parliaments could never be the same again.

SIXTEEN

James Perry of the Morning Chronicle, *1756–1821*

JAMES Perry, who was one of the three or four outstanding journalists of the early nineteenth century, has fared badly at the hands of the historical muse. For nearly forty-five years he was a working editor in charge of leading newspapers. For much of this period he was sole owner of the *Morning Chronicle*. Comments by contemporaries attribute to him an eminence comparable to that attained in the next generation of newspapermen by Thomas Barnes of *The Times*.[1] Despite this no more substantial biographical account followed the agreeable but conventional brief sketch of his life in the *Annual Biography and Obituary* for 1822.[2] Some ten years later, his old friend, Pryse Lockhart Gordon, well aware of his own unfitness to do more than turn a few interesting anecdotes, observed: 'It is remarkable that such a man as Mr Perry, who distinguished himself as an editor of a popular newspaper for thirty-five years, has not found a biographer among the multitude of talented persons who were intimate with him.'[3] Later in the century various historians of the newspaper press drew attention to the importance of his career;[4] but these notices and the sketch of him in the *Dictionary of National Biography* hardly constitute an adequate monument to his achievements. Only his eight-year term as editor of the *Gazetteer* has as yet been examined with the resources of modern scholarship.[5] An investigation of his long owner-editorship of the *Morning Chronicle* would probably yield

[1] Pryse Lockhart Gordon, *Personal Memoirs*, 2 vols (1830) I 236; William Jerdan, *Men I have known* (1866) pp. 229–30.

[2] VII (1822) 380–91.

[3] *Personal Memoirs*, I 236.

[4] E.g. Frederick Knight Hunt, *The Fourth Estate*, 2 vols (1850) II 104–6; Alexander Andrews, *The History of British Journalism . . . to . . . 1855*, 2 vols (1859) I 229–31; Bourne, *English Newspapers*, I 261–6.

[5] Haig, *The Gazetteer*, ch. XI.

a study richly rewarding for an understanding of the development of the British newspaper press during one of the most crucial and dramatic periods of its evolution. It might also provide some side-lights on whig party politics during these years; for Perry was closely connected with the party leaders, though little concerning his contacts with them seems to have been committed to paper. Indeed, for a man with such a wide circle of friends and acquaintances, astonishingly few letters seem to have survived,[1] and if this side of his activities is ever clearly elucidated, it will only be by much painstaking investigation. Until full-scale studies on these lines are undertaken, no more is possible than to present a brief but more rounded picture of Perry the man and journalist than has hitherto been available.

James Perry (originally his surname was Pirie), a native of Aberdeen, was born on 30 October 1756. His father was a joiner by trade and in business as a house-builder, and his mother's kinsmen included prosperous businessmen.[2] The elder Pirie was ambitious for his son and hoped to establish him in a career at the bar. James was given a good education. After attending Aberdeen high school, in 1769 he matriculated at Marischal College;[3] but after he had been there for about three years his father's business was ruined by unlucky speculations. Perry was obliged to leave without a degree and contribute to the family's income. For about a year he drudged in the office of a local advocate, Arthur Ding-

[1] There is a vast mass of whig party correspondence for the period of Perry's career, which may yield allusions to his activities. But there are no letters from him in the Brougham papers at University College, London, the Burdett collection in the Bodleian Library, or the Tierney papers in the Hampshire Record Office, only three in the papers of Earl Grey at the University of Durham, and one in those of Samuel Whitbread, jun., at Bedford Record Office. The Ilchester (Holland House) papers and the C. J. Fox papers in the British Museum have not yet been fully indexed, but any significant groups of letters would have been indicated by the indexing already done. A few single letters are to be found in other British Museum collections. The largest group known to me is one of about half a dozen in the papers of William Adam, calendared in the report made by Dr Donald E. Ginter on the Adam of Blair Adam muniments for the National Register of Archives (Scotland).

[2] Gordon, *Personal Memoirs*, I 254.

[3] Ibid.; *Fasti Academiae Mariscallanae Aberdonensis*, ed. P. J. Anderson, 3 vols (New Spalding Club, 1898) II 340.

wall Fordyce. According to one account, for a time he worked as an assistant in a draper's shop at Aberdeen.[1] Later he acted in theatrical companies touring Scotland under the management of Booth and Wilkinson, and although his figure was not considered good for the stage, he displayed talent and enjoyed fair success. Two explanations exist for his abandonment of this career: one, that he was disappointed in a love affair with an actress who later, as Mrs Sparks, achieved a considerable reputation;[2] the other, that when the company with which he was touring moved south of the Scottish border, he was advised to leave because his brogue made him incomprehensible to English audiences. In 1775, by means of the network of personal contacts which existed among Scottish migrants in England, he found a position as clerk to a Manchester cotton manufacturer. Here he spent two years, devoting his spare time to further self-education, improving his oratorical talent (and no doubt also his accent) in a local debating society, and putting together a few savings. In 1777, now aged about twenty-one, he resolved to try his fortune in London, the one place offering the fullest opportunities for the type of literary career to which he now felt himself drawn.

In London Perry was again well-served by introductions to fellow-Scots. After a brief period as a publisher's hack, his gifts as a writer of light-hearted, witty paragraphs were discovered by one of the proprietors of the *General Advertiser*, and he was given a regular engagement as writer and parliamentary reporter at a guinea a week, with an additional half-guinea for assisting on the *London Evening Post*.[3] Two years later came the stroke of good luck needed by every cub-reporter. In the autumn and winter of 1778–9 the naval and political world was rent by the mutual recriminations and counter-charges of the naval commanders, Keppel and Palliser, over their conduct during the battle of Ushant. This affair gave rise to two successive hearings before a court martial. Sent to Portsmouth to cover the proceedings against Keppel, Perry distinguished himself by the thoroughness with which he discharged his assignment, sending to London each day, so it was said, copy sufficient to fill eight columns during a period

[1] John Payne Collier, *An Old Man's Diary* . . . , 2 vols (1871–2) II 43.
[2] Ibid. However, this story does not seem to be in character.
[3] *European Magazine and London Review*, LXXIV (1818) 188.

of some six weeks. His reputation was made. It was not long before new opportunities were opened to him. In 1782 he founded the *European Review*. Less than a year afterwards he was tempted away from it to become editor of the prosperous and well-established *Gazetteer* at a salary of four guineas a week and took up his duties in January 1783. He was then twenty-five. About the same time, or soon afterwards, he also undertook and carried on for several years the editing of *The Parliamentary Register* published by John Debrett.

Already the development of Perry's personality made it clear that he would be an editor of a particular type. He was full of zest, cheerful, friendly, extrovert. Political discussion and activity were a vital part of his life. The debating talents which he had exercised during his stay at Manchester had since been cultivated in the debating club known as the Westminster Forum, and in other metropolitan debating societies. In a biographical sketch which it has been suspected, was inspired by Perry himself, it is stated that, about 1782, Pitt the younger was so struck by the young journalist's abilities that he tried to tempt him to seek election to the House of Commons.[1] Another, unidentified contemporary thought his command of the spoken word outstanding and considered him even better able to present argument verbally than in writing.[2] This was high praise; for the quality, the clarity and the force of his prose style are distinctive and their impact upon the pages of the *Gazetteer* unmistakable.[3] These abilities were directed by firm political convictions. Perry sympathised strongly with the opposition to North's administration. His journalistic apprenticeship was served in a period when the general body of the London newspaper press was hostile to North. Personal interest in journalistic liberty, as well as political ideals, caused many of its leaders to be connected with the Wilkite movement, particularly in so far as that movement was concerned with vindicating the right of free political comment. To Perry, as to many of his contemporaries, this cause was linked with the more general defence of English liberties established at the Revolution of 1689. In the early 1780s the cause of liberty had found a new hero. Perry's early years as a journalist coincided with the emergence of Charles James Fox as

[1] Ibid.; Bourne, *English Newspapers*, I 250 n. 1, 251.

[2] Hunt, *The Fourth Estate*, II 105–6. [3] Haig, *The Gazetteer*, pp. 187–96.

'the man of the people' and as the charismatic leader of the Westminster committee of association, which had been formed to resist supposed royal and ministerial violations of the constitution. Perry's admiration for Fox was unalloyed. When, on the sudden death of John Henley Wall, the proprietors of the *Gazetteer* offered Perry the vacant editorship, he stipulated 'that he was to be left to the free exercise of his political opinions, which were those asserted by Mr Fox'.[1]

Perry swung the *Gazetteer* firmly into line in support of Fox. The new political allegiance of the paper was made plain in an address to readers in the autumn of 1783, where, echoing the nickname conferred on Fox, he emphasised its role as 'the *Paper* of the *People*'.[2] At the same time he devoted his attention to making it a first-class all-round newspaper. After he took control in January 1783 the *Gazetteer* seldom appeared without a 'leading article', in which opinions were stated with unprecedented force and clarity. The type-face of the 'London' heading was enlarged to draw attention to editorial comment. The addition of two assistants to help him report parliamentary news – an unprecedented enlargement of regular reporting staff – enabled him to present somewhat fuller and much more accurate accounts of debates, giving him a decisive lead over his chief rival, William Woodfall of the *Morning Chronicle*; but he balanced this by extensions of the literary section at the expense of advertising, the space devoted to this being noticeably reduced. Essays and poetry were both accepted, Robert Burns being one of Perry's literary contributors. Fewer political essays were taken from outside contributors, but in place of these appeared the increasing editorial comment on political affairs by Perry himself in the 'London' column.[3] Constant support for the Foxites left the public in no doubt where the *Gazetteer* stood on political questions; and had Perry's editorial position been commensurate with his ambitions, he might have developed it into the party organ that the *Morning Chronicle* afterwards became.

According to Pryse Lockhart Gordon, Perry's resignation from the *Gazetteer* was due to a change of proprietors, leading to the adoption of a pro-ministerial policy.[4] Recent investigation has

[1] *European Magazine and London Review*, LXXIV 188.
[2] Haig, *The Gazetteer*, pp. 190–1. [3] Ibid., pp. 187–205.
[4] *Personal Memoirs*, I 240.

disproved this report. Some friction with the proprietors there may have been, not about politics but over Perry's policy of reducing the space allowed for advertisements; but in general his relations with them seem to have been good, and almost up to the last minute he was negotiating for the purchase of a half share in the paper and admission to partnership. By conceding this quickly the proprietors might have forestalled his withdrawal for a time at least. But, as the historian of the *Gazetteer* observes: 'Perry himself would probably not long have been satisfied with less than the full reward of his labour.'[1] There is some reason to believe that even while the purchase of the half share was under discussion, he was already angling for better prospects elsewhere.[2] Ambition led Perry to seek the complete control and the full profits to be enjoyed by owning his own newspaper. In November 1790 the chance arrived, and on the twenty-seventh Perry terminated his service with the *Gazetteer*.[3]

For the prospect now opened of becoming joint-owner, in partnership with one congenial, trusted friend, of the *Morning Chronicle*, a newspaper which his able editorship of the *Gazetteer* had done much to topple from its former eminence. William ('Memory') Woodfall had long sustained this paper by virtue of a somewhat unjustified reputation for accurate memorising and reporting of parliamentary debates; but he could not compete with Perry's reporting team, and it may well have been a sense of the impending failure of the paper that decided him to give up the conduct of it in 1789, and to attempt (unsuccessfully) to launch one of his own. No longer fortified by his reputation, the sales of the *Morning Chronicle* went into rapid decline, and the proprietors decided to salvage what little was possible of their capital.

Perry's partner in this new venture was James Gray, a gifted young man from Banffshire, a few years his junior. Son of a farmer, born at Deskford in 1761, Gray had been particularly fortunate in his schooling at Fordyce, and proceeded early in 1776 to King's College, Aberdeen, from which he emerged Master of Arts in March 1780. For much of the next ten years he was a school usher – for two years with a relative named Gerrard who ran an academy on the outskirts of London, and then, after a period as a

[1] Haig, *The Gazetteer*, pp. 216–17. [2] See p. 340 below.

[3] Haig, *The Gazetteer*, pp. 216–17.

private tutor, at the Charterhouse, where, for five years, he was 'Latin usher . . . with a handsome salary'. At some time during these years he was introduced to Perry by his intimate friend of college days, Pryse Lockhart Gordon, and it is to be surmised that by 1790 the two men had become close friends.[1] How far Gray may already have become involved in journalism by that date is not clear; that he may have done so seems to be indicated by the way in which Boswell, meeting him and Perry at another friend's dinner-table in August 1790, mistakenly bracketed them together as editors of the *Gazetteer*.[2]

Boswell's information, though wrong, may have some further significance. It seems possible that at this dinner party Perry and Gray were discussing their projected joint-ownership of the *Morning Chronicle*, although their ambition was not to be fulfilled for another three or four months. However, it appears likely that by this time their first bid had been made and rejected and they were now waiting for the fruit to ripen and fall into their hands. This seems indicated by the story told by Pryse Lockhart Gordon:[3]

> The reputation of the Chronicle was chiefly owing to the editor's [Woodfall's] extraordinary talent for faithfully reporting the debates in parliament; consequently when it got into another hand, the sale began to decline, and in a few months became a losing concern. This alarmed the proprietors, and it was privately offered for sale. Messrs George Robinson of Paternoster-row and George Nicol of Pall Mall, were the intimate friends of Messrs Gray and Perry, and thought that these gentlemen's talents were admirably adapted to conduct jointly this well-

[1] Gordon, *Personal Memoirs*, I 21–8, 236–40; *Officers and Graduates of University and King's College Aberdeen, 1495–1860*, ed. P. J. Anderson (1893) p. 255.

[2] Haig, *The Gazetteer*, p. 208. Haig states, but without reference, that Gray was by this time editor of the *Morning Chronicle*. There is no hint of this in Gordon's account of Gray's career. Gordon was writing forty years later and his memory can be proved faulty on other matters of detail; but he was an intimate of Gray and it seems unlikely that he would have overlooked a general point of this sort. However, one of Gray's obituary notices clearly indicates that he had been a parliamentary reporter (no journal is specified) before he became a partner in the *Morning Chronicle* (*Gentleman's Magazine*, 1796, II 617).

[3] *Personal Memoirs*, I 240–1.

established journal. They advised them to purchase it, and they did more – they made offer of their security for the price. I have heard also that they proffered 1,000*l* for this purpose, and were refused; but the losses were daily increasing, and in a few months it was offered for public sale, at Garraway's, to the best bidder. The worthy booksellers attended on the part of their friends, and had the good fortune to purchase it for 210*l*.

The two new partners found this sum and also the additional capital for launching the venture, perhaps £1,000 or so. This scale of outlay seems indicated by the generally received account that Perry 'borrowed £500 from Ransome and Co., bankers, and some more money from Bellamy, the wine merchant in Chandos Street, who was also caterer and doorkeeper to the House of Commons', and that Gray put in a legacy of £500 he had just received.[1] The deed of partnership provided 'that the whole property should go to the longest liver', an annuity for Gray's sister being reserved in the event of his prior decease.[2] A printer named Lambert in Shire Lane was found to undertake the printing of the paper, Perry lodging nearby with his sister and her husband, an Irish bookbinder named Luman, until the new editorial headquarters in Lancaster Court at the west end of the Strand were ready to receive him.[3]

At the outset of his long and distinguished career as owner-editor of the *Morning Chronicle*, Perry was just thirty-four. The evidence of friends and acquaintances indicates that he was a man of tremendous vitality: 'full of fire and energy', Gordon wrote; and Leigh Hunt, who knew him only in his later years, remarked on his liveliness.[4] In his business engagements he early established

[1] Bourne, *English Newspapers*, I 261–2, citing the *Monthly Magazine*, Jan. 1822, p. 567. However his facts are not exact, for Gray had received his legacy some years before and spent it on further education (Gordon, *Personal Memoirs*, I 238–9); he might have replaced this capital out of savings.

[2] Gordon, *Personal Memoirs*, I 241–2; Andrews, *History of British Journalism*, I 231.

[3] Gordon, *Personal Memoirs*, I 242; it is possible that Perry had been settled there before 1790, for an un-updated entry appears in *The Universal British Directory of Trade, Commerce and Manufacturers* . . . , 2nd ed. (1793) p. 235: 'James Perry, editor of the Gazetteer, 16 Shire lane, Temple bar.'

[4] Gordon, *Personal Memoirs*, I 241; Leigh Hunt, *Autobiography*, I 230.

a reputation for integrity, reliability and fair dealing: it became a current saying that he 'might be trusted with anything', and his kindness towards those he employed was widely acknowledged.[1] In appearance he was 'plain and homely (though like all the editors of those . . . days he was always well-dressed)' – indeed he had some reputation as a dandy.[2] Although not equal, pehaps, to Gray in taste and scholarship, he stood high among the editors of his day; and if there were occasional lapses when he tried to show off his learning, nevertheless he was a devoted and discriminating bibliophile and art collector, and a man of interesting and agreeable conversation. Convivial and a bon viveur, despite the rigours of his profession he still found energy to carry on a full social life, enlivened in earlier years by membership of various clubs and later by dinner parties at his house at which a notable circle of writers, artists and politicians were regular guests. With great warmth of manner he readily attracted friends, and his tact ensured that few were lost. The attractiveness of his personality is well reflected in the observation of one of the friends of his later days, Mary Russell Mitford, who described him in 1813 as 'a man so genial and so accomplished that even when Erskine, Romilly, Tierney, and Moore were present, he was the most charming talker at his own table'.[3] The 'twinkling eyes' which drew the attention of Leigh Hunt bore witness to a lively sense of humour, at one time strenuously exercised in his brain-child, the Humbug Club, where schoolboy burlesques of Masonic ritual were inflicted on aspiring members.[4] Although a 'red-hot' politician, he never let his ardour get the better of his good manners, and was, said William Jerdan, 'one of the coolest personages you could encounter in society'.[5] As a journalist he was bold and outspoken, but a certain native prudence preserved him on the whole from disagreeable encounters with the law courts or the Houses of Parliament.[6]

[1] *Annual Biography and Obituary*, VII (1822) 389; Gordon, *Personal Memoirs*, I 295–300; Hardcastle, *Life of John Lord Campbell*, I 49–50, 82, 179.

[2] William Jerdan, *Men I have known*, pp. 332, 334.

[3] A. G. L'Estrange, *The Life of Mary Russell Mitford in a selection from her letters*, 3 vols (1870) III 254.

[4] Gordon, *Personal Memoirs*, I 258–62.

[5] *Men I have known*, p. 330.

[6] Perry was only twice before the courts for libel, winning acquittal on both occasions. The House of Lords once inflicted penalties upon him.

With great firmness he set his face against the kind of vulgarity and personal abuse which was all too common in the newspapers of the time. 'I am deeply concerned', he wrote to Peel on one occasion,[1]

> at seeing in my paper of this day, a private allusion, in a political paragraph connected with your name which is highly indecorous and offensive. It is most painful to me when such personalities find place by oversight in my Journal. . . . I cannot express to you how much I am grieved at the circumstance, and entreat you to believe that it would not have appeared . . . if I had been at the Printing House last night.

Much contemporary testimony shows that this was not mere buttering of an important politician. Perry felt as he wrote; and he took a pride in the high standard of propriety maintained in the *Morning Chronicle*. 'After a service of twenty-nine years . . . I have never deviated from the principles of Whiggism and never outraged the decorums of private life', he replied in 1805 to a line of praise from the whig savant, Samuel Parr.[2] Some thirty years after his death an unnamed contemporary strikingly summed up the impression he made of fairness, openness, sensibility and right-dealing, of detachment from the sordid side of business activity, and devotion to a code of conduct:[3]

> Perry had a great deal of the feeling which you find in some of Walter Scott's characters, and which in this commercial age is rarely met with. You had no doubt or difficulty as to how he would act on a given occasion; but always considered yourself safe with him. Walter of *The Times* was a better man of business and Daniel Stuart of the *Post* and *Courier* knew better how to make money; but Perry was a thorough gentleman, who attracted every man to him with whom he was connected.

About his partner, Gray, there is less information. Gray's promise was cut short unfulfilled in 1796 at the early age of thirty-

[1] B.M. Add. MSS. 40402, fo. 21, n.d.

[2] *The Works of Samuel Parr . . .*, ed. John Johnston, 8 vols (1828) VIII 120.

[3] Quoted in Hunt, *The Fourth Estate*, II 105–6. Hazlitt left a well-known sketch of Perry's character, which has been drawn upon in all later accounts (*The Complete Works of William Hazlitt*, ed. P. P. Howe, 21 vols (1931–4) XVI 223).

six, and his brief obituary notices indicate little more than that he was a man who had kindled affection in his friends.[1] However, testimonies to his ability are not confined to his friend, Pryse Lockhart Gordon.[2] His talents perfectly complemented those of Perry. 'Gray', wrote Gordon, who was intimate with both, 'was a scholar, a profound politician, well-acquainted with the British constitution, industrious . . . and ready at composition. His colleague was . . . full of fire and energy.' In the view of their backer, George Robinson, 'such a coalition had never been before formed – they were like a ship well-trimmed. Gray was the *ballast* and Perry the *sail*.'[3] By another account, 'Gray was a more profound man than Perry, and wrote the serious articles. Perry was volatile and varied, but not profound.'[4] Like Perry, Gray was an admirer of Charles James Fox. On politics the two men thought as one.[5] Their partnership seemed cut out to be lasting and fruitful, and its early success seems to have been considerable.

Perry and Gray launched their enterprise in highly promising circumstances. British prosperity was buoyant, and the newspaper industry was enjoying boom conditions. Dangers of war seemed to be receding, as government in France dissolved into exciting but not yet menacing revolutionary disorder. The fascination and the sympathy awakened in many Englishmen by events in France whetted the demand for newspapers. The new editors of the *Morning Chronicle* were quick to exploit this situation. Within a few months, in the summer of 1791, they made the decision that Perry should go to Paris, in order to provide first-hand reports. Given introductions to French leaders in the capacity of a 'deputy' of the English Revolution Society which had been established to commemorate the centenary of 1689, Perry seems to have had a most successful sojourn in Paris and may have been there for the best part of a year.[6] Meanwhile Gray ran the paper in London.

[1] *Gentleman's Magazine*, 1796, II 617; *Morning Chronicle*, 29 June 1796.

[2] John Taylor remarked upon it in a conversation with Joseph Farington in Nov 1814 (*The Farington Diary*, ed. James Greig, 8 vols (1922–8) VII 286); and see below.

[3] Cited in Gordon, *Personal Memoirs*, I 241.

[4] Hunt, *The Fourth Estate*, II 103, quoting personal information from a 'veteran journalist'.

[5] Gordon, *Personal Memoirs*, I 240.

[6] *Burke Correspondence*, VI 451 n. 2.

The impact of these arrangements on its fortunes was remarkable. When the two partners took charge at the end of 1790, its circulation was so low that it was barely paying its way.[1] But in December 1793 the painter and diarist, Joseph Farington, noted in his journal that during the previous year Perry and Gray had cleared a profit of about £6,000 and had paid the government about £25,000 for stamped paper.[2] If the latter part of this statement were anything like correct, then the editors' achievement would have been extraordinary; for as the stamp duty on a sheet of newsprint was then twopence, this indicated an average daily sale during 1792 of over 9,600. Farington's information is certainly not always reliable, and this figure for the circulation is not credible; but there is no doubt that Perry's dispatches from Paris helped to make the *Morning Chronicle* a phenomenal success. Edmund Burke, who deplored its politics, referred angrily at this time to its 'amazing circulation'.[3]

This success owed a good deal at first to the patronage of the whig opposition.[4] Perry's attachment to Fox was now of long standing, and their new venture was understood from the first to be in the party's interest. Quarters were provided for the newspaper office by one of Fox's adherents, the Duke of Norfolk, at no. 474, Strand, on the corner leading into Lancaster Court by St Martin's church.[5] This seems to have been part of a fairly comprehensive business agreement. In return for a substantial subsidy, Perry and Gray agreed to sacrifice a considerable amount of

[1] Collier, *An Old Man's Diary*, II 44.
[2] *The Farington Diary*, I 28.
[3] *Burke Correspondence*, VI 451.
[4] Ibid.
[5] The description in the *Morning Chronicle* for 21 Feb 1791 of the new offices which were about to be opened makes it clear that they were at the west end of the Strand, on a site on its north side which was later razed for the widening of the road just east of Trafalgar Square. H. B. Wheatley (*London Past and Present*, 3 vols (1891) II 365) was confused by the existence of another Lancaster Court near Aldwych, subsequently demolished for the widening of Wellington Street, and incorrectly located Perry's office there. Cyrus Redding would appear to have been mistaken in his *Fifty Years Recollections* (I 96) in stating that the back of the house extended to the Thames: it was on the wrong side of the Strand for this to be possible. The general unreliability of Gordon's *Personal Memoirs* is again indicated by the fact that he placed this move 'three or four years' after Perry and Gray purchased the paper. Their printer, J. Lambert, continued to be based at no. 1 Shire Lane, which acted as a convenient office for clients in the City.

advertisement revenue in order to provide space for very full reports of parliamentary debates which would do justice to the opposition. They also entered into arrangements with the proprietors of the *Star*, acquiring a sufficient interest in this newspaper to ensure that the *Chronicle's* parliamentary reports were fully reprinted in it. The *Star*, which had been started the preceding year to support the government, was at this time the only evening daily, and the most important aspect of the deal was that it was the most convenient and earliest source from which provincial journalists could take their reports of the most recent debates; as a result, so Perry declared the following year, 'in the north particularly we have almost sole possession of the country.'[1] Perry and Gray acknowledged an obligation to follow party advice and kept in close touch with the chief party organiser, William Adam. As early as 7 January, only a few weeks after they had taken control, Perry was consulting Adam on a matter of editorial policy.[2] A letter from Gray to Adam of 22 September (during Perry's absence in France) showed a desire not to offend the party by the publication of 'outrageously' democratic items on French affairs.[3] But the path of the *Morning Chronicle* as a party newspaper was by no means smooth, for during the course of 1791 the pro-French and reformist sympathies of its proprietors became more and more offensive to the right-wing whigs. Portland, Fitzwilliam, Burke and others of their circle, suspected the two journalists of being paid agents of the French National Assembly, and at their insistence the party subsidy was dropped. This decision in turn led Perry to reconsider the arrangements which he had entered into about the beginning of 1791 and to point out the disadvantages he had shouldered in return for the subsidy. These included the loss of an annual income of about £500 in advertisements and also of an unknown but prob-

[1] Perry to William Adam, 8 June 1792, Blair Adam MSS., transcript of Professor D. E. Ginter.

[2] 'Mr Heywood called on me to say that if the *Morning Chronicle* would occasionally admit temperate letters from the Dissenters, they would push the paper in every part of the country. I told him that temperate letters I would chearfully admit, but nothing violent nor personal. Did I right?' (Blair Adam MSS., cited in Donald E. Ginter, 'The financing of the Whig Party organization, 1783–1793', *American Historical Review*, LXXI (1965–6) 437.

[3] Ibid.

ably large potential sale of the *Morning Chronicle*, since customers waited for the *Star* each evening in the confidence of its containing all the *Chronicle*'s debates. If the subsidy were not paid, it would be necessary to dissolve the connection with the *Star*, which would both reduce literary expenses and permit an increase in sales, and to open the paper more largely to advertisements, with a consequent reduction of the space available for debates. Whatever the outcome the *Chronicle* would support the party.[1] These assurances were of no avail. In the following months, as the editorial opinions of the paper swung slightly to the left of those held by Fox himself, the discontent increased. In October 1792 one of the party moderates was fuming about the absolute need 'to curb the insolence of Perry'.[2] However, Perry's connections with Adam were not severed, and as the whig party broke up during 1793 and 1794 his paper fell into line as the independent champion of the Foxite minority and of the reforming society of the 'Friends of the People'.

The golden harvest of these early years did not last for long. The excesses of the revolution in France and the outbreak of war at the beginning of 1793 diminished public sympathy for revolutionary ideas, and in the mid-1790s a strong right-wing reaction swept the country. Perry also faced private difficulties. Gray's health gave way under tubercular infection, and in June 1796 his death deprived the paper of its writer of serious 'leading articles'. About the same time the *Morning Chronicle* was challenged by a dangerous competitor, when Daniel Stuart purchased the *Morning Post* and began skilfully to build it up as a leading opposition newspaper. The following year the government created new difficulties by raising the stamp duty, a move deliberately aimed to curb the sale of newspapers. During 1797 Perry can have been making only a modest profit, for the average daily issue of the *Morning Chronicle* in March of that year was little over a thousand.[3]

[1] Ibid., pp. 437–8; Perry to Adam, 8 June 1792, Blair Adam MSS., transcript of Professor Ginter.

[2] Ginter, in *American Historical Review*, LXXI 438.

[3] Andrews, *History of British Journalism*, I 234, gives a sales figure for March 1797 of 1,148 daily. No source is given; but there is some confirmation in an observation by John Payne Collier suggesting that Robert Spankie helped to nurse the paper back to prosperity from a situation in which the daily circulation was only about 1,000 (*An Old Man's Diary*, II 44).

These difficulties were somehow overcome. Gray's place was filled, and during the next few years the *Morning Chronicle* was firmly established as one of the leading London newspapers. Perry's chief assistant in this period of reconstruction was Robert Spankie, a young graduate of St Andrews who, like many of his countrymen, had gravitated to London with the intention of studying for the bar and drifted into journalism to eke out his financial resources. As he matriculated at St Andrews in February 1789, he was probably born about 1774 and can hardly have arrived in London before the spring of 1793. His record at St Andrews had been outstanding.[1] The beginnings of his association with Perry have not been ascertained. Possibly he had been acting as a reporter from some time in 1793; otherwise he joined the *Morning Chronicle* within a year or so of Gray's death, for he was firmly established as a writer of leading articles before the end of 1798.[2] There is some conflict of evidence about his status, but Lord Campbell's later recollection that he was 'editor and part proprietor' must be rejected as inconsistent both with Campbell's own emphasis in his letters on Perry's primacy,[3] and with other statements that Perry was sole owner of the paper after Gray's death. Spankie seems to have been a man of fair ability. After serving Perry for some years, he completed his bar training in 1808 and made an honourable, though not outstanding, career in the law, becoming advocate general in Bengal (*c.* 1818–*c.*1823), a serjeant-at-law, and from 1832 till his death in 1842 standing counsel to the East India Company. He was M.P. for Finsbury in the first reformed parliament.

Information about Perry's reporting staff and circle of literary contributors is difficult to obtain, but there is some indication of a steady improvement in their quality as the years went by. During part, or perhaps the whole, of the period of his partnership with Gray, and for many years after, he was assisted with parliamentary reporting by two rumbustious but erratic Irishmen, Mark Supple and Peter Finnerty. Although both were well-educated men, their

[1] *Matriculation Roll of the University of St Andrews*, ed. J. M. Anderson (1905) p. 37; Hardcastle, *Life of John, Lord Campbell*, I 45.

[2] Ibid.; James Grant, *The Newspaper Press: its origin – progress – and present position*, 2 vols (1871) I 266.

[3] Hardcastle, *Life of John, Lord Campbell*, I 44, 49–50, 123, 179.

characters were not strong enough to withstand the temptations of life in London and both ended sodden and broken down by alcoholic excess. Pryse Gordon left lively, if anecdotal portraits of them. Supple had been a school usher in Ireland and took up newspaper work soon after his arrival in London some time in 1786. Despite his dissipated habits, 'he was found a most useful person on the spur of the occasion; for he never failed to bring with him a column of reports, even if he had been shut out of the gallery, which frequently occurred. A few hints from a brother reporter were quite sufficient for he grounded good speeches on them.' Even if he were present in the chamber, his reports were hardly exact. 'When Supple had funds', wrote Gordon,[1]

> he generally drank his wine at Bellamy's, and mounted to the gallery to his duties. In reporting the speeches he paid but little attention to their correctness. His style was flowery, and discovered the man of genius. Members, on perusing what they had delivered the previous evening, were surprised to find them dressed up with metaphors and 'prose-run-mad' passages which they had not uttered: but they were sometimes so beautifully turned, that they never found fault with the metamorphoses, pocketed the affront, and fathered the oriental orations.

On one not-to-be-forgotten occasion, when Bellamy's beeswing port had done its work too well, Supple reduced the House to helpless convulsions of laughter by bellowing out 'Mr Speaker, give us a song' during a lull in the debate.[2]

In view of the unsteadiness of Perry's Irish assistants, it was perhaps all the more natural that when he could, he should recruit help from the less brilliant but steadier ranks of his own countrymen.[3] Spankie, if the first, was but one of the talented young Scotsmen who helped to nurse the *Morning Chronicle* to renewed success. Briefly Perry was also served by William Spankie, presumably a brother of Robert.[4] At the beginning of 1800 John Campbell, the future lord chancellor, then a young man of twenty-

[1] Obituary notice, *The Times*, 4 Nov 1842, p. 5; *Royal Kalendars; Dod's Parliamentary Pocket Companion for 1833*, 3rd ed. (1833) p. 161.

[2] On Supple and Finnerty, see Gordon, *Personal Memoirs*, I 295–300.

[3] Perry himself contrasted Irishmen and Scotsmen in these terms, ibid., pp. 300–1.

[4] Collier, *An Old Man's Diary*, II 44.

one recently arrived in London with the aim of studying for the bar, exploited a college acquaintanceship with Robert Spankie to obtain employment as a reporter and theatre critic. A sober, serious-minded man – 'I hate to drink with a parcel of dissipated reporters', he wrote to his father soon after joining the newspaper – Campbell's diligence recommended him to Perry, who soon advanced him to a salary of three guineas a week, with four during the parliamentary session. Campbell also provided law reports. These he continued to supply after he withdrew from the House of Commons gallery in 1802 for fear that his role as a reporter, becoming common knowledge, might jeopardise his professional prospects. In July 1803 he became a salaried critic and writer at £100 a year, but his countributions soon tapered off and ceased altogether before his call to the bar in 1805.[1] For House of Lords reports Perry for long relied on one of the celebrated eccentrics of Fleet Street, a reporter named Proby, who was always in a perspiration and known as King Porus. His prejudices and eccentricities, it has been said, were 'innumerable. He had never been out of London, in a boat, or on the back of a horse in his life; to the end of bag wigs he wore a bag; and was the last man in London to walk with a cane as long as himself.' In the old tradition he made no notes and relied entirely on memory when preparing his accounts of debates.[2]

The general prejudice and contempt with which the journalistic profession was regarded at this time probably accounts in part for the paucity of surviving evidence in memoirs and manuscript collections about Perry's literary contributors. From a very early stage of his editorship the brilliant classical scholar, Richard Porson, who became professor of Greek at Cambridge in 1790 and who married Perry's divorced sister, Mrs Luman, in 1796, was contributing both political squibs and literary items. In 1793 he produced over a hundred epigrams upon the arrival drunk in the House of Commons of Pitt and Dundas on the day war was declared with France.[3] About 1800 Perry opened a connection with the young poet, Thomas Campbell, numbers of whose verses first saw light

[1] Hardcastle, *Life of John, Lord Campbell*, I 45–178.

[2] Andrews, *History of British Journalism*, II 70.

[3] M. L. Clarke, *Richard Porson: A Biographical Essay* (Cambridge, 1937) pp. 42–6.

in the *Morning Chronicle*.[1] Among other contributors to its columns were R. B. Sheridan, the poet, Thomas Moore, and the young radical lawyer-politicians, James Mackintosh and Joseph Jekyll.[2]

Buttressed by hard work, able management, a sound advertising policy, a balance of appeals to various interests, and the employment of some of the best talent on the market, the *Morning Chronicle* was carried to a leading place among the London daily newspapers. From little over a thousand in 1797 the circulation climbed back to 1,500 in the following year, and before long seems to have stabilised at between three and four thousand.[3] Early on, this recovery made Perry's personal financial position assured. In 1798 he felt sufficiently secure to marry Miss Anne Hull and start a family. It was presumably about this time that he acquired his leasehold residence of Tavistock House, at the north-east corner of Tavistock Square, and began to make it 'noted for its reunions of men of political and literary distinction'.[4]

The reviving fortunes of the Foxite party about the turn of the century and the growing intimacy of Perry with a number of its leaders probably also contributed to the prosperity of the *Morning Chronicle*, especially after Daniel Stuart began to stamp a rather less anti-ministerial character upon its great rival at that period, the *Morning Post*. Only a thorough investigation of a large number of collections of papers of members of Fox's party will enable the story of Perry's involvement with them to be told as fully as is possible. For the time being only certain bare outline facts can be given. There is little evidence for the period before 1800; but his

[1] Andrews, *History of British Journalism*, I 265–6.

[2] Redding, *Fifty Years Recollections*, I 96.

[3] Andrews, *History of British Journalism*, I 234, for 1798. In 1811, according to a governmental estimate, the circulation was about 3,000, but the figure was higher during the parliamentary session owing to the excellence of the reports of debates (Gray, *Spencer Perceval*, p. 132). J. P. Collier associated Spankie's career with the paper with an increase of circulation from 1,000 to 4,000 by the time he left it in 1808; and Collier also recalled a brief peak in circulation of about 7,000 as coming in 1810, on an occasion when Perry successfully pleaded his own defence against a charge of libel (*An Old Man's Diary*, II 44).

[4] Wheatley, *London Past and Present*, III 349; Gordon, *Personal Memoirs*, I 250; *Annual Biography and Obituary*, VII 390. The site is now commemorated by a plaque recording the residence of Charles Dickens, who later occupied part of the house.

association with the Foxites was sufficiently intimate in 1798 to give rise to 'a most kind and affectionate letter' of condolence from Fox on the occasion of his imprisonment in Newgate by the House of Lords on charges of libel and breach of privilege.[1] Up till 1802 fragments at least remain of a continuing correspondence with the party's man of business, William Adam.[2] Sheridan, Tierney and Mackintosh, Fox's *alter ego*, Richard Fitzpatrick, and the party's leading lawyer, Thomas Erskine, were among the politicians who thronged the celebrated gatherings at Lancaster Court and Tavistock House in the opening years of the new century.[3] By 1806 when, after over twenty years in opposition, the Foxites at last enjoyed a renewed if brief lease of power, Perry's services were felt to give him irresistible claims to reward, and he was found a place as secretary of one of the commissions with a salary of £600 a year. The party even sought – vainly – to secure him a baronetcy. Doubtless to have refused the appointment would have been impolitic; but to be tied daily even to a modest office attendance from eleven to five was tedious to Perry and he was glad to abandon it when his friends were forced out of power the following year.[4]

Some indication of the possible degree of Perry's involvement in the affairs of the party and the nature of the services he might perform is provided by a fragment of his correspondence which survives in the Whitbread papers. In 1804 the opposition was out for the blood of Charles Hope, the Scottish lord advocate. Judging by the dossier which survives in Samuel Whitbread's papers, he took a leading part in organising the attack and a good deal more information was gathered up about Hope's iniquities than seems eventually to have been used. Perry's news-gathering service was called into play, and some at least of Whitbread's ammunition was supplied from his files.[5] On 13 June Perry wrote to Whitbread:[6]

[1] Noticed in the report 'Adam of Blair Adam Muniments', by Donald E. Ginter, National Register of Archives (Scotland).

[2] Ibid.

[3] Hardcastle, *Life of John, Lord Campbell*, I 71, 179; Gordon, *Personal Memoirs*, I 242.

[4] *The Farington Diary*, IV 55, 104.

[5] Calendar, 'Bedford County Record Office, Whitbread Letters', National Register of Archives report no. 1123, items 5623–41.

[6] Whitbread MSS., Bedford Record Office. Another issue, the threat of action against a farmer who had acted against one of his labourers for

> Dear Sir, I take the liberty of submitting to you the Account of the trial of the Officer and Serjeants of the Ross and Cromarty Rangers, which I am persuaded will disclose to you a most flagrant breach of duty on the part of the Lord Advocate. I have written to Aberdeen and shall certainly have an answer by monday or tuesday next, when I shall have the honour to wait on you. The flight of ensign Lanigen is a material part of the case to which I beg leave to draw your attention. The introduction will shew you the outline of the case.

There is no other direct piece of evidence so far consulted which shows, in so detailed a way as this letter to Whitbread, how closely Perry at times was enmeshed in party activity; but there are some indications that this was probably not untypical, at least of the period from about 1804 to 1815. In 1807, during the general election which followed the dismissal of the 'Talents' ministry, Holland, Brougham and John Allen were in close touch with Perry, keeping him supplied with political squibs and paragraphs as part of a widespread newspaper campaign to try to sway public opinion in favour of the Foxites, and Brougham continued a prolific contribution of political paragraphs during the following two years.[1] Perry received reciprocal advantages. His close contact with Earl Grey enabled him to obtain intelligence in advance of the government about military events in Portugal in 1809, Grey for his part relaying information derived from his correspondence with Colonel Willoughby Gordon, a member of Wellington's staff.[2] It seems likely that these exchanges to mutual advantage went on for some years, though the only surviving evidence in Grey's papers is provided by three letters from Perry, extending over a few months of the summer and autumn of 1812; one of these seems to show Perry intimately involved with party election matters during the general election of that year.[3] The party's continued reliance on Perry is again indicated by discussions in the autumn of 1809

attending militia exercises, was made the chief subject of complaint against Hope (G. W. T. Omond, *The Lord Advocates of Scotland*, 2 vols 1883) II 208–12; Cobbett's *Parliamentary Debates* (continuation of *The Parliamentary History*), vol II, *1804*, 787–817).

[1] Aspinall, *Politics and the Press*, pp. 284–92.

[2] Ibid., p. 282.

[3] 12 Aug, 4 Sept, 21 Oct 1812, Grey MSS., University of Durham; Mitchell, *The Whigs in Opposition*, p. 48, n. 3.

about the possibility of his acquiring an evening newspaper to be conducted in its interest; and the leaders' knowledge of his willingness to fall in with their policy is shown by a note of slightly later date that same year concerning newspaper comment on Lord Grenville's candidature for the chancellorship of Oxford University.[1] In 1812, when the main corps of the party was under attack from the Burdettite radical wing, Perry came boldly forward in defence of traditional constitutional principles at a public meeting in Westminster on the subject of parliamentary reform, and 'spoke up with all the conviction of a Rockingham Whig for the party system which the Burdettites were attacking'.[2] Indeed, he had never been very far to the left. Many years before, in 1798, he had told William Adam, after his unfortunate brush with the House of Lords: 'I have not come to Newgate a Jacobin and I shall not go out of it a Jacobin.'[3] Consistently with this position he stressed the traditional whig preoccupation with government influence and played down the desirability of electoral reform.[4] His enrolment about the same time as a founder-member of the Hampden Club may have reflected party desires to try to keep the new society reformist and respectable.[5] These scattered fragments of information confirm the general impression held by Perry's contemporaries, summed up in 1811 in the words of Lord Glenbervie, that he was 'reckoned as a sort of *sous-ministre* of the Fox party'.[6]

After 1812 traces of his party activity became more scarce, and probably it slackened as ill-health began to overtake him in the last years of his life. The Prince of Wales's break with the party in 1811 was a disappointment to him.[7] However it does not seem to have weakened his general loyalty to it. He appears to have been a leading officer of the Fox Club,[8] a role which must have kept him in close touch with most of the leaders, and the monument its members

[1] H.M.C., *Fortescue MSS. at Dropmore*, IX 345, 399.
[2] Roberts, *The Whig Party*, pp. 288–9.
[3] 'Adam of Blair Adam Muniments', National Register of Archives (Scotland).
[4] Roberts, *The Whig Party*, pp. 288–9. [5] Ibid., pp. 292–3.
[6] *The Diaries of Sylvester Douglas*, ed. Francis Bickley, 2 vols (1928) II 118.
[7] *The Correspondence of George IV*, ed. A. Aspinall, 3 vols (1938) I 176–7.
[8] According to Mitchell, he was either treasurer or secretary (*The Whigs in Opposition*, p. 44).

later put up to his memory indicates a continued mutual loyalty and respect. Nevertheless, in these later years, and especially in 1817 and 1818, there was growing disappointment among the party leaders about Perry's failure to give full space to their speeches in the *Morning Chronicle.* It can hardly have been with complete equanimity that he learned of their intention to launch another party paper for this purpose; though he judged confidently, and rightly, that a journal directed to such specialist ends could not survive.[1]

For Perry, though a politician, was first and foremost a newspaperman, and sound principles of newspaper management continued in the last decade of his life to have first claim on his energies. The *Morning Chronicle* was his livelihood (and much else to him); and nothing could kill a newspaper stone-dead more quickly thah filling it with turgid parliamentary speeches to the exclusion of advertisements and all the other features that interested the public. He himself on one occasion referred to 'the enormous expense of the disgusting, though necessary, reports of parliamentary chattering',[2] and though the *Morning Chronicle* kept its unmatched reputation for this branch of journalism, he was careful not to let it get out of hand. In all departments the quality of writing for the paper was maintained and improved, and a new wave of talented young men helped to sustain its primacy against the growing challenge of *The Times*. From about 1810 Perry's reporting staff included his eventual successor as editor, John Black. Black, a classics scholar from Edinburgh, was dour and devoted, and is, perhaps, the only reporter known to have broken into the House of Commons on finding himself locked out of the gallery[3] – a step his predecessor, Mark Supple, would hardly have thought was necessary. Black's ability and application brought him to the unofficial position of assistant editor in 1817, when Perry's declining health forced him into semi-retirement, and in this role he was successful; but his editorial management after Perry's death revealed a lack of imagination, flexibility and flair which doomed the paper to a slow decline. About the same time, the talented

[1] Aspinall, *Politics and the Press*, pp. 294–304.

[2] To Thomas Moore, 4 Dec 1814, *Memoirs, Journal and Correspondence of Thomas Moore*, ed. Lord John Russell, 8 vols (1853–6) VIII 127.

[3] Gray, *Spencer Perceval*, p. 132 n.

miniature-painter and parliamentary reporter, Walter Henry Watts, began an association with the *Morning Chronicle* which was to last for some thirty years.[1] In 1813 the reporting staff was joined by the brilliant but misanthropic William Hazlitt, who, from 1814, also became responsible for the theatrical criticism. Hazlitt's talents were not always appreciated by Perry, who pulled long faces over his columns of criticism, and 'used to execrate "the damned fellow's damned stuff" for filling up so much of the paper at the very height of the advertisement season'.[2] In 1817 a difference of opinion over the merits of Sir Thomas Lawrence, from whom Perry had commissioned a portrait, caused Hazlitt's dismissal.[3]

During these last years Thomas Moore continued to be one of Perry's occasional contributors, being retained at a salary of £200 a year.[4] Writers of another kidney were also making their appearance. David Ricardo made his mark in 1810 with a series of letters on the depreciation of the currency and continued to provide specialist articles on political economy.[5] During the last three or four years of Perry's life the economist, John Ramsay McCulloch, also contributed frequent articles on commercial subjects.[6] Bentham also sent occasional articles; but Perry's one surviving letter to Bentham, written in 1820 to acknowledge the offer of an article on Spanish affairs, is brief and formal and suggests no personal intimacy.[7] Other material came from more miscellaneous sources. According to Lady Holland, when the Duke of Kent went on a Continental tour in search of a wife in 1818, he supplied the *Morning Chronicle* not only with foreign intelligence but also with news and comment about domestic affairs.[8] This perhaps was not an isolated instance: alone it would hardly have laid the ground for

[1] According to the *D.N.B.*, Watts started his journalistic career with the *Morning Post* in 1803 and did not join the *Morning Chronicle* till about 1813. However, according to *The History of The Times* (I 136), John Payne Collier demanded a salary of five guineas a week from John Walter II on the ground that Watts was receiving this as a reporter for the *Chronicle* – this was about 1808.

[2] *Life of Mary Russell Mitford*, II 47.

[3] Bourne, *English Newspapers*, I 365.

[4] *Memoirs of Thomas Moore*, VIII 127.

[5] Andrews, *History of British Journalism*, II 64–5.

[6] Grant, *The Newspaper Press*, I 229.

[7] Bentham MSS., University College, London, box CLXXIII 17.

[8] Aspinall, *Politics and the Press*, p. 282.

Hazlitt's sneer that Perry wished it to be thought everything in the newspaper not from his own pen 'came from a lord, or an acknowledged wit'.[1] In another vein is a story told in Cyrus Redding's *Recollections*. About 1817 a Portuguese politician asked Redding to write letters for inclusion in the English newspapers giving the Portuguese side of a controversy in which the Spanish side had been strongly represented in *The Times*. Redding's articles, about a column or so in length, were sent to the *Morning Chronicle*. Perry demanded, and obtained, twenty guineas for each insertion.[2] However, if Perry's principles were affronted, no money would buy a way into his columns. When the French minister, Decazes, made overtures to Perry in 1818 to get articles in favour of liberal opinions printed in the *Chronicle*, he was informed that he should have them inserted in French journals so that they might be read in France, and then he, Perry, 'would cheerfully and gratuitously copy them'. Perry, a French ambassador sadly remarked a year or so earlier, was 'incorruptible'.[3]

With able management and stimulating, talented contributors, Perry's paper continued to bring him handsome profits till the end of his life. In the last year it yielded him an income of £12,000; and as the circulation had long been stabilised at the then figure of three to four thousand, he had probably drawn a similar income for many years. One salient mistake in management, indeed, there was. In July 1813 the inventor, Friedrich Koenig, perfected his cylindrical, steam-driven printing-press to his satisfaction and issued invitations to a demonstration to the two leading London newspaper proprietors, Perry and John Walter II of *The Times*. Perry, however, 'did not consider a newspaper worth so many years' purchase as would equal the cost of the machine and declined to disturb himself with a visit to Whitecross Street'.[4] Walter was allowed to seize a decisive advantage in flexibility of production and ability to send late news to press, and by the year of Perry's death the circulation of *The Times*, though still very small by modern standards, had risen to about twice that of the *Morning Chronicle*.[5] In

[1] *Complete Works of William Hazlitt*, XVI 223.

[2] Redding, *Fifty Years Recollections*, II 116–17.

[3] *History of The Times*, I 467, 465.

[4] Ibid., p. 112.

[5] By 1820 *The Times* was normally selling about 7,000 copies (Aspinall, *Politics and the Press*, p. 313).

1813 Perry was in his late fifties, and perhaps advancing age was blunting the initiative and foresight which had been such conspicuous qualities of his journalistic career. He seems also to have been handicapped by a constitutional incapacity to rate his financial resources at their true worth; but others were surprised when, after his death, his executors obtained £40,000 for the newspaper. 'This', his old friend, Gordon, commented, 'is perhaps the most extraordinary instance of the rise of literary property on record.'[1]

Perry's wife predeceased him in 1814, leaving six young children, two sons and four daughters; another daughter, the eldest, had died a little before this in her early teens. Perry himself died on 6 December 1821, at the house in Brighton which he had taken after the breakdown of his health in 1817, when his doctors had warned him to spend several months of each year away from London. His property was said to be worth £130,000. It included freehold, leasehold and copyhold estate in the parishes of Wimbledon, Mitcham and Clapham, four freehold properties in St Mary le Strand, his leasehold residence of Tavistock House, and shares in Drury Lane Theatre, the Surrey and Croydon Iron Railway Corporation, and the British Fire and the Real Life Assurance Companies, as well as the *Morning Chronicle*.[2] In accordance with the wishes expressed in his will, he was interred in the vault which he had bought in Wimbledon churchyard, and the members of the Fox Club of Westminster subscribed to a memorial placed within the church. He left a reputation as one of the most notable journalists of his day. Even the cross-grained Brougham, often vexed to find his speeches ignored in Perry's columns, was moved to praise him as far superior to the ordinary run of newspaper-men.[3] Together with Daniel Stuart of the *Morning Post* and *Courier* and John Walter II of *The Times*, he was one of the tiny handful of men who, in the second half of George III's reign, stamped a new dignity upon the newspaper press and set new canons of conduct for the profession of journalism.

[1] Gordon, *Personal Memoirs*, I 262–3.

[2] Will of James Perry, proved on 19 Dec 1821, by Thomas Bentley, and by Mary Ann Bentley, the guardian of his children, P.C.C. 683 Mansfield.

[3] Aspinall, *Politics and the Press*, p. 304.

SEVENTEEN

*Horace Walpole: The Gossip as Historian**

'I HAVE . . . everything in the world to tell posterity', Horace Walpole once wrote to his cousin, Henry Seymour Conway. The phrase was rhetorical; but this and other similar pronouncements, scattered throughout Walpole's letters and memoirs, sound the keynote of his long career. Walpole deliberately set himself to chronicle the social and political history of his age. For almost sixty years, from his early manhood up till his death in 1797, he carried on, with certain picked friends, a copious and remarkable correspondence; and the great series of letters from his pen provides a running commentary upon social, cultural and political activities, a record almost always interesting, at times vivid, of the society in which he moved. Over a somewhat shorter period, his political memoirs, which were written from a highly personal point of view and merge at times into autobiography, form an important contribution to the narrative history of his times. The mass of this material is considerable. The two series, the letters and the memoirs, amount in themselves to a substantial body of literature. Mrs Paget Toynbee's edition of the letters, together with the supplements edited by her husband, contains over three thousand of them in nineteen substantial volumes;[1] and the printed memoirs, in the existing standard editions, fill another nine volumes.[2] These writings are by no means the whole of Walpole's literary output.

* This originally appeared in *History Today*, IV (1954) 291–300.

[1] *The Letters of Horace Walpole*, 16 vols (1903–5), suppl. vols (1918–25). Quotations for which no other source is cited are taken from these volumes. As a standard edition, this work is in course of being superseded by the new, sumptuous Yale edition of Horace Walpole's correspondence, now in progress.

[2] *Memoirs of the last ten years of the reign of George II*, ed. Henry Fox, 3rd Lord Holland, 2nd ed., 3 vols (1847); *Memoirs of the reign of King George III*, ed. G. F. R. Barker, 4 vols (1894); *The Last Journals of Horace Walpole during the reign of George III*, ed. A. F. Steuart, 2 vols (1910).

His versatility was remarkable. He was active in many fields – politics, social life, literature, architecture, antiquarianism, virtu, printing. He wrote five books that were pioneer works of their kind. But to the historian, the letters and memoirs are Walpole's primary achievement and legacy.

What were Walpole's qualifications for the task of chronicling his age? Born in 1717, he was the youngest son of Sir Robert Walpole, first Earl of Orford – the Walpole who was Britain's leading minister for over twenty years. Although not a rich man, he thus belonged by birth and breeding to the 'inner ring' of aristocratic eighteenth-century society, in the activities of whose members centred the nation's political and cultural life. Through the marriage alliances of his house, he gained connections with families prominent in politics and in the life of the court around which this society revolved. As a typical representative of the 'inner ring', he entered parliament at the first general election after he came of age. A legislator by, as it were, almost indefeasible right, he sat for over twenty-five years in the House of Commons – for Callington and Castle Rising, both of them boroughs at his family's command, and later for King's Lynn: at Lynn, so he once reported, the corporation held his father's memory in such reverence that they would not apply to his more distant relations, so long as sons of Sir Robert were still living and willing to accept the honour of election to parliament. Throughout those years Walpole was an enthusiastic politician. And although he was never really in the centre of politics, he had knowledge of most of the events worth knowing about that took place in parliament.

He had also leisure. We may note here another qualification in which he was thoroughly representative of the 'inner ring'. A main object of many courtiers and politicians was to batten on the state, whether by way of unearned pension or by salary in return for service. A prime minister's son had a flying start over them all. Before Sir Robert was forced out of office in 1742, he had assured to Horace a substantial and impregnably secure income for life, by obtaining his appointment to various patent offices under the crown. While still a schoolboy, Horace received the sinecure appointments of comptroller of the pipe and clerk of the estreats; and in his twentieth year he was made usher of the exchequer. These places were worth well over £1,000 per annum. In addition, he received a more than equal sum from his share in a collectorship of the customs held, after his father's death, by his brother Edward. Though not rich, he was at least comfortably provided, and he was perfectly content with what he had. These appointments imposed on him no duties whatsoever, but he had no qualms about drawing the salaries for which he made no return: for in his view his father was completely justified, after having been the faithful and trusted servant of two kings, in securing as part of the reward for his services the financial independence of his children. Unhampered by any need to work for his living, he could freely devote his energies to the pursuit of politics, and to his various fruitful hobbies – not least among them being the compilation of a record of his times.

In addition to these advantages, Walpole brought to his self-appointed task of chronicler his own indispensable personal contributions – wide and varied social and cultural interests; a mingled delight and amusement in the people around him; keen observation sharpened by a penetrating wit; the mastery of a pleasant, smooth-flowing, semi-conversational style of writing; together with an intense desire to portray the contemporary scene for the instruction and entertainment of posterity. At times, we feel that he had such zestful enjoyment in his own experiences that he could not bear to think that they might pass into oblivion.

Spreading out from the beginnings in the circle of his family and of his school and college acquaintances, Walpole's regular correspondence soon came to conform to a deliberate plan. Each main section of his activities and interests – politics, antiquarianism, literature, social life – was depicted in a series of letters to a carefully selected correspondent. Sir Horace Mann, the British representative at the court of Florence, was for forty-five years the ever-delighted recipient of Walpole's reports of political events. 'You will believe that I set the highest value upon them', Mann once wrote, 'when I assure you that I frequently highly entertain myself with the perusal of them.'[1] Walpole's old schoolfellow, George Montagu, was chosen as the recipient of a stream of letters mainly devoted to social anecdote and description. The poet Gray, a friend of school and college days, became his correspondent on

[1] Unpublished manuscript, cited by Cremer in *Horace Walpole* (1940) p. 127.

M2

literary matters, and the Cambridge scholar, the Rev. William Cole, on antiquarian topics. To quote Walpole's biographer, Mr R. W. Ketton Cremer, 'Each correspondence, in fact, became an encyclopædia of what Walpole had to say on one particular topic.' If death or estrangement parted Walpole from one of his friends, and closed one channel of correspondence, another correspondent was soon selected to carry on that subject. There was, perhaps, a certain cold-bloodedness about the way in which he picked and substituted recipients of his letters, in order to preserve the pattern of his correspondence. But posterity had to be served. Whatever his concern or grief for a departed friend, he lost no time in recruiting a substitute to fill his place.

Walpole's letters bring home immediately the flesh-and-blood reality of the society in which he moved. The members of it cease to be mere shadows or ciphers, and emerge as living beings with fads and foibles, figures of laughter as well as solemnity. 'They tell me', he once wrote, 'Mr Hume has had sight of King James's journal; I wish I could see all the trifling passages that he will not deign to admit into history. I do not love great folks till they have pulled off their buskins and put on their slippers, because I do not care sixpence for what they would be thought, but for what they are.' It was in this spirit that he approached, for instance, a great occasion like the coronation service and banquet of George III in 1761. The brilliance, the pomp and majesty of the scene, were dismissed in three or four lines: it was the amusing, the bizarre, the human details that caught his eye. For example, the peeresses – Lady Pembroke, 'alone at the head of the countesses . . . the picture of majestic modesty'; Lady Harrington, devoid of any taste in the use of jewellery, 'covered with all the diamonds she could borrow, hire or seize, and with the air of Roxana . . . the finest figure at a distance'; the Duchess of Bedford, whose rouge had been dabbed on for her, most appropriately in the painted chamber, by Lord Bolingbroke, 'like an orange-peach, half red and half yellow'. Nor were the peers any less his targets: for example, the Duke of Newcastle – poor, shortsighted Newcastle – blundering into the retiring chamber set aside in the Abbey for the Queen; or Lord Talbot, acting as king's champion during the traditional ceremonies of the banquet in Westminster Hall, reduced to a figure of ridicule, because, having trained his horse to go backwards so that he should not turn his back on the king when leaving the hall, the beast insisted on coming in tail first when he made his entrance; or again, the earl marshal, dropping the most shattering of bricks when George III criticised the many failures of organisation: 'told him', wrote Walpole, 'it was true there had been great neglect . . . but he had now taken such care of registering directions, that *next coronation* would be conducted with the greatest order imaginable. The King was so diverted with this *flattering* speech that he made the Earl repeat it several time.'

Thus, with deft touches, Walpole would skim the cream of the situation he described, producing, in Macaulay's phrase, 'an entertainment worthy of a Roman epicure, . . . nothing but delicacies, the brains of singing birds, the roe of mullets, the sunny halves of peaches'. The result is indeed delicious literary fare; but naturally it does not provide the reader with any systematic picture of Georgian society. And then the letters contain much that is ephemeral – births, marriages, illnesses, deaths, love affairs, elopements, separations, divorces – events common to the lives of all communities. Yet, as the accumulating strokes of a painter's brush on his canvas build up a picture, so the letters, by their accumulated detail, convey the flavour of that eighteenth-century aristocratic society, its gaiety and seriousness, its good and its evil, its robust self-confidence, its unmistakable panache. Here are Walpole's contemporaries at work and at play – the ruling class of Great Britain, busy with government, politics, court duties, the law, military service, or taking their leisure at balls and masquerades, at conversaziones and club meetings. Walpole revelled in the social gatherings at the great town houses, where the young came to dance, the old to play cards, and all to enjoy wit and good conversation, and resigned himself, as he grew older, to the dowagers' card-tables, at which whist and loo were the favourite pastimes. These parties were more decorous than those in the fashionable clubs – Almack's, Arthur's, Brooks's, 'the Coterie', the Maccaronis', the *Sçavoir vivre*, White's – scenes of wild gambling, where fortunes might change hands in a night, and where bets were offered and taken at the slightest provocation and upon the most curious occasions. 'They have put in the papers a good story made on White's', Walpole wrote to a friend on one occasion. 'A man dropped down dead at the door, was carried in; the club immediately made bets whether he was dead or not, and when they were going to bleed him, the wagerers for his death interposed, and said it would affect the fairness of the bet.'

Like most societies, the high society of the eighteenth century had its young people who panted after novelties of fashion. There were the young men of the Maccaronis' Club, 'who wear long curls and spying glasses', and 'who will have everything before the season'. French fashions were all the rage. 'Our greatest miracle', wrote Walpole in a letter of 1751, 'is Lady Mary Wortley's son . . . the most curious part of his dress, which he has brought from Paris, is an iron wig; you literally would not know it from hair. I believe' – and one can almost hear the writer's laugh – 'I believe it is on this account that the Royal Society have just chosen him of their body.' 'You are so thoughtless about your dress, that I cannot help giving you a little warning against your return', he wrote in 1759 to his cousin, Conway, then with the British forces in Germany. 'Remember, everybody that comes from abroad is *censé* to come from France, and whatever they wear at their first reappearance immediately grows the fashion. Now if, as is very likely, you should through inadvertence change hats with a master of a Dutch smack, Offley will be upon the watch, will conclude you took your pattern from M. de Bareil, and in a week's time we shall all be equipped like Dutch skippers.'

This love of novelty was not confined to clothes. There is more than one passage in the letters that reminds us of the interest then taken by Englishmen in the inventive genius of their fellows. 'I love the history of refinements', Walpole wrote to Mann in 1750. 'Mr Dodington has a steel machine to pick up his handkerchief.' Or again, he records how, in 1760, the hanging which ended the *cause célèbre* of the aristocratic murderer, Earl Ferrers, was made the occasion of an experiment with a new device, the dropping stage. 'As the machine was new, they were not ready at it', he reported. 'His toes touched it and he suffered a little . . . they pulled his legs so that he was soon out of pain, and quite dead in four minutes.'

When they were not up in London, busy with politics, service at court and other public duties, or relaxing in the social round, the lords and gentlemen of Walpole's world retired to the country to hunt, to manage their estates, to make improvements, and to build – vast sums were spent on the building or enlarging of country houses and on the laying out of parks. Farming was never one of Walpole's interests: for its annals we must turn to the pages of Arthur Young. But Walpole, whose antiquarian pursuits took him about a great deal, visited many of the great houses, old and new, and often wrote descriptions of them to his friends. He was captivated by Sir George Lyttelton's park at Hagley, with its lake and its streams, and the specially constructed castle ruins, and rhapsodised over it to his friend, Richard Bentley. 'You might draw', he wrote to him, 'but I can't describe, the enchanting scenes of the park; it is a hill of three miles, but broke into all manner of beauty; such lawns, such wood, rills, cascades, and a thickness of verdure quite to the summit of the hill, and commanding such a vale of towns and meadows and woods, extending quite to the Black Mountains in Wales, that I quite forgot my favourite Thames. . . . There is a ruined castle, built by Miller, that would get him his freedom even of Strawberry: it has the true rust of the Baron's Wars. . . . I wore out my eyes with gazing, my feet with climbing, and my tongue and my vocabulary with commending.' At Chatsworth, so he recorded after a visit in 1760, 'the expense of the works now carrying on will amount to £40,000.' At Osterley Park, the residence of the banker, Robert Child, we have a glimpse, through Walpole's eyes, of the prolific ostentation with which the newly rich surrounded themselves in their efforts to vie with the old aristocracy. 'The old house I have often seen', Walpole reported, ' . . . but it is so improved and enriched, that all the Percies and Seymours of Sion must die of envy. There is a double portico that fills the space between the towers of the front and is as noble as the Propyleum of Athens. There is a hall, library, breakfast-room, eating-room, all *chefs-d'œuvre* of Adam, a gallery one hundred and thirty feet long, and a drawing-room worthy of Eve before the Fall. Mrs Child's dressing-room is full of pictures, gold filigree, china, and japan. So is all the house; the chairs are taken from antique lyres, and make charming harmony; there are Salvators, Gaspar Poussins, and to a beautiful staircase a ceiling by Rubens . . . and then, in the drawing-room I mentioned, there are door-cases, and a crimson and gold frieze, that I believe were borrowed from the Palace of the Sun.'

This desire to build was shared by Walpole himself; but not

having the income to indulge in great houses and parks, he contented himself with the adornment and extension of his little house at Strawberry Hill, encrusting the surfaces of the old fabric with Gothic, rather in the manner of a chef icing a wedding-cake. 'Imagine the walls', he wrote, 'covered with (I call it paper, but it is really paper painted in perspective to represent) Gothic fretwork.' To the outside he added battlements, lightly made of plaster. They crumbled quickly, but were just as easily replaced. Many years before his death, it was said that 'Mr Walpole has already outlived three sets of his battlements.'[1] The craving to create, the delight in design, the glow and pride of achievement, which on every side inspired this rage for building, breathe through every letter in which he describes his beloved Strawberry.

While Walpole's letters are, from their nature, a jumble of disjointed fragments, the political memoirs, planned with deliberation, sustained in composition, and confined in subject to a narrower field, have a greater coherence and completeness of form. To these memoirs the letters written about political matters form an indispensable adjunct, especially the great series to Mann at Florence, of which Walpole secured the return at intervals to assist him in his historical writing. Not only do the letters contain information discarded during the composition of the memoirs and which thus supplements them, but they are also essential aids to making a critical assessment of the material in the memoirs, providing as they do, from a current, contemporary record, evidence regarding Walpole's initial thoughts and opinions about political matters, which sometimes differed greatly from those to which the memoirs gave expression. The letters report his immediate impressions; the memoirs recollections and reflections, which were not always arrived at in a state of mental tranquillity.

In the standard published editions, Walpole's political memoirs comprise the *Memoirs of the last ten years of the reign of George II*, covering the years 1751–60; the *Memoirs of the reign of King George III*, carrying his story up to 1771; and the *Last Journals*, for the years 1771–83. In these writings he bequeathed to posterity a continuous narrative of political events covering a period of over thirty years. As sources of historical information, these various memoirs vary greatly in quality. Some parts are very good indeed;

[1] W. S. Lewis, *Collector's Progress* (1952) p. 92.

almost always there is useful information to be culled from them, though often it supports conclusions very different from those reached by Walpole himself. It was Walpole's deliberate intention to leave a record for future generations of the political events in which he had taken some part, a record which should be, so far as possible, unbiased. Many readers, he once wrote, might be offended at the liberty he had taken in painting men as they were: 'Yet this, I fear, must always be the case in any history written impartially by an eye-witness: and eye-witnesses have been generally allowed the properest historians.' 'If I write, I must write facts.' Or again: 'Whatever tends to a knowledge of the characters of remarkable persons, of the manners of the age, and of its political intrigue, comes properly within my plan. I am more attentive to deserve the thanks of posterity than their admiration.'[1] Where he himself had participated in events, the reader was to be clearly informed of the part he had taken. In later years he pleaded a further justification for the memoirs. No longer himself engaged in politics, disgusted at the poor leadership which had produced the American crisis and the War of Independence, and nursing unfounded suspicions about the intentions of the king and certain politicians close to the court, he declared that he wrote also 'to warn posterity (however vain such zeal) against the folly and corruption and profligacy of the times I have lived in'. And before the end of his career, under the stress of his desire to warn posterity, he had come to scorn 'the cold impartiality recommended to historians'.

Impartiality was, however, an ideal in the pursuit of which Walpole was never remarkably successful. There were always strong dislikes and resentments, which distorted his verdicts and added gall to his criticisms of the men whose careers he discussed – for instance, his hatred of the Pelhams, who had, so he considered, betrayed his father; his animosity towards Henry Fox, who had spurned his advice and subsequently persecuted him; his resentment at the failure of the Duke of Grafton and leaders of the Rockingham party to appreciate his services and his counsel.

Then, too, the political memoirs suffer from another limitation – one that, to do him justice, Walpole often admitted. He was never at the centre of the political stage – only once or twice even

[1] *Memoirs of George II*, I XXIX, 238; II 249.

in the wings. The only politician in a high ministerial position with whom he was ever in intimate intercourse was Henry Seymour Conway, his first cousin and very dearly cherished friend. Between 1764 and 1768 Conway – with Walpole close at his elbow in the role of political mentor – became first a leading figure in the parliamentary opposition, and then a secretary of state. These circumstances gave an exceptional value to Walpole's memoirs of those years. After 1768 the eclipse of Conway and the retirement from parliament of Walpole himself greatly reduced the information at his disposal. For this reason the *Last Journals* are of much less value as a historical narrative. To quote one instance: under the year 1780 Walpole gives an account of *pourparlers* for a coalition between Lord North, the prime minister, and the leader of the opposition, the Marquis of Rockingham. The general tenor of this account does not spare the Marquis's political reputation. Walpole received his information from Conway, who had received his from the Duke of Richmond. Nothing had been either lost or added in the telling: what Conway learned he reported with accuracy. But what had he learned? Documents in the Marquis of Rockingham's papers, recently become available, show that Conway received information and opinions from Richmond at a moment when Richmond had not yet been fully informed of the course of events and was blaming Rockingham for sins of omission and commission of which he was very largely innocent. Consequently Walpole recorded Richmond's incomplete knowledge as if it were a true account of Rockingham's activities.

In reading the *Memoirs of the Reign of George III*, allowance has to be made for yet another circumstance. The *Memoirs* were written between 1766 and 1772 and underwent literary revision in the early months of 1775. But nearly ten years later Walpole went over his manuscript once again; and a series of alterations, which can be dated to the year 1784, were made for a very different purpose. His letters show that about the middle of 1775, just at the outbreak of hostilities with the American colonies, his political opinions underwent a sudden transformation, and he began to accept a completely new interpretation of the course of political events since 1761. Leading incidents now all seemed to him to fall into place as parts of a deliberate scheme of George III, his mother, and his favourite, the Earl of Bute, to pervert the constitution, win absolute power, and suppress the hard-won liberties of his countrymen. That is to say, Walpole had swallowed, hook, line and sinker, what one might term 'the Burke legend' from the fact that the first exposition of it had been published five years before, in 1770, in Burke's pamphlet, *Thoughts on the Cause of the Present Discontents*. When in 1784 he took up his manuscript again, brooding over the now completed dismemberment of the British empire, and anxious to make clear to posterity the errors that had produced the disaster, some restatement of his narrative seemed necessary, to illustrate and emphasise the various stages of the royal conspiracy. Additions to the opening sections laid stress on the influence of Bute and on the campaign against liberty involved in the persecution of the political journalist, John Wilkes. Comment inserted in the later sections criticised royal influence over the North administration, during the life of which America was lost. His later journals for the years after 1771 were coloured throughout by this new point of view. But this reinterpretation is not supported by the more intimate manuscript information which has since come to light concerning the politics of those years. Walpole's interpolations and revisions obscured the story told in his memoirs, instead of clarifying it.

Nevertheless, the *Memoirs* and the *Letters* together yield a wealth of information on mid-eighteenth-century politics. Much light is thrown on the intricate manœuvres of the various factions in parliament, upon political transactions which would otherwise remain obscure, upon the often trivial motives of political conduct. They include valuable reports, generally proved authentic, concerning parliamentary debates of which sometimes no other record is known to exist. Then there are the graphic character-sketches of leading political figures. In a letter to Mann, for instance, a pen portrait of the young George III soon after his accession is skilfully drawn in half a dozen phrases: 'His person is tall and full of dignity; his countenance florid and good-natured; his manner is graceful and obliging; he expresses no warmth or resentment against anybody; at most coldness.' This description supplements the character-study of the king at about the same period outlined by Walpole in the first volume of the *Memoirs of Geogre III*. 'So far as could be discerned of the King's natural disposition', Walpole wrote, 'it was humane and benevolent . . . he accepted services with grace and appearance of feeling; and if he forgot them with unrestrained facility, yet he never marked his displeasure with harshness. . . . He had neither passions nor activity. He resigned himself obsequiously to the government of his mother and Lord Bute: learned and even entered with art into the lessons they inspired, but added nothing of his own. When the task was done he relapsed into indifference and indolence till roused to the next day's part.'[1]

Walpole's assessments of his great contemporaries were often partial and prejudiced. With his cousin, Conway, he would hardly find any fault. With almost all others, he was perhaps rather too inclined to expose the imperfections but fail to praise the virtues; and the reader may even suspect at times something of the gleeful malice of a little boy in the act of 'debunking' one of his seniors. But his descriptions are always lively and apt, and his power to diagnose weaknesses of character acute. Of the elder Pitt (with a metaphor that brilliantly fits the man) he wrote that 'Lord Chatham was a meteor and a glorious one. . . . A minister that inspires great actions must be a great minister; and Lord Chatham will always appear so – by comparison with his predecessors and successors.' And of one of those successors, Lord North: 'Two large prominent eyes that rolled about to no purpose (for he was utterly short sighted), a wide mouth, thick lips, and inflated visage, gave him the air of a blind trumpeter. . . . But within that rude casket were enclosed many useful talents. He had much wit, good-humour, strong natural sense, assurance, and promptness both of conception and elocution. . . . His indolence prevented his forming any plan. His indifference made him leap from one extreme to another; and his insensibility to reproach reconciled him to any contradiction.'[2] Or again, the meretricious brilliance of Charles Townshend is dissected and pinned down in a couple of scarifying sentences: 'Townshend . . . had parts that embraced all knowledge with such quickness, that he seemed to create knowledge instead

[1] This description of George III by Walpole invites comparison with the more penetrating character-sketch, based on much more intimate acquaintance, recorded in his memoirs two or three years before by the second Earl Waldegrave, Walpole's nephew by marriage (quoted by Sir Lewis Namier in his article, 'King George III, a study in personality', in *History Today*, III IX (Sept 1953) 615. Walpole had access to those memoirs and clearly drew upon them.

[2] *Memoirs of George III*, IV 52–4.

of searching for it.' 'He had almost every great talent, . . . he must have been the greatest man of this age . . . had his faults been only in a moderate proportion – in short if he had had but common truth, common sincerity, common honesty, common modesty, common steadiness, common courage, and common sense.'[1] And to conclude these illustrations, nothing could better convey the essential childlike naïvety of the Duke of Newcastle than this description of him on the solemn occasion of King George II's funeral: 'This grave scene was fully contrasted by the burlesque Duke of Newcastle. He fell into a fit of crying the moment he came into the chapel, and flung himself back in a stall, the Archbishop hovering over him with a smelling-bottle – but in two minutes his curiosity got the better of his hypocrisy, and he ran about the chapel with his glass to spy who was, or was not there, spying with one hand and mopping his eyes with the other. Then returned the fear of catching cold, and the Duke of Cumberland, who was sinking with heat, felt himself weighed down, and turning round, found it was the Duke of Newcastle standing upon his train to avoid the chill of the marble.'

Walpole wrote both for the entertainment and the enlightenment of posterity. The entertainment was provided in his letters – interesting, witty, informative, always extremely readable, a source of continuous fresh enjoyment. The memoirs he intended as more solid historical fare. He understood perfectly that even incomplete information was better than no information at all; and he was well aware that although he could give a fairly complete account of some transactions in which he himself had played a leading part, there were many about which he was largely ignorant. 'Yet that very ignorance', he wrote in the *Memoirs of George III*, 'may guide future historians to the search after authentic papers.' To serve that purpose was an ample justification of the labours which he expended upon the memoirs. Although Walpole performed no official services in return for the comfortable salaries he received, which were charged upon his country's revenues, it can perhaps with justice be contended that in the service of posterity the outlay incurred was more than fully requited.

[1] Ibid., II 195; III 72.

erts are timed for us. He had almost every great talent ... he must have been the greatest man of this age ... had his talents been only in a moderate proportion [illegible] had but common truth, common sincerity, [illegible] common modesty, common steadiness, common courage, and common sense.' And to conclude these illustrations, nothing could better convey the essential [illegible] the Duke of Newcastle than this description of him on the solemn occasion of [illegible] [illegible] Duke of Newcastle [illegible] into the [illegible] the Archbishop hovering over him [illegible] his curiosity [illegible] with his glass [illegible] with one hand and mopping his eyes with the other. Then returned the fear of catching cold; and the Duke of Cumberland, who was sinking with heat, [illegible] was the Duke of Newcastle [illegible] to avoid the chill of the marble.

While he was [illegible] comedy [illegible] of posterity. The [illegible] [illegible] [illegible] [illegible] [illegible] he was well aware that [illegible] transactions [illegible] were many about which he was largely ignorant. 'Yet, that very ignorance,' he wrote in the *Memoirs of George II*, [illegible] historians [illegible] that [illegible] was an ample [illegible] of the labours which he expended upon the memoirs. Although Walpole [illegible] informal services [illegible] for the [illegible] the salaries he received, which were [illegible] upon the country's revenues, it can perhaps with justice be contended that [illegible] to the [illegible] of posterity the [illegible] [illegible] was more than fully repaid.

[1] Ibid., [illegible]

Index